THE STATS BASEBALL SCOREBOARD

THE STATS™ BASEBALL SCOREBOARD

John Dewan, Don Zminda, and STATS, Inc.

Illustrations by John Grimwade

Ballantine Books • New York

Copyright © 1990 by Sports Team Analysis and Tracking Systems, Inc.

All rights reserved under International and Pan-American Copyright Conventions. Published in the United States by Ballantine Books, a division of Random House, Inc., New York and simultaneously in Canada by Random House of Canada Limited, Toronto.

STATS Inc. is a trademark of Sports Team Analysis and Tracking Systems, Inc.

Library of Congress Catalog Card Number: 89-90920

ISBN: 0-345-36434-1

Cover design by Dale Fiorillo

Manufactured in the United States of America
First Edition: April 1990

10 9 8 7 6 5 4 3 2 1

Dedication

To Sue Dewan — her assistance, support and patience extend far beyond Babe Ruth's longest home run.

To Sharon Zminda — the best teammate a ballplayer ever had.

ACKNOWLEDGMENTS

Behind the essays and statistics within this book there is another story. It's the story of all the people at STATS who put the information together and helped crunch the data and analyze it so that we could answer all the questions in this book.

Dr. Richard Cramer is the founder and Chairman of the Board of STATS and is responsible for the design and growth of the computer system that we marvel at every day — the system that all this begins with. Dick is an accomplished baseball analyst; his expertise developing ideas and massaging our computer to get the answers was indispensable.

Bob Mecca is another very key person in the making of this book. He helped develop many of the questions and wrote lots and lots of programs to get the answers. If you like the detailed appendices in the back of the book, he's the one to applaud. Bob played *the* major role in compiling the appendices which took long hours of dedicated work. Thanks Bob.

One of the things that makes this book different from other baseball books is the graphics of John Grimwade. We think you'll agree that he has an awesome talent to take an idea and develop it into a stunning graphic. His pictures are certainly worth a thousand words. STATS met John through mutual work with *Sports Illustrated* where you can see his sports graphic talent displayed weekly. We're overjoyed to have John work with us on this book.

The core staff of the STATS office, Sue Dewan, Carmen Corica, and Matt Greenberger, kept the other STATS projects running smoothly while we took the time to complete this book. Carmen and Matt also helped put many of the final touches on the book.

Special thanks to all the STATS scorers who supplied the play by play to our computer system throughout the season.

Thanks to Bill James for his consultation and support of STATS Inc.

Table of Contents

INTRODUCTION 1

I. GENERAL BASEBALL QUESTIONS 3

DO BASE STEALERS HAVE AN ADVANTAGE ON ARTIFICIAL TURF? 4
HOW DO RUNS SCORE? 6
WHICH PLATOONS WERE IN COMPANY "A"? 8
WHICH UMPIRES ARE OFFENSIVE? 10
HOW DO TEAMS PERFORM IN THE LATE INNINGS OF CLOSE GAMES? 12
WILL THE DOME LIFT THE JAYS TO THE SKIES? 14
DO HITTERS SPEND MOST OF THEIR TIME JUST STANDING AROUND? 16
WHICH TEAMS BUNT MOST IN THE EARLY INNINGS? 18
WHICH PLAYERS HAD THE BIGGEST CHANGE IN PERFORMANCE FROM 1988 TO '89? 20
WHAT WERE THE FASTEST GAMES IN THE MAJORS LAST YEAR? 23
WHICH TEAMS BLOW THE MOST LEADS IN THE LATE INNINGS? 26
WHO WANTS TO PLAY LEFT FIELD? 29
WHAT ARE BASEBALL'S MOST AND LEAST COMMON PLAYS? 32
HOW RARE IS A TWO STRIKE HOMER? 35
WHICH TEAMS HAVE THE BEST BENCH PLAYERS? 38
ARE PITCHERS' THROWS TO FIRST A WASTE OF TIME? 40
DO GROUNDBALL HITTERS DO BETTER AGAINST FLYBALL PITCHERS? 42
WHICH STADIUMS PRODUCE THE MOST FOULOUTS? 44
HOW DOES TEMPERATURE AFFECT OFFENSIVE PRODUCTION? 46

WHICH TEAMS PERFORM BEST WITH RUNNERS IN SCORING POSITION? 48
DOES THE PURPOSE PASS PAY OFF? 51
DOES RUNNING AGGRESSIVELY MEAN MORE RUNS? 54
HOW DO TEAMS PERFORM VS. LEFTIES AND RIGHTIES? 56
WHICH TEAMS RUN LATE? 58
WHICH IS THE BEST DIVISION IN BASEBALL? 60
DOES ARTIFICIAL TURF PRODUCE MORE GROUNDBALL HITS? 62
WHAT ARE THE BEST HITTERS' COUNTS? 64
WHICH PLAYERS TURNED IN THE BEST MONTHLY PERFORMANCES OF 1989? 66
DO SACRIFICES SACRIFICE TOO MUCH? 68
WHICH TEAMS SHOWED THE MOST IMPROVEMENT DURING THE SECOND HALF OF 1989? 70
WHY SHOULD FIELDERS PLAY SHALLOW WHEN WILL CLARK IS HITTING? 72
WHEN ARE TWO OUTS BETTER THAN ONE? 74
WHEN DO GOOD TEAMS SCORE? 76

II. QUESTIONS ON OFFENSE   79

WHICH HITTERS SWING AND MISS MOST OFTEN? 80
WHO CAN POP IN THE CLUTCH? 82
WHAT IS THE AVERAGE OFFENSIVE PERFORMANCE FROM EACH POSITION? 84
WHICH HITTERS PERFORM BEST AGAINST THE TOP PITCHERS? 86
WHO ARE THE MAJOR LEAGUE LEADERS IN GO-AHEAD RBIS? 88
WHICH HITTERS ARE AT HOME ON THE ROAD? 90
WHICH PLAYERS CREATE THE MOST RUNS? 93
WHO ARE THE MOST CONSISTENT GROUNDBALL HITTERS IN BASEBALL — AND WHO ARE THE BEST FLYBALL HITTERS? 96
WHICH PLAYERS HOMER TO THE OPPOSITE FIELD MOST OFTEN? 98
WHO ARE THE BEST LEADOFF HITTERS IN BASEBALL? 100
TO WHOM DOES THE GREEN MONSTER BECKON? 102
WHO ARE BASEBALL'S MOST (AND LEAST) AGGRESSIVE BASERUNNERS? 104
WHICH HITTERS ARE EASIEST TO DOUBLE UP? 106
WHICH BATTERS HAVE THE BIGGEST DAY/NIGHT DIFFERENCES? ... 108

WHICH HITTERS HAVE THE BEST STRIKEOUT TO WALK RATIOS? 111
WHO WERE THE HOTTEST (AND COLDEST) SECOND-HALF
HITTERS LAST YEAR?.. 114
WHAT WOULD AN AVERAGE MAJOR LEAGUE LINEUP LOOK
LIKE?... 116
WHO ARE THE LEADERS IN SECONDARY AVERAGE? 118
WHO ARE THE BEST RBI MEN WITH RUNNERS IN SCORING
POSITION?.. 120
IS IT BETTER TO PULL OR GO THE OTHER WAY?............................... 122
WHO LEADS THE LEAGUE IN LOOKING?... 124
WHY DON'T THEY STEAL THIRD MORE OFTEN?................................ 126
WHO ARE THE BEST BUNTERS IN BASEBALL? 128
WHICH PLAYERS PRODUCE THE MOST RBI PER HOME RUN? 130
IF LINEOUTS WERE HITS . . .?.. 132
WHO HIT THE LONGEST HOMERS DURING 1989? 134
WHO ARE THE BEST CLEANUP HITTERS IN BASEBALL? 136
WHO ARE THE LEADERS IN "POWER PERCENTAGE"? 138
DOES PLATOONING MAKE SENSE? 140
WHAT GOOD IS A FOUL BALL?.. 142

III. QUESTIONS ON PITCHING   145

HOW IMPORTANT IS A FIRST PITCH STRIKE?...................................... 146
WHO ARE THE BEST HITTING PITCHERS IN BASEBALL? 148
HOW EFFECTIVE ARE PITCHOUTS?... 150
DO THEY STILL BRUSH 'EM BACK?.. 153
WHO THROWS GROUNDBALLS? 156
WHICH STARTERS ALLOW THE FEWEST BASERUNNERS?................... 158
WHO WAS BETTER IN '89 — STORM DAVIS OR DOYLE
ALEXANDER?... 160
CAN A PITCHER INDUCE A DOUBLE PLAY GROUNDER? 162
WHO ARE THE BEST RELIEVERS AT HOLDING THE FORT FOR
THEIR LATE MEN? 164
WHICH RELIEVERS HAVE THE HIGHEST SAVE PERCENTAGES? 166
WHO ARE THE TOUGHEST PITCHERS TO HIT? 168
WHO HAS THE BEST STARTING STAFF IN BASEBALL? THE BEST
RELIEF STAFF?... 170
WHICH RELIEVERS HAVE THE BEST ENDURANCE?............................. 172

WHAT IS FIRST BATTER EFFICIENCY? 174
HOW MUCH REST IS BEST? 176
WHICH PITCHERS SHOULD NEVER LEAVE HOME? 179
WHICH PITCHERS MAKE THE LEAST OF THEIR INHERITANCE? 182
IS THE QUALITY START A QUALITY STAT? 184
WHICH LEFTY RELIEVERS ARE TOUGHEST AGAINST
LEFTHANDED HITTERS? 186
WHICH PITCHERS PERFORM BEST AGAINST THE TOP HITTERS? 188
WHICH PITCHERS ARE VICTIMIZED MOST BY THEIR OWN
BULLPENS? 190
WHAT HAPPENS AFTER A HOME RUN? 192
WHO ARE THE TOUGHEST (AND EASIEST) PITCHERS TO STEAL
ON? 194
DO PITCHERS HAVE TROUBLE AFTER A HIGH PITCH OUTING? 196
WHOSE HEATER IS THE HOTTEST? 199
WHO THROWS TO FIRST? 200
WHICH PITCHERS THROW THE MOST DOUBLE PLAY
GROUNDERS? 202
WHICH PITCHERS ARE THE BEST "LONG DISTANCE RUNNERS"? 204

IV. QUESTIONS ON DEFENSE   207

WHICH CATCHERS THROW OUT THE MOST BASERUNNERS? 208
WHO LED THE LEAGUE IN FUMBLES? 210
CAN CATCHERS HELP A PITCHER'S ERA? 212
WHICH INFIELDERS HAVE THE BEST RANGE? 215
WHICH OUTFIELDERS ARE THE TOUGHEST TO RUN ON? 220
WHO ARE THE PRIME PIVOT MEN? 222
WHICH CATCHERS ARE BEST AT BLOCKING PITCHES? 224
WHICH PARKS PRODUCE THE MOST ERRORS? 226
WHICH FIRST BASEMEN RECORD THE MOST 3-6-3 DOUBLE
PLAYS? 228
WHICH OUTFIELDERS HAVE THE BEST RANGE? 230

About STATS Inc.   233

APPENDIX   235

INTRODUCTION

Hi, and welcome to our new book. We already know you like baseball. Now we'd like to help you understand the game a little better — and to have some fun while we're doing it.

We work for STATS, Inc., an outfit which has been gathering and analyzing baseball statistics for a decade. A lot of us at STATS got involved in this work through Bill James — first by being fans of Bill's, then by being lucky enough to work with him. We don't claim to be him; there's only one Bill James. But *The STATS Baseball Scoreboard* does start with the same approach that Bill has done: we want to use the statistics of the game to unlock some of its mysteries. That means keeping an open mind as much as possible. It means starting with the question, rather than beginning with the notion that we know all the answers. We gather as much data as we can on each subject — and then we go wherever it leads us. We think you'll agree that it takes us to some pretty interesting places.

The format of our book is simple: 101 questions and answers, divided by subject matter. The questions are the kind fans are always asking: Who are the best clutch hitters? Which second basemen are best on the pivot? Which teams like to sacrifice in the early innings, or go for a stolen base when the game is on the line? (That's just a small sample.) We discuss each subject, and supply you with pertinent information to answer the question. Often we'll include an illustration that can give you a quick overview and a visual feel for the topic. Finally, since we know many of you will want more data so that you can study the issues yourself, we include an appendix. The appendix has additional detailed data for most of the topics.

To delve into these subjects we need good and complete information. At the risk of appearing immodest, we can say without contradiction that the STATS database is the most detailed record ever kept on major league baseball. You're probably familiar with some of our final products: bits of it appeared regularly last year in *Sports Illustrated*, *The Sporting News*, and many daily newspapers. But that was just the tip of the iceberg. Our scorers record every pitch, every pitchout, every throw to first. When a ball is hit, we not only note what happened; we record where the ball landed on the field, and how far it traveled. That information is logged into our computer on a daily basis, and continually checked for accuracy.

Our database helps make this book like no other baseball book you've ever seen. Have you always wondered whether the pitchout is an effective strategy? We have the data, and we present and discuss it in these pages. Have you ever seen a batter foul off a lot of pitches, and asked whether hanging in there increases his chances of eventual success? We go into that subject as well. Do you get annoyed when pitchers throw to first, and think it's a total waste of time? We look at that issue also, with some results you might find surprising. And that's just the beginning.

While we'll present you with a lot of statistics, there's no need to feel overwhelmed. Baseball is a fun game, and this is meant to be a fun book, not a Ph.D. thesis. We're sure you'll enjoy the illustrations by John Grimwade; if you did nothing but study John's charts, you'd still learn a lot about baseball. The essays are meant to be entertaining as well as informative. We don't take everything seriously, and we're not above tweaking a few noses from time to time — including our own.

So enjoy the book. We like to think that you can turn to any page, and find something of interest. Our hope is that this is just the beginning, that we can return each year and delve into some new subjects, as well as present fresh information on some of the older ones. Feel free to give us your feedback — we'd like to know what interested you most, what interested you least, what subjects you'd like us to explore in the future. This is your book as well as ours, and we'll do our best to give you what you want.

John Dewan and Don Zminda

I. GENERAL BASEBALL QUESTIONS

DO BASE STEALERS HAVE AN ADVANTAGE ON ARTIFICIAL TURF?

Everyone, it seems, hates artificial turf. Every year we hear how plastic grass shortens careers, increases injuries, causes numerous phony hits and makes players with creaky knees long for a new home address. The actual evidence for some of these claims is a little skimpy, but turf is clearly out of fashion. Dick Allen might have been speaking for a generation when he said, "If a horse can't eat it, I don't want to play on it."

There is, however, a devious minority which can't get enough of that artificial stuff: the nation's base thieves. The evidence clearly shows that runners are significantly more successful when attempting to steal on artificial turf. Here are the major league totals for the last three seasons:

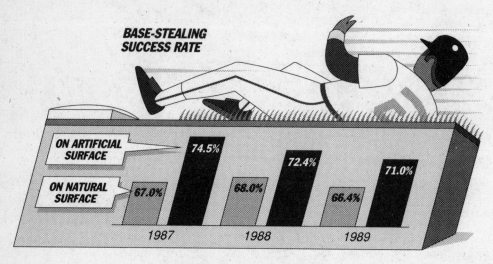

Base-Stealing Success Rate 1987 to 1989	
Natural	67.1%
Artificial	72.7%

The consistent advantage on turf has real strategic implications. Those who've studied the subject know that a 67 percent success rate, the figure on a natural surface, gives a team a negligible strategic advantage. But a 73 percent rate, the figure on turf, makes stealing an effective weapon. Other things being equal, managers would do well to limit the running game on natural surfaces, except for their outstanding baserunners.

You might wonder how those outstanding runners steal on a natural surface vs. turf. Here are the totals for the eleven players who stole 40 or more bases last year:

	Natural			Artificial		
Player, Team	SB	CS	%	SB	CS	%
Rickey Henderson, Yanks-Oak	63	10	86.3	14	4	77.8
Vince Coleman, StL	14	1	93.3	51	9	85.0
Cecil Espy, Tex	40	19	67.8	5	1	83.3
Devon White, Cal	38	13	74.5	6	3	66.7
Gary Pettis, Det	39	12	76.5	4	3	57.1
Steve Sax, Yanks	37	15	71.2	6	2	75.0
Juan Samuel, Phi-Mets	23	9	71.9	19	3	86.4
Roberto Alomar, SD	21	13	61.8	21	4	84.0
Howard Johnson, Mets	25	5	83.3	16	3	84.2
Tim Raines, Mon	9	3	75.0	32	6	84.2
Tony Gwynn, SD	25	11	69.4	15	5	75.0
TOTAL	334	111	75.1	189	43	81.5

There are some player-to-player differences, but overall the greyhounds do significantly better on turf as well.

The reason for the advantage on artificial turf is pretty simple: you can run faster on it. The traction on the turf areas between bases is better for running than the dirt between bases on grass fields. Runners can accelerate better, and that shows up in their success rate.

It's interesting to note that when turf fields began appearing in the mid-sixties, the infields had the traditional dirt paths between bases. That, of course, meant no stealing advantage over grass. It wasn't until the opening of Riverfront Stadium in 1970 that turf was used to cover the infield, except for the small dirt cutouts right around the bases. The Reds, we recall, had no great reason for covering the infield; they simply thought it looked better. Other turf teams followed suit, and the game was changed in a small, but (as we can see from these figures) significant, way.

A complete listing for this category can be found on page 237.

HOW DO RUNS SCORE?

Ask the average fan which event produces most runs, and he'll probably say, "singles." Surprisingly, this isn't always true. The following 1987-89 chart breaks down runs by the six events that produce 90 percent of the scoring. Among other things, you'll discover that in 1987, the home run — not the single — was the big run producer:

American League

Year	Single	Double	Triple	Homer	Sac Fly	Error	Total Runs
1987 Runs	3189	1479	273	4140	631	881	11112
Percent	28	13	2	37	5	7	
1988 Runs	3064	1500	272	2992	676	830	9858
Percent	31	15	2	30	6	7	
1989 Runs	3305	1380	272	2715	706	900	9732
Percent	33	14	2	27	7	9	

National League

Year	Single	Double	Triple	Homer	Sac Fly	Error	Total Runs
1987 Runs	2671	1310	262	2873	483	765	8777
Percent	30	14	2	32	5	8	
1988 Runs	2566	1129	255	1959	589	671	7522
Percent	34	15	3	26	7	8	
1989 Runs	2444	1208	276	2168	536	679	7673
Percent	31	15	3	28	6	8	

The American has been the home run league, but that may be starting to change. From '87 to '89 the percentage of runs scoring on homers in AL games dropped by a full 10 percent, from 37 to 27. In 1989, American League home run production went down while NL production went up. As a result, the percentage of scores resulting from homers was actually higher in National League games last year.

Another interesting thing you can see in the chart is that, while the number of runs scoring on homers went way down in 1988, the number coming home on sacrifice flies went up. This suggests that there's some validity to the theory that the ball was more lively in '87. In '88, long flies stayed in the park more often, resulting in fewer homers but more sac flies.

There's a considerable amount of variance from team to team in how they score their runs. Here are some team figures from 1989 on scoring by event, and the percentage of total team runs. We list the five top teams in each event, and the single worst:

	Singles	Runs	%	**Doubles**	Runs	%	**Triples**	Runs	%
The Five Best	Royals	264	38	Red Sox	131	16	Pirates	36	5
	Red Sox	262	34	Cardinals	119	18	Cubs	32	4
	White Sox	262	37	Giants	117	16	Giants	30	4
	Yankees	262	37	Rangers	114	16	Cardinals	28	4
	Rangers	242	34	Mariners	113	16	White Sox	27	3
Worst	Giants	186	26	Phillies	70	11	Dodgers	7	1

	Homers	Runs	%	**Sac Flies**	Runs	%	**Sac Hits**	Runs
The Five Best	Blue Jays	237	32	Athletics	61	8	Cubs	10
	Giants	233	33	Red Sox	58	7	White Sox	9
	Padres	213	33	Twins	58	7	Brewers	6
	Reds	211	33	Brewers	54	7	Dodgers	4
	Angels	211	31	Blue Jays	53	7	Giants	4
Worst	Cardinals	116	18	Giants	39	5	4 with	0

Things *are* changing: the top five teams in scoring on singles were all American League clubs, while three of the top four in scoring on homers played in the National. The swifter NL still leads the way in scoring on triples, however, taking four of the five top spots.

Scoring on sacrifice hits, of course, means squeeze plays, and the two Chicago teams are the master of those, with 31 percent of the major league total between them. Other unusual methods of scoring in 1989:

- There were 31 steals of home, 22 of them, surprisingly, in the American League. The Brewers stole home six times, easily the highest total in the majors.
- A total of 55 runs scored on balks, well down from the 133 in balk-happy 1988.
- There were 243 runs scored on wild pitches. The Mets led in this category with 16, and apparently lost numerous contests waiting for that "clutch wild pitch" to bring home the game-winner.
- Double play grounders scored 112 runs, 11 of them hit by the Cardinals. Whitey Herzog will take a run whatever way he can get it.

A complete listing for this category can be found on page 238.

WHICH PLATOONS WERE IN COMPANY "A"?

Once considered controversial, platooning two players at one position is now an accepted part of baseball strategy. Combinations such as Woodling-Bauer, Lowenstein-Roenicke and Dykstra-Wilson often worked in tandem to outperform all but the biggest stars at their positions. But though still very popular, platooning took it on the chin in 1989 — at least in terms of forging effective combinations. As usual, many teams alternated a lefty and a righty at one position or more. But all too many platoons were like San Francisco's right field combo of Pat Sheridan and Candy Maldonado, one notorious for its lack of production.

What follows is a listing of the most effective platoon combinations of 1989. The requirements were two players sharing a position for at least half the year, with one ordinarily going against lefties and the other versus righties. And both players had to make offensive contributions. The stats given are the players' totals only when playing that position:

Chicago Cubs — LF	AB	H	HR	RBI	Avg
Dwight Smith	242	71	5	26	.293
Lloyd McClendon	134	42	7	25	.313

Both players started the season in the minors, so this combination didn't develop until well into the season. Both players also played other positions; their full-season stats add up to a .307 average, 21 homers and 94 RBIs in 602 at bats, the sort of numbers Woodling and Bauer would have been proud of. The two turned a Cub weakness into one of its strengths, and their play was a vital factor in Chicago's division championship.

California Angels — RF	AB	H	HR	RBI	Avg
Claudell Washington	375	104	12	36	.277
Tony Armas	155	41	6	19	.265

This was not a classic platoon, since Washington sometimes played against lefties. But the two were used often enough as a platoon to qualify for our rankings, and they were unquestionably very effective. Armas, whose career seemed finished a couple of years ago, has forged a role for himself as an effective platooner.

Toronto Blue Jays — C	AB	H	HR	RBI	Avg
Ernie Whitt	345	94	11	51	.272
Pat Borders	174	46	2	20	.264

A longtime productive platoon since Borders took over from Buck Martinez, it's now broken up with Whitt's trade to Atlanta. An original Blue Jay, Whitt had 13 seasons as a top-level platoon player for the same club, a stint of longevity we believe unprecedented.

Minnesota Twins — RF	AB	H	HR	RBI	Avg
Randy Bush	224	60	7	24	.268
Carmen Castillo	151	43	7	24	.285

The stats here underrate the contributions of these two veteran platooners, since, like Smith-McClendon, both also played other positions. Overall the pair hit .262 with 22 homers, 87 RBIs and 63 walks in 609 at bats, quietly helping a Twin offense that was the second best in baseball. These two are the type of player Earl Weaver would love.

Seattle Mariners — LF	AB	H	HR	RBI	Avg
Greg Briley	314	81	11	43	.258
Henry Cotto	150	39	3	15	.260

Like Smith-McClendon, this platoon didn't develop until well into the year, when Briley came up from the minors to take the place of the slumping Mickey Brantley. Briley had excellent numbers for a rookie, and Cotto, always a good defensive player, has finally become a useful hitter.

Surprisingly, that's about it for effective 1989 combinations. There were others like Dave Magadan-Tim Teufel (1B-Mets), Joe Orsulak-Mike Devereaux (RF-Orioles) and Jeff Treadway-Jeff Blauser (2B-Braves) that had some good numbers, but really didn't play enough as a platoon to make our rankings. As we said before, many clubs platooned last year, but not too many platooned effectively. Often they were combinations like Montreal's Dave Martinez-Otis Nixon and Tom Foley-Damaso Garcia platoons, where one player did good work while the other struggled. No one had more trouble than the Giants' Roger Craig, who platooned in both right field (Sheridan-Maldonado) and at catcher (Terry Kennedy-Kirt Manwaring) and got almost no production from any of the four. Craig fortunately had powerful hitters at other positions, but most managers were not so lucky.

WHICH UMPIRES ARE OFFENSIVE?

There's a lot of talk in baseball circles about "pitcher's umpires" and "hitter's umpires," but no one ever lets us in on the secrets of distinguishing between the two. So, we've had to come up with our own methods. The chart lists what we call "Dream Crews," one for pitchers and one for hitters, based on the number of runs scored per nine innings for home plate umpires. There are more differences — huge differences — as the tables on the next page indicate (minimum 20 games behind the plate for each ump).

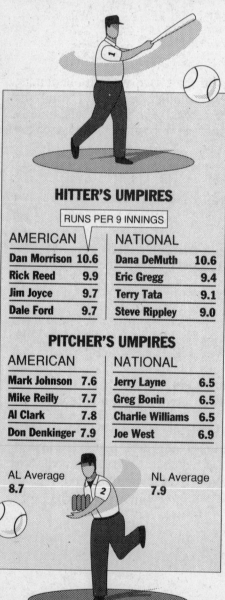

HITTER'S UMPIRES
RUNS PER 9 INNINGS

AMERICAN		NATIONAL	
Dan Morrison	10.6	Dana DeMuth	10.6
Rick Reed	9.9	Eric Gregg	9.4
Jim Joyce	9.7	Terry Tata	9.1
Dale Ford	9.7	Steve Rippley	9.0

PITCHER'S UMPIRES

AMERICAN		NATIONAL	
Mark Johnson	7.6	Jerry Layne	6.5
Mike Reilly	7.7	Greg Bonin	6.5
Al Clark	7.8	Charlie Williams	6.5
Don Denkinger	7.9	Joe West	6.9

AL Average 8.7   NL Average 7.9

The strike zone is supposed to be universal — remember how they made a big deal of the "new strike zone" that the rulesmakers came up with in 1988? And yet the differences between umpires is fairly amazing, especially considering that they're carefully picked and all come from the same one or two umpire schools. With National League umpire Dana DeMuth working the plate last year, the average hitter batted about like Tim Raines. But when rookie Jerry Layne was working, the same hitters looked like Raines's slumping teammate Mike Aldrete.

Since DeMuth and Layne are both fairly young umpires (DeMuth has been around for six years), one might wonder whether there's an evening out among umps who've been around a long while. This does seem to be the case. Bob Engel, Doug Harvey, John Kibler and Harry Wendelstadt have all worked between 24 and 28 years in the National League. (Kibler is now retired.) There were some real differences between them, but on the whole the vets tended to slightly favor the pitcher. Larry Barnett, Don Denkinger, Larry McCoy and Dave Phillips are the senior American League arbiters, with between 19 and 21 years each. There are some real differences between them as well — Denkinger, in particular, very much favors the pitcher — but the rest of the group has a slight but not extreme pitchers' bias. The big differences tend to be among the younger umps.

The most "average" umpire in the major leagues seems to be Larry Young, a five and a half year veteran. In every category — batting average, on-base and slugging percentages, runs per game, strikeouts and walks — Young's figures are right around the American League average. We watch numerous games around the STATS office, and yet Young has made almost no impression on us. There's a cliche about umps that goes: you know he did a great job if you never even noticed him. In Young's case, that seems to be true.

American League

	Batting Average		Slugging Average		Strikeouts per Nine Innings	
Top Three	Tim Tschida	.281	Dan Morrison	.417	Steve Palermo	11.8
	Jim McKean	.280	Tim Tschida	.412	Dale Scott	11.8
	Ken Kaiser	.279	Jim Joyce	.406	Joe Brinkman	11.6
Bottom Three	Mark Johnson	.248	John Hirschbeck	.367	Durwood Merrill	10.4
	Steve Palermo	.248	Ted Hendry	.359	Dave Phillips	10.1
	Don Denkinger	.247	Greg Kosc	.355	Rick Reed	10.0

National League

	Batting Average		Slugging Average		Strikeouts per Nine Innings	
Top Three	Dana DeMuth	.283	Dana DeMuth	.417	Terry Tata	12.9
	Paul Runge	.258	Bruce Froemming	.390	Bob Davidson	12.9
	Dutch Rennert	.256	Paul Runge	.388	Ed Montague	12.5
Bottom Three	Charlie Williams	.230	Joe West	.336	Bruce Froemming	10.7
	Joe West	.226	Charlie Williams	.329	Charlie Williams	10.3
	Jerry Layne	.222	Jerry Layne	.317	John McSherry	10.3

A complete listing for this category can be found on page 239.

HOW DO TEAMS PERFORM IN THE LATE INNINGS OF CLOSE GAMES?

Crunch time comes in the late innings of a close game, when a key hit can mean the difference between victory and defeat. About 30 percent of all major league games last year were decided by one run, meaning that either team could have won with a strong performance at the finish. If the Red Sox (13-25 in one run games) had performed as well as the Padres (30-18), Boston would have won the American League East. Here are the late-and-close statistics for each team during 1989:

Team	Hitting			Pitching		
	AVG	HR	RBI	AVG	HR	RBI
Baltimore	.243	16	97	.234	14	84
Boston	.269	17	111	.248	20	105
California	.222	15	76	.233	18	102
Chicago	.265	9	103	.253	24	100
Cleveland	.216	18	89	.250	21	109
Detroit	.215	17	96	.272	18	99
Kansas City	.280	17	111	.225	12	90
Milwaukee	.255	12	84	.275	18	90
Minnesota	.287	24	118	.260	16	108
New York	.271	20	114	.296	20	108
Oakland	.237	18	94	.219	16	90
Seattle	.236	24	93	.273	13	102
Texas	.257	16	94	.238	17	97
Toronto	.255	19	118	.240	15	114
AL Average	.250	17	100			
Atlanta	.217	19	96	.261	19	124
Chicago	.239	14	79	.237	21	106
Cincinnati	.242	18	110	.232	14	100
Houston	.233	23	115	.214	14	83
Los Angeles	.222	12	76	.238	13	93
Montreal	.250	21	122	.262	21	110
New York	.230	27	88	.234	18	93
Philadelphia	.240	17	102	.228	14	79
Pittsburgh	.230	15	96	.239	23	123
St. Louis	.257	8	96	.233	13	100
San Diego	.259	16	106	.225	23	92
San Francisco	.254	19	99	.233	16	90

NL Average	.236	17	99	.236	17	99
MLB Average	.243	17	100			

In close contests both hitting and pitching are important, but a mound staff which can stop the opposition seems to be the crucial element. Last year the best American League teams in one-run games were the A's, Angels and Royals; those three teams also had the lowest opponents' batting averages in the late innings of close games. (The Angels had one of baseball's best records in one run games despite only a .222 late-and-close batting average on offense.) Three other American League pitching staffs held opponents to a batting average of .240 or less (Orioles, Rangers, Blue Jays); all had winning records both in one-run and extra-inning games. The top two National League clubs in one-run games were the Padres and Astros; those two teams also had the best late-and-close mound staffs. The Cardinals and Giants also stopped the opposition in the late innings (opponents' BAs of .233) and had strong records in one-run games.

Before we get carried away, we should point out that there are some exceptions to this generalization. The Phillies' mound staff was outstanding in close games (.228 BA), but had only a 20-23 one-run record. On the other hand, Twin pitchers were strictly mediocre in late-and-close games (.260), but Minnesota's late-inning attack was so strong (.287) that they had one of the best won-lost records in those games. The Cubs also did well in one-run games despite a pitching staff that, by National League standards, was mediocre in the late innings (.237).

On the whole, major league hitters have a lot of trouble in late-and-close situations. The major league average in these situations last year was only .243, a full 11 points under the leagues' overall .254 mark.

A complete listing for this category can be found on page 240.

WILL THE DOME LIFT THE JAYS TO THE SKIES?

Ballplayers moving to a new park after a trade face numerous adjustment problems. Often they'll take half a year or so to get used to their new park's dimensions. But what happens when a whole ballclub moves during the middle of a season? For the Toronto Blue Jays, the move from Exhibition Stadium to the SkyDome last June couldn't have gone much better. Not only did the Jays draw fans in record numbers, but they played so well that they won a division title. Now the Jays hope they can follow the example of the 1970 Reds. Cincinnati moved from Crosley Field to Riverfront Stadium in the middle of the season, won a pennant that fall . . . and went on to chalk up six division championships, four league titles and two World Series wins before the seventies were over.

Toronto's upswing was notable because Exhibition Stadium and the SkyDome are two very different ballparks. Here are offensive figures recorded by the Blue Jays and their opponents in Toronto home games during 1988 and '89:

	Avg	OBP	Slg	R/G	HR/G	K/G	BB/G
Exh (4/88 to 6/4/89)	.261	.328	.399	8.80	1.69	11.27	6.55
Sky (6/5/89 on)	.247	.311	.379	7.47	1.53	10.22	6.13

Exhibition Stadium was a fairly neutral park during its last years, ranking in the middle of the spectrum in its effect on runs and batting average, but a little above average in home runs. Based on its 55-game sample from '89, the SkyDome looks like it's going to be one of the best pitchers' parks in the majors. The home run rate at the Dome was right around the league average, but that's probably because the Jays, a fine home run team, were playing there. In truth the Dome will probably turn out to be a below-average home run park, and a very bad park for scoring and batting average. One effect noted by Tony Kubek was that pitchers became more aggressive. They stayed in the strike zone more and just let the batter hit the ball; the result was that both the walk and strikeout rate declined.

Here are comparisons in both parks for four key Toronto hitters. The Exhibition Stadium figures, once again, are from the start of 1988 until the move last year:

		Avg	OBP	Slg	HR/G	K/G	BB/G
Bell	Exh	.292	.331	.457	0.12	0.38	0.25
	Sky	.318	.356	.475	0.09	0.30	0.23
Fernandez	Exh	.277	.329	.378	0.03	0.39	0.31
	Sky	.238	.285	.359	0.04	0.33	0.28

		Avg	OBP	Slg	HR/G	K/G	BB/G
Gruber	Exh	.276	.331	.401	0.07	0.62	0.27
	Sky	.292	.297	.454	0.13	0.45	0.06
McGriff	Exh	.267	.372	.534	0.22	0.84	0.55
	Sky	.275	.411	.560	0.25	0.67	0.75

While the overall effect of the Dome was to penalize hitters, it didn't seem to hurt sluggers Bell, Gruber and McGriff. On the whole, their figures actually got better in the new park. Tony Fernandez's numbers declined, but a lot of that may have been due to the fact that he was still recovering from an early-season beaning.

Happily for the Jays, the Dome also had a positive effect on three of the four top Toronto pitchers:

		Avg	OBP	Slg	ERA	HR/G	K/G	BB/G
Cerutti	Exh	.267	.318	.417	3.34	0.94	0.86	2.50
	Sky	.255	.305	.361	2.11	0.59	3.64	2.35
Henke	Exh	.215	.314	.349	2.83	1.09	10.45	4.35
	Sky	.218	.238	.327	1.95	0.65	13.99	0.98
Key	Exh	.259	.286	.399	3.57	0.70	4.09	1.13
	Exh	.289	.319	.462	4.65	0.75	5.15	1.63
Stieb	Exh	.214	.294	.316	3.55	0.60	6.11	3.16
	Sky	.162	.259	.262	1.29	0.64	5.14	3.70

In the Dome Cerutti, Henke and Stieb all went from good pitchers to great ones — at least during the last four months of '89. Key went the other way, but like Fernandez, he was injured much of the year.

The SkyDome figures were, of course, based on a small sample. But the overall outlook for the Jays is very good. We'll monitor the figures again this year and perhaps keep an eye on something else: how the park differs when the Dome is open or closed. Here's Toronto's 1989 won-lost record based on whether the Dome is open or closed:

1989 SkyDome Games	Dome Status	Toronto Record
Regular Season	Open	29-19
	Closed	10-0
	Closed during Game	2-0
Playoffs	Closed	1-2

DO HITTERS SPEND MOST OF THEIR TIME JUST STANDING AROUND?

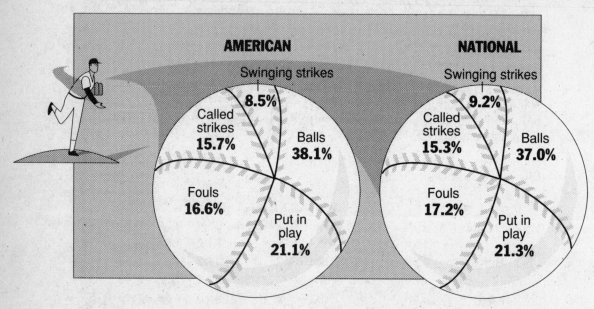

Major League hitters make contact on less than 40 percent of all pitches thrown to them. More than half the time, the hitter is sitting in the batter's box hoping the pitch will be called a ball. And if your name is Rickey Henderson, you stand with your bat on your shoulder for over 70 percent of all pitches. The above chart shows a breakdown of all plate appearances, with some interesting results. You'll note from the chart that an average strike/ball ratio (each pitch swung at is considered a strike) would be about three to two. A pitcher with a two-to-one ratio is doing a good job; one closer to the 50-50 point is apt to have a rough time, and especially likely to walk a lot of batters. That's something to keep in mind when you hear a pitch breakdown during a broadcast.

Here are the league leaders in each of the categories:

American League

Pitch Result	Pitcher	%	Hitter	%
Ball	Charlie Hough, Tex	42.0	Rickey Henderson, Yanks-Oak	49.0
Called Strike	Frank Tanana, Det	19.8	Rickey Henderson, Yanks-Oak	22.0
Swing Strike	Nolan Ryan, Tex	14.1	Bo Jackson, KC	22.4
Fouls	Bret Saberhagen, KC	23.5	Gary Gaetti, Min	22.5
In Play	Jerry Reuss, WSox-Mil	27.0	Ozzie Guillen, WSox	31.1

National League

Pitch Result	Pitcher	%	Hitter	%
Ball	Don Carman, Phi	42.5	Jack Clark, SD	46.8
Called Strike	Rick Sutcliffe, Cubs	18.8	Tony Gwynn, SD	21.5
Swing Strike	Mike Scott, Hou	14.3	Dale Murphy, Atl	15.3
Fouls	Don Robinson, SF	21.4	Garry Templeton, SD	24.0
In Play	Derek Lilliquist, Atl	25.6	Andres Thomas, Atl	29.2

There are some unique individuals among the leaders. It's no surprise that Henderson and Jack Clark are the leaders in taking pitches for balls; each is traditionally among his league's walk leaders. It's no shock, either, that Nolan Ryan and Mike Scott make the batters swing and miss more than any other pitcher, though it is surprising that Mike is even tougher than Nolan. But we wouldn't have guessed that the winners of the Luke Appling trophy — for most foul balls — would be Gaetti and Templeton. And it's a total puzzle that Tony Gwynn topped the NL in pitches taken for strikes. How was that possible for a hitter who seldom either walked (only 40 unintentional BB) or struck out (30 Ks)?

One interesting thing about the "Pitcher" and "Hitter" columns is that, in every case but one, the leading hitter has a higher percentage than the leading pitcher. No pitcher gets more called balls or called strikes than Rickey Henderson does as a hitter. As much as Mike Scott makes hitters swing and miss, that's still not as much as Dale Murphy fans the air against National League pitchers. (Bo Jackson is on a planet of his own in this category, as he is in so many others.) And as easy as Jerry Reuss' pitches are for hitters to put in play, Ozzie Guillen puts pitches in play even more often. What does all this mean? That the hitter is more responsible for the outcome of a plate appearance than the pitcher is. Those who argue that pitching is 80 percent of baseball, or some other foolish figure, will have a hard time explaining these results.

A complete listing for this category can be found on page 241.

WHICH TEAMS BUNT MOST IN THE EARLY INNINGS?

Despite considerable evidence that they're costing their clubs runs, some teams continue to lay down bunts in the early innings. Here's a chart showing a breakdown of sacrifice hits by innings by the average team during 1989:

Sacrifice Hits by the Average Team

Inning	1	2	3	4	5	6	7	8	9	10+	Total
AL	4.4	2.9	5.9	3.7	6.6	5.4	8.6	6.9	4.7	3.0	51.9
NL	3.7	8.0	10.9	6.3	10.5	7.0	9.1	7.9	6.7	4.8	74.9
Total	4.0	5.2	8.2	4.9	8.4	6.1	8.8	7.3	5.6	3.8	62.5

The chart seems to indicate that National League clubs bunt much more often than AL clubs, and that a lot of sacrifices are laid down as early as the second or third inning. However, that's a little deceptive. An inordinate number of bunts are laid down by National League pitchers, who will often be pinch hit for in the later frames. So let's revise the chart by eliminating the ninth hitter from consideration:

Sacrifice Hits by the Average Team
(With #9 hitter eliminated)

Inning	1	2	3	4	5	6	7	8	9	10+	Total
AL	4.4	2.4	3.9	2.6	4.6	4.1	6.4	5.6	3.4	2.4	39.6
NL	3.6	1.4	2.0	1.7	2.3	3.8	5.0	6.0	5.6	4.5	35.8
Total	4.0	1.9	3.0	2.2	3.5	4.0	5.7	5.8	4.4	3.4	37.9

The late innings, as would figure, are the most popular for sacrificing — at that point in a game, one run will often mean victory. But what's surprising is that with the ninth hitter eliminated, the higher-scoring American League clubs actually sacrifice more than their National League counterparts. That's something we didn't expect.

Individual managers, of course, have widely differing views on how to use the sacrifice bunt. Here's another chart comparing club sacrifices by innings.

Sacrifices by Inning
(excluding the #9 hitter)

Team	1	2-4	5-7	8+	Total
Baltimore	3	14	15	5	37
Boston	5	8	14	12	39
California	7	7	16	14	44
Chicago	11	14	22	21	68

Sacrifices by Inning
(excluding the #9 hitter)

Team	1	2-4	5-7	8+	Total
Cleveland	11	7	22	17	57
Detroit	2	4	12	11	29
Kansas City	0	8	11	13	32
Milwaukee	4	11	18	10	43
Minnesota	4	10	16	12	42
New York	4	17	18	11	50
Oakland	3	4	7	7	21
Seattle	0	4	7	8	19
Texas	5	9	24	12	50
Toronto	2	6	9	7	24
Atlanta	3	3	14	10	30
Chicago	3	8	12	13	36
Cincinnati	4	3	9	15	31
Houston	2	5	11	23	41
Los Angeles	1	3	15	17	36
Montreal	3	5	4	19	31
New York	0	2	9	8	19
Philadelphia	2	2	8	9	21
Pittsburgh	6	7	11	20	44
St. Louis	4	6	7	14	31
San Diego	14	5	13	30	62
San Francisco	1	12	20	15	48

Gene Mauch was famous for the strategy known as "little ball" — playing for one run even in the first inning. Mauch's legacy is kept alive by Jeff Torborg, Jack McKeon and the currently-unemployed Doc Edwards. Those were the only skippers to have more than ten first-inning sacrifices last year. On the other hand, John Wathan's Royals, Dave Johnson's Mets and Jim LeFebvre's Mariners didn't have any. A manager's background often plays a large part in how he'll view the sacrifice, and Johnson was clearly influenced by playing under the bunt-hating Earl Weaver. But Torborg and LeFebvre, who hold opposing views toward the sac hit, both played for Walt Alston's light-hitting Dodgers. Lifelong Dodger Tommy Lasorda, meanwhile, won't bunt much early, except with his pitchers. But Lasorda will sacrifice quite often in the later frames.

A complete listing for this category can be found on page 242.

WHICH PLAYERS HAD THE BIGGEST CHANGE IN PERFORMANCE FROM 1988 TO '89?

Some players' careers are like the stock market, with the figures wildly fluctuating up and down. Often there's a good reason for a dramatic advance or decline — an injury or the recovery from an injury, personal problems, a new attitude that results from a trade. Young players sometimes mature overnight; older players can simply lose it. Here are the players who improved and declined the most in batting average from 1988 to '89 (minimum 251 plate appearances each year):

IMPROVED MOST	1988	1989	Change
Ivan Calderon, WSox	.212	.286	+.074
John Kruk, SD-Phi	.241	.300	+.059
Fred Manrique, WSox-Tex	.235	.294	+.059
Tony Phillips, Oak	.203	.262	+.059
Carney Lansford, Oak	.279	.336	+.057
Howard Johnson, Yanks	.230	.287	+.057
Steve Jeltz, Phi	.187	.243	+.056
Greg Brock, Mil	.212	.265	+.053
Ruben Sierra, Tor	.254	.306	+.052
Willie Randolph, LA	.230	.282	+.052

DECLINED MOST	1988	1989	Change
Ron Gant, Atl	.259	.177	-.082
John Shelby, LA	.263	.183	-.080
Kirk Gibson, LA	.290	.213	-.077
Wally Backman, Min	.303	.231	-.072
Alan Trammell, Det	.311	.243	-.068
Rance Mullinicks, Tor	.300	.238	-.062
Jody Davis, Atl	.230	.169	-.061
Vance Law, Cubs	.293	.235	-.058
Cory Snyder, Cle	.272	.215	-.057
Dave Henderson, Oak	.304	.250	-.054

Recovering from injury in 1989 were Calderon, Brock, Phillips and Randolph; injured and suffering were Gibson, Backman and Trammell. A trade seemed to revive John Kruk, the lack of a trade (and a big new contract) helped Howard Johnson. Carney Lansford was aided by the arrival of Rickey Henderson, though he was hitting pretty well even before the A's obtained Rickey. Ruben Sierra arrived as a great player at age 24 in '89; Steve Jeltz and Fred Manrique simply looked like new players. (Can that continue?)

Some of the decliners have no easy excuses for their big drop in 1989. Squarely on the hotseat this year are John Shelby, Rance Mullinicks and Jody Davis, veterans who have slipped badly. Each of them will have to show something quickly in the spring if they expect to get much playing time. Vance Law has slipped even farther, all the way to Japan — Vance's biggest 1990 adjustment may involve getting used to being referred to as "Vance Raw." Dave Henderson had a good '89 even hitting .250, which is more his norm anyway. And anyone who can figure out how to revive Ron Gant and Cory Snyder should call Atlanta or Cleveland.

The following pitchers showed the biggest change in ERA from 1988 to '89 (minimum 81 IP each year):

IMPROVED MOST	1988	1989	Change
Bert Blyleven, Cal	5.43	2.73	-2.70
Frank DiPino, StL	4.98	2.45	-2.54
Ted Power, StL	5.91	3.71	-2.20
Willie Fraser, Cal	5.14	3.24	-2.17
Mark Williamson, Bal	4.90	2.93	-1.96
Neal Heaton, Pit	4.99	3.05	-1.94
Todd Stottlemyre, Tor	5.69	3.88	-1.81
Bud Black, Cle	5.00	3.36	-1.64
Bret Saberhagen, KC	3.80	2.16	-1.64
Chuck Finley, Cal	4.17	2.57	-1.60

DECLINED MOST	1988	1989	Change
Danny Jackson, Cin	2.73	5.60	+2.87
Wes Gardner, Bos	3.50	5.97	+2.47
Dave LaPoint, Yanks	3.25	5.62	+2.37
Brian Holton, Bal	1.70	4.02	+2.32
Dave Schmidt, Bal	3.40	5.69	+2.29
Don August, Mil	3.09	5.31	+2.22
Lance McCullers, Yanks	2.49	4.57	+2.08
Bob Knepper, Hou-SF	3.14	5.13	+1.99
Charlie Leibrandt, KC	3.19	5.14	+1.95
Mike Henneman, Det	1.87	3.70	+1.83

The "improved most" category includes some real comeback stories, especially Blyleven, Black, Power and DiPino. Several of the others are young pitchers who are maturing. For pitchers like Stottlemyre and Finley, the improvement is expected to be permanent. But who would have thought Bret Saberhagen, who wasn't bad in '88, would be one of the most improved pitchers in 1989? The frail Saberhagen has yet to have two solid years in a row and is unlikely to maintain his '89 form. But you never know.

The pitcher whose performance declined the most, Danny Jackson, was injured in '89, and so was Mike Henneman. But most of the others find their careers in jeopardy, especially LaPoint, Schmidt, Knepper and Leibrandt, who are aging finesse pitchers — a group that tends to lose it in a hurry. The others are young enough to come back, although Don August, a soft thrower, probably pitched over his head in '88 and is a long shot to come all the way back.

One noticeable thing about the "improved most" category is the presence of three California Angel pitchers. In each case some improvement was understandable: Blyleven had been injured in 1988, and Fraser and Finley were talented young pitchers who suddenly matured. But there was another factor at work, the presence of new California manager, Doug Rader. Rader had also produced dramatic improvement in several pitchers during his rookie season at Texas, 1983:

PITCHER	1982	1983	Change
Rick Honeycutt	5.27	3.03	-2.24
John Butcher	4.87	3.51	-1.36
Dave Stewart	3.81	2.60	-1.21
Mike Smithson	5.01	3.91	-1.10
Frank Tanana	4.21	3.16	-1.05

Honeycutt and Stewart's figures include their work for the Rangers and Dodgers in '83 — they were traded for each other in midseason. Each had much lower ERAs pitching for Rader than they did for L.A. that year (Honeycutt was a league-leading 2.42 before the trade, then 5.77 with LA; Stewart was 2.96 with the Dodgers before the deal, then 2.14 after arriving in Texas).

I don't know what it is about Rader, a former third baseman, but he seems to have a knack for turning pitchers around. It's no exaggeration to say he turned around the careers of Honeycutt and Tanana, who'd gone 5-17 and 7-18, respectively, in 1982. Smithson, who was 28 and had appeared in only eight major league games before 1983, and Butcher, who'd won five games in three years before Rader's arrival, were traded to the Twins after the '83 season and continued to win in double figures for a couple of seasons. The only one who slid back after 1983 was Stewart, and that was mostly due to Dave's personal problems. Whatever Doug Rader does with pitchers, it seems to have a lasting positive effect.

WHAT WERE THE FASTEST GAMES IN THE MAJORS LAST YEAR?

Draw up any list of frequently-heard complaints about baseball, and right near the top would be, "The games are too darn long." It's an old complaint, one voiced even in the early fifties, when the average nine inning game took less than two hours and fifteen minutes. As you can see, the situation's getting worse:

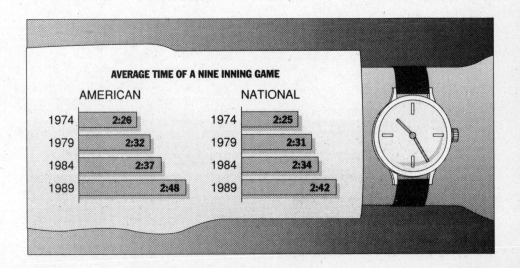

American League games tend to be longer because they're higher-scoring. About the only chance for a fast game these days is a low-scoring pitchers' duel. Only nine major league games took less than two hours in 1989, and five of them were 1-0 or 2-1 games. As you can see, your chances of getting home early last year were greatly enhanced if Tom Browning was on the hill:

Date	Site	Score (Starting Pitcher)	Time
7/4	Phi	Reds 2 (Browning), Phillies 1 (Mulholland)	1:44
6/29	Cin	Braves 2 (Clary), Reds 1 (Browning)	1:48
9/17	Hou	Astros 1 (Portugal), Reds 0 (Browning)	1:49
10/1	Bos	Red Sox 5 (Dopson), Brewers 1 (Navarro)	1:50
4/27	Chi	Cubs 1 (Maddux), Dodgers 0 (Hershiser)	1:55
6/17	Cle	Indians 4 (Bailes), Royals 3 (Gubicza)	1:56
5/31	Atl	Braves 3 (Smoltz), Cubs 2 (Kilgus)	1:56
9/27	LA	Dodgers 1 (Belcher), Giants 0 (Garrelts)	1:56
10/1	Phi	Phillies 5 (Combs), Expos 3 (B. Smith)	1:58

Obviously, the starting pitcher is the key to a fast game, though the current vogue of the hitter stepping out of the batter's box after every pitch doesn't help much. (Neither do those ever-increasing television commercials.) And the catcher is also important, as anyone who's watched the s-l-o-w pace of Carlton Fisk would know. But the manager probably plays as important a role as anyone. Some skippers, like Bobby Valentine, prefer a leisurely pace. Others, like the exiled Pete Rose, push the pace along. Here are the average times of nine inning games for each of the major league teams. You'll notice some big differences:

American League		National League	
Team	Time	Team	Time
Cle	2:38	Cin	2:34
KC	2:41	Atl	2:38
Min	2:43	SD	2:39
Sea	2:45	SF	2:41
Cal	2:47	Pit	2:42
Mil	2:47	LA	2:43
Oak	2:47	StL	2:43
Tor	2:48	Hou	2:44
NY	2:50	Phi	2:44
Bos	2:51	Chi	2:45
Det	2:52	NY	2:46
Chi	2:54	Mon	2:47
Bal	2:57		
Tex	2:57		

Bobby Valentine's Rangers were involved in the longest nine inning game last year, a 9-6 victory over the Tigers which took a tedious four hours and six minutes; the starting pitchers in that game were Charlie Hough and Jack Morris, who are old enough to know better. We're glad you won, Bobby, but should it take that long to beat the Tigers? As fans who love baseball but don't like to spend our *entire lives* watching it, we salute Tom Browning and hope other pitchers — and managers, too — will emulate this winner's brisk pace.

Here's the box score for the fastest major league game of 1989:

July 4 At Philadelphia (N)

Cincinnati	ab	r	h	bi	Philadelphia	ab	r	h	bi
Harris, 3b	4	1	0	0	Dykstra, cf	4	0	0	0
Daniels, lf	4	1	2	1	Herr, 2b	3	0	0	0
Winningham, lf	0	0	0	0	V. Hayes, rf	3	0	0	0
Larkin, ss	4	0	1	0	Jordan, 1b	3	0	0	0
Davis, cf	3	0	0	0	Ready, lf	3	0	0	0
O'Neill, rf	4	0	0	1	C. Hayes, 3b	3	0	0	0
Benzinger, 1b	4	0	0	0	Thon, ss	3	1	1	0
Quinones, 2b	3	0	2	0	Lake, c	3	0	0	0
Diaz, c	2	0	1	0	Mulholland, p	2	0	0	0
Browning, p	3	0	0	0	Jeltz, ph	1	0	1	1
Franco, p	0	0	0	0					
Totals	31	2	6	2	Totals	28	1	2	1

Cincinnati   200 000 000—2
Philadelphia 000 000 001—1

Cincinnati	IP	H	R	ER	BB	SO
Browning (W, 7-6)	8.1	2	1	1	0	4
Franco (Save 22)	0.2	0	0	0	0	0

Philadelphia	IP	H	R	ER	BB	SO
Mulholland (L, 1-3)	9	6	2	2	4	5

E-Thon. DP-Cincinnati 1, Philadelphia 1. LOB-Cincinnati 8, Philadelphia 0. 2B-Daniels, Quinones, Thon. SH-Browning. HBP-by Mulholland (Quinones). T-1:44 A-14,636.

A complete listing for this category can be found on page 243.

WHICH TEAMS BLOW THE MOST LEADS IN THE LATE INNINGS?

Over a decade ago, when Nolan Ryan was still with the Angels, the California press department started trumpeting the "ahead after seven" statistic. The gist of it was that Ryan was so invincible in the late innings that when leading after seven, his won-lost record was 84 and 5, or something like that. The Yankee publicity men soon picked up on the idea and used the same stat to demonstrate the invincibility of relievers Goose Gossage and Ron Davis.

We should have known better, but most of us accepted these stats at face value; after all, it was easy enough to believe in any numbers which indicated how Ryan and Gossage were Supermen. It wasn't until a few years later that Bill James, that old spoilsport, took a thorough look at the subject. Bill discovered that *everybody* had an overwhelming record when ahead after seven. The figures for 1989 show that the average major league club wins ninety percent of its games when leading after seven innings. But some records are a little more overwhelming than others:

American League

Team	Ahead after 7 inn.			Behind after 7 inn.			Tied after 7 inn.		
	W	L	Pct	W	L	Pct	W	L	Pct
Orioles	72	5	.935	6	62	.088	9	8	.529
Red Sox	70	5	.933	4	63	.060	9	11	.450
Angels	75	8	.904	7	55	.113	9	8	.529
White Sox	54	7	.885	4	76	.050	11	9	.550
Indians	60	7	.896	5	68	.068	8	14	.364
Tigers	40	6	.870	9	85	.096	10	12	.455
Royals	71	4	.947	6	58	.094	15	8	.652
Brewers	68	5	.932	5	70	.067	8	6	.571
Twins	64	7	.901	10	70	.125	6	5	.546
Yankees	63	5	.927	7	77	.083	4	5	.444
Athletics	90	4	.958	3	52	.055	6	7	.462
Mariners	61	9	.871	6	70	.079	6	10	.375
Rangers	68	9	.883	9	62	.127	6	8	.429
Blue Jays	69	9	.885	9	57	.136	11	7	.611
League Total	925	90	.911	90	925	.089	118	118	.500

National League

Team	Ahead after 7 inn.			Behind after 7 inn.			Tied after 7 inn.		
	W	L	Pct	W	L	Pct	W	L	Pct
Braves	52	9	.852	3	74	.039	8	14	.364
Cubs	79	9	.898	5	55	.083	9	5	.643
Reds	56	4	.933	6	73	.076	13	10	.565
Astros	63	9	.875	12	62	.162	11	5	.688
Dodgers	62	6	.912	6	65	.085	9	12	.429
Expos	65	5	.929	11	64	.147	5	12	.294
Mets	73	7	.913	6	58	.094	8	10	.444
Phillies	51	5	.911	6	82	.068	10	8	.526
Pirates	60	9	.870	5	64	.072	9	15	.346
Cardinals	67	8	.893	6	62	.088	13	6	.650
Padres	69	4	.945	9	63	.125	11	6	.647
Giants	79	7	.919	7	54	.115	6	9	.400
League Total	776	82	.904	82	776	.096	112	112	.500

The data shows that there's not a lot of difference between the best clubs and the worst. The lead group (Royals, Athletics, Reds and Padres) lost only four games when leading after seven innings last year; the bottom group (Mariners, Rangers, Braves, Cubs and Pirates) lost nine. Five games a year is nothing to sneeze at, and in truth the difference between the best teams and the worst is much greater than that in many seasons. But among other things, you wonder why the Royals, with a .947 percentage when ahead after seven, were so hot to get Mark Davis. Why didn't they go after some hitters who could help them *get* ahead after seven?

The other two columns show much more variance. In a separate essay we show you that the Twins were the highest scoring team in the late innings last year. The late punch helped them win 10 games when trailing after seven, the most in the AL. The National League Astros (12) and Expos (11) won even more than that. On the other hand, the world champion A's only won three games all season when trailing after seven innings, the same number as the Atlanta Braves. That figure indicates that you don't have to be a come-from-behind team to be a great one. Oakland's philosophy was simple: bludgeon the opponent in the early and middle innings, then turn the game over to Dennis Eckersley. With an invincible bullpen that lost only 11 games all year when tied or leading after seven, the A's didn't need to do any more than that.

Two clubs that really had problems in the late innings were the Braves and Pirates. Pittsburgh lost 24 games in which they were leading or tied after seven innings, Atlanta 23. Not much would have helped salvage the

Braves' season, but the same isn't true of Pittsburgh. The average National League club last year lost 16 games when tied or leading after seven. If the Pirates had met even that modest standard, they would have gone 82-80 instead of 74-88 — a considerable difference. So while we emphasize that you can make too much of late-inning statistics, it's obvious that this one can tell you a few things about a club's strengths and weaknesses.

WHO WANTS TO PLAY LEFT FIELD?

Every team starts a season with optimism; each position has one regular or a two-man platoon penciled in. But sometimes those well-intentioned plans end in disaster. Four 1989 teams went to the revolving door, using at least seven players a significant amount of time (ten or more games each) at a single position. Each team fell short of expectations, and the "problem position" was a key reason. Here are the league average for the position, the team's average for the position (both based on 600 plate appearances), and the stats for the key players at that position only:

Dodgers — Left Field	Avg	OBA	Slg	AB	HR	RBI
National League average in LF	.268	.347	.420	527	15	64
Dodgers LF (total players - 11)	.272	.338	.410	537	13	58
Kirk Gibson	.215	.310	.375	200	8	22
Mickey Hatcher	.312	.358	.450	109	2	11
Lenny Harris	.282	.292	.366	71	1	6

As defending World Champions, the Dodgers figured that one slot was solid — left field, where MVP Kirk Gibson cavorted. Unfortunately, Gibson spent 1989 cavorting on the trainer's table, and the Dodgers wound up using 11 left fielders . . . all but one of whom hit better than Gibson. Thanks to Mickey Hatcher (.312), Lenny Harris (.282), Kal Daniels (38 AB, .342), Franklin Stubbs (51 AB, .333), Mike Davis (51 AB, .314), Chris Gwynn (36 AB, .278) and Jose Gonzalez (4 AB, .500), the Dodgers out-hit the league batting average, and got close to the other league figures for the position. Mariano Duncan (4 AB, .250), Mike Huff (18 AB, .222) and Billy Bean (25 AB, .200) didn't quite work out. But overall, Los Angeles was satisfied. They would have hoped for MVP-type production from a healthy Gibson, but the subs played well with Gibson out. The Dodgers are good at this. Back in 1953, they sold their left fielder, Andy Pafko, and then won three pennants in four years with guys like Sandy Amoros and Dick Williams patrolling the position. Who's up for 1990, Jack Nicholson?

Padres — Right Field	Avg	OBA	Slg	AB	HR	RBI
National League average in RF	.257	.326	.409	535	16	70
Padres RF (total players - 9)	.286	.361	.390	520	9	57
Tony Gwynn	.335	.405	.398	266	1	27
Chris James	.242	.276	.434	99	4	15
John Kruk	.190	.338	.286	63	2	5

"Moonlighting" was a terrific TV show, but less than a terrific idea for Padres right fielder Tony Gwynn. Gwynn spent much of 1989 moonlighting in center field, where he played well enough to win another Gold Glove and yet another batting title, but where his knees ached and he wasn't happy. The other Padres' right fielders didn't exactly take up the slack: both James (.242) and Kruk (.190) are now with other teams, as are Marvell Wynne (46 AB, .348) and Luis Salazar (27 AB, .333). Other 1989 right fielders were Bip Roberts (44 AB, .295), Jerald Clark (14 AB, .286) Jack Clark (36 AB, .111) and Shawn Abner (3 AB, .000). This is no way to win a pennant, and the Padres begin 1990 with Joe Carter in center and Gwynn returned to right field. Both Gwynn and the Padres hope "Moonlighting" is canceled for good.

Tigers — Third Base	Avg	OBA	Slg	AB	HR	RBI
American League average at 3B	.263	.330	.380	536	11	54
Tigers 3B (total players - 8)	.224	.283	.311	547	8	42
Rick Schu	.208	.271	.319	226	6	14
Doug Strange	.238	.306	.287	164	1	14
Chris Brown	.193	.203	.246	57	0	4

For years Sparky Anderson either won division titles or had winning Tigers ballclubs, and for the entire time the Tigers had a third baseman, Tom Brookens, who had the type of figures that drove sabermetricians crazy. So in 1989, Sparky went modern; he got rid of Brookens, and handed his third base job to a man of today, Chris Brown. Well, it didn't work; not only was Brown not one of Sparky's beloved "we" ballplayers, he didn't even hit as expected (.193). Alternatives such as Rick Schu (.208) and Doug Strange (.238) were almost as bad, as were Al Pedrique (25 AB, .240), Mike Brumley (22 AB, .227) and Torey Lovullo (33 AB, .182). Keith Moreland (33 AB, .333) and Mike Heath (2 for 3, 1 HR) did better, but all in all it made a fellow pine for Tom Brookens. Who'd have imagined it . . . or imagined that the Tigers would sink to last place?

White Sox — First Base	Avg	OBA	Slg	AB	HR	RBI
American League average at 1B	.269	.350	.430	524	18	77
White Sox 1B (total players - 7)	.257	.317	.397	540	14	75
Greg Walker	.253	.333	.407	150	4	16
Ron Kittle	.370	.426	.685	92	8	28
Ivan Calderon	.375	.420	.512	80	1	13
Steve Lyons	.160	.190	.247	81	1	8

The White Sox figured 1989 would have its problems, but they thought that first base wouldn't be one of them. Guess again. Greg Walker, long a solid performer, looked like he'd come back strongly from a frightening 1988 seizure. Walker strived mightily, but suffered a shoulder injury and couldn't regain his old form. The Sox found a surprisingly effective replacement in Ron Kittle (.370), but then Kittle himself was lost for the season with an injury. After that, manager Jeff Torborg went to that old Merv Griffin game, "Play Your Hunch." Billy Jo Robidoux (38 AB, .132) hit like Billy Jo Rope-a-Dope; Ivan Calderon hit like Jimmie Foxx (.375), but fielded like Dick Stuart; Carlos Martinez (83 AB, .217) and Russ Morman (56 AB, .196) neither hit nor fielded; and Steve Lyons didn't hit (.160), but entertained sleepy Sox fans by playing Tic-Tac-Toe with opposing first basemen. A Sox fan's plea for 1990: if you can't give us Kittle, Jeff, give us Tic-Tac-Toe!

WHAT ARE BASEBALL'S MOST AND LEAST COMMON PLAYS?

What do Alex Trevino, Bip Roberts and Julio Franco have in common? They were the three batters during baseball's least common play of 1989: they made it to first on an error after a dropped third strike. That did not necessarily make them better players than the Yankees' Steve Sax, who grounded out 236 times — the most common event of the year. The chart below lists the most and least common plays of 1989. It's sobering to note, that including foulouts, players popped out more than three times as often as they homered. Or that, in an age of streamlined gloves and manicured

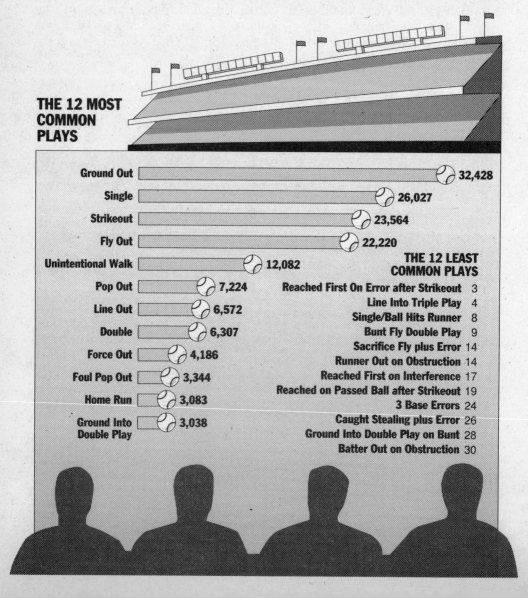

THE 12 MOST COMMON PLAYS

Play	Count
Ground Out	32,428
Single	26,027
Strikeout	23,564
Fly Out	22,220
Unintentional Walk	12,082
Pop Out	7,224
Line Out	6,572
Double	6,307
Force Out	4,186
Foul Pop Out	3,344
Home Run	3,083
Ground Into Double Play	3,038

THE 12 LEAST COMMON PLAYS

Play	Count
Reached First On Error after Strikeout	3
Line Into Triple Play	4
Single/Ball Hits Runner	8
Bunt Fly Double Play	9
Sacrifice Fly plus Error	14
Runner Out on Obstruction	14
Reached First on Interference	17
Reached on Passed Ball after Strikeout	19
3 Base Errors	24
Caught Stealing plus Error	26
Ground Into Double Play on Bunt	28
Batter Out on Obstruction	30

fields, there were 24 three base errors last year. And single/ball hits runner (eight times) — isn't that only supposed to happen in pinball?

We thought you might like to see the list of leaders in the most common plays of '89. The Yankees Steve Sax, who ruled both of the most popular categories, must be the obsessive-compulsive type:

Most groundouts	Steve Sax, Yanks	236
Most singles	Steve Sax, Yanks	171
Most strikeouts	Bo Jackson, KC	172
Most flyouts	Wally Joyner, Cal	155
Most unintentional walks	Rickey Henderson, Yanks-Oak	121
Most pop outs	Joe Carter, Cle	64
Most lineouts	Greg Jefferies, Mets	55
Most doubles	Wade Boggs, Bos	51
Most forceouts	Ozzie Guillen, WSox	32
Most foul pop outs	Cal Ripken, Bal	30
Most home runs	Kevin Mitchell, SF	47
Most grounded into DP	Julio Franco, Cle	27

This is a list of pretty good ballplayers ... proof, we guess, that if you're good at something, you keep doing it over and over again. In many cases, leading in one of the out categories is a dubious achievement — much as we love Joe Carter, we'd guess that there's not much value in being the best popper-upper in the major leagues. But all those groundouts from Sax probably pleased him; Steve knew that when he was in a groove, he kept hitting the ball on the ground. The result was that Sax also led the majors in singles while batting a solid .315.

The second least common play of '89 was lining into a triple play. That happened only four times, two of them with Cub hitters (Vance Law and Domingo Ramos) at bat. That was a strange way to drive toward a division title, but hey, it worked. (At least the Cubs never had three men on third, as the old Brooklyn Dodgers once did.) The Yanks' Steve Balboni and the Braves' Bruce Benedict were the other players to line into triple plays last year. Benedict and Law are no longer in the majors ... do you think Ramos and Balboni are hearing footsteps?

One uncommon play that a few players sometimes specialize in is reaching first on catcher's interference. Batters who swing late and stand deep in the batters' box might reach first a half dozen times a year when the the catcher accidentally tips their bat. But this play occurred only 17 times in 1989, and only two players, the Brewers' Jim Gantner and the Yanks'

Roberto Kelly, who did it twice, reached base more than one time this way.

A complete listing for this category can be found on page 244.

HOW RARE IS A TWO STRIKE HOMER?

Traditionally, hitters are supposed to "shorten their stroke" when the count gets to two strikes. The idea is that the batter has only one strike left, so he has to give in to the pitcher a little bit and just try to make contact. (They used to tell the hitter to choke up on the bat with two strikes. But that seems to have gone by the wayside . . . along with a lot of other things in baseball.) The gist of all that advice was that, with two strikes, the hitter should forget about trying to hit a homer.

We often hear that modern hitters ignore such council and swing from the heels whatever the count. The evidence suggests otherwise. Only 25.8 percent of all homers were hit with two strikes last year. That's far less than a normal distribution, which would be 33.3 percent. That figure caused us to wonder what sort of hitters buck the trend and hit a lot of two-strike homers. The following players were the 1989 leaders in two strike homers (minimum 10 homers):

Player, Team	– Home Runs –		
	Two Strike	Total	%
Tony Fernandez, Tor	7	11	63.6
Darrell Evans, Atl	6	11	54.5
Tom Brunansky, StL	10	20	50.0
Danny Tartabull, KC	9	18	50.0
Terry Pendleton, StL	6	13	46.2
Glenn Wilson, Pit-Hou	5	11	45.5
Hubie Brooks, Mon	6	14	42.9
Howard Johnson, Mets	15	36	41.7
Bobby Bonilla, Pit	10	24	41.7
Steve Balboni, Yanks	7	17	41.2

There's no one single trait that binds together this odd assortment of hitters. They fall into several groupings:

1. Occasional home run threats (Fernandez, Pendleton, Wilson, Brooks). Pitchers respect these hitters, but they're not afraid to challenge them, even with two strikes. These guys have the power to respond if the offering is too fat.

2. Hitters who take a lot of pitches (Evans, Johnson, Bonilla, Brunansky, Tartabull). These are selective hitters who aren't afraid to take a walk. They get an inordinate amount of at bats with two strikes, so it's no surprise that they hit a lot of two strike homers.

3. Wild swingers who don't get cheated no matter what the count (Balboni). Hey, the man seems to have started life with two strikes on him, so why is it a surprise that he does well in this category?

Among the big home-run hitters, we find varying percentages of two strike homers. Bo Jackson, Joe Carter and Darryl Strawberry, all of whom would fit nicely into group three, each hit between 34 and 38 percent of their homers with two strikes. Don Mattingly and Fred McGriff were right around the major league average of 25 percent; McGriff looked like a good candidate for group two, but he seems to shorten up with two strikes. Way down on the list of two-strike homer hitters were Mark McGwire, Glenn Davis and Kevin Mitchell — all less than 20 percent. It's possible they're unusually disciplined. But it's more likely that since there were no other viable home run threats batting behind these three for most of the season, pitchers simply refused to give them much to hit when the count got to two strikes.

The logical question to ask next is, what sort of pitchers allow a lot of two-strike homers? Managers go crazy over two-strike homers, since the pitcher is supposed to have an advantage. So you'd expect more inexperienced hurlers to dominate this list. They do, but not completely:

Player, Team	Two Strike	Total	%
Ken Patterson, WSox	6	11	54.5
Jim Abbott, Cal	7	13	53.8
Doug Drabek, Pit	10	21	47.6
Chuck Cary, Yanks	6	13	46.2
Bryan Clutterbuck, Mil	5	11	45.5
Ramon Martinez, LA	5	11	45.5
Bobby Ojeda, Mets	7	16	43.8
Mike Bielecki, Cubs	7	16	43.8
Bob Knepper, Hou-SF	7	16	43.8
Jerry Reuss, WSox-Mil	8	19	42.1

(HR Allowed)

Paterson, Abbott and Martinez were all raw rookies, so their lapses are understandable. Cary and Clutterbuck are a little older, but without a lot of major league experience. Ojeda, Knepper and Reuss are out-and-out finesse pitchers who usually just serve up the ball and say "hit it," no matter the count; in the cases of Knepper and Reuss, the batters usually did just that. The surprises on this list are Drabek and Bielecki. They're both very effective workmen who've been around a few years, but they're not finesse pitchers either. It's possible they suffered lapses of concentration with two strikes; we'll know more if they repeat (or eliminate) the pattern this year.

A complete listing for this category can be found on page 245.

WHICH TEAMS HAVE THE BEST BENCH PLAYERS?

In baseball's formative years, it was standard for a club to pick eight starting players and use them day after day until someone got injured. Platooning began creeping in around the time of World War I, but it was many years before it really became commonplace. These days platooning is accepted strategy, and with a longer schedule and coast-to-coast travel both causing wear and tear, every club has to depend on its bench players. But as the following table from 1989 shows, there's a lot of variance in how much teams use their benches:

USE STARTERS MOST				USE BENCH MOST			
Team	Starters AB	Bench AB	Starters %	Team	Starters AB	Bench AB	Staters %
Cardinals	4,420	707	86.2	Reds	2,975	2,221	57.3
Angels	4,490	1,055	81.0	Padres	3,163	1,882	62.7
Blue Jays	4,275	1,306	76.6	Braves	3,036	2,096	59.2

"Starters" would be defined as the most-used regular at each position. As you can see, the Cardinals had by far the most set lineup in the majors. St. Louis pretty much went with Guerrero-Oquendo-Pendleton-Smith in the infield, Coleman-Thompson-Brunansky in the outfield, and Pena behind the plate. Only one Redbird regular had fewer than 500 at bats, Tony Pena with 424. The only Cardinal bench hand to bat more than 120 times was Willie McGee, who had 199. The Reds, by contrast, had only one player, Todd Benzinger, who batted more than 500 times. Cincinnati got at least 100 at bats from no less than 17 different players.

While the Cardinals seem to like going with a set lineup, the teams in the "use bench most" column did not necessarily do so out of choice. All were losing teams who tried one combination after another in an attempt to play better ball. The Tiger starters, to use a good example, batted only .248, so Detroit felt forced to experiment.

A better way to compare starters vs. bench players would be in terms of overall effectiveness, rather than just usage. The following clubs had the best (and worst) starters or benches:

THE BEST STARTERS				THE BEST BENCHES			
Team	Avg	OBP	Slg	Team	Avg	OBP	Slg
Red Sox	.288	.368	.432	White Sox	.267	.331	.374
Twins	.287	.338	.427	Red Sox	.257	.321	.349
Cubs	.282	.340	.430	Yankees	.257	.310	.377

THE WORST STARTERS				THE WORST BENCHES			
Team	Avg	OBP	Slg	Team	Avg	OBP	Slg
Dodgers	.245	.314	.350	Tigers	.222	.283	.319
Astros	.247	.319	.359	Braves	.226	.291	.335
Brewers	.251	.314	.379	Giants	.228	.275	.345

The Red Sox had the best offense in the American League last year, and you can see why: they got strong contributions from both their starters and bench players. The Cubs led the National League in scoring, but that was mainly due to their heavy-hitting starting lineup. Cub bench players hit only .248, with Lloyd McClendon (.286) the best among them. The need for more useful bench players was a key factor in Chicago's late-season deal for Luis Salazar and Marvell Wynne (although Salazar ended up as a regular), and their offseason trade for Dave Clark.

One can tell from looking at the figures that a good bench doesn't necessarily make for a good offense, and a weak bench doesn't doom a club's chances for success. The White Sox had the best bench corps in the majors, but finished last anyway. The Giants, meanwhile, won the National League pennant while having one of the weakest reserve corps in the majors. Having lost ace pinch-hitter Ken Oberkfell to free agency, the Giants will have to scrounge around to find better bench players in 1990.

One sign of a strong bench is a good pinch-hitting corps. This is especially true in the National League, where pinch-swingers are used so frequently to bat for the pitcher. There's a big difference in how teams fared last year in pinch roles. White Sox pinch-swingers batted a solid .282 last year; Tiger pinch-hitters managed only a .156 mark. The valuable Oberkfell batted .360 in pinch roles last year, with a major league-leading 18 pinch hits — why'd the Giants let him get away? Mark Carreon of the Mets had an even higher average (.370), including four pinch homers.

A complete listing for this category can be found on page 246.

ARE PITCHERS' THROWS TO FIRST A WASTE OF TIME?

In the era of the three-hour-and-twenty minute pitchers' duel, nothing seems to make a contest drag on like those endless throws to first any time a swift runner reaches base. "Speed slows down the game," says Tim McCarver, and he's right: put Rickey Henderson on base, and everything stops while the pitcher toes the rubber, scowls toward first, fakes a throw, steps off, scrapes the rubber again, and finally makes a half-dozen futile tosses to the first baseman. The batter, meanwhile, yawns . . . the fans fall asleep . . . the writers miss their deadlines. And then Rickey steals second anyway. Or so it seems.

At the risk of encouraging pitchers like Rick Sutcliffe — who seems to make 30 or 40 pickoff tosses every time Vince Coleman gets on base — our data show that throwing to first really does work. While pickoff tosses don't stop the top thieves from stealing, they decidedly decrease the runners' chances of stealing successfully. We looked at players with 40 or more stolen bases in 1989 and separated their second base steal attempts between times when the pitcher made at least one throw to first, and times in which no pickoff tosses were made. The difference was startling: when the pitcher made his presence known at least once, the success rate for the top stealers dropped from 89 to 65 percent. For all baserunners, the success rate dropped from 73 to 63 percent when the pitcher threw to first. Here are the figures for the top base stealers:

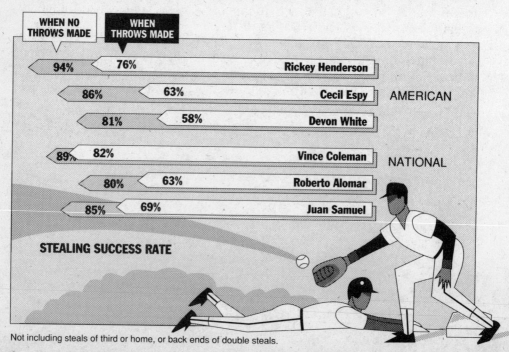

	WHEN NO THROWS MADE	WHEN THROWS MADE		
Rickey Henderson	94%	76%	AMERICAN	
Cecil Espy	86%	63%		
Devon White	81%	58%		
Vince Coleman	89%	82%	NATIONAL	
Roberto Alomar	80%	63%		
Juan Samuel	85%	69%		

STEALING SUCCESS RATE

Not including steals of third or home, or back ends of double steals.

Some additional detail:

	No Throws Made			Throws Made		
American League	SB	CS	%	SB	CS	%
Rickey Henderson, Yanks-Oak	33	2	94	19	6	76
Cecil Espy, Tex	12	2	86	26	15	63
Devon White, Cal	13	3	81	18	13	58
Steve Sax, Yanks	20	2	91	12	8	60
Gary Pettis, Det	17	0	100	19	15	56
National League	SB	CS	%	SB	CS	%
Vince Coleman, StL	25	3	89	23	5	82
Roberto Alomar, SD	16	4	80	19	11	63
Juan Samuel, Phi-Mets	23	4	85	18	8	69
Howard Johnson, Mets	24	3	89	14	3	82
Tim Raines, Mon	18	0	100	11	7	61
Tony Gwynn, SD	22	5	81	10	11	48
Totals (Top 11)	223	28	89	189	102	65
All Runners	1,401	526	73	1,175	681	63

Note: The figures don't include steals of third or home, or the back ends of double steals.

Interestingly, there were no exceptions among the top eleven stealers: each runner's success percentage decreased when a throw to first was made. Obviously, throwing to first, even only once, gets the runner leaning back to first a little — and that gives the catcher a much better chance to throw the man out. With a runner like Henderson on base, the pitcher would be well advised to make at least one toss to first before going to the plate, because Rickey often takes off on the first pitch.

Note to Rick Sutcliffe, whose mind is probably buzzing: there's no evidence that *repeated* throws to first will decrease the success percentage even more. One or two will suffice, buddy!

A complete listing for this category can be found on page 247.

DO GROUNDBALL HITTERS DO BETTER AGAINST FLYBALL PITCHERS?

One popular theory these days is that groundball hitters perform better against flyball pitchers. And that flyball hitters do better against groundball pitchers. The idea is that each type of hitter or pitcher performs better, as a general rule, against its opposite. Existing data on this, presented by The Elias Sports Bureau, is interesting, but incomplete in some areas. We'd like to take another look at the subject using data involving *all* major league batters and pitchers from 1989, with one exception — pitchers' batting, which we did not consider meaningful in a study such as this. Hopefully this study will shed a little more light on the situation.

We began by separating both hitters and pitchers into three groups: Groundball, Average and Flyball, depending on how extreme their groundout/flyout ratio is. We define a groundball batter or pitcher as one with a G/F ratio of 1.5 to one, a flyball batter or pitcher as one with a ratio of less than one, an average player as anyone in between. Because they depend on a fixed definition, the groups are not equal in size. In 1989 the average groups accounted for around half the at bats, the groundball groups around 30 percent, the flyball groups about 20 percent. These groups differ in skills; here is how they compared overall in 1989:

| | Avg | OBA | Slg | | — Opponent — | | |
					Avg	OBA	Slg
Groundball Batters	.264	.312	.351	Groundball Pitchers	.265	.315	.376
Average Batters	.257	.307	.387	Average Pitchers	.257	.304	.379
Flyball Batters	.248	.303	.414	Flyball Pitchers	.249	.305	.393

Out of these groupings, we have nine different matchups. Here they are, with 1989 data for batting, on base and slugging averages:

Matchup	Avg	OBA	Slg
Groundball Batter vs. Groundball Pitcher	.264	.310	.343
Average Batter vs. Groundball Pitcher	.265	.316	.382
Flyball Batter vs. Groundball Pitcher	.265	.319	.417
Groundball Batter vs. Average Pitcher	.267	.316	.354
Average Batter vs. Average Pitcher	.255	.300	.381
Flyball Batter vs. Average Pitcher	.245	.298	.414
Groundball Batter vs. Flyball Pitcher	.259	.308	.358
Average Batter vs. Flyball Pitcher	.252	.309	.406
Flyball Batter vs. Flyball Pitcher	.229	.292	.411

Let's look at the first group, groundball pitchers. The opponents' batting average against each kind of hitter are almost identical. But that's deceiving. Overall, flyball batters are much weaker hitters for average (.248) than groundball batters are (.264). They improve markedly when going against groundball pitchers, while the groundball batters' average declines against groundball pitchers. So it's indeed true that flyball batters do better against the "opposite" group, groundball pitchers.

Now let's look at the second group, average pitchers. This group has its most trouble with groundball hitters. Groundball batters hit .264 overall; they hit .267 against this group. Flyball batters hit .248 overall; they hit .245 versus this group. The slugging averages don't vary from how groundball and flyball batters normally perform.

Finally we come to flyball pitchers. This group has great success in lowering the batting averages of the "same-same" group, flyball batters. It lowers the batting averages of the groundball batters as well, but not nearly as much. However, flyball batters actually hit for more power against flyball pitchers than they do against pitchers overall. This is not apparent from the slugging averages because slugging averages include singles. The "power percentage" or isolated power (slugging average minus batting average) of flyball hitters overall is .166; the power percentage of flyball batters against flyball pitchers is .182. But considering how groundball and flyball batters perform overall, flyball pitchers do have more trouble against the opposite group, groundball batters.

In conclusion, we can say that pitchers do have more trouble against their "opposite" group. The difference is primarily in the area of batting average — flyball batters hit for power against whatever group they're matched against.

A complete listing for this category can be found on page 248.

WHICH STADIUMS PRODUCE THE MOST FOULOUTS?

If baseball were football, the Chicago Cubs would play on a 75-yard field, and people would rave about the great Chicago offense. (Think about it, Ditka.) Meanwhile the Houston Astros would play in a 140-yard cavern and everyone would think they had the greatest defense in the world. They don't, of course, but that's the NFL's loss. Unlike football stadiums, ballparks don't have the same dimensions. The left field wall at Fenway entices hitters in the same division where Death Valley at Yankee Stadium destroys dreams. It's not "fair"; it's baseball.

And in baseball, foul isn't fair either. In some parks the seats are on top of the action, in others they're a mile away. As people finally have some understanding of the effects of fair territory — that Wrigley Field is not the Astrodome, in other words — they at least have a grasp on the fact that foul territory varies as well. But these effects are still somewhat misunderstood. Ask a knowledgeable fan which park produces the most foulouts, and he'll almost certainly say, "Oakland"; ask him which yard produces the fewest, and "Fenway" will be the answer.

We keep track of foulouts, and the common perceptions are not quite right. We rank ballparks for foulouts in the same way Bill James does park factors for run scoring. The idea is to total the number of foulouts recorded in each team's home park (by both the home club and the visitors) and compare that with the number recorded by the same team and its opponents in its road games. Then we divide the home total by the road total and round it off to the nearest one percent. Doing it that way eliminates any bias that would be caused by a club whose pitching staff produces a more (or less) than-normal amount of foulouts; we're comparing ratios here, not raw totals. A park factor higher than 100 means it has a more than normal amount of foulouts; a factor less than 100 means that it has fewer than normal. Here are foulout park factors for each of the 26 clubs, based on data from the last three seasons (1987- '89):

FOULOUT PARK FACTORS, 1987-1989

Team	Foulouts Home Games	Foulouts Road Games	Park Factor	Team	Foulouts Home Games	Foulouts Road Games	Park Factor
Detroit	572	425	135	San Diego	389	399	97
San Fran.	555	431	129	NY Mets	435	460	95
Oakland	531	422	126	St. Louis	422	452	93
Minnesota	556	465	120	Cincinnati	406	443	92
Los Angeles	531	453	117	Cleveland	414	457	91
Seattle	525	456	115	Chi. W. Sox	397	464	86
Atlanta	495	429	115	NY Yankees	359	419	86
Pittsburgh	452	395	114	Texas	365	422	86
Kansas City	441	417	106	Toronto	398	465	86
Milwaukee	409	394	104	California	357	419	85
Philadelphia	430	424	101	Boston	379	465	82
Montreal	437	435	100	Chi. Cubs	343	437	78
Baltimore	449	456	98	Houston	411	554	74

Ballparks with high park factors should tend to favor the pitcher, at least in the sense of reducing the total number of hits. And parks with low factors would be expected to produce higher batting averages. Tiger Stadium has always been an outstanding home run park, so people tend to think it's great for hitters. But as far as batting average is concerned, Detroit has had one of the best pitchers' parks in the majors in recent years. Candlestick and the Oakland Coliseum are also notorious for their negative effects on batting average ... which makes the performance of Will Clark last year all the more impressive.

The rest of the chart, however, is a little bit murky. Would anyone suspect that the Astrodome, and not Wrigley or Fenway, produces the fewest foulouts? It's not as strange as it seems. The Astrodome is very tough on homers and extra base hits in general. But its negative effect on batting average, while definite, is not nearly so great. The Houston park is clearly a lot tougher on fair balls than fouls.

The Astrodome and Tiger Stadium are clearly exceptional parks, however. In general the older stadiums (Fenway, Wrigley, Comiskey, Cleveland) don't have much foul territory and don't produce many foulouts. But six of the top eight park factors belong to parks that are (or were, in the case of Oakland) used for both football and baseball.

HOW DOES TEMPERATURE AFFECT OFFENSIVE PRODUCTION?

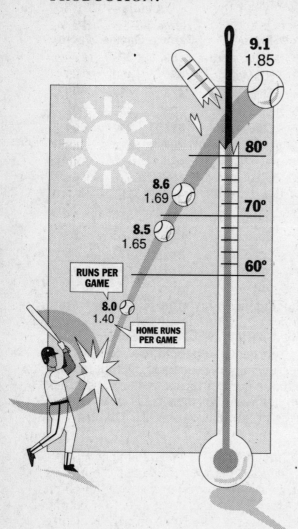

To put it bluntly, the higher the temperature, the hotter the bats. We have recorded the temperature for well over 3,800 games since 1987. Measuring offensive production against temperature for those three years (both leagues) we get:

Temp.	BA	Runs*	HRs*
90+	.263	9.1	1.83
80-89	.263	9.1	1.85
70-79	.259	8.6	1.69
60-69	.253	8.5	1.65
<60	.248	8.0	1.40

* per game

As you can see, the relationship is clear. With one slight exception, all the key aspects of offense increase as the temperature rises. That exception, for games when the temperature is 90 or above, is partly explained by the fact that the sample for those games is smaller, partly by the fact that so many of them are games involving one team, the Texas Rangers. Nonetheless the generalization holds: heat equals hitting.

Most affected, by far, is home run production. Over 30 percent fewer four-baggers are belted in cool (59-degree or lower) weather than are hit when it's in the eighties. Ever wonder why hitters have usually faded late in the year when making a run at sixty homers? In good part it's because any challengers to Ruth and Maris not only have to deal with the pressure, but have to fight the elements as well. In cool September weather, the ball simply doesn't travel as far.

This data has a couple of other implications. One is that we shouldn't get too excited when a new season starts out with a spate of low-scoring, cold-weather games: that's the norm, not the exception. Ordinarily the hitters will dominate the warm weather months. Late in the year, the hurlers reassert themselves — think of Orel Hershiser's performance in September of '88. Postseason games tend to be low-scoring, pitcher-dominated contests, the '89 World Series notwithstanding. Cool weather, especially in October night games, may be the biggest single reason for this.

On the other hand, pitchers should beware when the springtime is unusually hot and sultry. That was the case in 1987, the year of the home run. It may or may not be true that the ball was livelier that year. One thing not in dispute is that the warm weather was a major factor in that season's offensive explosion. So if you're a fan who likes offense, just wait a few years. The "Green-House" effect — discovered by Gene Green and Frank House, two bullpen catchers of the 1950s — states that temperatures will rise significantly in the next century. If the theory is true, we'll have more weather patterns similar to 1987 . . . and more long seasons for pitchers. Global warming may have some serious negative effects for the planet as a whole, but it's going to make a lot of sluggers very happy.

A complete listing for this category can be found on page 249.

WHICH TEAMS PERFORM BEST WITH RUNNERS IN SCORING POSITION?

Batting

Performance with runners in scoring position is crucial, because a hit with a runner on second and/or third will almost always score a run. There should be a strong correlation between the teams which are successful with runners in scoring position and those which score the most runs. In general, there is. But, as a look at last year's averages with runners in scoring position shows, the relationship is not quite perfect:

American League	BA	OBA	SLG	HR	Runs
Brewers	.283	.351	.407	29	707
Red Sox	.281	.365	.404	28	774
White Sox	.276	.342	.384	23	693
Yankees	.270	.347	.370	24	698
Royals	.267	.352	.378	27	690
Rangers	.266	.337	.387	26	695
Athletics	.264	.340	.375	28	712
Orioles	.261	.356	.389	34	708
Angels	.261	.328	.376	27	669
Blue Jays	.260	.337	.394	36	731
Twins	.259	.333	.385	32	740
Mariners	.257	.328	.375	25	694
Tigers	.240	.324	.331	21	617
Indians	.228	.321	.330	23	604

National League	BA	OBA	SLG	HR	Runs
Cubs	.277	.359	.385	16	702
Cardinals	.273	.355	.396	19	632
Expos	.261	.370	.386	24	632
Pirates	.261	.363	.386	17	637
Giants	.257	.358	.418	38	699
Braves	.257	.349	.373	21	584
Astros	.257	.349	.368	20	647
Reds	.253	.355	.411	36	632
Mets	.251	.342	.383	30	683
Phillies	.250	.338	.374	29	629
Padres	.241	.336	.384	38	642
Dodgers	.231	.331	.350	24	554

The most surprising team is the Brewers, who only ranked sixth in scoring despite their mighty .283 RSP batting average. Milwaukee's problem is that they were far more effective in this specialized situation than they were overall. The Brewers' ranked below the league average in batting, on-base and slugging percentages; that was too big a burden to overcome.

Similarly the White Sox, suffering from a lack of power, had an ineffective attack despite hitting .276 with ducks on the pond. On the other hand, the power-hitting Mets and Padres had relatively good offenses despite poor marks in this category; they simply slugged their way to a lot of runs. Hitting with runners in scoring position, we conclude, is important, but not the only key to an effective attack.

Pitching

Here's how the 26 pitching staffs ranked against opposing hitters with runners in scoring position. We include their overall ERAs for comparison purposes:

American League	BA	OBA	SLG	HR	ERA
Athletics	.230	.319	.320	17	3.09
Angels	.232	.309	.316	20	3.28
Indians	.254	.321	.363	22	3.65
Royals	.254	.325	.359	19	3.55
Brewers	.254	.325	.380	37	3.80
Rangers	.260	.353	.356	23	3.91
Blue Jays	.264	.331	.384	25	3.58
Mariners	.264	.351	.384	27	4.00
Orioles	.265	.350	.382	31	4.00
White Sox	.266	.326	.392	33	4.23
Red Sox	.268	.343	.378	27	4.01
Twins	.273	.340	.405	30	4.28
Tigers	.277	.377	.408	34	4.53
Yankees	.307	.386	.448	38	4.50

National League	BA	OBA	SLG	HR	ERA
Dodgers	.222	.323	.338	24	2.95
Mets	.236	.331	.363	28	3.29
Cubs	.239	.333	.346	21	3.43
Expos	.239	.328	.375	28	3.48
Giants	.240	.317	.383	35	3.30
Padres	.250	.340	.380	29	3.38

National League	BA	OBA	SLG	HR	ERA
Braves	.252	.332	.367	23	3.70
Astros	.252	.348	.359	19	3.64
Reds	.258	.353	.371	29	3.73
Pirates	.259	.352	.390	34	3.64
Cardinals	.260	.349	.386	22	3.36
Phillies	.271	.377	.400	27	4.04

Once more there is a sound relationship between success in this category and preventing scoring. But that relationship is not quite perfect. The Cardinals, to use the most obvious example, had the fourth best ERA in the National League despite ranking 11th with men in scoring position. St. Louis's key was that they kept the ball in the park, allowing a major-league low 84 home runs.

The Yankees' wretched .307 opponents' batting average with men in scoring position was the worst mark in recent memory. No club has approached it in the six years we've been keeping the figure, not even during the hit-happy '87 campaign.

A complete listing for this category can be found on page 250.

DOES THE PURPOSE PASS PAY OFF?

Nothing distinguishes one manager from another like his opinions about the intentional walk. Sparky Anderson and his "vacation" replacement, Dick Tracewski, ordered 91 intentional passes last year; the Angels' Doug Rader ordered 19. In the National League the intentional walk is more popular, primarily because it's often used to bring the pitcher to the plate. But Pete Rose and Tommy Helms of the Reds called for 105 intentional walks in '89, Davey Johnson of the Mets only 45.

The philosophy of the intentional walk is to get an advantage by working to a weaker hitter. Ordinarily there's a runner on second, or runners on second and third, and a dangerous hitter at the plate. Here are the average statistics of a 1989 intentional walk recipient (per 600 plate appearances):

Average Overall Statistics of Intentional Walk Recipients

	BA	HR	RBI
NL	.257	14	66
AL	.273	15	71
MLB	.263	15	68

The intentional walk recipient was a much more dangerous hitter than the average batsmen (NL ave .246-12-65, AL .261-13-71). Now here are the average season stats for the batter who would be coming up following the intentional walk (per 600 plate appearances):

Average Overall Statistics of the Batters Following An Intentional Walk

	BA	HR	RBI
NL	.224	10	57
AL	.254	13	66
MLB	.237	11	60

The batter for whom the intentional walk was set up is far less dangerous, especially when you consider that, more often than not, the pitcher has a platoon disadvantage versus the hitter being walked and and a platoon advantage against the next man. So in terms of bringing up a less dangerous batsmen, the move seems to make sense.

But does the batsman, out of extra determination or whatever, become more dangerous following the walk? Here are how these hitters actually performed in their at bats following an IW (again, per 600 plate appearances):

Results of At Bat Following an Intentional Walk

	BA	HR
NL	.239	10
AL	.309	10
MLB	.268	10

We eliminate the RBIs here because they're based on batting with two or three men on base and thus not comparable with the other situations. The average American League hitter, however, turns from a .254 to a .309 batter following the walk, though with reduced power. National League hitters decline in average, but remember that a great many of those are weak-hitting pitchers who become even weaker when the opposing hurler is really bearing down on them. Overall, the new hitter turned out to be better for average than the IW recipient was. He showed less home run power, but remember that there was an extra man on base because of the walk. Of course, situations vary, but as a general rule it's hard to see how the manager gains anything by this strategy. The exceptions would be when the walk recipient is much, much more dangerous than the following batter. From that point of view, the 32 intentional passes given Kevin Mitchell last year — ordinarily to get to guys like Candy Maldonado — make sense. But that situation, and walking a dangerous number eight man to get to a pitcher, are about the only sensible uses of the IW.

Because of the hitters who bat ahead of them (an especially dangerous hitter or a guy who bats from the opposite side), some players find themselves coming up a lot after an intentional walk. Here are the batters with ten-plus appearances after an IW last year and what they did:

Players with 10+ Plate Appearances after an IW

Player	PA	AB	H	HR	RBI	Avg
Craig Worthington	13	13	9	0	10	.692
Jeff Hamilton	12	11	5	1	11	.455
Jack Clark	15	12	5	2	11	.417
Kevin McReynolds	15	12	4	0	8	.333
Candy Maldonado	11	10	3	0	3	.300
Kevin Mitchell	11	10	3	1	5	.300
Jody Reed	11	7	2	0	4	.286
Mike Marshall	12	11	3	0	4	.273
Chris James	16	16	4	0	6	.250
Jose Lind	19	18	4	0	4	.222

Players with 10+ Plate Appearances after an IW

Player	PA	AB	H	HR	RBI	Avg
Tom Brunansky	10	9	2	0	2	.222
Glen Wilson	13	11	2	0	4	.182
Bo Jackson	10	9	1	0	2	.111
Matt Williams	10	10	1	0	1	.100
Jeff Leonard	13	12	0	0	1	.000

The number of at bats here is extremely small, so we can't make any dramatic conclusions. But this *is* a clutch-hitting situation of sorts. A hitter batting after an intentional walk almost always has two or three men on base, at least one of them in scoring position. And there's the added determination a batter is supposed to have after the "insult" of putting a runner on base to pitch to him. Jack Clark has always been known as a great clutch hitter, and Craig Worthington has had that reputation since his days in the middle minors. These figures do nothing to belie those reputations.

A complete listing for this category can be found on page 251.

DOES RUNNING AGGRESSIVELY MEAN MORE RUNS?

The Boston Red Sox led the major leagues in runs scored in 1989. And they really had to work at it, considering that they were also the major leagues' most conservative team on the bases. We looked at the number of extra bases on hits and outs each team took out of the number of chances they had, and discovered how incredible the Red Sox effort was:

AMERICAN	RUNS Rank	BASERUNNING Rank	PERCENTAGE*
Red Sox	1	14	38.8
Twins	2	3	44.7
Blue Jays	3	7	43.3
Athletics	4	1	46.2
Orioles	5	9	41.9
AL AVERAGE			42.9

NATIONAL	RUNS Rank	BASERUNNING Rank	PERCENTAGE*
Cubs	1	2	46.9
Giants	2	4	44.4
Mets	3	3	45.3
Astros	4	5	44.0
Padres	5	6	43.7
NL AVERAGE			44.3

* 'Percentage' represents how often baserunners take an extra base on a hit or an out per opportunity.

Despite the Red Sox performance, there is a good relationship between how aggressive a team is on the bases and how many runs they score. Boston was helped considerably by having over 200 more opportunities to advance than any other major league team. It makes a difference to have Wade Boggs and Ellis Burks and Dwight Evans to continually get on base for you, and Nick Esasky and Evans to drive them in.

Along with Boston's unbelievable figures, a couple of other things show up in the data. One is that National League teams are generally more aggressive than their American League counterparts. That would figure.

NL clubs tend to play in bigger parks where home runs are harder to hit. And without the DH, there is one less offensive weapon in the lineup. So the games tend to be lower-scoring, and the teams tend to take more chances in trying to manufacture runs. A curious exception to this rule is the Cardinals, managed by the normally-aggressive Whitey Herzog. With an attack revolving around sluggers Pedro Guerrero and Tom Brunansky, Herzog is sensibly showing more caution.

The other notable factor is that there is a strong managerial bias in this data. The American League team with the highest advance ratio was Oakland, led by Tony LaRussa; the leading National League team was Pittsburgh, managed by Jim Leyland, who was once LaRussa's third base coach with the White Sox. The number two and number four National League teams, the Cubs and Giants, were skippered by longtime colleagues Don Zimmer and Roger Craig. The third ranking National League team was the Mets, managed by Davey Johnson; the runnerup American League team, Texas, was led by Johnson's ex-coach Bobby Valentine.

Looking at this data must make the White Sox brass wince. Not only is this another category dominated by the crosstown Cubs, but back in 1983, the Sox had general manager Roland Hemond (now holding the same job in Baltimore), manager LaRussa, third base coach Leyland, and hitting coach Charlie Lau. Lau unfortunately passed away; the White Sox fired the others, and are now paying the price for their bad judgment.

A complete listing for this category can be found on page 252.

HOW DO TEAMS PERFORM VS. LEFTIES AND RIGHTIES?

Batting

In order to succeed, major league teams need to hit effectively against both left and righthanded pitching. Any weakness against either side will cause the opposition to save starting pitchers to exploit that weakness. Here are the top five teams in each league in batting average versus left and righthanded pitchers; you'll notice the world champion A's aren't really close to the top in either category. You'll also see that teams in general hit lefties better than they do righties (.259 overall vs. LHP, .252 vs. RHP):

Leading Teams vs. Lefthanded Pitchers

American League	BA	OBA	SLG	HR	W-L
Yankees	.298	.362	.427	42	30-28
Twins	.288	.341	.422	34	23-23
Brewers	.284	.342	.424	39	33-16
Red Sox	.279	.345	.296	28	21-21
A's	.266	.335	.389	33	32-14

National League	BA	OBA	SLG	HR	W-L
Cubs	.282	.346	.424	41	31-17
Expos	.272	.339	.410	43	27-18
Padres	.267	.340	.387	32	27-19
Astros	.257	.327	.375	31	27-21
Cardinals	.253	.314	.361	30	25-33

Leading Teams vs. Righthanded Pitchers

American League	BA	OBA	SLG	HR	W-L
Red Sox	.277	.354	.405	80	62-58
Twins	.271	.331	.393	83	57-59
White Sox	.270	.329	.388	68	46-56
Angels	.262	.317	.395	96	66-46
Blue Jays	.261	.327	.411	106	62-48

National League	BA	OBA	SLG	HR	W-L
Cardinals	.261	.326	.365	43	61-43
Cubs	.252	.309	.372	83	62-52
Giants	.250	.314	.389	92	56-50
Reds	.250	.310	.374	83	55-61
Mets	.246	.310	.389	96	54-48

It's apparent that there is no great relationship between batting effectiveness against left or righthanders and a good won-lost record. The Yankees — the best team versus lefties in the major offensive categories — had only a 30-28 record versus southpaws. It always helps to have a little pitching and defense to go along with the offensive power.

Pitching

As in the previous category, the good pitching staffs will ordinarily be good against both left and righthanded hitting. The Rangers and A's ranked one-two in the American League against both lefties and righties; the Angels were fifth against lefties, third against righties. In the National League, the Mets were second against lefties, first against righties, the Dodgers fourth vs. LHB, second vs. RHB. Here are the top teams in each league versus each type of hitting in 1989:

Leading Teams vs. Lefthanded Batting

American Lg.	BA	OBA	SLG	HR	National Lg.	BA	OBA	SLG	HR
Rangers	.224	.318	.333	48	Braves	.242	.316	.341	35
A's	.226	.300	.320	35	Mets	.242	.314	.359	37
Indians	.247	.312	.354	39	Expos	.243	.311	.363	52
Royals	.249	.311	.345	33	Dodgers	.246	.317	.341	41
Angels	.258	.311	.368	44	Pirates	.247	.324	.347	33

Leading Teams vs. Righthanded Batting

American Lg.	BA	OBA	SLG	HR	National Lg.	BA	OBA	SLG	HR
A's	.249	.309	.370	68	Mets	.225	.292	.342	78
Rangers	.249	.328	.370	71	Dodgers	.229	.291	.337	54
Angels	.250	.313	.355	69	Giants	.231	.287	.359	73
Red Sox	.252	.318	.378	74	Astros	.234	.303	.346	59
Blue Jays	.253	.307	.373	70	Cardinals	.234	.287	.354	51

The Rangers' dominance of the American League categories is a little deceptive. Texas held opponents to a .239 average, which tied them for first in the league with Oakland. But the Rangers walked 654 men, the most in baseball, and gave up 119 homers, a middling total. Ranger pitchers could blow away hitters, but gave away too many gifts.

In the National League, the dominance of the Dodgers and Mets is well documented. The Giants had the third best overall ERA, barely behind the Mets (3.30 to 3.29), but did so despite a relatively weak performance against lefthanded batters (.257).

A complete listing for this category can be found on page 253.

WHICH TEAMS RUN LATE?

One measure of managerial aggressiveness is a willingness to go for a stolen base in the late innings, when getting thrown out may rub out the tying or lead run. As these tables of 1989 steals by inning show, the success rate is high in the seventh, eighth and ninth . . . but the number of attempts is low:

Stolen Bases by Inning

American League	1	2	3	4	5	6	7	8	9	10+
Stolen Bases	277	131	218	179	189	168	161	150	79	35
Attempts	399	244	313	263	277	240	218	210	97	52
Success Percent	69	54	70	68	68	70	74	71	81	67

National League	1	2	3	4	5	6	7	8	9	10+
Stolen Bases	297	109	199	174	153	159	159	141	92	46
Attempts	413	199	291	249	239	235	223	201	126	68
Success Percent	72	55	68	70	64	68	71	70	73	68

Both Leagues	1	2	3	4	5	6	7	8	9	10+
Stolen Bases	574	240	417	353	342	327	320	291	171	81
Attempts	812	443	604	512	516	475	441	411	223	120
Success Percent	71	54	69	69	66	69	73	71	77	68

One can make several more observations from examining the tables. The attempt rate is highest in the first, which would figure, because that's the inning in which the best base stealers will almost certainly come to bat. Usually they're the leadoff men, and if they reach base, there are no outs and no one clogging the basepaths ahead of them. On the other hand, the success rate is lowest in the second, when the low-percentage stealers who bat in the middle of the lineup will most likely come up. In addition, teams will sometimes send a low percentage stealer in the second inning for lineup reasons. If the eighth hitter on a National League team is up, for example, a steal attempt is a low-risk situation. Even if the runner is tossed out, the club avoids having the pitcher lead off the next inning.

Here's a by-team breakdown of '89 stolen base attempts:

Steal Attempts By Inning

	1-3	4-6	7-8	9	10+	Total
Baltimore	67	58	37	7	4	173
Boston	34	29	24	4	0	91
California	46	52	26	0	5	129
Chicago	61	53	27	4	4	159
Cleveland	49	45	27	2	2	125
Detroit	68	51	16	14	4	153
Kansas City	91	76	20	9	9	205
Milwaukee	91	68	53	13	2	227
Minnesota	82	49	29	3	1	164
New York	84	60	36	14	3	197
Oakland	83	68	47	10	4	212
Seattle	50	51	28	5	2	136
Texas	67	51	21	6	5	150
Toronto	83	69	37	6	7	202
Atlanta	63	43	20	5	6	137
Chicago	96	57	27	10	3	193
Cincinnati	80	59	31	20	9	199
Houston	75	64	48	16	3	206
Los Angeles	55	46	26	2	6	135
Montreal	73	74	48	24	11	230
New York	86	66	44	11	4	211
Philadelphia	60	58	33	2	3	156
Pittsburgh	86	87	34	10	7	224
St. Louis	85	57	50	12	5	209
San Diego	85	64	39	8	7	203
San Francisco	59	48	24	6	4	141

In the late innings, the most aggressive teams by far were the Reds and Expos. Those two clubs were responsible for 23 percent of all the ninth inning steals last year. What's interesting is that each club was both very aggressive and very successful. That suggests that other teams might do well to take more chances at the end of a game.

The height of conservatism was represented by the California Angels. Though the Halos were slightly above the American League average in stolen base percentage, they attempted no steals at all in the ninth inning. That was despite the fact that California played 54 one-run games, most in the American League.

A complete listing for this category can be found on page 254.

WHICH IS THE BEST DIVISION IN BASEBALL?

Hard as it is to believe, it's the American League West, the division once described by Bill James — and accurately so — as "the third world of baseball." In 1979, the Oakland Athletics went 54-108 and drew only 306,000 fans, an attendance figure right out of the 1930s. A decade later, the A's won the World Championship and drew 2.7 million. In baseball, at least, the meek have inherited the earth.

In didn't happen overnight, either for the A's or the division. After playing punching bag for the AL East for much of the 1980's, the West started punching back. On a steady climb since hitting bottom in 1983 (with a slight downturn in 1986), the West posted an all-time high winning percentage against their Eastern cousins in 1989, culminating in Oakland's title:

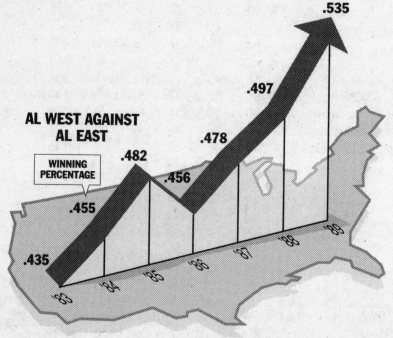

How did the turnaround take place? It was a combination of good fortune and good management. The dominant American League East teams of the early eighties — the Yankees, Orioles and Tigers — all either drafted poorly, made free agent signings that didn't pan out, or gave away a lot their best players in foolish trades. The clubs that were supposed to take up the slack — the Blue Jays, Brewers and Red Sox — haven't really done so. The void at the top was made to order for teams like the A's, which have been managed brilliantly. Of course, it didn't hurt that the A's and most of the other western clubs were getting a crack at the best draft choices.

With the AL West flexing its muscles, there's been comment in baseball circles that the talent is moving westward — toward warmer climates, newer ballparks and affluent, enthusiastic fans. If that were the case, we'd expect to see a similar upturn in the fortunes of the National League. Here's how the NL West has fared against the NL East over the same period:

NL WEST AGAINST NL EAST

Year	1983	1984	1985	1986	1987	1988	1989
Percentage	.528	.456	.483	.497	.434	.499	.495

While the American League West has made steady progress, its National League counterpart has basically stagnated, not winning over half of the interdivisional games since 1983. Still, there are hopeful signs. The Dodgers won the world championship in 1988, and the Giants reached the World Series in '89; that was the first time the West won back-to-back pennants since 1978. In addition, the Padres now look like a force to be reckoned with. While it's way too early to toss in the towel on clubs like the Cubs, Mets and Cardinals, the West in both leagues is clearly on the rise.

A complete listing for this category can be found on page 255.

DOES ARTIFICIAL TURF PRODUCE MORE GROUNDBALL HITS?

A common criticism of artificial turf, one often voiced by broadcaster Tony Kubek, is that it produces numerous phony hits. (Kubek has assumed the posture held by Frankie Frisch in Tony's day: nothing good has happened in baseball since I retired.) If artificial turf does indeed help the hitter, more groundballs should become hits on turf than they do on grass. With our database, we can measure whether this is actually the case.

We counted the number of groundballs hit at each stadium last year, the number of grounders that became base hits, and then divided the two figures to create a "groundball hit percentage." We rated the parks in our usual way: by counting both teams' data in the club's home park, and comparing that with the total recorded by both teams in the club's road games. This eliminates a bias that would be created by groundball pitching staffs or infielders of varying skill. Based on 1989 data, here is the groundball hit percentage in each team's home park (for both teams), the GBH percentage in the team's road games (again, both teams), and the difference between the two figures. If artificial turf produces more groundball hits, turf parks should produce the greatest positive difference:

		% GB Hits to Groundballs		
Team	Surface	Home	Road	Difference
Cincinnati	Turf	24.6	20.6	+4.0
Minnesota	Turf	24.1	20.7	+3.4
NY Yanks	Grass	25.2	22.3	+2.9
Seattle	Turf	23.5	21.3	+2.2
Houston	Turf	23.1	21.2	+1.9
Kansas City	Turf	24.5	22.8	+1.7
NY Mets	Grass	23.4	21.8	+1.6
Montreal	Turf	22.6	21.3	+1.3
Philadelphia	Turf	23.0	22.1	+0.9
Texas	Grass	23.5	22.8	+0.7
Cleveland	Grass	21.5	21.1	+0.4
Oakland	Grass	21.6	21.3	+0.3
Baltimore	Grass	22.6	22.5	+0.1
Milwaukee	Grass	21.6	21.5	+0.1
Chicago Cubs	Grass	23.5	23.5	+0.0
California	Grass	21.9	22.0	-0.1
San Diego	Grass	22.6	23.0	-0.4
Los Angeles	Grass	22.6	23.1	-0.5

San Francisco	Grass	19.2	20.6	-1.4
Toronto	Turf	19.6	21.9	-2.3
Atlanta	Grass	21.7	24.1	-2.4
Pittsburgh	Turf	21.0	23.4	-2.4
St. Louis	Turf	21.4	23.8	-2.4
Boston	Grass	22.0	24.9	-2.9
Chicago W. Sox	Grass	22.5	25.4	-2.9
Detroit	Grass	18.9	22.9	-4.0

The data shows that most turf parks indeed produce more groundball hits. Five of the top six parks, and seven of the top nine in the rankings, are artificial turf stadiums. Meanwhile the bottom three parks are all grass fields.

However, this difference isn't universal, and in any case it isn't overwhelming. Three of the ten turf parks (Toronto, Pittsburgh and St. Louis) actually have *negative* biases. And in most instances the home/road difference is fairly small. In the most extreme case, Cincinnati, the four percent difference would produce about an eleven point increase in batting average. But the Cincinnati difference is unusually high. Overall the turf parks produced an average groundball hit increase of only 0.8 percent — a difference that would add only two points to the park batting average.

So if turf parks produce more groundball hits — and it appears they do — the overall advantage is slight. Turf doesn't help a hitter nearly as much as the friendly confines of Wrigley helps home run hitters, or as much as the caverns of the Astrodome hurts them. If we're supposed to rip up the plastic grass to be more fair, shouldn't we first tear down the wall at Fenway?

And another thing. Our data strongly indicates that groundskeepers in grass stadiums can produce as great a negative effect on hits as any turf stadium produces a positive one. The negative groundball bias in Tiger Stadium — a result of keeping the grass long to help the Tigers' aging moundsmen and middle infielders — is exactly the same as the positive bias in the turf park at Cincinnati. Isn't that sort of difference just as "phony"? If Astroturf is unfair, then so is Detroit's knee-high grass . . . maybe more so.

A complete listing for this category can be found on page 256.

WHAT ARE THE BEST HITTERS' COUNTS?

In another essay we show the importance of throwing the first pitch for a strike. But what about the count as a whole? Is the batter virtually finished once the count goes to 0-and-2? Is swinging at a 3-0 pitch a foolish move? Does the hitter, or the pitcher, have the advantage on 3-and-2? Thanks to the STATS database, we can finally begin to answer these questions.

Let's look at the ball-and-strike data in two different ways. The first is to log each plate appearance according to the count it ended on. This means, in looking at 2–1 counts, for instance, that we're studying all the times the batter either reached base, or was put out, or was hit by a pitch on 2-and-1; if he took the pitch, or swung and missed, or hit a foul, the appearance would continue and that would not be a part of this particular study. Looked at in that somewhat limited way, here are the major league results from 1989:

Situation	Batting Average	On-Base Average	Slugging Percentage
At 0-0 count	.313	.313	.470
At 0-1 Count	.304	.309	.440
At 0-2 Count	.161	.168	.224
At 1-0 Count	.307	.310	.465
At 1-1 Count	.305	.306	.449
At 1-2 Count	.172	.177	.237
At 2-0 Count	.324	.333	.508
At 2-1 Count	.311	.311	.474
At 2-2 Count	.191	.193	.272
At 3-0 Count	.372	.927	.631
At 3-1 Count	.332	.664	.534
At 3-2 Count	.225	.458	.340

As you can see, there are some dynamite hitters' counts, and a few where the pitchers are in complete control. Putting the first pitch into play, as we've discussed earlier, produces good batting and slugging averages, though a weak on-base percentage due to the fact that the batter is giving up his chances for a walk. Swinging at 3-and-0, often thought to be unwise, turns out be an excellent idea, at least when the ball is put into play — .372 average with a hefty .631 slugging mark. Looking at the results from 3-and-1, you can see why managers like to give their hitters the green light — the result is a high average with great power. But while 3-2 counts produce numerous walks (.458 on-base average), the advantage is otherwise very much with the pitcher — only a .225 average, with .340 slugging.

Of course, this is a fairly narrow way of examining the subject, for while many plate appearances start out 2-and-0, they usually don't end there. Let's look at the end results of plate appearances according to how they begin (or, stated another way, this is how they hit after "passing through" this count):

Situation	Batting Average	On-Base Average	Slugging Percentage
After (0-1)	.229	.269	.331
After (0-2)	.177	.206	.249
After (1-0)	.267	.372	.400
After (1-1)	.236	.301	.347
After (1-2)	.185	.230	.262
After (2-0)	.285	.491	.436
After (2-1)	.254	.382	.384
After (2-2)	.201	.294	.291
After (3-0)	.291	.729	.449
After (3-1)	.278	.579	.437
After (3-2)	.225	.459	.340

As you can see, this data paints a slightly different picture. Any time the pitcher jumps out ahead — 0-1, 0-2, or 1-2 — he's basically taking the bat out of the hitters' hands. But interestingly, pitchers also control the "even" counts, 1-1 and 2-2. It's only when the hitter gets ahead that he gains an advantage . . . and even that advantage dissipates on 3-and-2. As we might have expected, most of the offensive damage occurs when the count begins 2-0, 3-0 or 3-1.

Studying both charts compels one to endorse the virtues of patient hitting. The first chart shows that attacking pitches early in the count — 0-0, 1-0, 1-1, even 0-1 — produces good averages and moderate power. By putting the first or second pitch in play, the hitter can also avoid falling behind in the count, which puts the hurler in command. But by doing that, the hitter is also sacrificing his chances for a walk, always an important offensive weapon. More significantly, he's cutting down on his opportunities for the long ball. The big power numbers generally occur on 2-0, 3-0 or 3-1 pitches. This sounds elementary, but you can't get a three-ball count without taking at least three pitches. Elementary or not, some hitters never seem to grasp the concept.

A complete listing for this category can be found on page 257.

WHICH PLAYERS TURNED IN THE BEST MONTHLY PERFORMANCES OF 1989?

Too bad the National League didn't have a "Player of the Month" Award back in 1955 — winning it would have been Bob Speake's one glorious moment in the sun. Speake, a rookie Cub outfielder, bashed out 11 home runs that May, and Cub fans revived their eternal dream of a pennant. A new nickname, "Tris" Speake, was even being considered among the bleacherites. But then June arrived, and Speake's bat spoke no more. Bob managed only one more homer the rest of the year, and soon faded into oblivion. The Cubs wound up finishing sixth.

Bob Speake's experience underscores the notion that one month does not a season make. Fortunately there are no Speakes in our list of the best one-month hitters and pitchers. But for a few of these guys, the month practically *was* the season:

1989

	HITTERS	HR	RBI	AVG.	ML Avg.	PITCHERS	W	L	ERA	ML Avg.
APRIL	Pete O'Brien	2	10	.400	.250	Kirk McCaskill	4	1	0.74	3.68
MAY	Carney Lansford	0	3	.406	.253	Rick Reuschel	6	0	0.84	3.64
JUNE	Tony Gwynn	2	16	.448	.261	Scott Bankhead	4	0	1.05	3.65
JULY	Robin Yount	5	24	.396	.256	Mike Boddicker	4	0	1.10	3.82
AUG.	Jim Eisenreich	3	17	.402	.252	Marty Clary	1	1	1.21	3.65
SEP.	Paul Molitor	2	18	.476	.252	Bret Saberhagen	6	1	0.98	3.63

Qualifications: 80 at bats or 30 innings pitched during the month

Molitor's amazing September wasn't noticed because his team was out of the pennant race, but it was some month nonetheless. There is no truth to the rumor that the Mariners and Dodgers thought our figures were *full-season* averages when they threw all those millions at O'Brien and

Hubie Brooks, who hit .384 last September. Heck, if these guys could do this for the whole season, we'd forget about Ty Cobb.

Three more players didn't quite made the leaders list, but had such outstanding all-around months that we thought you'd like to see their figures:

Player, Team	Month	AB	R	H	HR	RBI	SB	CS	Avg
Jose Oquendo, StL	July	97	16	40	0	16	1	1	.412
Barry Larkin, Cin	June	112	20	44	1	11	3	0	.393
Pedro Guerrero, StL	Aug.	113	11	41	4	26	1	0	.363
Rickey Henderson, Oak	July	86	31	31	3	16	17	1	.360
Howard Johnson, Mets	June	100	25	34	11	24	6	1	.340

Henderson's extraordinary July not only announced that he was back in Oakland with a big exclamation point, it gave the A's a big push at a time they really needed it, and was a crucial factor in Oakland's drive toward a championship.

On the pitching side, a good monthly ERA does not necessarily transfer into a great won-lost record. In four of the top ten performances during a month, the pitcher won only one or two games, though none had a losing record. In addition to Marty Clary, shown in the chart, Jose Rijo only went 1-0 in April despite a 0.87 ERA while Mike Morgan and Derek Lilliquist each went 2-1 in May with ERAs under 1.40. Considering everything, the best all-around months were Reuschel's May and Saberhagen's September. The outstanding month for a relief pitcher was probably Dennis Eckersley's August: no earned runs over eleven appearances and 13.1 innings, with ten saves.

The most consistent starters of 1989 were Saberhagen, Scott Garrelts and Orel Hershiser. Saberhagen's highest monthly ERA during the season was a quite-respectable 3.35. The remarkable Hershiser's worst month, May, produced a 3.06 mark (Orel's best ERA was in April, 1.96), while Garrelts never had a monthly mark higher than 3.25.

A complete listing for this category can be found on page 258.

DO SACRIFICES SACRIFICE TOO MUCH?

We've discussed which teams like the sacrifice bunt, even in the early innings. But how does sacrificing affect a team's overall scoring potential? And how about the situations where a sacrifice is attempted, but doesn't succeed? Rather than work with mathematical models, we'd like to present data from the last three seasons, 1987-89. We looked at the two most obvious sacrifice situations, a runner on first with none out and runners on first and second with none out.

Because National League pitchers have to bat, we felt it essential to separate the data by leagues. We show the results for each league both with the first through eighth hitters up, and then with the number nine hitter up. We present two figures in each case — the average number of runs that scored in the inning, and the percentage of innings that at least one run scored. We do this because the sacrifice is regarded as a "one run" strategy. If the traditional view of sacrifices holds up, teams will score fewer runs per inning when they sacrifice, but score at least one run a greater percentage of the time. Here are the first two tables, for each league, based on all games from 1987 through '89:

		—— #1 thru #8 ——		—— #9 hitter ——	
	0 Out - Man on 1st only	Runs per Inning	% At Least One Run	Runs per Inning	% At Least One Run
AL:	Innings with successful SH	0.69	39.5	0.76	42.7
	Innings with failed SH	0.51	31.4	0.67	32.8
	Innings, SH not attempted	0.85	40.6	0.88	39.9
NL:	Innings with successful SH	0.71	40.1	0.75	40.4
	Innings with failed SH	0.45	24.5	0.37	20.2
	Innings, SH not attempted	0.77	38.9	0.77	39.8

The data is basically what's expected. When teams don't sacrifice, their overall scoring potential is greater . . . but except for a slight surprise with the first eight hitters in an American League lineup up, the percentage of innings when one run scored is greater during an inning when a sacrifice is successful. The missing links are the innings where a sacrifice is attempted, but fails: both figures go way down. This happens about 13 to 15 percent of the time, not at all a trivial percentage. Since the possibility of scoring one run with a successful sacrifice increases only slightly, the overall conclusion would be that sacrificing with a man on first only is a wasteful endeavor, unless one run (and no more) is badly needed.

Here's the data from the other situation, with runners on first and second with none out:

	#1 thru #8		#9 hitter	
0 Out - Men on 1st and 2nd	Runs per Inning	% At Least One Run	Runs per Inning	% At Least One Run
AL: Innings with successful SH	1.60	65.8	1.62	65.8
Innings with failed SH	1.05	43.9	1.96	65.2
Innings, SH not attempted	1.36	56.8	1.49	53.3
NL: Innings with successful SH	1.50	63.7	1.49	64.8
Innings with failed SH	1.02	48.0	0.58	27.5
Innings, SH not attempted	1.27	54.0	1.13	50.0

This situation is completely different. Sacrificing with men on first and second and none out not only scores at least one run more often, but scores more runs per inning overall. The failed sacrifice happens in this situation about 17 percent of the time, except when a National League number nine hitter is up; the failure rate in those cases jumps to 31 percent, not surprising since it usually involves a pitcher batting. But even including the failure rate, bunting in this situation is the better move. Major league managers do this routinely except when their very best hitters are up, and clearly they know what they're doing.

A complete listing for this category can be found on page 259.

WHICH TEAMS SHOWED THE MOST IMPROVEMENT DURING THE SECOND HALF OF 1989?

When a team shows a big improvement from the first half of the season to the second, team officials say, "We're on the right track." When a team shows a big decline, they say, "We had a lot of injuries." When it shows neither a major advance nor a decline, they say, "We're a steady ballclub. That's a sure sign of stability." The following clubs were either on the right track, suffering from injuries, or were very steady during 1989. You'll notice they number 26:

Team	Win/Loss Percentage Through 6/30	July 1-end	+/-
Toronto	.474	.619	+.145
San Diego	.488	.610	+.122
Chicago White Sox	.375	.481	+.106
Philadelphia	.360	.460	+.100
Chicago Cubs	.526	.619	+.083
Milwaukee	.468	.530	+.062
Boston	.480	.540	+.060
St. Louis	.507	.552	+.045
Oakland	.595	.627	+.032
Pittsburgh	.446	.466	+.020
Los Angeles	.474	.488	+.014
New York Mets	.533	.540	+.007
Kansas City	.571	.565	-.006
Minnesota	.506	.482	-.024
Atlanta	.410	.378	-.032
Cleveland	.468	.435	-.033
Seattle	.468	.434	-.034
Baltimore	.566	.512	-.044
San Francisco	.595	.542	-.053
California	.592	.535	-.057
Detroit	.395	.337	-.058
New York Yankees	.494	.429	-.065
Texas	.551	.476	-.075
Houston	.570	.494	-.076
Montreal	.557	.446	-.111
Cincinnati	.526	.405	-.121

Officials from every major league team can undoubtedly give good, and glowing, explanations for what happened to their clubs over the course of the season. But what fans want to know is whether they can predict what will happen the next year from a team's first half/second half tendencies.

Do teams which show a big improvement over the second half continue to improve the next year? The answer is sometimes yes, sometimes no. From 1984 through '88, a total of 13 teams showed a really sharp improvement from July 1 on — that is, they had a winning percentage that was at least 100 points better over the second half. Seven of those 13 clubs actually won *fewer* games the next year. Two of the exceptions were the '87 Padres, who improved by 18 wins in 1988, and the Padres again in '88 — this time they improved by six wins in 1989. Since San Diego also showed a large first half/second half jump in 1989, they'll bear watching next year.

But remember, continued improvement the next year is unpredictable. How about clubs which show a major drop (100 points or more) from the first half to the second? There were four clubs like this in 1987-1988, and three of them won fewer games the next year. The '88 Tigers and Yankees showed serious declines the next season, winning 21 and 11 fewer games, respectively. The '87 Astros were the exception; their winning percentage during the second half of that year dropped by 119 points, but their record improved in 1988 by six victories.

In truth, such Jekyll/Hyde performances over the course of a season are a sign of instability, no matter in which direction a club goes. Solid organizations don't ordinarily need half a year for their rosters to jell — they're far more likely to be ready to go from the start of the season. Look at the clubs which made big jumps over the second half of '89 — the Blue Jays, Padres, White Sox, and Phillies — and you'll see teams in upheaval.

While the Padres continue to improve, they've had turmoil at the managerial, front office and ownership level over the last few years. With more stability, San Diego might have won a divisional title in 1989. After a long power struggle, Jack McKeon finally seems to be in control of the franchise. With stable leadership, the Padres' chances of getting off to a good start are much better than they've been in several years. So are their hopes for a championship.

The other side of the coin is represented by the Yankees, who've shown a first half/second half drop of at least 65 percentage points during each of the last three years. The Yanks seem to begin each season the same way — a new crop of undependable ballplayers, a manager on shaky ground, an owner ready to start meddling at the first downturn. No wonder things fall apart during the second half of every year.

A complete listing for this category can be found on page 260.

WHY SHOULD FIELDERS PLAY SHALLOW WHEN WILL CLARK IS HITTING?

Imagine a pitcher winding up and delivering a ball northward from a pitching mound in Rio de Janeiro, Brazil. Now imagine that the pitch traveled a distance equal to that of all pitches thrown in 1989. Your first question, geography students: where would home plate be? If you said San Francisco (6,650 miles away), you can give yourself a gold star. Now suppose that our San Francisco batter — let's call him "Will the Thrill" — swung at the pitch and hit the ball southward a distance equal to that of all 1989 batted balls. Here's your second question: where would the ball have landed? If you guessed Lima, Peru, 4,500 miles from San Francisco and a good 2,000 miles short of Rio, you can go to the head of the class. We guess Will just didn't get a hold of that one.

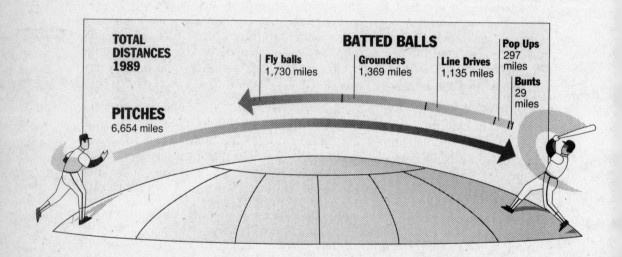

TOTAL DISTANCES 1989

BATTED BALLS
- Fly balls 1,730 miles
- Grounders 1,369 miles
- Line Drives 1,135 miles
- Pop Ups 297 miles
- Bunts 29 miles

PITCHES 6,654 miles

The chart above shows total distance for batted balls hit during 1989. As a guide for fielders, here's approximately where they should have been stationed to make the play on a ball hit from San Francisco:

Type	Miles	Where the Ball would Land
Grounders	1,369	Sierra Madre Mountains, Mexico (Bogey grabs ball with Gold Glove discovered by Walter Huston, but has ball and glove stolen by banditos)
Line Drives	1,135	Quinones, Baja peninsula, Mexico (Rey Quinones spears this screamer, begins his comeback)
Fly Balls	1,730	Guadalajara, Mexico (In Guadalajara, the fielder will be a bit shallow, but it's a pleasant place to stand)
Pop Ups	297	Santa Barbara, California (Another pleasant place to wait for the ball to come down)
Bunts	29	San Jose, California (The entire Giants team may soon be here to make the play)

Though they're only men, these players contributed mightily to all those miles:

Grounders — Steve Sax, 9.66 miles of groundballs hit during 1989, Tony Gwynn 8.5. Considering their batting averages (.315 and .336), it was worth it.

Pop Ups — Joe Carter, 2.56 miles worth of popups, Kevin McReynolds 2.05. This is the total horizontal, not vertical, distance, but it's pretty impressive. Rumor has it that the Indians offered Carter a million dollars for each popup mile; he was insulted, and demanded a trade to San Diego.

Line Drives — Don Mattingly, 7.56 miles on line drives alone, Gregg Jefferies, 7.28 miles. It hurts your glove hand just to think about it.

Flyballs — Wally Joyner 12.39 miles of flyballs, Todd Benzinger, 9.55 miles. Joyner needs a new nickname; how about "Lord of the Flies"?

Bunts — Steve Lyons 0.52 bunting miles, Oddibe McDowell 0.51. That might not seem like much, but you could probably say that Oddibe bunted his way from Cleveland to Atlanta last year.

WHEN ARE TWO OUTS BETTER THAN ONE?

A few years ago, when Hubie Brooks drove in 100 runs for Montreal, the Expo media boys trotted out an interesting statistic. Of Hubie's 100 ribbies, they said, a whopping 41 of them came after two men were out. The stat was given a lot of press, and presented as evidence to show what a great clutch hitter Brooks was.

We don't want to spill the beans on Hubie — especially after the Dodgers just finished paying him millions of dollars. But it turns out that driving in 41 percent of your runs with two out is, in fact, a below average performance. Here is how the major league teams scored their runs after two outs during 1989:

Run Scoring after Two Outs

American League			National League		
Team	Two Out Runs	Percent of Total Runs	Team	Two Out Runs	Percent of Total Runs
Baltimore	349	49	Atlanta	285	49
Boston	357	46	Chicago	348	49
California	327	49	Cincinnati	303	48
Chicago	301	43	Houston	316	49
Cleveland	260	43	Los Angeles	273	49
Detroit	300	48	Montreal	301	48
Kansas City	307	44	New York	306	45
Milwaukee	331	47	Philadelphia	292	47
Minnesota	323	44	Pittsburgh	293	46
New York	320	46	St. Louis	325	51
Oakland	319	45	San Diego	257	40
Seattle	333	48	San Fran.	311	44
Texas	316	45			
Toronto	314	43			
AL Average	4,457	46	**NL Average**	3,610	47

With few exceptions, there is a remarkable uniformity in the way teams score: about 16-18 percent of their runs with no outs, 34-38 percent with one out, and 44-48 percent after two out. This only makes sense: the longer an inning goes, the more chances a club has to put men on base. More runners are apt to be on with two out — so naturally, more runs will be scored.

An interesting question is whether the higher-scoring teams are simply the ones which are more efficient with two out. This chart lists the five top scoring clubs in each league, and shows how they ranked vs. their league in scoring by out:

Team	League Rank in Scoring Runs			
	Total Runs	With 0 Out	With 1 Out	With 2 Out
Red Sox	1st	5th	1st	1st
Twins	2nd	3rd	2nd	6th
Blue Jays	3rd	2nd	9th	10th
A's	4th	1st	11th	8th
Orioles	5th	6th	10th	2nd
Cubs	1st	4th	5th	1st
Giants	2nd	3rd	1st	4th
Mets	3rd	2nd	4th	5th
Astros	4th	8th	6th	3rd
Padres	5th	1st	8th	12th

The highest scoring club in each league was, in fact, the one that scored the most with two out. But even though the Blue Jays, Twins and A's weren't very good two-out clubs, they had the three next best offenses anyway. In the National League the Padres were dead last in two-out scoring, but had the fifth-best attack because of an unequaled ability to score before a man was retired. The results show that a club can have a good offense even without being especially productive with two out.

A complete listing for this category can be found on page 261.

WHEN DO GOOD TEAMS SCORE?

Back in the twenties and thirties, when games generally started at three in the afternoon, the champion Yankees had a reputation for what was known as "Five O'Clock Lightning." Often behind as the end of the game drew near, the Yanks would mount a rally and pull the contest out. Or so we've been told.

That — and the current emphasis on late-inning performance — caused us to wonder when the best teams do their scoring. Is late punch indeed the key to success? Here's a chart showing the total runs scored by each team in 1989, and the club's scoring breakdown by early, middle and late innings:

American	Total Runs	1-3	4-6	7+
Orioles	708	252	252	204
Red Sox	774	310	263	201
Angels	669	223	257	189
White Sox	693	255	215	223
Indians	604	226	195	183
Tigers	617	223	210	184
Royals	690	241	231	218
Brewers	707	240	246	221
Twins	740	236	234	270
Yankees	698	230	262	206
Athletics	712	261	238	213
Mariners	694	255	244	195
Rangers	695	234	265	196
Blue Jays	731	239	241	251
AL Average	695	245	239	211

National	Total Runs	1-3	4-6	7+
Braves	584	202	196	186
Cubs	702	285	256	161
Reds	632	209	202	221
Astros	647	227	208	212
Dodgers	554	192	200	162
Expos	632	211	219	202
Mets	683	253	242	188

Phillies	629	221	219	189
Pirates	637	228	212	197
Cardinals	632	212	219	201
Padres	642	195	249	198
Giants	699	278	228	193
NL Average	639	226	221	192
ML Average	669	236	231	202

Teams generally score about 35 percent of their runs in the first three innings, 35 percent in the middle three, and 30 from the seventh inning on. Late inning scoring is lower for two reasons: home clubs often don't bat in the last of the ninth, and the teams are using their premier relievers — who overall have lower ERAs than starting pitchers — in the final frames. Let's look at the highest-scoring clubs in each league during the three segments:

American League

Innings 1-3		Innings 4-6		Innings 7+	
Red Sox	310	Rangers	265	Twins	270
Athletics	261	Red Sox	263	Blue Jays	251
WSox-Mariners	255	Angels	257	White Sox	223

National League

Innings 1-3		Innings 4-6		Innings 7+	
Cubs	285	Cubs	256	Reds	221
Giants	278	Padres	249	Astros	212
Mets	253	Mets	242	Expos	202

If late-inning performance is the crucial element in a club's success, it's hard to see it from these breakdowns. In each league, only one of the three best late-inning clubs had a winning record. Only one of those six clubs, the Blue Jays, won a division title — and the Cubs, who won the National League East, were the lowest-scoring club in the majors from the seventh inning on. Now look at the *first* three innings. The top two American League teams and all three National League teams played better than .500 ball. The number two American League club was the world champion; the top two National League clubs were its division winners. Now do you still believe it's only the *late* innings which are important?

You may wonder if there's a bias at work: since bad teams are more apt to be losing at home in the ninth, they'll have more total innings to score. There is a small bias because of this, but not a crucial one. Even if we eliminate the ninth from our late-inning totals, the Giants rank only fifth in the NL in late runs, and the Cubs are still last; in the American League the Blue Jays and A's would rank second and fifth in late runs.

We're not saying the late innings are unimportant. Late punch was certainly a crucial element in Toronto's division title. But late-inning stats are probably being given too much weight. We're now even seeing figures like "Batting average from the seventh inning on" — regardless of whether the game was close or not. Hey fellows, baseball is a nine-inning, not a three-inning game. And if any innings need to be emphasized more, this study shows that it's the *first* three. Perhaps the correct phrase, updated for the modern game, should be "Eight O'Clock Lightning."

A complete listing for this category can be found on page 262.

II. QUESTIONS ON OFFENSE

WHICH HITTERS SWING AND MISS MOST OFTEN?

It would figure: the man whose hobby is making defenders grab nothing but air is the leading major leaguer at hitting . . . nothing but air. Last year Bo Jackson swung and missed a grand total of 452 times — 25 percent more futile swings than any other player. Move over, Nike: Bo's next endorsements may be Fedders or Carrier for air conditioners.

Not to knock Bo, who made great strides during the 1989 baseball season, but consider the top five at swinging and missing last year: Jackson, Devon White, Dale Murphy, Pete Incaviglia and Jeffrey Leonard. Except for Murphy, a legitimate superstar on the way down, there's a common denominator: enormous potential, largely unfulfilled. A coincidence? Here's numbers six through ten: Rob Deer, Andres Galarraga, Cory Snyder, Jack Clark, Juan Samuel. Some fearsome sluggers, but none of them hit higher than .257 last year. The third five rate a little better: Danny Tartabull, Jesse Barfield, Glenn Davis, Joe Carter, Dave Henderson. But you have to get down to number 19, Will Clark, to find someone who would — potential aside — currently be regarded as a complete major league hitter.

Is there a lesson in this? We think there is, though it probably should be taken with a note of caution. There's a relationship between swinging hard and getting big results, like Jackson's awesome All-Star Game homer last year. But such a swing takes a long time to uncoil, and becomes easy for a clever pitcher to fool. The end result, ordinarily, is a lot of home runs, offset by a low batting average. Usually these guys chase a lot of bad pitches as well, so they don't draw many walks, either. (Jack Clark is a major exception.) At best, that adds up to a dangerous hitter, but not a great hitter.

The note of caution is that it's hard for a lot of these hitters to change. At this point of his career, Joe Carter could learn "discipline" about as easily as he could learn to throw a knuckleball. But it's less easy to say that about Cory Snyder, or Devon White, or Bo himself, all of whom were born within two months of each other in late 1962. Without question, Snyder's and White's lack of discipline have cost them dearly . . . at this point, their careers are stagnating. As for Bo, he's still fairly inexperienced at baseball, so there's a good chance he'll continue to improve. But that improvement will probably be muted unless he can learn to cut down on his massive swing a little.

A complete listing for this category can be found on page 263.

WHO CAN POP IN THE CLUTCH?

To answer this question, the first thing we'll have to do is define our terms. The STATS definition of a clutch situation is, first of all, a plate appearance in the seventh inning or later — no first-inning game-winning RBIs here. In addition, the batting team must be tied or have no more than a one run lead, or else have the tying run on base, at bat or on deck. You'll notice an intentional similarity to the save definition. Here are the top clutch hitters in batting average for 1989 (50 or more plate appearances), along with something you seldom see — the leaders for the category in home runs and RBIs:

Player, Team	Ave.	AB	H	HR	RBI
Danny Tartabull, KC	.403	67	27	5	21
Al Newman, Min	.386	70	27	0	8
Bob Boone, KC	.379	66	25	0	8
Randy Milligan, Bal	.370	46	17	2	9
Mike Greenwell, Bos	.364	77	28	2	9
Ozzie Smith, StL	.361	83	30	0	8
Luis Salazar, SD-Cubs	.359	64	23	2	9
Barry Larkin, Cin	.358	53	19	1	7
Kirby Puckett, Min	.352	91	32	3	16
Tony Gwynn, SD	.351	94	33	0	13
Harold Reynolds, Sea	.351	77	27	0	6

Home Run Leaders: Eric Davis 8, Glenn Davis 7, Lou Whitaker 7, Jack Clark 6, Andres Galarraga 6, Kent Hrbek 6, Kevin Mitchell 6.

RBI Leaders: Eric Davis 26, Jack Clark 24, Pedro Guerrero 23, Don Mattingly 21, Danny Tartabull 21, George Bell 20, Will Clark 20.

Listing the home run and RBI leaders gives a little more balanced view of this category; Jack Clark batted only .221 in the clutch, but he certainly swung a heavy bat. Considering run production, the best clutch hitters last year were probably Tartabull, Eric Davis (a .325 hitter in these situations), Puckett, Guerrero (.282) and Mattingly (.303). And Clark would have to be considered because of his heavy RBI total. Not a bad group of ballplayers by any measuring system.

That said, we agree with those who say you can make too much of the notion of trying to quantify clutch performance. Because players have a limited number of at bats, pure chance can be a big factor; that's why you don't see much year to year consistency among the leaders in this category. Though we applaud Al Newman's performance last year, we suspect that he's not about to become the next three million dollar ballplayer. Nonetheless, a glimpse at the RBI leaders shows you that *something* meaningful is being measured.

Those were the heroes — now who were the goats? A look at last year's ten worst clutch hitters is going to embarrass some famous names. We also include the worst RBI men (50 or more PA):

Player, Team	Ave.	AB	H	HR	RBI
Rey Quinones, Sea-Pit	.115	52	6	1	3
Vance Law, Cubs	.131	61	8	0	5
Jesse Barfield, Tor-Yanks	.133	75	10	3	11
Darryl Strawberry, Mets	.134	82	11	3	8
Jody Davis, Atl	.135	52	7	0	3
Cory Snyder, Cle	.141	99	14	0	3
Darrell Evans, Atl	.143	63	9	0	3
John Shelby, LA	.143	77	11	1	3
Mitch Webster, Cubs	.160	50	8	1	3
Andre Dawson, Cubs	.164	61	10	3	9

Fewest RBIs: Omar Vizquel 0 (52 AB), Rick Schu 0 (51 AB), Jose Uribe 1 (56 AB), Lenny Harris 1 (57 AB), John Cangelosi 2 (67 AB), Kurt Stillwell KC 2 (67 AB), Fred Lynn 2 (57 AB), Jose Gonzalez 2 (53 AB), Bill Spiers 2 (50 AB).

For many of these players, the tough times continued when the season ended. As we went to press, Quinones was a man without a team, Webster had been traded to Cleveland, Law was mulling over an offer to play in Japan, and Jody Davis was about to lose his job to that fine young catching prospect, 37-year-old Ernie Whitt. On the other hand, Barfield signed a hefty new contract with the ever-believing Yankees. Meanwhile, the Mets, Indians and Cubs are figuring that what they saw last year from Strawberry, Snyder and Dawson was just an aberration. For their sake, we hope so, too.

The weak clutch performances of Webster and Dawson might make you wonder how the Cubs won a division title last year. Mark Grace (.348) did his best to compensate for Vance and Andre, but clutch hitting was the Wrigleys' achilles heel last year. The Cubs batted only .239 in late-and-close situations in 1989, a far cry from their .261 overall average. Don Zimmer's boys survived mainly because their pitchers held the opposition to an even lower clutch average, .237. In the playoffs the hitters continued their season-long tendencies (especially Grace and Dawson), but the hurlers couldn't continue to take up the slack.

A complete listing for this category can be found on page 264.

WHAT IS THE AVERAGE OFFENSIVE PERFORMANCE FROM EACH POSITION?

You're a National League manager with a mediocre, weak-hitting team. Your catcher is a sound defensive player, but last year he hit .240, barely got his on-base average over .300 and hit only ten homers. Is it time to find a replacement... maybe someone with a little more pop in his bat?

Judging by the average level of performance among NL catchers, finding a replacement is the last thing you should consider. In fact, you'd be better off shaking that catcher's hand and congratulating him on his fine hitting. In baseball, everything is relative, and all our mythical catcher's figures were better than the National League norm for 1989. That means that if you could get that valuable receiver to settle for less than two million a year, you'd consider yourself lucky.

Before you know what's good or bad, it helps to know what average is. Here are the average offensive performances at each position last year. To give you a better mental picture of how those stats stack up, we include the name of the player whose '89 figures came closest to the average:

American League

Pos	Batting Average	On-Base Average	Slugging Percentage	HR per 600 AB	Most Typical Performer
C	.249	.310	.360	11	Don Slaught
1B	.269	.350	.430	18	Greg Brock
2B	.273	.336	.363	6	Jim Gantner
3B	.263	.330	.380	11	Brook Jacoby
SS	.247	.299	.334	6	Alan Trammell
LF	.266	.329	.402	14	Greg Briley
CF	.264	.327	.386	11	Mike Devereux
RF	.266	.327	.416	16	Claudell Washington
DH	.256	.322	.392	15	Jeffrey Leonard

National League

Pos	Batting Average	On-Base Average	Slugging Percentage	HR per 600 AB	Most Typical Performer
C	.236	.299	.335	9	Terry Kennedy
1B	.271	.354	.429	17	Andres Galarraga
2B	.261	.326	.366	8	Greg Jefferies
3B	.251	.312	.392	14	Ken Caminiti
SS	.249	.300	.348	8	Garry Templeton
LF	.268	.347	.420	15	Kevin McReynolds

CF	.251	.313	.352	8	Herm Winningham
RF	.257	.326	.409	16	Mike Marshall

Looking at the figures can give one a little better perspective about what constitutes good production. For instance, any shortstop who bats over .250 is exceeding the norm. If he can get on base a little or pop an occasional homer, he's a real offensive plus. He doesn't have to hit like Cal Ripken to have value.

On the other hand, some teams never seem to grasp the notion that, while .250 with ten homers is fine for a shortstop, it's just not going to cut it at first base or the outfield. The Pirates, to use a good example, got only a .243 average and 13 homers out of their numerous first basemen last year. Their excuse was that Sid Bream got hurt . . . but, of course, Bream himself was only a marginal performer compared to the standards of first basemen.

Here are the strongest, and weakest team performances from each position last year:

	The Strongest					The Weakest				
Pos	Team	BA	OBA	SLG	HR	Team	BA	OBA	SLG	HR
C	White Sox	.274	.325	.422	16	Braves	.185	.258	.246	7
1B	Blue Jays	.270	.398	.526	37	Braves	.231	.312	.333	14
2B	Rangers	.316	.384	.472	16	Pirates	.219	.266	.275	3
3B	Red Sox	.326	.422	.442	4	Tigers	.224	.283	.311	8
SS	Phillies	.254	.328	.395	16	Braves	.222	.246	.325	15
LF	Giants	.289	.379	.595	45	Rangers	.234	.296	.393	18
CF	Brewers	.310	.377	.495	20	Dodgers	.207	.267	.286	6
RF	Rangers	.307	.348	.542	29	Giants	.215	.281	.342	13
DH	White Sox	.263	.346	.453	23	Blue Jays	.212	.299	.295	6

The gap between strong and weak is enormous, with the weak teams often turning crucial positions into automatic outs. The offseason flurry of trades and free agent signings (Atlanta's acquisition of Ernie Whitt and Nick Esasky, the Giants' signing of Kevin Bass, to cite two examples) were meant to close that substantial gap.

A complete listing for this category can be found on page 265.

WHICH HITTERS PERFORM BEST AGAINST THE TOP PITCHERS?

In the past few years we've seen a multitude of statistics which measure various aspects of clutch hitting. But one list we doubt you've seen is one we call Top Gun, because it matches the best against the best. The idea was pretty simple. We took a representative list of fifteen top pitchers in each league — the top ten ERA qualifiers, plus the top five relievers in saves — and measured how each batter performed against them. Does the cream really rise to the top? Here are the best and worst hitters hitters, with a minimum of 60 at bats against the top hurlers:

HITTERS VERSUS STAR PITCHERS
Minimum 60 at bats.

BATTING AVERAGE

BEST:
- .420 Phil Bradley
- .385 Mark Grace
- .372 Will Clark
- .361 Barry Larkin
- .351 Tony Gwynn

WORST:
- .164 Wally Backman
- .163 Andres Thomas
- .162 Darryl Strawberry
- .154 Cory Snyder
- .130 Mike Pagliarulo

Aside from the leader, Phil Bradley, the list fits very well with our notion of who the toughest hitters are. Five of the ten best played on division champions, while most of the others have solid reputations as pressure players. The numbers posted by Mark Grace, Will Clark and Kevin Mitchell (.333 batting average), in particular, are right in line with what we would have expected. Mitchell had an awesome .733 slugging percentage against the top hurlers, which underscores once more what an outstanding season he had.

One thing that jumps out when looking at the leaders list is that the on-base percentages, for the most part, are barely higher than the batting averages — in the cases of Clark and Barry Larkin, they're actually lower, thanks to no walks and at least one sacrifice fly:

Batter	Batting Average	On-Base Average
Bradley	.420	.478
Grace	.385	.393
W. Clark	.372	.363
B. Larkin	.361	.359
T. Gwynn	.351	.355

These hitters aren't at the plate to walk against the top pitchers, and the hurlers seem inclined to take up the challenge. A major exception was Mitchell with a .533 on-base average; Kevin was hampered all season by weak hitters behind him in the lineup.

Though they didn't make the leaders list, some other hitters posted notable numbers against the top pitchers. Bo Jackson embellished his reputation as a prime time performer by batting .313 with five homers. Howard Johnson had eight homers and 18 RBIs against the leading hurlers, while Joe Carter had five four-baggers and 16 RBIs.

The worst five hitters in the list were simply overmatched when going up against the best in 1989. For any fan following these hitters last year, the numbers aren't surprising. Snyder and Pagliarulo, considered coming stars a few years ago, have reached a point of struggle in their careers where it's no shock that the best pitchers simply knock the bats out of their hands. And Darryl Strawberry's deep decline last year is eloquently reflected in his sad numbers.

A complete listing for this category can be found on page 266.

WHO ARE THE MAJOR LEAGUE LEADERS IN GO-AHEAD RBIS?

Here's a list that's banned in Boston, and everywhere else in the world of official baseball statistics. Presenting the 1989 leaders in game winning RBIs:

American League	GW RBI	National League	GW RBI
Chili Davis, Cal	17	Will Clark, SF	20
George Bell, Tor	16	Pedro Guerrero, StL	19
Don Mattingly, Yanks	15	Bobby Bonilla, Pit	18
Joe Carter, Cle	14	Kevin McReynolds, Mets	18
Alvin Davis, Sea	14	Kevin Mitchell, SF	18
Dave Henderson, Oak	14	Barry Bonds, Pit	14
Cal Ripken, Bal	14	Andre Dawson, Cubs	14
Ruben Sierra, Tex	14	Howard Johnson, Mets	14
Five with	13	Milt Thompson, StL	14

For ill or good, the GWRBI has fallen on the scrap heap of discredited statistics. The argument against it has always been that it's supposed to be a measure of clutch hitting, but that a player frequently got credit for a "game-winner" that occurred in the first few innings. Looked at from a narrow point of view, that argument has considerable merit. Here is a distribution chart of game-winning RBIs by inning in 1989:

Inning:	1	2	3	4	5	6	7	8	9	10+
Total GW RBIs:	421	231	219	177	155	152	139	157	141	178

As you can see, more gamers occurred in the first inning than any other — and among games decided in nine innings, nearly half the GWRBIs were recorded in innings one to three. Since we tend to assume that there is no particular pressure on a hitter in the early innings, we usually throw out the gamer as a measure of clutch performance. But look at the chart another way. A lot of emphasis in recent years has been put on late-inning performance, as though that's when most games were decided. By this argument, runs scored before the seventh are sort of generic; it's like they appear automatically on the scoresheet, in a predictable fashion. (Like the baskets in the first 46 minutes of an NBA game, maybe.) But as we can see, nearly half the time, one team takes the lead by the end of the third inning and is never headed — that's precisely what the game winning RBI measures. So why discount performance which ultimately has such a great impact on the winning of a game?

A more fundamental argument against the GWRBI is stated by Bill James. Any good statistic, Bill feels, should measure a skill. But compare two situations. In situation A, Jones hits a two-run single in the eighth which puts his club ahead 4-3; the lead holds up. In situation B, Smith hits a two-run single in the eighth which puts his club ahead 4-3; his club's bullpen doesn't hold the lead. So how can you give Jones credit but not Smith, since they did exactly the same thing? (This same argument can be made against pitchers' wins and losses. With good reason.)

So, if it's important to drive in a run which puts your team ahead — and it is, unquestionably, a crucial factor in the winning and losing of games — why not just measure go-ahead RBIs? We do, and here are the 1989 leaders. We add total RBIs, the percentage of total RBIs which put the team ahead, and GWRBIs, for comparison purposes:

Player, Team	Go-ahead RBI	Total RBI	%	GWRBI
Pedro Guerrero, StL	40	117	34.2	19
Will Clark, SF	39	111	35.1	20
Kevin Mitchell, SF	36	125	28.8	18
George Bell, Tor	30	104	28.8	16
Lou Whitaker, Det	30	85	35.3	10
Kirby Puckett, Min	28	85	32.9	13
Cal Ripken, Bal	28	93	30.1	14
Chili Davis, Cal	27	90	30.0	17
Mark Grace, Cubs	26	79	32.9	11
Bo Jackson, KC	26	105	24.8	12
Don Mattingly, Yanks	26	113	27.4	15
Eddie Murray, LA	26	88	29.5	11
Rafael Palmeiro, Tex	26	64	40.6	12

We think it's important to note that, 40 times last year, Pedro Guerrero drove in a run that gave the Cardinals the lead. If that's not important — and a measure of clutch performance — what is? We also salute Rafael Palmeiro. In many ways he had a disappointing year. But, without a doubt, he drove in a big number of important runs.

A complete listing for this category can be found on page 267.

WHICH HITTERS ARE AT HOME ON THE ROAD?

A hitter will make himself more valuable if he can take advantage of what his home ballpark has to offer. Of course, it helps if his talents are suited to the park. A flyball power hitter like Tom Brunansky is going to be hurt in a stadium with deep power alleys, like the Cardinals' Busch Stadium. Nonetheless, some players show a great ability to adapt to their home yard. The following hitters had the biggest home advantage in batting average during 1989 (minimum 150 at bats both home and road):

BA Change	Player, Team	Home BA	HR	RBI	Road BA	HR	RBI
+.133	Luis Polonia, Oak-Yanks	.372	1	26	.239	2	20
+.120	Alvin Davis, Sea	.365	13	56	.245	8	39
+.107	Kirby Puckett, Min	.390	7	52	.283	2	33
+.104	Mickey Tettleton, Bal	.310	15	41	.207	11	24
+.096	Glenn Davis, Hou	.317	15	42	.221	19	47
+.092	Carlton Fisk, WSox	.343	4	32	.251	9	36
+.090	Wade Boggs, Bos	.377	2	27	.287	1	27
+.090	Darryl Strawberry, Mets	.272	15	41	.183	14	36
+.088	Paul O'Neill, Cin	.316	11	45	.228	4	29
+.084	Bob Boone, KC	.317	1	24	.233	0	19

For some of these players, this sort of performance is old hat. In '88 Puckett hit .406 at home, only .308 on the road; Glenn Davis had a 53-point home advantage in '88; and Wade Boggs has always hit extremely well in Fenway — his .377 mark last year was his *lowest* at home since 1986. Alvin Davis' power stats have always been much better in the Kingdome, and he's usually hit for a higher average as well. And though he was playing his first season in Kansas City, Bob Boone had hit over .400 on artificial turf in 1988. (Boonie must be learning to take advantage of his great speed.) On the other hand, Darryl Strawberry's road difficulties were a new occurrence; the Straw man's home figures were a typical home performance for him.

It's possible to read too much into these figures. Often they're a one-or-two year phenomenon. For instance, Carlton Fisk's high batting average at Comiskey was unusual for him — in 1988 he hit .273 at home, .280 on the road. (Pudge's home run disadvantage in Chicago has been a much more consistent pattern.) While Puckett has had two years of big numbers in the Metrodome, in 1987 he hit .362 on the road, only .301 at home. We're on pretty safe ground in saying that Boggs and the Davises really know how to use their home parks, because they've shown a home field advantage over a period of years. But Polonia, Tettleton and O'Neill haven't been playing in their ballparks long enough to draw any longterm conclusions about their home-road tendencies.

Boggs's good, but not sensational, road figures are probably the biggest reason why he's been difficult to trade. Playing in Boston, Wade is a genuine superstar, but that reputation is built on his ability to consistently hit from .375 to .410 at Fenway. Boggs is thus worth much, much more to the Red Sox than he would be to anyone else, which severely limits his trade value. Though he's not a power hitter, Boggs is in somewhat the same situation that Fred Lynn was in a decade ago. Lynn was 28 and probably on track for a Hall of Fame career when salary considerations prompted the Red Sox to deal him away after the 1980 season. Lynn couldn't take Fenway with him, and his career was never the same.

The following players had the biggest home field *disadvantage*, based on home/road batting averages, during 1989:

BA Change	Player, Team	Home BA	Home HR	Home RBI	Road BA	Road HR	Road RBI
-.131	Dave Martinez, Mon	.208	1	7	.339	2	20
-.129	Dion James, Atl-Cle	.220	1	16	.349	4	24
-.101	Greg Briley, Sea	.207	5	23	.309	8	29
-.088	Steve Lyons, WSox	.217	0	15	.305	2	35
-.086	Barry Bonds, Pit	.204	7	28	.290	12	30
-.078	Glenn Braggs, Mil	.211	8	36	.289	7	30
-.073	Lloyd Moseby, Tor	.180	4	13	.254	7	30
-.072	Darren Daulton, Phi	.163	2	20	.235	6	24
-.070	Ivan Calderon, WSox	.248	2	34	.318	12	53
-.067	Kurt Stillwell, KC	.226	2	30	.293	5	24

In assessing this group, we find little year-to-year consistency. There is some: Calderon hit 42 points better on the road in 1988, Martinez has shown a pronounced disadvantage on turf fields during his career, and Braggs has hit better away from County Stadium for three straight seasons, though the difference was never this pronounced in the past. On the other hand, Lyons had nearly equal home/road splits in '87 and '88, Bonds was better at home during both those years, and Stillwell was a better home hitter during 1988, his first season in Kansas City. In 1987 Calderon was 42 points better at home, Darren Daulton 112 points better. Greg Briley was a rookie in 1989, and the switch to new parks make the numbers of Dion James and Lloyd Moseby impossible to assess.

One factor that might be at work here is that struggling players sometimes relax more on the road, where they're away from hostile fans and constant media attention. The performances of Moseby, Braggs, Bonds, Daulton and (to some extent) Calderon have disappointed their clubs, and all have been the subjects of trade rumors; Moseby in fact has already signed with a new team. For such players, the pressure to succeed is much greater at home.

That, of course, doesn't explain the performance of Darryl Strawberry. But then, what does?

A complete listing for this category can be found on page 268.

WHICH PLAYERS CREATE THE MOST RUNS?

Two of the most time-honored individual statistics are runs scored and RBIs. Both stats are useful measurements of a player's offensive contributions, and we like them as much as anyone. But both are also subject to powerful illusions. A player batting at the top of the batting order has a better chance to score runs; a player batting in the middle of the order has an increased chance of recording more RBIs. Some have tried to combine the two stats with a number called "runs produced" — runs plus RBIs minus homers. This stat is pretty bogus, since it needlessly penalizes players who hit homers. How is it that when player A triples and player B brings him home with a groundout, two runs are "produced," since each gets credit for an RP . . . but when player A homers, only one run is produced? By the "runs produced" formula, the Chicago White Sox produced 29 more runs than the Chicago Cubs did last year — even though they scored nine fewer! We think that's pretty dumb. Even if you didn't subtract the homers, runs produced, like runs scored, is very team-dependent: players on good teams have a much better chance to record high totals than players on bad teams do.

To eliminate some of those illusions, Bill James invented the stat known as "runs created." Runs created uses individual statistics to evaluate the number of runs each player's contributions imply. There are several versions of the formula for runs created; we use the most exact, and technical version, the definition of which appears at the end of this article. This definition has been sharpened over time, and it takes into account almost everything a player does, both positively and negatively, to produce runs. The formula works about as well as anything we've seen. As with runs scored and RBIs, a player with a total of 100 runs created or thereabouts is having an outstanding season. The 1989 leaders in runs created were:

Player, Team	Runs Created
Will Clark, SF	136.4
Kevin Mitchell, SF	135.8
Howard Johnson, Mets	127.0
Robin Yount, Mil	125.3
Wade Boggs, Bos	122.2
Ruben Sierra, Tex	121.6
Fred McGriff, Tor	120.8
Lonnie Smith, Atl	112.9
Rickey Henderson, Yanks-Oak	109.9
Alvin Davis, Sea	109.0

You can see right away why we like this stat; any listing of the top offensive players of 1989 would have to begin with these guys. Different types of players are represented, from sluggers to leadoff men. The top two National League players in the MVP voting rank one-two in runs created, though Clark barely edges Mitchell here. The top two American League players in the MVP voting rank first and third in A.L. runs created. Not bad.

Bill also has a refinement of runs created called "offensive winning percentage." (The definition is included below.) What this stat does is use runs created as a base for answering a question: if all players on his team hit like this player, what would the team's winning percentage be? You can see that a team of Kevin Mitchells last year would have had a nifty winning percentage of .843, which translates into a 137-25 record for a team's season:

Player, Team	Offensive Winning Pct.
Kevin Mitchell, SF	.843
Will Clark, SF	.839
Lonnie Smith, Atl	.824
Howard Johnson, Mets	.807
Alvin Davis, Sea	.776
Jack Clark, SD	.765
Robin Yount, Mil	.764
Fred McGriff, Tor	.760
Mark Grace, Cubs	.757
Pedro Guerrero, StL	.757

Mitchell moves ahead of Clark in this ranking, and Alvin Davis moves to the top of the American League standing. The difference is that this is a percentage, based on number of plate appearances, while runs created is strictly a total. Either way, all these guys had stellar years. The value of Jack Clark, who's often underrated because of his low batting average, really shines through here.

You might wonder which regulars were the weakest offensive performers. Here are the five lowest in offensive winning percentages (minimum 400 plate appearances):

Player, Team	Offensive Winning Pct.
Andres Thomas, Atl	.212

Omar Vizquel, Sea	.227
Felix Fermin, Cle	.259
Jose Uribe, SF	.280
Ozzie Guillen, WSox	.290

Not surprisingly, all five are shortstops. But Cory Snyder, a "hard-hitting outfielder," ranked just below Guillen at .292.

Technical Version Of Runs Created Formula

Runs created is A times B divided by C where

A = Hits plus Walks plus Hit Batsmen minus Caught Stealing minus Grounded into Double Plays,

B = Total Bases plus (.26 times the Sum of Hit Batsmen and Unintentional Walks) plus (.52 times the sum of Sacrifice Hits, Sacrifice Flies and Stolen Bases),

C = At Bats plus Walks plus Hit Batsmen plus Sacrifice Hits plus Sacrifice Flies.

Offensive Winning Percentage

To figure a player's offensive winning percentage, start by figuring the number of runs the player created per 27 outs. Then find the offensive context of his team by adding the number of runs scored by his team to the number they allowed (say 700 plus 650) and divide that total by 324 (162 games X 2). Divide the number of runs created per 27 outs by the offensive context figure.

Square this new figure. Then divide the squared figure by the sum of itself plus one to obtain the offensive winning percentage.

A complete listing for this category can be found on page 269.

WHO ARE THE MOST CONSISTENT GROUNDBALL HITTERS IN BASEBALL — AND WHO ARE THE BEST FLYBALL HITTERS?

If baseball would only pass a rule that any balls hit on the ground were automatic hits, then Felix Fermin and Steve Sax would be the new Babe Ruth and Lou Gehrig. Last year Fermin and Sax hit the ball on the ground far more consistently than any hitters in baseball — they averaged 4.17 and 3.99 grounders, respectively, for every flyball. The next best ratio (minimum 350 plate appearances) belonged to Groundball Billy Ripken, whose G/F ratio was 2.62. "Forget my brother Cal. My idol is Felix Fermin," Billy Rip has been rumored to say. And indeed Billy outhit Felix last year, .239 to .238, outhomered him 2 to 0, and drove home 26 big runs to Fermin's 21. Is Billy Ripken the emerging king of groundball hitting?

The leading groundball and flyball hitters of 1989 were:

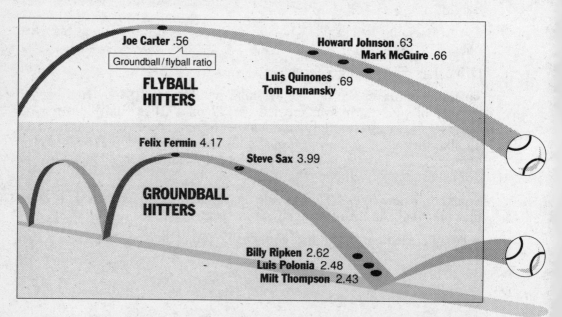

Look at the groundball hitters. What a weird group of players this is. About the only thing they have in common is that all are considered good bunters — but these ratios actually exclude bunts! That's the only real similarity for the group as a whole. Fermin and Ripken were, by any measuring system, two of the weakest offensive players in the major leagues last year, while the others hit very well: Sax .315, Polonia .300, and Thompson .290. Sax, Polonia and Thompson are all good base stealers and the kind of hitters frequently urged to "hit it on the ground and use your speed." But Fermin doesn't have a lot of speed, and Ripken is an average runner, if that. Since their results are so meager, what are those two accomplishing by attempting to hit the ball on the ground?

The opposite end of the spectrum is represented by the extreme flyball hitters. This is, of course, a totally different group of players. These players are obvious uppercutters who can hit the ball out of the park — Carter, Johnson, and McGwire had over 30 homers, Brunansky had 20 while playing in a park that destroyed his power, and even Quinones had 12 dingers in only 340 at bats. On the other hand, they're low-average hitters, all in the .230s and .240s except for Johnson, who batted .287. HoJo aside, these players seem to make a conscious choice to go for the longball at the expense of being a better all-around hitter. On the whole, however, it's hard to knock the results.

If there's a lesson in this, it's that it's possible to have an extreme style as a hitter, either flyball or groundball, and still be very productive. In most cases, one suspects, the hitters are simply sticking to their natural hitting style. But Fermin, Ripken and perhaps Quinones may be trying to adapt a style that isn't really suited for them. Like most things in baseball, it's only good if it works.

A complete listing for this category can be found on page 270.

WHICH PLAYERS HOMER TO THE OPPOSITE FIELD MOST OFTEN?

Most home runs are pulled. According to our data, only 10.5 percent of the 3,083 home runs hit in the major leagues last year went to the opposite field — even though we count left or right center (depending on whether the hitter's a lefty or a righty) as part of the opposite field. There are, however, a few players who go the other way and reach the seats on a fairly regular basis. The following players hit the greatest percentage of their four baggers to the opposite field last year (five opposite field homers minimum):

Player, Team	Opposite Field Home Runs	Total Home Runs	% to Opposite Field
John Kruk, SD-Phi	6	8	75%
Bo Jackson, KC	16	32	50
Robin Yount, Mil	10	21	48
Phil Bradley, Bal	5	11	46
Julio Franco, Tex	5	13	39
Harold Baines, WSox-Tex	6	16	38
Pete Incaviglia, Tex	7	21	33
Fred McGriff, Tor	10	36	28
Mickey Tettleton, Bal	7	26	27

The most interesting player on this list, of course, is Bo Jackson. A good half of Bo's homers went to right and right center, which is very, very rare for a big power guy. Only Fred McGriff, who went the other way a little more than half as often as Jackson, showed much opposite-field tendency among last year's big home run hitters. And even McGriff is something of a freak. Here are the opposite field totals for the other 30-homer hitters in 1989: Kevin Mitchell six of 47, Howard Johnson one of 36, Eric Davis five of 34, Mark McGwire four of 33, Nick Esasky three of 30. Jose Canseco, probably the only hitter in baseball who can rival Bo when it comes to sheer power, went the other way on only two of his 17 four-baggers. In this category, as in so many others, Bo stands alone.

One might wonder whether Bo is costing himself a lot of homers by sticking with this distinctive hitting style. That's not an easy question to answer. On the one hand, you have all these big power guys pulling consistently while Jackson bucks the trend . . . it's almost like he's thumbing his nose at the Ted Williams school of hitting every time he rounds the bases. On the other hand, why would you tamper with success? Bo ranked third in the American League in home run percentage last year, despite the fact that his home ballpark was costing him dearly. Jackson hit

21 of his 32 homers on the road last year; only Mitchell, with 25, had more home runs on foreign soil. As they used to say about Babe Ruth, when Bo hits 'em, they stay hit — whichever direction they go. And, anyway, if he *tried* pulling, he might mess himself up and get discouraged and quit to play professional polo or something. Which would be a loss for us all.

Among the other opposite field leaders, the only real surprise is Pete Incaviglia. Inky keeps experimenting with his game, trying to figure out a way to get over the hump somehow. It's not working right now, but you have to admire his determination.

The opposite extreme from Bo and John Kruk is represented by the guys who hardly ever go the other way. There are some real surprises here. Rob Deer hit only two of his 26 homers to the opposite field last year, which is no big shock. But Ryne Sandberg, of all people, outdid him, with only two of 30 to right and right center. The following players hit only one opposite field homer last year: Kelly Gruber, Cory Snyder, Don Mattingly, Jesse Barfield, Bobby Bonilla, Von Hayes. Mattingly has probably adapted himself to Yankee Stadium's friendly right field wall better than any player since Bill Dickey. Last year Don hit 19 of his 23 homers at the Stadium.

Finally, what do Eddie Murray, Lou Whitaker, Dave Parker, Andre Dawson, Dwight Evans, Kevin McReynolds, Cal Ripken and Alvin Davis have in common? Last year they all hit at least 20 homers, but none — that's zero — to the opposite field. Charlie Lau must be turning over in his grave.

A complete listing for this category can be found on page 271.

WHO ARE THE BEST LEADOFF HITTERS IN BASEBALL?

A leadoff man's job is to score runs, and the best way to do that is to get on base as often as possible. A lot of seemingly smart baseball men never seem to grasp that concept; year after year we see the likes of Billy Hatcher and Alfredo Griffin in the number one slot, dragging their clubs' offenses down with them. The following players were the major league leaders in on-base percentage while batting first during 1989:

Player, Team	OBA	AB	R	H	BB	HB
Wade Boggs, Bos	.414	497	85	155	86	4
Rickey Henderson, Yanks-Oak	.411	539	112	147	126	3
Tim Raines, Mon	.399	244	35	71	44	2
Bip Roberts, SD	.388	294	69	88	43	1
Jerry Browne, Cle	.385	456	67	138	61	1
Gregg Jefferies, Mets	.380	165	30	56	12	0
Kevin Seitzer, KC	.376	139	19	38	21	3
Gary Pettis, Det	.373	436	75	111	82	0
Steve Sax, Yanks	.366	364	49	118	25	1
Paul Molitor, Mil	.366	475	63	140	53	4

(Note: minimum 150 pate appearances in the leadoff slot of the lineup.)

Although Boggs led the way, his overall on-base percentage of .430 was his lowest in five years. Curiously, Wade got on base much more when he was batting in other positions in the batting order (OBA .493) than when he was batting first (.414). Troubled by trade rumors and the Margo Adams circus, he didn't have a typical Wade Boggs year. That, however, is the only bad thing you could say about his season.

While Boggs was outstanding, the real ace among leadoff men was Rickey Henderson. Henderson's on-base average while batting first was only three points lower than Wade's, and he more than made up for that with his ability to steal and run the bases. With the A's, Henderson's OBA was .425, and he scored a fantastic 72 runs in only 85 games.

The other leaders deserve some comment. One wonders why Montreal keeps pulling Tim Raines, arguably the best leadoff man in National League history, out of the number one spot. One wonders, also, whether Greg Jefferies and Gary Pettis can keep up their '89 performances; the free-swinging Jefferies is an unlikely leadoff man, and Pettis has never before shown such a great ability to draw walks. They'll have to do it again in 1990. Bip Roberts and Jerry Browne were surprise stars in '89, and the jury is still out on them, as well. Kevin Seitzer, Steve Sax and Paul

Molitor are all proven performers, however, and among the best leadoff men in the game.

The leadoff Hall of Shame is represented by the five players who ranked the lowest while batting leadoff during 1989 — but perhaps we should include their managers as well:

Player, Team	OBA	AB	R	H	BB	HB
Ron Gant, Atl	.214	160	18	29	7	0
Doug Dascenzo, Cubs	.230	134	19	22	12	0
Ozzie Guillen, WSox	.271	214	25	53	7	0
Mookie Wilson, Mets-Tor	.280	180	19	46	5	1
Alfredo Griffin, LA	.283	291	35	69	19	0

Your guess is as good as ours as to why Griffin, Wilson and Guillen got so many plate appearances in the number one slot. A few guesses: they're "ignitors," they "make things happen," they're "catalysts." Yeah, but they don't get on base, and they don't help their teams much.

A complete listing for this category can be found on page 272.

TO WHOM DOES THE GREEN MONSTER BECKON?

The Green Monster in Fenway Park has turned many fly balls that would have been outs elsewhere into hits. And which batters would benefit most by a move to Boston? Based on the direction and distance of flyouts he hit in 1988 and 1989, Kevin McReynolds would have picked up an additional 20 hits had he played all his games in Fenway. The chart shows the top five players in "Green Monster hits" in 1988-'89. Interestingly, two bat righthanded, two lefthanded, and one is a switch hitter — good evidence that Fenway can help any kind of hitter.

Certainly the Red Sox would love to have McReynolds and Brett. It's easy to fantasize how, playing in Fenway, McReynolds could move into the 30-home run bracket at last. And a Brett career at Fenway might have produced several more batting titles and hefty increases on George's already-impressive .310 career average and 267 lifetime home runs.

Always an outstanding hitters' park, Fenway remains somewhat misunderstood. It's an excellent park for scoring runs, and traditionally the best field in the majors for inflating batting averages. People have begun to realize that Fenway is a better park for lefthanded hitters than for righties. Of the seven Red Sox hitters who have led the American League in batting since World War II (Ted Williams, Billy Goodman, Pete Runnels, Carl Yastrzemski, Fred Lynn, Carney Lansford, Wade Boggs), six have batted lefty.

FLYOUTS ELSEWHERE THAT WOULD HAVE BEEN HITS IN FENWAY

Kevin McReynolds 20
George Brett 16
Chris Sabo 15
Chili Davis 14
Jack Howell 14

But because of the wall, Fenway has a reputation as a great home run park, and that reputation is probably greater than it should be. In recent years the Red Sox and their opponents have often hit more home runs away from Boston than in Fenway. The problem is that its longball effects are much better for some hitters than for others. Given the right lineup, like the one the Red Sox had in the late forties and early fifties, the home run balls will fly. A good example is Bobby Doerr, the righthanded-hitting Red Sox second baseman of the forties. Doerr hit 223 homers in his career — 145 of them at Fenway, only 78 on the road. But over the last five seasons Dwight Evans, no longer the great pull hitter he was in his youth, has hit 55 homers in Fenway, 75 on the road.

A home/road comparison for last year's leading Red Sox hitters shows how the park helps some hitters much more than others:

Player	Home				Road			
	BA	OBA	SLG	HR	BA	OBA	SLG	HR
Wade Boggs	.377	.475	.547	2	.287	.386	.358	1
Dwight Evans	.273	.403	.430	8	.295	.392	.493	12
Nick Esasky	.300	.379	.541	15	.253	.331	.459	15
Jody Reed	.300	.384	.415	2	.276	.368	.370	1
Ellis Burks	.319	.376	.480	6	.287	.353	.462	6
Mike Greenwell	.325	.387	.465	6	.291	.352	.421	8

Five of the six hit better at Fenway than on the road. Boggs, the quintessential Fenway hitter, belted 51 doubles — 37 of them at home. But of the four power hitters, none hit more homers in Boston. These days the Red Sox don't have the kind of righty power hitters who can hit the ball over the Wall. Where have you gone, Dick Stuart?

He left his heart in Fenway: Todd Benzinger, who went over to Cincinnati in the Esasky trade, had eleven "Green Monster" hits last year, which put him in a tie with the Astros' Craig Biggio for the most in the category during 1989. Unfortunately, Benzinger couldn't bring the park with him.

A complete listing for this category can be found on page 273.

WHO ARE BASEBALL'S MOST (AND LEAST) AGGRESSIVE BASERUNNERS?

Running the bases is one of baseball's hidden mysteries. There are no official statistics for it and, until now, no unofficial ones either. According to the stats, having Ernie Whitt on first base is exactly the same as having Rickey Henderson . . . even though all of us understand that isn't so.

Fortunately, STATS has taken a step to help our understanding of this important subject. What we've done is count each situation where a runner has an opportunity to take an extra base: basically, those would be, a runner on first when a double is hit, or a runner on first or second when a single is hit — there must also be no other runners impeding the base ahead. The system, as with all statistics, is not perfect; it doesn't take into account what field the ball was hit to, how hard it was hit, how deeply it was hit, or whether the field was grass or turf. But it's a start, and a good one. The following players took an extra base on hits most often during 1989:

Player, Team	Opportunities to Take An Extra Base	Number of Times An Extra Base Taken	Extra Bases Percent
Shawon Dunston, Cubs	26	25	96.2
Luis Polonia, Oak-Yanks	42	35	83.3
Gary Pettis, Det	41	32	78.0
Pat Sheridan, Det-SF	30	23	76.7
Milt Thompson, StL	40	30	75.0
Ken Caminiti, Hou	49	36	73.5
Phil Bradley, Bal	47	34	72.3
Jim Eisenreich, KC	36	26	72.2
Devon White, Cal	42	30	71.4
Bip Roberts, SD	48	34	70.8

While this list is not full of terribly-familiar names, all the players are known for having good speed and excellent baserunning judgement. Shawon Dunston's development into a fine all-around ballplayer really shows in this category, and the inclusion of such players as Gary Pettis, Milt Thompson and Devon White is no real surprise. But they are not alone. The ten players stole a total of 235 bases, with an average success rate of 73.4 percent, an excellent percentage. These are "smart" baserunners, and that intelligence is reflected in the figures.

If you're wondering where some famous names are, they rate just a little below the top group: Tim Raines 66.7 percent, Ozzie Smith 63.2, Rickey Henderson 62.5, Bo Jackson 61.1, Ryne Sandberg 57.6, Robin Yount 57.1. Those may seem like low figures, but remember that they're dependent on a number of factors, as well as managerial philosophy. And all these players were above the major league average of 51.7.

The dregs of the category are represented by the leadfoots, the guys who strictly go one base at a time. Ever hear the phrase, "he runs like a catcher"? Perhaps it should be amended to, "he runs like a well-paid first baseman."

Player, Team	Opportunities to Take An Extra Base	Number of Times An Extra Base Taken	Extra Bases Percent
Alvin Davis, Sea	62	13	21.0
Eddie Murray, LA	40	10	25.0
Garry Templeton, SD	27	7	25.9
Ernie Whitt, Tor	30	8	26.7
Bob Boone, KC	33	9	27.3
Kevin Romine, Bos	25	7	28.0
Mark McGwire, Oak	46	13	28.3
Kent Hrbek, Min	34	10	29.4
Damon Berryhill, Cubs	26	8	30.8,
Rick Cerone, Bos	29	9	31.0

The only real surprises in this group are Garry Templeton, a very sore-kneed shortstop, and Kevin Romine, who in his first extensive trial with Boston has already gotten into the Red Sox scheme of things. Romine fits right in with teammates Dwight Evans (45.1), Wade Boggs (42.2), Marty Barrett (36.4) and Nick Esasky (32.1). Fenway Park has always been a tough place to take an extra base in, but the Boston philosophy has been to play things conservatively and wait for the big inning.

A complete listing for this category can be found on page 274.

WHICH HITTERS ARE EASIEST TO DOUBLE UP?

Released by the Red Sox, Jim Rice ended 1989 with hopes of signing on with another major league team. Rice might want to reconsider if he wants to avoid one of baseball's more ignominious records. Jim has grounded into a staggering 315 double plays during his career. Nine more will give him the American League record; 14 and he'll break the major league mark. Rice must be comforted by the fact that the American League record-holder is Carl Yastrzemski, while the all-time leader is Henry Aaron. That kind of company won't embarrass anyone.

The stereotype of a big GDP man would be a lumbering righthanded pull hitter — your basic Ernie Lombardi. So it's surprising to note the biggest potential challenger to Aaron, Rice and Yaz is a swift base stealer (21 for 24 last year) who's only 28 years old. After just eight seasons, Julio Franco has grounded into 167 double plays, a nifty average of 21 per year. Without even factoring in an inevitable loss of speed, Franco will be closing in on the immortals when he passes his 35th birthday. Sort of gives you goose bumps, doesn't it?

The major league leaders in double play percentage last year (a GDP opportunity is an at bat with a runner on first, and less than two out) were:

Player, Team	GDP Opp.	GDP	% GDP per Opp.
Julio Franco, Tex	110	27	24.6
Keith Moreland, Det-Bal	86	21	24.4
Steve Buechele, Tex	93	21	22.6
Rance Mullinicks, Tor	54	12	22.2
Mike Heath, Det	82	18	22.0
Lenny Harris, Cin-LA	64	14	21.9
Dave Valle, Sea	60	13	21.7
Charlie O'Brien, Mil	52	11	21.2
Tony Pena, StL	94	19	20.2
Kevin Romine, Bos	56	11	19.6

(Note: Minimum 50 opportunities)

Franco notwithstanding, most of the hitters do fit the model: eight righthanded hitters, four catchers, four players 32 or older. Aside from Julio, the oddball of the group is Lenny Harris, a lefty swinger with excellent speed.

A lefty swinger with excellent speed — that's the perfect mental image of a player who hardly ever grounds into double plays. The players who were toughest to double up in '89 show once again how full of surprises this category can be:

Player, Team	GDP Opp.	GDP	% GDP per Opp.
Dan Pasqua, WSox	59	0	0.0
Darrell Evans, Atl	61	1	1.6
Dave Martinez, Mon	51	1	2.0
Cecil Espy, Tex	75	2	2.7
Tom Foley, Mon	72	2	2.8

The two leaders, naturally, were Darrell Evans, the oldest position player in the majors last year, and Dan Pasqua, who lumbers down to first while wearing a knee brace. Evans and Pasqua are proof that it's hard to ground into a double play if you don't hit the ball on the ground.

Jim Rice, bless him, grounded into only four DPs last year. Is that how the Red Sox knew he was washed up?

A complete listing for this category can be found on page 275.

WHICH BATTERS HAVE THE BIGGEST DAY/NIGHT DIFFERENCES?

NEED GLASSES?	DAY	NIGHT
Rolando Roomes	.386	.206
Harold Baines	.405	.277
Dion James	.365	.248
Luis Polonia	.358	.266
Alvin Davis	.371	.281

HAVE NIGHT VISION	DAY	NIGHT
Jim Presley	.136	.272
Carlos Martinez	.214	.336
Mike Felder	.173	.275
Dwight Evans	.219	.320
Andy Allanson	.179	.258

Qualifications: 100 PA during day and 200 PA at night.

Probably the biggest change in baseball over the last 50 years has been the shift from day to night baseball. Even the Cubs have lights now, and day games are generally only played a couple of times a week. Nonetheless, there are still plenty of day games, and a complete player needs to be productive under both natural and artificial light. The chart at the top of the page lists the players who had the biggest day/night differentials last year. Here are more complete stats for those players; note that all except Evans had at least twice as many at bats during night games:

	----- Day -----					----- Night -----					Difference
	AB	H	HR	RBI	BA	AB	H	HR	RBI	BA	
Roomes	101	39	3	14	.386	214	44	4	20	.206	+.180
Baines	126	51	4	21	.405	379	101	12	51	.277	+.128
D. James	137	59	2	14	.365	278	69	3	26	.248	+.117
Polonia	159	57	1	15	.358	274	73	2	31	.266	+.092
A. Davis	132	49	9	34	.371	366	103	12	61	.281	+.090

Presley	103	14	2	8	.136	287	78	10	33	.272	−.136
C. Martinez	103	22	2	10	.214	247	83	3	22	..336	−.122
Felder	104	18	1	4	.173	211	58	2	19	.275	−.102
Dw. Evans	183	40	8	28	.219	337	108	12	72	.320	−.101
Allanson	106	19	1	3	.179	217	56	2	14	.258	−.079

There seems to be little park bias to the data. Both Baines, in the "plus" group and Martinez, in the "minus," played for the White Sox; similarly, James and Allanson both toiled for the Indians, and Davis and Presley for the Mariners. Even so, we can't draw too many sweeping conclusions from the stats. The problem is that the data shows little consistency from year to year. Of the five players in the plus group, four actually hit better at night during *both* 1987 and '88; the fifth, Roomes, had an insignificant number of at bats. In the minus group, only Presley and Evans hit better at night during each of the last three seasons — and during the period from 1984 to '86, each of them hit better during the daytime.

Despite such evidence, some clubs seem to believe that failure to hit at night is a sign that the hitter, indeed, needs glasses. With the White Sox in 1986, Tim Hulett hit .295 during the day and .205 at night. The Sox had Hulett undergo an eye exam and fitted him for glasses, but in '87 Tim continued to hit much better in the daytime (.282 to .189). The Sox got rid of Hulett, and maybe his eye doctor as well.

There is one player who preferred day baseball so much that he practically threw himself on the Cubs' doorstep. (Perhaps it was on the advice of his optometrist.) As the stats from the last three seasons show, Andre Dawson knew what he was doing:

	----- Day -----					----- Night -----				
Year	AB	H	HR	RBI	BA	AB	H	HR	RBI	BA
1987	390	123	35	94	.315	231	55	14	43	.238
1988	362	106	12	43	.293	229	73	12	36	.319
1989	229	64	12	45	.279	187	41	9	32	.219
Total	981	293	59	182	.299	647	169	35	111	.261

Even Dawson hit better in night games during one of the last three years. But Andre's daytime production is much better overall, and even with the lights at Wrigley, he's with the team who helps him achieve maximum production.

Now that the Cubs are playing more night games than ever, you might wonder how they're making the adjustment. Here are the Cubs' percentages over the last three years, as they've gone from zero to eighteen night games at Wrigley:

Year	----- Day -----			----- Night -----		
	BA	OBA	SLG	BA	OBA	SLG
1987	.268	.329	.447	.258	.320	.405
1988	.262	.311	.379	.259	.309	.390
1989	.274	.334	.400	.246	.302	.372

The Cubs remain a better day team, though most of that is due to the park effects of the friendly confines of Wrigley. In 1989, the divisional championship year, the gap was greater than ever. Clearly the Cubs were utilizing their familiarity with day baseball to the maximum extent.

A complete listing for this category can be found on page 276.

WHICH HITTERS HAVE THE BEST STRIKEOUT TO WALK RATIOS?

One sign of a quality pitcher is a good strikeout-to-walk ratio: if it's two-to-one or thereabouts, you're usually talking about a quality workman. But a good strikeout-to-walk ratio is the sign of a quality hitter as well — it indicates an outstanding ability to make the pitcher work for his outs. The following major league hitters had the best strikeout-to-walk ratios in 1989 (minimum 251 plate appearances):

Player, Team	SO	BB	SO/BB Ratio
Marty Barrett, Bos	12	32	0.38
Wade Boggs, Bos	51	107	0.48
Carney Lansford, Oak	25	51	0.49
Alvin Davis, Sea	49	101	0.49
Mark Grace, Cubs	42	80	0.52
Tim Raines, Mon	48	93	0.52
Rickey Henderson, Yanks-Oak	68	126	0.54
Tony Gwynn, SD	30	56	0.54
Mike Scioscia, LA	29	52	0.56
Spike Owen, Mon	44	76	0.58

While the group contains a couple of punch-and-judy types in Barrett and Owen, it also contains some of the best — and most intelligent hitters — in the game. Boggs, Lansford, Davis, Grace, Henderson, Gwynn . . . we're talking high quality here. Tim Raines may return to that group soon, and Mike Scioscia has always been a useful offensive performer for a catcher.

Now contrast that group with this one, the players with the *worst* strikeout/walk ratios:

Player, Team	SO	BB	SO/BB Ratio
Rolando Roomes, Cin	100	13	7.69
Mookie Wilson, Mets-Tor	84	13	6.46
Mariano Duncan, LA-Cin	51	8	6.38
Cory Snyder, Cle	134	23	5.83
Andres Thomas, Atl	62	12	5.17
Matt Williams, SF	72	14	5.14
Jim Presley, Sea	107	21	5.10
Greg Gagne, Min	80	17	4.71

Player, Team	SO	BB	SO/BB Ratio
Charlie Hayes, SF-Phi	50	11	4.55
Bo Jackson, KC	172	39	4.41

Any group that contains Matt Williams and Bo Jackson, as well as the Mookster, can't be beyond hope. Bo's SO/BB ratio last year was the best of his career, so he's making progress. And at 24, Williams remains a hitter of enormous potential. But both will have to improve in the area of plate discipline if they want to continue to improve. To recognize that, all they have to do is look at Snyder and Presley. A few years ago each was considered one of the game's best young power hitters. But pitchers learned that they'd swing at anything, and in 1989 Cory and Jim were among the easiest outs in baseball. Both are young enough to recover, but for Presley, especially, time is getting short. That goes double for Duncan and Thomas, two middle infielders whose careers have stagnated.

In looking at the group of players with the best K/W ratios, one criticism would be that only Alvin Davis, who had 21 homers, was a real power hitter. Veteran fans might long for the "good old days" and players who both hit homers *and* had great strikeout/walk ratios. Like these three:

Player, Team	HR	SO	BB	SO/BB Ratio
Ted Williams, Bos	521	709	2019	0.35
Stan Musial, StL	475	696	1599	0.44
Joe DiMaggio, Yanks	361	369	790	0.48

We'll admit that there's no one like these guys in the modern game. (There was no one like them back then, either). But the following four hitters combined both power and discipline to an unusual degree in 1989:

Player, Team	HR	SO	BB	SO/BB Ratio
Alvin Davis, Sea	21	49	101	0.49
Don Mattingly, Yanks	23	30	51	0.59
Kent Hrbek, Min	25	35	53	0.66
Lou Whitaker, Det	28	59	89	0.66

While we won't burden him with the label of a modern-day DiMaggio, Don Mattingly is putting up some figures that wouldn't embarrass even the Yankee Clipper. In less than eight seasons Mattingly has belted 164 homers while striking out only 238 times; over the last six he's averaged

27 four-baggers, only 34 Ks and a strikeout/walk ratio of 0.70. That's not quite DiMaggio, but it's plenty good.

A complete listing for this category can be found on page 277.

WHO WERE THE HOTTEST (AND COLDEST) SECOND-HALF HITTERS LAST YEAR?

The "salary drive" is an honor-bound part of baseball tradition. Players who can't do a thing for half a year will suddenly get their acts together and turn it on late in the campaign. Then they can hit their club for more money at contract time. Even in an era of multi-year contracts, the salary drive is as popular as ever. The following players showed the biggest jump in performance during last year's second half (minimum 150 at bats in each half):

BA Change	Player, Team	First Half BA	HR	RBI	Second Half BA	HR	RBI
+.094	Jim Gantner, Mil	.237	0	20	.331	0	14
+.091	Oddibe McDowell, Cle-Atl	.216	3	22	.307	7	24
+.089	Shawon Dunston, Cubs	.225	4	22	.313	5	38
+.085	John Kruk, SD-Phi	.253	3	20	.338	5	24
+.081	Chris James, Phi-SD	.201	2	26	.282	11	39
+.081	Roberto Alomar, SD	.256	2	20	.337	5	36
+.080	Dickie Thon, Phi	.227	6	27	.307	9	33
+.078	George Brett, KC	.231	3	23	.309	9	57
+.077	Mookie Wilson, Mets-Tor	.206	3	15	.283	2	20
+.074	Jose Oquendo, StL	.252	0	16	.326	1	32

Performing like this does not always favorably impress a player's bosses. Four of the top ten were traded in midseason, and Chris James has now been peddled yet again. Jim Gantner's brilliant second half was derailed by a serious knee injury, so he'll have to prove himself all over again in 1990. But the late-season performances of Dunston and Wilson were key factors in their clubs' drives for division titles; Alomar and Oquendo are now looked on as coming stars; and the comebacks of Thon and Brett have heightened hopes that both can return to their old All-Star form.

Though he didn't make the top ten, another player who really helped himself with a big second half was Robin Yount. Robin had a decent start last year (.301, 8, 45), but then he really got rockin' with a .333-15-58 finish. The result was an MVP award, a long bidding war for his services, and finally a megabuck contract to re-sign with the Brewers. The salary drive lives!

It also lives in reverse. The following players showed the biggest *drop* in batting average over the second half of last year, and maybe a lump of coal in their first contract offers:

BA Change	Player, Team	First Half BA	HR	RBI	Second Half BA	HR	RBI
-.130	Billy Doran, Hou	.272	8	46	.141	0	12
-.111	Ernie Whitt, Tor	.319	5	31	.208	6	22
-.085	Rafael Palmeiro, Tex	.315	5	47	.230	3	17
-.085	Jim Presley, Sea	.275	5	20	.190	7	21
-.084	Terry Steinbach, Oak	.313	4	24	.229	3	18
-.082	Dave Gallagher, WSox	.303	1	26	.221	0	20
-.080	RJ Reynolds, Pit	.313	3	20	.234	3	28
-.078	Junior Felix, Tor	.297	6	36	.218	3	10
-.071	Lenny Dykstra, Mets-Phi	.281	4	16	.210	3	16
-.069	Robby Thompson, SF	.275	9	27	.205	4	23

Most of these players jeopardized formerly solid reputations with their poor finishes. Bill Doran's inexplicable decline made him the focus of offseason trade rumors; the same was true of Presley, Gallagher and Dykstra. Whitt, an original Blue Jay, has been shuffled off to Atlanta, and Rafael Palmeiro is no longer being talked about as a future batting king. About the only players still on solid footing are Steinbach and Thompson. Baseball, indeed, is a game of "what have you done for me lately?"

Avoiding both extremes, our last group of players were jewels of consistency in '89:

BA Change	Player, Team	First Half BA	HR	RBI	Second Half BA	HR	RBI
+.001	Dave Henderson, Oak	.250	7	39	.251	8	41
+.001	Darryl Strawberry, Mets	.224	16	36	.225	13	41
.000	Billy Hatcher, Hou-Pit	.231	3	33	.231	1	18
-.001	Tony Pena, StL	.260	3	22	.259	1	15
-.001	Bobby Bonilla, Pit	.281	9	40	.280	15	46
-.001	Todd Benzinger, Cin	.246	8	39	.245	9	37
-.001	Jerry Browne, Cle	.300	2	30	.299	3	15

Darryl Strawberry is proof that consistent performance won't make the right impression if your average is .225. Ditto for Billy Hatcher, who switched clubs late in the year. But the steadiness of Henderson, Bonilla and Browne did a lot to enhance their reputations going into '90. And Tony Pena made no salary drive, but he got a big free agent salary from the Red Sox anyway.

A complete listing for this category can be found on page 278.

WHAT WOULD AN AVERAGE MAJOR LEAGUE LINEUP LOOK LIKE?

	LEAD-OFF	2	3	CLEAN-UP	5	6	7	8	9
	NATIONAL								
AVG.	.254	.261	.278	.266	.248	.250	.247	.233	.168
RUNS	79	71	75	73	63	57	49	50	36
HR	8	9	15	22	14	12	10	6	4
RBI	41	48	71	85	70	60	60	50	34

Based on 600 plate appearances.

When a major league manager fills out his lineup card, what he can expect depends a lot on what league he's managing in. Looking at the average productivity from each spot in the batting order, it's obvious from the charts that American League managers can expect to see a lot more punch.

There is one obvious reason for the disparity: the designated hitter. Because of the DH, even the number nine hitter in an American League lineup possesses some potency — no .168 hitters here. The big offensive hole in National League lineups means that the number eight hitters can often be pitched around, which effectively takes the bat out of their hands. By contrast, an AL lineup is "seamless," giving the pitcher a continuous challenge.

But the difference goes deeper than that. The American League shows better production from every lineup spot except number four, and there the difference is slight and mostly due to one player, Kevin Mitchell. In good part the AL's better hitting can be attributed to the ballparks. We've pointed out in other essays that American League parks tend to be smaller, and better for the hitter; National League parks, most of them with artificial surfaces, tend to favor the pitcher and the running game. You could describe National League games as being "stolen base oriented" and American League games as being "home run oriented" and not be far off the mark. Certainly American League games are higher-scoring, and its pitchers have to work more carefully. Even without the DH, the offensive statistics for the American League would be better.

At this point, it's almost certainly true that the American League is the better hitting league — big parks or small, DH or no DH. Last year Johnny

	LEAD-OFF	2	3	CLEAN-UP	5	6	7	8	9
				AMERICAN					
AVG.	.269	.265	.287	.266	.263	.262	.244	.246	.238
RUNS	77	71	75	74	68	65	57	57	62
HR	6	7	17	19	16	16	12	9	6
RBI	42	51	84	84	70	70	62	56	51

Bench lamented that National League scouts tended to look first at how a hitting prospect ran and threw, rather than how he hit. Bench is probably right. Just as the American League took years to make up the NL's advantage in signing black and Latin players, now the AL has the jump in corralling the good hitters. After years of being pushed around, the Americans have won five of the last seven World Series and have begun to assert themselves in the All Star game as well. The AL is now the "Junior Circuit" in name only.

If you study baseball history back to the days of Ruth and Cobb, one thing that jumps out at you is that the stronger-hitting league has almost always been the stronger and more popular league overall, and the one that has dominated interleague confrontations. For a long time, the American was a loser in the All-Star game, a loser in the World Series, and a loser at the box office. All that is changing. In 1990 the Blue Jays figure to shatter the Dodgers' longstanding one-season attendance record, and may even approach the four million mark for the first time in baseball history. The National League now appears to be the one that will have to play catch-up.

A complete listing for this category can be found on page 279.

WHO ARE THE LEADERS IN SECONDARY AVERAGE?

Secondary average is a tool created by Bill James to reflect offensive contributions that are not represented in the primary figure — batting average. The idea is to give proper credit to extra base hits and stolen bases on a per at bat basis. The formula is:

$$\text{Secondary Average} = (2B + 3B \times 2 + HR \times 3 + BB + SB - CS) / AB$$

As a guide, the 1989 major league secondary average was .228. The spread tends to be greater than with batting averages, however. The best hitters in secondary average will be around .450 or higher, while the worst will be below .150. The 1989 leaders in secondary average (minimum 350 plate appearances) were:

Player, Team	Secondary Average
Jack Clark, SD	.516
Kevin Mitchell, SF	.503
Fred McGriff, Tor	.477
Rickey Henderson, Yanks-Oak	.475
Howard Johnson, Mets	.464
Eric Davis, Cin	.437
Mickey Tettleton, Bal	.431
Von Hayes, Phi	.428
Mark McGwire, Oak	.408
Randy Milligan, Bal	.403

Who does well in secondary average? Guys who hit homers, draw walks and steal bases — usually two of the three in heavy quantities, or all three in lesser ones. Thus it's possible to do well in this category and not be a great "all around" ballplayer. But you have to do more than just knock out singles, which is one way to rack up a good batting average. Jack Clark is a good example of a ballplayer who sticks out in the secondary average statistics. Jack's batting average has been only .242 during each of the last two seasons. But Clark consistently hits between 20 and 30 homers and draws well over 100 walks. His secondary average, in truth, may exaggerate his value a little. But his batting average clearly underrates it, and that's what this figure is intended to correct.

Another good example of a fine secondary average hitter is Gary Redus, now of the Pirates. Redus has played for four teams and is considered a disappointment in some quarters because his career average is only .250. But Redus makes up for that low average in other ways. He's one of the best base stealers in the game; he draws a more-than-normal number of walks; and he has always had good extra-base power. All in all, Redus is an offensive plus, and that value is reflected in his '89 secondary average of .391, a normal figure for him. Yet people will deride Redus, and extol someone like Mickey Hatcher (secondary average .138) as a "good" hitter. Hatcher indeed bats around .300, but the batting average really describes almost his entire value. We don't discount hitting .300. But overall, Hatcher is a player of much less value than Redus.

The following players — perhaps we should call them the "Mickey Hatcher All Stars" — were the worst 1989 performers in secondary average (minimum 350 plate appearances):

Player, Team	Secondary Average
Alvaro Espinoza, Yanks	.078
Omar Vizquel, Sea	.106
Felix Fermin, Cle	.112
Ozzie Guillen, WSox	.122
Dave Gallagher, WSox	.123

Dave Gallagher of the White Sox is famed as the inventor of a batting device called the "Stride Tutor" — no truth to the rumor that it's a 250-foot wire which attaches to the ball to keep it from going too far. Center fielder Gallagher at least proves that you don't have to be a middle infielder to be a member of this club. But it helps.

A complete listing for this category can be found on page 280.

WHO ARE THE BEST RBI MEN WITH RUNNERS IN SCORING POSITION?

The run batted in is the glamour statistic in baseball, the one figure that consistently transfers to votes in the Most Valuable Player balloting. But like all counting stats, RBI figures are somewhat subject to distortion. The main problem is that they don't measure the number of opportunities each hitter gets to drive in runs . . . and that number can vary greatly from hitter to hitter.

So we decided to count the number of baserunners in scoring position — the most obvious RBI opportunity — presented to each hitter. We then counted the number of those runners the hitter drove in, and computed an "RBI percentage." We didn't count the times the hitter drove in himself with a home run, or any runners who were driven in from non-scoring position (that is, first base). We were simply looking for a way to compare production to opportunity, and the results were pretty interesting. Here were the top ten hitters in RBI percentage last year (minimum 150 opportunities):

Batter	Runners in Scoring Position		
	Driven In	Opportunities	Percent
Pedro Guerrero, StL	89	248	35.9
Ruben Sierra, Tex	72	206	35.0
George Bell, Tor	78	225	34.7
Johnny Ray, Cal	52	155	33.5
Will Clark, SF	67	206	32.5
Don Mattingly, Yanks	77	239	32.2
Julio Franco, Tex	66	206	32.0
Robin Yount, Mil	68	216	31.5
Brian Harper, Min	45	150	30.0
Kent Hrbek, Min	45	152	29.6

The first thing you'll probably notice about this list is a name that's missing — Kevin Mitchell, last year's major league RBI leader with 125. Though his overall stats were awesome, Mitchell drove in only 53 of 226 runners from scoring position last year; his percentage of 23.5 percent was only a little above the major league average of 22.6. So how did Kevin drive in so many runs? In part because he drove in himself 47 times with home runs, and in part because he drove in 26 runners from first base, an outstanding total. If Mitchell wasn't the most productive player with runners in scoring position last year, he certainly found plenty of other ways to bring runs home.

Among the top ten, there aren't too many surprises. Guerrero hit .400 with runners in scoring position last year, Sierra .335, Bell .337, Clark .389, Franco an amazing .407. The surprises are Johnny Ray and Brian Harper. Neither had big RBI totals last year (Ray had 62, Harper 57), but that was due in good part to lack of opportunities. The figures show that Ray and Harper made the most of them.

If you're wondering which players had the most chances to drive in runners from scoring position last year, one word will suffice: Boston. Mike Greenwell and Nick Esasky of the Red Sox each came up with 252 runners on second or third last year, while teammate Dwight Evans ranked fourth, after Guerrero, with 245. Jack Clark and Joe Carter each had 244, Mattingly 239, Todd Benzinger 231, Cal Ripken 229, and Mitchell 226 to round out the top ten. Compared to those totals, Will Clark's 206 opportunities were pretty meager. Yet Will drove in 111 runs overall, while Todd Benzinger, to name one player, had only 76 ribbies. As he showed in last year's playoffs, Clark makes the most of his chances.

Meanwhile, some other players were making the least. The following hitters brought up the rear among players with at least 150 opportunities:

| | **Runners in Scoring Position** | | |
Batter	Driven In	Opportunities	Percent
Jack Howell, Cal	22	259	13.8
Robby Thompson, SF	24	169	14.2
Jesse Barfield, Tor-Yanks	32	204	15.7
Vince Coleman, StL	26	164	15.9
Lloyd Moseby, Tor	26	161	16.1

Caveat emptor: Moseby and Barfield both signed lucrative contracts during the offseason. Despite being a power hitter who's played with good hitting ballclubs, Barfield has driven home more than 84 runs only once in his career. Meanwhile Moseby's driven in 85 runs, total, over the last two seasons. The struggles of Coleman, Thompson and Howell — especially Thompson's anemic figures with runners in scoring position — have been well documented over the last couple of years. These figures only serve to amplify their problems.

A complete listing for this category can be found on page 281.

IS IT BETTER TO PULL OR GO THE OTHER WAY?

Use the whole ballfield! That's one of the most common pieces of advice given out by hitting coaches. But many hitters achieve good results while showing a pronounced preference for either pulling the ball or going the opposite way. The average major leaguer pulls the ball (that is, hits to the left of second if he's batting righty or to the right of second if he's a lefty) about 59 percent of the time. The following hitters were the most pronounced pull hitters and opposite field hitters in baseball during 1989, based on a minimum of 200 balls put in play:

The list is a little surprising. Balboni, Davis and Barfield would figure, but Von Hayes doesn't have the reputation of being a big pull hitter. And Tom

PULL HITTERS	Percentage of balls pulled	GO THE OTHER WAY	Percentage of balls hit to the opposite field
Steve Balboni	73.7%	Wade Boggs	69.0%
Von Hayes	73.3%	Kevin Seitzer	60.6%
Glenn Davis	72.9%	Felix Fermin	60.4%
Tom Foley	72.6%	John Kruk	60.2%
Jesse Barfield	71.5%	Luis Polonia	56.3%

Minimum 200 balls put into play.

Foley, who hit .229 and smashed all of seven homers last year? Of the five players, four hit for good power, but none batted higher than .269. So you might guess that pull hitters, except for Tom Foley, were basically low-average sluggers. Guess again. Ranking just below this group, in the 68-69 percent pull range, were such good all-around hitters as Ruben Sierra, Carlton Fisk, Brian Downing, Howard Johnson and Bobby Bonilla. None of those fellows hit less than .281 in 1989.

How about the hitters who consistently go the other way? Wade Boggs would figure; part of the secret of his success is lining balls off the left field wall at Fenway. The degree of his edge over anyone else, however, is quite surprising. The other players on this list are mostly singles hitters, although Kruk has a little power. Kevin Seitzer, who batted a career-low .281 last year and saw his doubles total drop from 32 to 17, may have to start pulling more to return to his previous success. Tony Gwynn, incidentally, ranked a little below this group, going the opposite way 54 percent of the time.

Then there are the hitters who listen to the coaches' advice and neither pull nor go to the opposite way consistently. The following hitters rate right down the middle:

Hitter	Pulls	Hits to the Opposite Field
Julio Franco, Tex	52%	48%
Ivan Calderon, WSox	50%	50%
Willie Randolph, LA	50%	50%
Kirby Puckett, Min	49%	51%
Bo Jackson, KC	48%	52%

Despite the conventional wisdom, the stats show it's possible to be a successful hitter while using a variety of hitting styles.

A complete listing for this category can be found on page 282.

WHO LEADS THE LEAGUE IN LOOKING?

Baseball begins with the chess game between pitcher and batter. The hitter tries to get a good pitch to hit, to foul off or take the ones he can't handle. The pitcher, meanwhile, tries to work on the hitter's weaknesses, to get ahead on the count and make the batter chase bad pitches if possible. It's a continual war, and so it's startling to discover that the average plate appearance takes only about three and half pitches. Extremely patient hitters will average about four pitches per appearance; wild swingers will average about three. Not much difference — and yet all the difference in the world.

The following hitters averaged the most pitches per plate appearance in 1989 (minimum 300 plate appearances):

Hitter	Pitches per PA
Randy Milligan, Bal	4.23
Jesse Barfield, Tor-Yanks	4.18
Wade Boggs, Bos	4.15
Gary Pettis, Det	4.12
Darrell Evans, Atl	4.11
Rickey Henderson, Yanks-Oak	4.10
Brian Downing, Cal	4.08
Steve Jeltz, Phi	4.08
Brady Anderson, Bal	4.08
Mickey Tettleton, Bal	4.05

As would figure, these are hitters who draw a lot of walks; they also tend to strike out more than the average hitter. The most consistent high average hitter in baseball (Wade Boggs) is a member of the group, as is baseball's premier leadoff man in Rickey Henderson. But even those who hit for low averages help their teams by getting on base often via the walk. One hitter, Gary Pettis, both revived his career and found free agent riches by making a conscious effort to take more pitches last year.

One fact that should be noted is that there are three Baltimore Orioles on the list. Two more O's, Craig Worthington and Jim Traber, ranked in the top fifteen. Clearly Frank Robinson stressed patience to the young Oriole hitters, and that patience paid off in the team's performance.

Although there's a strong relationship between pitches per plate appearances and drawing walks, it doesn't always work out that way. Brian Downing ranked high in the PPA standings last year, but drew only 56 walks, his lowest total in eight years. And amazingly, both Jose

Canseco (one walk per 11.2 PA) and Jack Clark (one walk per 4.5) averaged 3.93 pitches per plate appearance last year. Jose seems to have the patience to wait for his kind of pitch, but rather than walk, he'll foul off offerings until he gets it.

We've discussed the patient hitters. The opposite group consists of the hackers, the players who average the fewest pitches per plate appearance:

Hitter	Pitches per PA
Alvaro Espinoza, Yanks	2.76
Kirby Puckett, Min	2.78
Ozzie Guillen, WSox	2.91
Tony Pena, StL	2.92
Scott Bradley, Sea	2.93
Brian Harper, Min	2.95
Andres Thomas, Atl	2.98
Jim Eisenreich, KC	2.99
Jim Gantner, Mil	3.00
Jeff Hamilton, LA	3.02

There are some good hitters in this group, and one great one in Kirby Puckett. So it's possible to be an effective offensive performer while seeing a minimum number of pitches. But it's not easy, especially since the hitter is giving up numerous opportunities for free passes to first.

While only one Milwaukee Brewer made the "least patient" group, several other Brewers ranked near the bottom — Bill Spiers, B.J. Surhoff and Gary Sheffield. The young Brewer hitters appear to be coached differently than the young Orioles are, and judging from the results, it's not to their advantage.

A complete listing for this category can be found on page 283.

WHY DON'T THEY STEAL THIRD MORE OFTEN?

Great baserunners often say that, despite the shorter throw, it's actually easier to steal third base than second. And they're right; last year runners were successful 68 percent of the times they tried to steal second, but 74 percent of the times they went for third. Here are the major league leaders at stealing third base in 1989, along with their totals when going for second:

Player, Team	Third Base			Second Base		
	SB	CS	%	SB	CS	%
R. Henderson, Yanks-Oak	24	5	82.8	53	8	86.9
Vince Coleman, StL	17	2	89.5	48	8	85.7
Devon White, Cal	11	0	100.0	32	16	66.7
Steve Sax, Yanks	11	6	64.7	32	11	74.4
Tim Raines, Mon	9	1	90.1	32	7	82.1
Otis Nixon, Mon	9	3	75.0	28	8	77.8
Jim Eisenreich, KC	7	0	100.0	20	7	74.1
Tony Gwynn, SD	7	0	100.0	33	16	67.3
Roberto Alomar, SD	7	1	87.5	35	15	70.0
Barry Bonds, Pit	7	1	87.5	25	9	73.5
Dave Martinez, Mon	7	1	87.5	16	3	84.2
Gerald Young, Hou	7	1	87.5	26	24	52.0
Major League Average			73.7			68.4

Not surprisingly, nine of the twelve leaders were more successful when attempting to steal third . . . and two of the others had third base success rates of 83 and 75 percent. The only runner who had a poor percentage when going for third was Steve Sax, not always the most prudent of baserunners.

Given that kind of success, you might wonder why there aren't more third base steal attempts. Last year runners attempted to steal third only 518 times, about once every four games. By contrast, they tried to steal second 4,557 times, or 8.8 times as often. Admittedly, the opportunities to steal third are less frequent, but not *that* less frequent. Given a 74 percent chance for success, why aren't more runners like Rickey Henderson, who seems willing to go for third whenever he thinks he can make it?

The answer is that it usually isn't worth the risk. Pete Palmer and John Thorn in *The Hidden Game of Baseball* estimate, as do most statisticians, that runners attempting to steal second will cost their team runs unless they're successful at least two thirds of the time. But stealing third, they figure, requires an 80 to 90 percent success rate to justify the risk of removing a valuable runner from second base. Except for runners in the elite class, like Henderson or Coleman, attempting to steal third is going to be a losing proposition.

A complete listing for this category can be found on page 284.

WHO ARE THE BEST BUNTERS IN BASEBALL?

BEST	Bunt tries	Good bunts	PCT.
Tony Gwynn	20	15	75%
Jody Reed	23	15	65%
Marty Barrett	32	19	59%
WORST			
Kevin Seitzer	59	10	17%
Otis Nixon	61	9	15%
Luis Polonia	45	6	13%

'Good bunts' are bunt singles and sacrifice hits.
'Bunt tries' are bunts in play plus fouled and missed bunts. Minimum 15 bunts in play.

Bunting is considered a lost art, with good reason. Look at a tape of a World Series game from the forties or fifties, and your eyes may well up with tears watching all the perfectly-laid bunts being executed. These days bunting still has its skillful practitioners who carry on the tradition of Phil Rizzuto. But it also has an ever-increasing number of hacks who consider even a request to bunt as a personal insult. The above chart lists the best and worst bunters of 1989. The fact that only two hitters had a "good percentage" higher than 60 indicates how hard it is lay one down without a hitch. Last year less than one third of all bunts (32.5%) attempted in major league games were good bunts.

An interesting point about the chart is that two of the three best bunters are American League players. One would expect that the better hitting American League would have fewer skillful bunters, but that isn't so — in fact the American League had a slightly better good bunt percentage (32.7) than the NL did (32.4). (The American League did, however, produce five of the worst six bunters.) The fact that the AL has more grass fields may help its good and marginal bunters; grass is much more conducive to bunting than artificial turf is. All but one of last year's five best bunters played on grass. Another factor for the lower NL percentage would be pitchers bunting. You would expect that the average pitcher would be a poorer bunter than the average hitter, despite a lot more practice.

One thing our chart doesn't show is the number of bunt hits recorded by each batter. Here are the major league leaders in bunt hits for 1989:

Player, Team	Bunt Hits
Brett Butler, SF	22
Vince Coleman, StL	19
Jerome Walton, Cubs	18
Oddibe McDowell, Cle-Atl	16
Steve Lyons, WSox	13
Junior Felix, Tor	11
Craig Biggio, Hou	10
Robbie Thompson, SF	10
Ron Karkovice, WSox	9
Wally Backman, Min	8
Cecil Espy, Tex	8

National League players come to the forefront in this category, taking the top three and a half places if we count McDowell for both leagues. There are a few surprises in this list, but the biggest may be the presence of two catchers, Biggio and Karkovice.

It's hard to knock the results of Vince Coleman, what with 19 bunt hits. But a breakdown of his attempts shows that getting all those bunt singles took considerable effort. Coleman fouled off a total of 55 bunt attempts and missed 19 pitches completely in his attempts to lay one down. As a result Vince's "good percentage" was only 23.8. Coleman at least has the right idea in taking lots of opportunities to use his speed.

Since they often get a chance to help themselves with a bunt, one group that deserves special examination are the National League pitchers. The following NL moundsmen laid down at least ten good bunts last year:

Pitcher, Team	Bunt Hits	Sac Hits
Rick Reuschel, SF	1	16
Tom Browning, Cin	1	14
Orel Hershiser, LA	2	10
Rick Sutcliffe, Cubs	1	10
Tim Belcher, LA	0	10
Ken Howell, Phi	0	10
Mike Bielecki, Cubs	1	9
Jose DeLeon, StL	1	9

A complete listing for this category can be found on page 285.

WHICH PLAYERS PRODUCE THE MOST RBI PER HOME RUN?

Every team wants home run hitters in the middle of their lineup; the third, fourth and fifth hitters are the players most likely to come up with men on base, and a longball in those situations can mean the difference between a win and a loss. Because a home run with men on base is often a gamebreaker, whatever the inning, the ability to come through in such situations is an important, and often underrated, measure of clutch hitting ability. The following players produced the most RBI per home run in 1989 (minimum 15 homers):

Player, Team	RBI per HR	HR	RBI
Eddie Murray, LA	2.15	20	43
Dale Murphy, Atl	2.10	20	42
Jack Clark, SD	2.08	26	54
Nick Esasky, Bos	1.97	30	59
Paul O'Neill, Cin	1.93	15	29
Gary Gaetti, Min	1.89	19	36
Matt Williams, SF	1.89	18	34
Eric Davis, Cin	1.79	34	61
Jeffrey Leonard, Sea	1.79	24	43
Jesse Barfield, Tor-Yanks	1.78	23	41
Andres Galarraga, Mon	1.78	23	41

Not surprisingly, some battle-hardened veterans lead the way. Though his skills are obviously in decline, Eddie Murray remains one of the most dangerous hitters in baseball. The active leader in grand slam home runs, Murray has always possessed a knack for coming through with men on base. His performance in this category last year was all the more impressive because the Dodgers possessed a very weak attack. With Kirk Gibson and Mike Marshall out for much of the year, Murray was the club's only power threat for much of the season.

Most of the other players have well-deserved reputations as good clutch hitters. But they can also tip their hats to some productive teammates. Dale Murphy had a poor year overall, but he was able to come through with the longball with men on base; Murphy had the considerable advantage of Lonnie Smith batting ahead of him. Jack Clark produced in clutch situations in 1989, as he has so often in the past; the on-base abilities of Bip Roberts, Roberto Alomar and Tony Gwynn helped him get many opportunities with ducks on the pond. Similarly, Nick Esasky was often able to swing for the fences with Wade Boggs on ahead of him. Gary Gaetti was fortunate to bat behind Kirby Puckett, and Matt Williams had the advantage of coming up after Will Clark and Kevin Mitchell. But Gaetti and Williams have shown in the postseason that they can come through with the best in pressure situations. The same goes for Jeffrey Leonard, who belted four home runs in the '87 playoffs.

The other side of the coin is represented by the players who produced the fewest RBI per home run in 1989:

Player, Team	RBI per HR	HR	RBI
Ryne Sandberg, Cubs	1.27	30	38
Bobby Bonilla, Pit	1.29	24	31
Steve Buechele, Tex	1.31	16	21
Ken Griffey, Jr., Sea	1.31	16	21
Danny Tartabull, KC	1.33	18	24
Dave Henderson, Oak	1.33	15	20
Lonnie Smith, Atl	1.33	21	28

Though we are safe in labeling the first group of players as good clutch hitters, it is probably unfair to label these players as ones who fold under pressure; anyone who labels Ryne Sandberg or Dave Henderson as poor clutch players deserves to go to the back of the class. Lonnie Smith often batted at the top of the lineup, so he didn't have as many opportunities with men on base as other players. And Ken Griffey was a raw rookie, still feeling his way around the majors. But Danny Tartabull definitely had a disappointing season, dropping from 102 RBI to 62 overall, and Bobby Bonilla often came to the plate last year troubled by his problems afield. Steve Buechele has consistently produced between 50 and 60 total RBIs for the Rangers, but his overall performance has been disappointing. His numbers in this category are one more example of how he's struggled.

A complete listing for this category can be found on page 286.

IF LINEOUTS WERE HITS...?

Talk to a hitter who's having a tough season, and he's likely to say, "Yeah, but I'm hitting into a lot of tough outs." Excuses are easy to make, but our statistics show that sometimes this one has merit. We keep track of exactly how each out is recorded — not only to whom the ball was hit, but whether it was a lineout, flyout or whatever. Most base hits are line drives, so we decided to see how the batting races would have been changed if every lineout had dropped safely. Here are the restructured batting races, with the player's actual average, the number of lineouts he recorded and what his new average would have been if those liners had been hits. You'll immediately notice that some players get robbed a lot more than others:

American League

Player, Team	AB	H	Avg.	Lineouts	New Avg.	Gain
Lansford, Oak	551	185	.336	36	.401	.065
Boggs, Bos	621	205	.330	43	.399	.069
Puckett, Min	635	215	.339	25	.378	.039
A. Davis, Sea	498	152	.305	34	.373	.068
Franco, Tex	548	173	.316	31	.372	.056
Molitor, Mil	615	194	.315	34	.371	.056
Sax, Yanks	651	205	.315	36	.370	.055
Mattingly, Yanks	631	191	.303	40	.366	.063
Yount, Mil	614	195	.318	28	.363	.055
Sierra, Tex	634	194	.306	36	.363	.057

National League

Player, Team	AB	H	Avg.	Lineouts	New Avg.	Gain
Gwynn, SD	604	203	.336	41	.404	.068
L. Smith, Atl	482	152	.315	32	.382	.067
Herr, Phi	561	161	.287	50	.376	.089
Grace, Cubs	510	160	.314	31	.375	.061
W. Clark, SF	588	196	.333	20	.367	.033
Jefferies, Mets	508	131	.258	55	.366	.108
Guerrero, StL	570	177	.311	27	.358	.047
Oquendo, StL	556	162	.291	36	.356	.065
Randolph, LA	549	155	.282	39	.353	.071
Treadway, Atl	473	131	.277	35	.351	.071

The average player will lose 52 points on his batting average due to lineouts. The interesting cases are the ones who vary from that figure.

Some players lose only 25 points, others more than 100. The classic line-drive hitters like Wade Boggs obviously suffer the most, but there is a lot of variance even among this group.

The most interesting case of all may be Gregg Jefferies. Despite a torrid finish, Jefferies hit only .258, an enormously disappointing figure for a player who was tabbed for Cooperstown — at least by some people — before he'd ever played a major league game. But that .258 could have easily been a lot higher. Jefferies lined out 55 times last year, the highest total in the majors. If all those liners had fallen in, he'd have batted .366. Of course, that's an unrealistic assumption. But if Jefferies had hit into only 30 lineouts, an average figure for a player with his total of at bats, he would have batted .307 and no one would have been disappointed. Not the most popular of players, Jefferies has started getting a reputation as something of a whiner. That's not an admirable trait, but it's easy to see that Greg had something to complain about.

The other extreme is represented by two Davis boys. Eric Davis of the Reds hit into only 12 lineouts last year and would have gained only 26 points if those balls had been hits. Eric is an outstanding player, but it's justifiable to say that his .281 average was helped by a little luck . . . maybe more than a little. In the same vein, another Davis — Chili of the Angels — hit only 17 lineouts in 560 at bats. Chili's .271 average could have easily been a lot lower.

The elite group of tough luck hitters would consist of the players who hit into at least 40 lineouts last year. That group is composed of Jefferies (55), Tommy Herr (50), Boggs (43), Tony Gwynn, Ozzie Guillen and Cal Ripken (41 each), and Don Mattingly (40). Most of them had good seasons anyway, but not everyone. Strawberry, especially, had a miserable year all around, and it wasn't just bad luck. But we can see that Straw hit into a lot of tough outs while batting a career-low .225 last year.

A complete listing for this category can be found on page 287.

WHO HIT THE LONGEST HOMERS DURING 1989?

One of the more popular scoreboard items of recent years has been the "Tale of the Tape." It always amazes us when a ball disappears into the ozone, and ten seconds later a message will flash on that board saying, "That homer by Joe Shlabotnick traveled 443 feet!"

You won't see our distance figures on any scoreboard; not yet, anyway. But we do keep track of the direction and distance of every ball put in play. While we agree that the "Tale of the Tape" stuff is fun, we don't feel confident in recording the distance down to less than the nearest ten feet. But we can still have some fun with it. According to our data, only 19 players hit a ball at least 450 feet last year. Here they are:

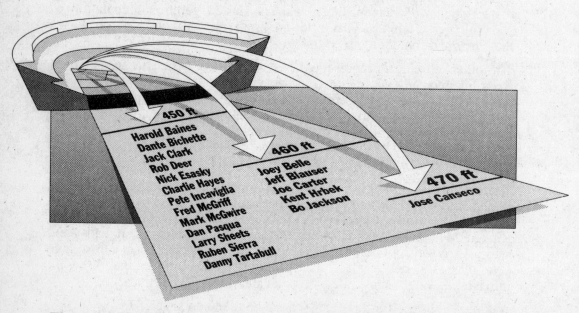

450 ft
Harold Baines
Dante Bichette
Jack Clark
Rob Deer
Nick Esasky
Charlie Hayes
Pete Incaviglia
Fred McGriff
Mark McGwire
Dan Pasqua
Larry Sheets
Ruben Sierra
Danny Tartabull

460 ft
Joey Belle
Jeff Blauser
Joe Carter
Kent Hrbek
Bo Jackson

470 ft
Jose Canseco

These are figures for the regular season only, of course. There are mighty sluggers in this list, and Canseco at the top is pretty fitting — only Bo Jackson can rival Jose when it comes to sheer power. Players like Joey Belle and Jeff Blauser are less likely candidates to belt a tape measure shot, but these guys have the power to drive a ball a long way. It's when we decrease the distances just a little that some really bizarre names start to crop up. Here are the longest balls hit by some other major league hitters last year, including some very unlikely heroes:

440 feet: The list of players to hit a ball this far includes such big names as Bobby Bonilla, Eric Davis, Mike Greenwell, Kevin Mitchell, Kirby Puckett and Cal Ripken. But it also includes those two famous sluggers, Dick Schofield and Randy Velarde.

430 feet: Steve Balboni, George Brett, Glenn Davis, Dwight Evans, Kirk Gibson, Rickey Henderson, Howard Johnson, Ron Kittle, Wally Joyner and Ryne Sandberg belted a ball 430 feet last year, among others. The "others" include Joel Skinner and Rob Richie. Or was it Bob Skinner and Rich Robbie?

420 feet: Matched pairs at this distance include Eddie Murray and John Smoltz, Andre Dawson and Joe Orsulak, Gary Gaetti and Jeff Wetherby, Darryl Strawberry and Tom Brookens. A new focus on Strawberry's '89 season: he couldn't hit a ball any farther than Tom Brookens.

Who were the 97-pound weaklings of the '89 season? National League pitchers, of course. The most anemic, undoubtedly, was Jay Howell of the Dodgers, who succeeded in putting three balls in play — none of them longer than 60 feet. Considering Howell's problems in the 1988 playoffs, maybe he should put the pine tar on his bat instead of his glove. (Or maybe he could try hitting with the glove.)

As a pitcher, Howell at least has an excuse. But for all around ineptitude among position players, it's hard to top a man with a fascinating name, Mike Blowers of the Yankees. In 38 September at bats, Blowers managed to record ten hits for a .263 average, which was enough to make the Yankees consider him a candidate for their third base job this year. (The Yankees are like that.) We wish Mike well, but we hope Blowers spent the winter eating his Wheaties. All of his ten hits were singles, and none of the 25 balls he put in play traveled farther than 290 feet. Blowers is going to have to flex his muscles a little if he's going to make the Yankee Stadium crowd forget those mighty pokes by Randy Velarde and Tom Brookens.

WHO ARE THE BEST CLEANUP HITTERS IN BASEBALL?

Baseball lineups are constructed so that the number four hitter is the man most likely to come up with men on base. The cleanup hitter's job is simple: hit the ball as hard as possible, preferably for extra bases, and bring those runners home. These are the sluggers, so we rank them by slugging percentage. The following players had the best slugging percentages in baseball while batting in the cleanup position — the last category is at bats per RBI, the lower the number the better:

While Batting Cleanup

Player, Team	Slugging Average	Batting Average	On-Base Average	AB	H	HR	RBI	AB per RBI
Kevin Mitchell, SF	.636	.290	.385	541	157	47	125	4.3
Eric Davis, Cin	.581	.296	.361	179	53	14	45	4.0
Ruben Sierra, Tex	.552	.311	.354	585	182	26	110	5.3
Robin Yount, Mil	.546	.330	.394	273	90	11	46	5.9
Mickey Tettleton, Bal	.537	.281	.407	281	79	17	43	6.5
Gary Gaetti, Min	.508	.299	.335	177	53	10	37	4.8
Bobby Bonilla, Pit	.491	.281	.357	613	172	24	85	7.2
Glenn Davis, Hou	.490	.266	.349	575	153	34	86	6.7
Bo Jackson, KC	.487	.256	.317	359	92	22	81	4.4
Kent Hrbek, Min	.480	.262	.346	256	67	15	57	4.5

(Minimum: 150 plate appearances while batting cleanup)

Some of these players were such reliable cleanup hitters that they never batted anywhere else all season. Mitchell, Mr. Cleanup of 1989, had only two at bats all year out of the fourth slot — both as a pinch hitter — while Bonilla and Glenn Davis had only three and six at bats, respectively, in other lineup spots. The rest were used in other batting positions with mixed results. Gaetti, for example, had 308 at bats in the fifth slot, and you'd hardly know it was the same player; Gary hit only .218 with .341 slugging batting fifth, with fewer home runs (nine) and RBIs (36) in 308 at bats than he produced in 177 fewer at bats hitting fourth. Mickey Tettleton, a solid .281 hitter with good power batting cleanup, was only a .208 hitter batting in other spots. On the other hand, Kent Hrbek, a good cleanup hitter, was a devastating force batting fifth: 7 homers, 15 RBIs and .843 slugging in only 51 at bats.

The following players were like Pigpen — they never cleaned up anything:

Player, Team	Slugging Average	Batting Average	On-Base Average	AB	H	HR	RBI	AB per RBI
K. Moreland, Det-Bal	.299	.248	.310	157	0	1	17	9.2
Alan Trammell, Det	.324	.246	.320	281	1	3	24	11.7
Pete O'Brien, Cle	.332	.233	.338	232	0	5	24	9.7
Dale Murphy, Atl	.357	.224	.296	482	0	16	72	6.7
Dave Parker, Oak	.367	.222	.367	180	0	6	26	6.9

Since the average cleanup man hit .266 with 20 homers and 84 RBIs and a .442 slugging average in 1989, these guys were clearly hurting their teams. Dave Parker had a 97-RBI campaign last year, but he was a dud as a cleanup man. The Cobra was much more effective hitting third: .321-13-57 with .526 slugging. Keith Moreland, the least effective of all cleanup hitters, was outstanding when he batted fifth: .344 with .532 slugging. Even Pete O'Brien, no power guy wherever he batted last year, was a .286 hitter in the fifth spot.

It seems obvious from these stats that some players are much more effective in certain lineup spots than they are in others. Sometimes it's a case of who hits before, or after them. Sometimes a case of how comfortable they feel. And sometimes it's just a matter of blind luck. In the old days, lineups were so set that the scorecards would be printed with the batting order already typeset. Those days are long gone — now managers move players in and out, looking for the right combination. It's only when they find a 1989-style Kevin Mitchell that they can stop the juggling act.

A complete listing for this category can be found on page 288.

WHO ARE THE LEADERS IN "POWER PERCENTAGE"?

The problem with batting averages, as everyone knows, is that they don't measure how far or how hard the batter is hitting the ball. According to last year's batting averages, Pat Tabler (.259) was a better hitter than his teammate Bo Jackson (.256). Even people who don't follow football or buy sneakers know this isn't so.

To measure power hitting, the slugging percentage was invented. It's a good stat, sensibly based on total bases divided by at bats. But it has a weakness: total bases include singles, and a player who hits a *lot* of singles, like former batting champion Rod Carew, can look like a slugger when he really isn't. Conversely, a low average power hitter, like Mark McGwire, suffers. So statisticians have gone one step farther, and invented the "power percentage," also known as power factor or isolated power. The basic formula for power percentage is simple; it's just slugging average minus batting average (the exact formula is [2b plus 3bx2 plus HRx3] divided by AB). What that subtraction does is to eliminate the effect of singles, and create a percentage based strictly on extra base hits. This identifies the McGwire-Dave Kingman types, the low-average sluggers, for what they are.

In 1989, major league batters had an overall power percentage of .121. The leaders (minimum 400 at bats) were:

Player, Team	Power %
Kevin Mitchell, SF	.344
Howard Johnson, Mets	.271
Eric Davis, Cin	.260
Fred McGriff, Tor	.256
Mickey Tettleton, Bal	.251
Darryl Strawberry, Mets	.241
Bo Jackson, KC	.239
Mark McGwire, Oak	.237
Ruben Sierra, Tex	.237
Andre Dawson, Cubs	.224
Glenn Davis, Hou	.224

One of the themes we've stressed in this book is that things may be changing in baseball, that power may at long last be returning to the National League. An encouraging sign for NL fans is that the top three players in power percentage all played in their league. Certainly they can brag about Kevin Mitchell. Based on 34 doubles, 6 triples and 47 home runs, Mitchell's power percentage was the best in the majors since Willie Stargell's .347 back 1973. (Don't get too puffed up, Kevin. Back in 1921, Babe Ruth's power percentage was .472.)

Aside from rewarding Mitchell's achievements, the leaders list gives credit to some overlooked players. Guys like McGwire and Glenn Davis are recognized as sluggers, but probably not to the extent that they should be. Their unimpressive batting averages limit their recognition; these high power percentages should help make up for that.

Can you have a good power percentage and yet still have a bad year overall? It's possible. You could argue that point about both Darryl Strawberry and Andre Dawson last year. Each had low batting averages and RBI figures, as well as shortcomings in other areas. The power percentages indicated that when they connected, the ball went a long way; that might not have made up for their other weaknesses, but both swung heavy bats.

You're probably dying to know who swung the lighest bats. Here are the players with the lowest power percentages last year, again based on a 400 at bat minimum:

Player, Team	Power %
Felix Fermin, Cle	.023
Gerald Young, Hou	.043
Dave Gallagher, WSox	.048
Bob Boone, KC	.049
Al Newman, Min	.049

Fermin and Gallagher seem to make all these "bottom of" lists, don't they? Bob Boone is probably a surprise because he hit .274, but it was a very singles-oriented .274; ditto for Gallagher's .266 and Al Newman's .253. Gerald Young had a very forgettable year in 1989, and this stat is one more indication of that.

A complete listing for this category can be found on page 289.

DOES PLATOONING MAKE SENSE?

The instinctive answer to this question is yes. Even a cursory glance at baseball statistics show that the underlying reasons for platooning seem to be sound. While every player is different, on balance lefthanded hitters do better against righthanded pitchers than they do against southpaws. And righthanded hitters perform better against lefthanded pitching. The figures bear it out, in terms of batting average and overall effectiveness.

But a deeper look at the numbers reveals a few surprises. Here are batting, on-base and slugging averages for major league players in 1989, broken down according to platoon differences. We add one more category, home run percentage:

	Batting Average	On-Base Average	Slugging Percentage	Home Run Percentage*
LHB vs. LHP	.240	.307	.341	1.62
LHB vs. RHP	.260	.332	.381	2.05
RHB vs. RHP	.243	.303	.363	2.31
RHB vs. LHP	.264	.329	.391	2.24

* home runs per 100 at bats

The percentages tell the familiar story. Both left and righthanded hitters do better against pitchers from the other side. But righthanded batters fare better overall: they hit lefties better than lefthanded batters hit righties, and the righty swingers' performance against righties outpaces the lefthanded hitters' performance against southpaws. This makes a certain intuitive sense: righthandedness is natural for the vast majority of people, so we might expect the overall level of skill among righties to be higher.

The most surprising statistic, however, is home run percentage. Righthanded batters hit more many more homers against righties than lefthanded hitters do against southpaws. But the shocker is that righthanded hitters belt more homers on a percentage basis against *righthanded* pitchers than they do against lefties. That's something you wouldn't expect, and might lead one to think that platooning is overrated. After all, if a righty swinger is more likely to homer against a righthanded pitcher than against a southpaw, isn't the whole thing being overused?

We don't think it is, and we feel there is a logical way to explain this surprising result. In the modern era, an increasing number of hitters are becoming switch-hitters. Despite the example of Mickey Mantle, most of the switchers are natural righthanded singles hitters who have learned to turn around to take advantage of their speed. (They also turn around, in many cases, because they simply have trouble hitting.) Let's separate batters into "pure" hitters who bat lefty or righty all the time, and switch-hitters. This is how each group does against opposite-side pitching:

	Batting Average	On-Base Average	Slugging Percentage	Home Run Percentage
Pure LHB vs. RHP	.262	.336	.393	2.40
Switch-hitters vs. RHP	.256	.325	.362	1.49
Pure RHB vs. LHP	.265	.331	.400	2.50
Switch-hitters vs. LHP	.260	.321	.366	1.48

You can see the difference that removing the switch-hitters makes. The switch-hitters tend to have a decent average against both lefties and righties, but with little power either way. The pure hitters, both left and right, have much more power — they hit about one more homer per 100 at bats than the switchers do. More to the point, you'll note that the pure righthanded hitters have a higher home run percentage against lefties (2.50) than they do against righties (2.31 from the first chart). For the normal righthanded hitter with average power, platooning thus makes perfect sense all the way around.

A complete listing for this category can be found on page 290.

WHAT GOOD IS A FOUL BALL?

When a pitcher gets two strikes on the hitter, he gains a big advantage. On two-strike counts last year, major league hitters batted only .183, slugged a piddling .261, and reached base less than 25 percent of the time. Often hitters will prolong a two-strike appearance by fouling off a pitch or two, or even more. But is that just delaying the inevitable? Do the hitter's chances of reaching base improve the longer he hangs in there? The chart at the right shows the outcome of all two strike plate appearances based on the number of fouls (1989 data) — additional details are in the table below.

No. of 2-strike fouls	Total PA	Avg	Slg	OBA
0	44,799	.176	.249	.229
1	15,259	.189	.278	.265
2	4,852	.209	.303	.304
3	1,600	.213	.340	.318
4	537	.204	.291	.315
5	170	.241	.414	.394
6+	98	.269	.526	.408
Total	67,315	.183	.261	.246

Except for a slight dip at four foul balls, the batter's figures improve with every foul ball hit. It's an uphill struggle, but starting at about five foul balls, the advantage finally shifts from the pitcher to the hitter. Now you know how Luke Appling, the legendary shortstop and foul ball champion, compiled his .310 career average.

NUMBER OF TWO-STRIKE FOULS DURING AT BAT

BATTING AVERAGE / ON-BASE AVERAGE

- 0: .176 / .229
- 1: .189 / .266
- 2: .209 / .304
- 3 OR MORE: .215 / .326

Who are the modern-day Applings? The following players hit the most two-strike fouls during 1989:

Player, Team	2-Strike Fouls	Avg	OBA
Phil Bradley, Bal	211	.277	.364
Wade Boggs, Bos	202	.330	.430
Howard Johnson, Mets	199	.287	.369
Kevin Seitzer, KC	196	.281	.387
Joe Carter, Cle	184	.243	.292
Paul Molitor, Mil	183	.315	.379
Brett Butler, SF	181	.283	.349
Brian Downing, Cal	179	.283	.354
Dave Gallagher, WSox	179	.266	.320
Pedro Guerrero, StL	176	.311	.391

What does two-strike fouling indicate? Good bat control, primarily; all these players have it except for Joe Carter, the one oddball on the list. Learning that kind of skill takes time and experience. There are no rookies here: six of the ten are 31 or older, and none is younger than 28. All of them — except Carter and perhaps Dave Gallagher, who still hasn't established himself — are quality hitters with a strong ability to get on base. (Carter is a quality hitter, but one with a low on-base average.) Obviously these players know how to wear out a pitcher in more ways than one.

The longest batter-pitcher duel of 1989 was between Boston's Marty Barrett and Toronto's David Wells at Fenway on June 4. It was one of the wildest games of the year, tied 11-11 with men on first and second and two out in the bottom of the ninth. Wells was brought in to pitch to Danny Heep, and Joe Morgan countered by pinch-hitting with Barrett.

Barrett took the first pitch for a strike. Then he fouled off one pitch, then another. Wells missed for ball one. Barrett hit a third foul, then a fourth and a fifth. He stepped out of the box and glanced at the scoreboard, where STATS' up-to-the-minute "Batting Figures by Two Strike Fouls" chart was being prominently displayed. He looked puzzled, so third base coach "Rac" Slider came over and said, "Hey, Marty, after five foul balls your chances of getting on base are a lot greater!" Barrett grinned and said, "Thanks, Coach. Now watch me rack this slider!" With renewed confidence, he stepped back in.

Wells delivered, and Barrett fouled it off. Wells look worried and missed for ball two. The crowd was going crazy. Another foul, then another, and another, and still one more. Ten foul balls! Still Wells wouldn't weaken. But neither would Barrett. He delivered, and Barrett fouled it off again. Then two more pitches, and two more fouls. Thirteen foul balls in the at bat. The crowd was on its feet. Wells delivered, Barrett swung . . . and grounded out to third.

The game went into extra innings, and the Jays pushed across two runs to win it, 13-11 in the 11th. Toronto was so inspired, they went on to win the division.

A complete listing for this category can be found on page 291.

III. QUESTIONS ON PITCHING

HOW IMPORTANT IS A FIRST PITCH STRIKE?

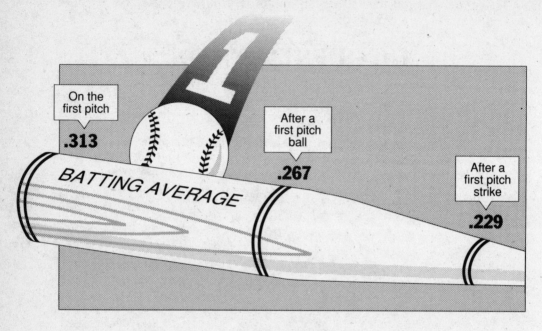

One of the first sermons that a pitching coach will preach to a young hurler is *The Lesson of the First Pitch Strike*. "Once you get ahead of the hitter," the coach will intone, "it's more than likely you won't have much trouble with him. But get behind on the count," he'll warn sternly, "and you invite an early shower. So throw strikes!"

Pretty corny stuff, but it happens to be true. The following chart shows the results of 1989 plate appearances after the first pitch was a ball, and then after it was a strike:

	After a First Pitch Ball	After a First Pitch Strike
Batting Average	.267	.229
On-Base Average	.372	.269
Slugging Percentage	.400	.331

The evidence is convincing. When the count starts with a strike, the batter hits for a low average, doesn't get on base much via walks, and doesn't hit for much power, either. But when the count starts with a ball, the result is exactly opposite: this time the hitter gains a decided advantage.

All this would be very neat and clean, if there weren't a third possibility — that the hitter will swing and put the ball in play. Because the pitcher is trying so hard to get ahead, the first pitch is usually a good one, and the batter often ends up doing pretty well:

	First Pitch in Play
Batting Average	.313
On-Base Average	.313
Slugging Percentage	.470

As the results show, the first pitch is a good candidate to be hit, and hit hard. A lot of home runs, in particular, are belted off first pitches. So it's not quite enough to say, "Get that first pitch over for a strike!" More sage advice is, "Get it over, but put a little something on it!"

A complete listing for this category can be found on page 292.

WHO ARE THE BEST HITTING PITCHERS IN BASEBALL?

Going back to Babe Ruth, good hitting pitchers are part of the lore of baseball. The twenties and thirties gave us such splendid batsmen as Red Lucas (.281 lifetime, 114 pinch hits), Wes Ferrell (.280, 38 home runs), and Red Ruffing (.269, 36 homers). Recent times have produced lower batting averages overall, but there was nothing wrong with the swat work of Bob Gibson (.206, 24 homers), Warren Spahn (.194, 35 home runs) and Don Drysdale (.186, 29 homers). A look at the top ten among current major league pitchers (100 or more at bats), however, shows that pitchers' hitting is rapidly becoming a lost art:

Pitcher	BA	AB	H	HR	RBI
Don Robinson	.243	510	124	11	57
Dan Schatzeder	.239	238	57	5	29
Rick Rhoden	.238	760	181	9	74
Tim Leary	.221	163	36	1	19
Bob Forsch	.213	569	121	9	61
Rick Aguilera	.203	138	28	3	11
Sid Fernandez	.201	319	64	1	25
Neal Heaton	.200	130	26	0	10
Greg Maddux	.195	231	45	0	11
Orel Hershiser	.192	449	86	0	29

Among the top ten, seven are over 30 years of age. And while some have respectable averages, only Robinson among all active pitchers has reached double figures in homers; in fact only Robinson, Rhoden, Forsch, Bob Knepper and Fernando Valenzuela have hit more than five. We can probably blame the age of specialization, exemplified by the DH rule, for this. It's a little depressing to think that the future of "good hitting pitchers" is now represented by Greg Maddux, who will be 24 shortly after the 1990 season starts. Maddux's .195 average with no home runs while playing in Wrigley Field indicates that he's no Wes Ferrell.

The future of pitchers' hitting, alas, might be better summarized by looking at the bottom five:

Pitcher	BA	AB	H	HR	RBI
Don Carman	.047	193	9	0	4
Andy McGaffigan	.048	126	6	0	5
Mike Bielecki	.052	154	8	0	4
Jim Deshaies	.081	234	19	0	9
Steve Bedrosian	.083	145	12	0	1

The worst hitting pitcher of all time, ex-Giant Ron Herbel (6-for-206, .029 lifetime average) might find his record being threatened one of these days.

A complete listing for this category can be found on page 293.

HOW EFFECTIVE ARE PITCHOUTS?

With runners stealing bases at record rates, managers often resort to an old weapon: the pitchout. San Francisco's Roger Craig, in particular, has a reputation for his ability to sense when a runner is going. According to the accepted wisdom, Craig calls more successful pitchouts than any other skipper.

Does the pitchout really work . . . and does Craig deserve his reputation? Here's some data on each team's pitchout calls during 1989. We list the total number of pitchouts made, the stolen base figures when the runner was going on the pitchout, and the percentage of times the pitchout did what it was designed to do — throw out the runner:

Team	Total Pitchouts	Pitchouts on SB Attempts			% of total Pitchouts with CS
		SB	CS	Percent	
Baltimore	167	4	6	.400	3.6
Boston	235	12	9	.571	3.8
California	144	3	0	1.000	0.0
Chicago	50	3	3	.500	6.0
Cleveland	86	4	2	.667	2.3
Detroit	203	6	6	.500	3.0
Kansas City	254	8	6	.571	2.4
Milwaukee	109	2	5	.286	4.6
Minnesota	91	0	5	.000	5.5
New York	132	4	2	.667	1.5
Oakland	135	3	5	.375	3.7
Seattle	130	6	5	.545	3.8
Texas	135	2	7	.222	5.2
Toronto	174	13	10	.565	5.7
Total AL	2045	70	71	.496	3.5
Atlanta	215	3	9	.250	4.2
Chicago	229	2	8	.200	3.5
Cincinnati	182	4	7	.364	3.8
Houston	178	5	3	.625	1.7
Los Angeles	174	2	8	.200	4.6
Montreal	299	12	14	.462	4.7
New York	192	4	4	.500	2.1
Philadelphia	175	8	10	.444	5.7

Pittsburgh	222	12	15	.444	6.8
St. Louis	98	3	1	.750	1.0
San Diego	140	3	4	.429	2.9
San Fran.	270	16	25	.390	9.3
Total NL	**2374**	**74**	**108**	**.407**	**4.5**
Total MLB	**4419**	**144**	**179**	**.446**	**4.1**

Clearly the pitchout is a very popular call, especially among National League managers. There were almost as many pitchouts last year (4,419) as there were stolen base attempts (4,557). But the two seldom linked up; the runner was actually going on only about seven percent of the calls. And since the runner stole the base anyway on about 45 percent of the pitchouts, the pitchout actually worked — in the sense of throwing out the runner — in only 4.1 percent of the total cases. Craig is indeed the best at this game. The runner was actually going on 15 percent of his pitchout calls, and the Giants threw the runner out in 9.3 percent of Craig's total calls. Both figures were easily the best among skippers. On the other hand, the Angels' Doug Rader called 144 pitchouts, guessed right only three times, and all three runners were safe!

You may conclude from this that the pitchout is a wasted call. It costs the pitcher an automatic ball, and that's a considerable disadvantage; according to our data from last year, a pitchout with an 0-0 count would turn the average batter from a .254 hitter to a .267 hitter, with an even higher increase in on-base percentage. If it's only going to work four percent of the time, is it really worth it? Those are valid points, but this viewpoint is somewhat narrow. One thing the data doesn't show is that a pitchout makes a runner more cautious. The success rate among all stealers last year was .683. There were 233 cases last year where a runner didn't go on the pitchout, but attempted to steal later in the at bat. In those subsequent attempts, the success rate was only .657. Clearly the pitchout reduced the runners' lead, and made them easier to throw out. But 233 cases out of 4,557 steal attempts (and 4,419 pitchouts) isn't very many.

Does the threat of a pitchout cause opponents to become more conservative on the basepaths? It might be useful to compare the three teams which called the most pitchouts with the three who called the fewest. If the pitchout has an intimidation factor, you would suspect that clubs which call a lot of pitchouts would reduce the number of steal attempts, and lower the overall success rate. Here's the comparison:

The Most	Pitch-outs	SB Att.	SB %	The Least	Pitch-outs	SB Att.	SB %.
Montreal	299	236	.703	Chi. W. Sox	50	145	.634
San Fran.	270	152	.631	Cleveland	86	176	.716
Kansas City	254	136	.581	Minnesota	91	164	.701

The data is not very consistent, but it would be stretching things to say we could see an intimidation factor at work here. The Expos called the most pitchouts, but runners went more often against Montreal than against most clubs (the major league average was 175 steal attempts), and were successful more often as well (the overall SB percentage was .683). The White Sox called the fewest pitchouts, but had both fewer steal attempts and a higher throw-out percent than most teams. Of course, the data might have been a lot different if Ron Karkovice and Nelson Santovenia had switched teams. But it's hard to see how all those pitchout calls helped the Expos much, considering that each one was making the batter a better hitter.

The data for the other clubs make the pitchout look a little better. You could certainly see how it helped the Giants. Take away Craig's correct calls, and the steal success rate for San Francisco's opponents would have shot up from .631 to .733 — a huge jump. The pitchout also seemed to help the Royals, although probably not as much as having Bob Boone behind the plate. The figures for the Indians and Twins were mixed. Both called few pitchouts and had higher than normal opponents' stolen base percentages, but each allowed only an average or below average number of attempts. You could argue that calling more pitchouts would have lowered the success rate, but given the Montreal numbers, it's a difficult argument to make.

So is calling pitchouts worth the cost of making the batter a better hitter? Perhaps, if you call them as well as Roger Craig. But the data indicates that, for most managers, this is a losing proposition.

DO THEY STILL BRUSH 'EM BACK?

To hear the ballplayers of the sixties tell it, today's players are wimps — especially when it comes to the issue of "pitching inside." Dodger broadcaster Don Drysdale, in particular, argues that today's hurlers are afraid to work the inside part of the plate. As a result, he says, hitters can dig in without fear and home run balls fly out of the park.

Is this a fair argument? We don't think so. Hit by pitch totals, a good measure of a hurler's willingness to work inside, actually increased during every year from 1985 through 1988. The total dropped again last year (see chart), but that may be because the home run rate has been declining. As the table below shows, there appears to be some relationship between how many balls fly out of the park, and how many hitters get plunked:

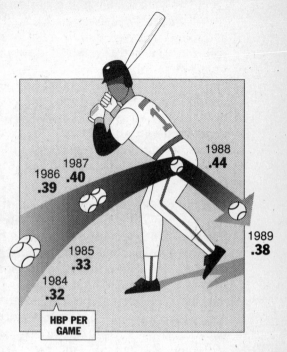

	— National —		— American —	
Year	HBP per Game	HR per Game	HBP per Game	HR per Game
1989	.33	1.40	.43	1.52
1988	.38	1.32	.49	1.68
1987	.35	1.88	.43	2.32
1986	.32	1.57	.44	2.02
1985	.29	1.47	.37	1.92
1984	.26	1.32	.37	1.75
1983	.30	1.44	.38	1.68
1982	.31	1.34	.33	1.83
1981	.29	1.12	.37	1.42
1980	.27	1.28	.35	1.63
1979	.34	1.47	.37	1.78
1978	.34	1.31	.39	1.49
1977	.34	1.68	.41	1.78

Over the 13 seasons, home run production first went downward, began a rise in the early eighties that reached its peak in 1987, and then declined again over the past two years. The hit batsmen rate, meanwhile, basically followed the same trend — down until the mid eighties, then up in the years 1986-88, and down again in '89. A year after the big home run explosion of '87, hit batsmen jumped to their highest level of the 13-year period. At the same time the home run rate went down. There are year-to-year variations, of course, but there appears to be a correlation between the two. And that's logical. When home run production goes up, hitters become more aggressive in trying to get an inside pitch to jerk out of the yard. Pitchers become just as aggressive in moving the batter off the plate.

One noticeable thing about the chart is that in every season, both the home run rate and the hit batsmen rate have been higher in the American League. This certainly underscores the notion that the two figures are related. But of course, the American League uses the designated hitter. That's a big factor in their dominance of the home run figures. Some people have argued that, because pitchers don't have to hit in the AL, they're more likely to be fearless about throwing at hitters. There's an easy way to see if this argument has merit. Let's compare the home run and hit batsmen figures for the last two years that American League pitchers hit, 1971 and '72, and compare them with the first two years of the DH, 1973 and '74:

	— National —		— American —	
Year	HBP per Game	HR per Game	HBP per Game	HR per Game
1974	.37	1.32	.43	1.41
1973	.37	1.60	.41	1.60
1972	.38	1.46	.42	1.26
1971	.41	1.42	.44	1.53

There is clearly no relationship between the hit batsmen rate and the DH. Though the home run rate jumped way up when the DH arrived in '73, the hit batsmen rate remained virtually the same.

Bill James feels that the rulesmakers and the umpires are the biggest factor in controlling the battle for the inside part of the plate. The evidence says he's right. In the sixties — the era of Drysdale — pitchers hit a lot of batters even in years when the home run rate was down. But then the umps cracked down, in part to increase offense, and in part to control a beanball level that had reached record proportions.

| | — National — | | — American — | |
Year	HBP per Game	HR per Game	HBP per Game	HR per Game
1969	.45	1.51	.45	1.69
1968	.43	1.10	.52	1.36
1967	.44	1.36	.49	1.48
1966	.45	1.70	.40	1.69
1965	.50	1.62	.39	1.69
1964	.40	1.49	.45	1.91
1963	.46	1.50	.42	1.84
1962	.46	1.78	.42	1.92
1961	.41	1.93	.39	1.89

If it's any comfort to Drysdale, the American League hit batsmen rate of recent years would have fit right in with the hair-on-their-chest sixties. And five-times hit batsmen leader Dave Stieb would have been right at home with Drysdale, Bob Gibson and Jim Bunning. Pitchers in both leagues hit many more batters than hurlers did in the days of Ruth and DiMaggio. They're not afraid to pitch inside — to the extent that the rules allow.

A complete listing for this category can be found on page 294.

WHO THROWS GROUNDBALLS?

We always hear how important it is for pitchers to keep the ball low and get a lot of grounders. So it's a little disconcerting to discover that the three leading groundball pitchers in the majors last year were Billy Swift, Kevin Brown and Bruce Ruffin, none of whom were featured on any Cy Young Award ballots. The list of leaders in groundball/flyball ratio, fortunately, includes a few familiar names:

Pitcher	Groundballs	Flyballs	Ratio
Billy Swift, Sea	312	61	5.11
Kevin Brown, Tex	391	118	3.31
Bruce Ruffin, Phi	267	89	3.00
Zane Smith, Atl-Mon	278	96	2.90
Scott Terry, StL	288	110	2.62
Mark Gubicza, KC	451	182	2.48
Mike Morgan, LA	280	117	2.39
Orel Hershiser, LA	445	192	2.32
Greg Maddux, Cubs	432	193	2.24
Pascual Perez, Mon	337	252	2.22

(Note: minimum 350 balls in play.)

Of the ten, only Maddux won more than 15 games, and only four had winning records. Zane Smith was 1-13. There were some good ERAs among the group (Hershiser 2.31, Morgan 2.53), but some lousy ones as well (Swift 4.43, Ruffin 4.44). Most of these guys are finesse pitchers who don't record many strikeouts, but Gubicza and Hershiser each fanned more than 170. Almost all have excellent control, which would figure. The ten had a modest won-lost record of 100-107 last year, although their ERA was a fine 3.21.

Can we learn anything by studying this group? Only that "keeping the ball down," by itself, is not the secret of pitching success. If it were, Billy Swift would have made us forget Bret Saberhagen (G/F Ratio of 1.04) by now.

Now look at the ten pitchers with the *lowest* ground/fly ratio in 1989:

Pitcher	Groundballs	Flyballs	Ratio
Sid Fernandez, Mets	151	310	0.49
Tom Browning, Cin	258	382	0.68
Scott Sanderson, Cubs	162	217	0.75
Steve Rosenberg, WSox	158	204	0.77
John Smiley, Pit	223	288	0.77

Roy Smith, Min	184	239	0.77
Jim Deshaies, Hou	243	302	0.80
Scott Bankhead, Sea	233	286	0.81
Don Carman, Phi	173	212	0.82
Dennis Cook, SF-Phi	142	171	0.83

Seven of the ten pitchers in this group had winning records, and overall they were a fine 107-92; that record would have been a lot better except for Carman (5-15) and Rosenberg (4-13). But this group's ERA, while decent at 3.58, was higher than the groundballers' 3.21; the flyballers' ERA was inflated a lot by Carman (5.24) and Rosenberg (4.94). The flyballers tended to strike out more batters than the groundball group, but they also gave up a lot more walks and home runs. Overall, they were probably a slightly better group than the groundball pitchers, but it's close.

Despite the slight advantage for this particular group of flyball pitchers, it's likely that, overall, there is no great advantage to being either a groundball or flyball pitcher. Each group has some outstanding performers . . . and some guys who can hardly get anyone out.

A complete listing for this category can be found on page 295.

WHICH STARTERS ALLOW THE FEWEST BASERUNNERS?

A pitcher's goal is to allow as few runs as possible. Although we find an occasional hurler who puts a lot of guys on base but still has a low ERA (like Pete Vuckovich in 1982), the most effective workmen tend to be those who don't allow many baserunners. The major league starters who allowed the fewest baserunners per nine innings last year (162 or more IP) were:

Pitcher	Baserunners per 9 IP	IP	Total Baserunners
Bret Saberhagen, KC	8.71	262.1	254
Scott Garrelts, SF	9.08	193.1	195
Jose DeLeon, StL	9.53	244.2	259
Mike Scott, Hou	9.63	229.0	245
Sid Fernandez, Mets	9.77	219.1	238
Bryn Smith, Mon	9.81	215.2	235
John Smiley, Pit	9.95	205.1	227
Ed Whitson, SD	9.95	227.0	251
Nolan Ryan, Tex	10.12	239.1	269
John Smoltz, Atl	10.13	208.0	234

There aren't too many surprises on this list, starting with the fact that the two ERA champs top the category. For the most part these pitchers have low opponents' batting averages and good strikeout totals; those with lower strikeout totals, like Smith, Smiley and Whitson, make up for that with excellent control.

Pitchers who do well in this category do more than make rotisserie league managers happy. They show a fundamental dominance of the hitter, and for that reason the category is a good predictor of continued success in the future. While their won-lost records can ebb and flow depending on the kind of support they get, most of these guys turn in solid work year after year.

Now let's look at the five worst performers in the category during 1989:

Pitcher	Baserunners per 9 IP	IP	Total Baserunners
Bob Knepper, Hou-SF	14.62	165.0	268
Andy Hawkins, Yanks	13.82	208.1	320
Bobby Witt	13.80	194.1	298
Melido Perez, WSox	13.75	183.1	280
Storm Davis, Oak	13.71	169.1	258

The Cardinals' megabuck signing of Bryn Smith was ridiculed in some corners as throwing money at a "mediocre" pitcher. But how about Storm Davis? In another section, we discuss the awesome offensive support that was largely responsible for Storm's 19-7 record last year. That record shouldn't have fooled many people, but apparently it fooled Kansas City. You can get a better handle on how Davis pitched in 1989 by noting that if Storm had pitched 93 more innings without allowing either a hit or a walk — get that, 93 innings with *no* hits and *no* walks — his ratio still wouldn't have been as good as his new teammate Bret Saberhagen. Davis is going to have to pitch much, much better if he's going to earn his keep in 1990.

A complete listing for this category can be found on page 296.

WHO WAS BETTER IN '89 – STORM DAVIS OR DOYLE ALEXANDER?

On the surface, this appears to be an absurd question; after all, Alexander's record was a pathetic 6-18, while Davis's was a mighty 19-7. And yet, the two had similar ERAs (4.44 for Alexander, 4.36 for Davis), they allowed about the same number of baserunners per inning (1.46 for Doyle, 1.52 for Storm), and both permitted slightly over one home run per nine IP (Alexander 1.13, Davis 1.01). The main difference between them, in truth, had nothing to do with their pitching. While Davis was on the mound, the A's were scoring an average of 6.5 runs per nine innings pitched. Meanwhile, the Tigers could manage only 3.0 runs per game when Alexander was on the hill.

Although many baseball people won't accept this, the difference between Alexander and Davis in 1989 was largely a matter of luck. Good as they were, the A's averaged only 4.4 runs per game in 1989, not the 6.5 they scored behind Davis. When Curt Young was on the hill, Oakland averaged only 2.8 runs a contest — even poorer support than the Tigers gave Alexander. Young had a 3.73 ERA, which was much better than Davis', but he could manage only a 5-9 record. Does anyone think Storm Davis' record would have been 19-7 if he'd received Alexander and Young's kind of offensive support?

And yet many folks cling to the notion that, somehow, Storm Davis "learned how to win" in 1989, while Doyle Alexander presumably forgot. This sort of thinking leads to distorted evaluations of pitchers, even by people who should know better. Here's a good example. From 1985 through 1987, Danny Jackson had ERAs that were, on average, an impressive 0.71 runs below the American League average. Yet Jackson's won-lost record over that period was only 34-42; Danny was one of the most poorly supported pitchers in baseball during each of the three years. The Royals, however, apparently concluded that Jackson "couldn't win," and traded him to Cincinnati. In 1988, his first year with the Reds, Jackson pitched about the same as he had the previous three years — his ERA was 0.72 below the National League average. But Jackson's team finally scored some runs for him, and the result was a 23-8 record. Of course, all we heard that summer was that Danny had finally learned how to pitch. (He apparently forgot over the winter of '88-'89.)

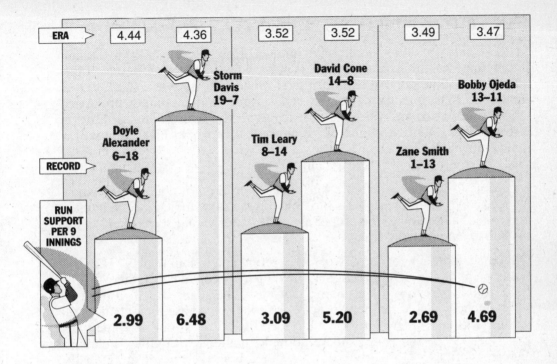

Here are a couple more comparisons from 1989:

Pitcher	ERA	W/L Record	Run Support per 9 innings
Allan Anderson	3.80	17-10	6.86
Jimmy Key	3.88	13-14	4.54
Jack Morris	4.86	6-14	3.54
Andy Hawkins	4.80	15-15	5.10

In some of these cases, a pitcher's ERA was helped or hindered by the park he pitched in — Anderson's Metrodome 3.80 mark, for instance, is a lot more impressive than Key's SkyDome 3.88. But the basic premise holds: a pitcher's won-lost record is extremely dependent on how many runs his team scores behind him. A winning record is not necessarily the mark of a "winner," nor does a losing record automatically denote a "loser."

A complete listing for this category can be found on page 297.

CAN A PITCHER INDUCE A DOUBLE PLAY GROUNDER?

In the classic baseball book Late Innings, Bob Gibson talks to author Roger Angell about his career and his philosophy of pitching. In one of the more fascinating stories, Gibson relates what he'd do when there was a runner on first, less than two out and a righty hitter coming up. After telling third baseman Mike Shannon to get ready, Gibson would throw a down and in sinker. And just like that, the batter would invariably pull a double play ball to Shannon.

Gibson's story, which he made seem like an elementary skill of pitching, caused us to wonder whether a hurler can indeed get a double play when he needs one. Intuition says it's possible. As the story indicates, if a pitcher makes the right pitch to the proper area, the batter would seem likely to hit the ball in a predictable fashion.

Of course, many factors are involved in producing a double play. The ball has to be hit in the right direction at the proper speed, and even then sloppy fielding or aggressive baserunning can upset the plan. But if Gibson is right, pitchers should, at the very least, be able to increase their chances of getting a groundball when they really need one. Let's look at some data from the '89 season, and compare normal situations with GDP situations (runner on first, less than two out). We measured the rate of groundballs hit per batter faced in each of the two situations:

All Major League Pitchers	Grounders per Batter Faced
All Situations	.332
GDP Situations	.333

Under normal circumstances, a batter will hit a groundball about one third of the time. But in GDP situations, when the pitcher is supposedly trying to induce a groundball, the rate is almost exactly the same. Pitchers as a group can't produce more groundballs, even when the need for one is present.

What about specific groups of pitchers? We thought that perhaps pitchers with high groundball ratios — those who have demonstrated a skill for getting the batter to hit the ball on the ground — might be more effective in DP situations. (Bob Gibson, of course, would *not* be part of this group.) We divided hurlers into those with high, average and low groundball/flyball ratios. Here is the same comparison done for each of the three groups:

Grounders per Batter Faced by Pitcher Type

	High G/F Ratio	Average G/F Ratio	Low G/F Ratio
All Situations	.400	.321	.257
GDP Situations	.396	.325	.252

The style of the pitcher makes no difference. Both the high and low-ratio groups have their groundball average actually go *down* in DP situations, while the middle group goes up by a very slight amount. The slight differences are most likely due to chance; for all practical purposes, pitchers in each group get the same percentage of groundballs in each situation.

The only conclusion we can reach is that what worked for Bob Gibson doesn't work for pitchers as a whole, whatever their style. In fact we have only Gibson's word that it worked for him. But we'll, uh, take your word for it, Mr. Gibson. Sir.

****

One question we answered as a separate part of this study is how often a ground double play occurs when there's a double play situation:

In 1989, the batter hit into a groundball double play about 10.5% of the time he came up with a runner on first and less than two out.

A related question is: Given that the batter has hit a grounder in a GDP situation, how often is the grounder turned into a double play?

In double play situations, about 32 percent of all groundballs hit actually end up as double plays. The style of pitcher makes little difference in how often the DP is turned.

WHO ARE THE BEST RELIEVERS AT HOLDING THE FORT FOR THEIR LATE MEN?

At the age of 35, Rick Honeycutt has a career record of 95-125, and is probably best known for getting caught with a thumbtack in his glove during an ill-concealed attempt to doctor the ball. Even when he led the American League in ERA in 1983, Honeycutt's reward was a ticket out of town before the season was even finished. But last year, in his 13th season, Honeycutt was one of the most valuable pitchers in the American League. Unfortunately, few noticed his splendid relief work, and Rick failed to received a single vote for the Cy Young Award.

Working out of the deep Athletics' bullpen last year, Honeycutt handled a variety of roles, all of them well. His 64 games were a career high, and his 2.35 ERA was his lowest ever. He racked up 12 saves, another career best, mostly as a substitute during super-reliever Dennis Eckersley's tenure on the disabled list. But Honeycutt's most valuable work was in middle relief, where he was arguably the major leagues' best set-up man. It wasn't his fault that few people noticed.

As befits his lot in life, Honeycutt led the majors last year in a stat few people even know exists — "holds." A hold is simply a save opportunity passed on to the next pitcher. The intent is to give credit to a reliever who comes into a close game and preserves the lead, but doesn't finish the contest. Here were the major league leaders in holds during 1989:

HOLDING THE FORT — HOLDS

Player	Holds
Rick Honeycutt	24
Rob Dibble	23
Ken Dayley	22
Chuck Crim	17
Larry Anderson	16
Ken Rogers	16
Calvin Schiraldi	16
Greg Minton	15
Steve Wilson	15
Juan Agosto	14

This is a pretty strong group of pitchers. Dibble was sensational in '89, richly earning the reputation as the best set-up man in the National League. Dayley, Schiraldi and Minton have all been effective closers at times during their careers, and most of the others have solid reputations as middle men. Times have changed. Once starters got all the glory. Then late men came on the scene to grab a little of the spotlight. Middle relievers were considered strictly fill-ins, the lowest forms of pitching life. Now the middle men are the vital bridge between starter and closer, and no team can win without good ones.

If things keep up like this, perhaps someday we'll be awarding the Rick Honeycutt Award to the major league leader in holds. Maybe a trophy featuring a lovely silver pitchers' glove, with a little hole in it where the thumbtack used to be?

A complete listing for this category can be found on page 298.

WHICH RELIEVERS HAVE THE HIGHEST SAVE PERCENTAGES?

The fragile life of the relief pitcher might be put in better perspective by examining the top ten pitchers in save percentage during 1989. Six of the ten — including the top three — have modeled at least three uniforms, and only two are still with their original teams. The '89 leaders (20 or more opportunities):

Pitcher, Team	Saves	Opportunities	Save Percentage
Mark Davis, SD	44	48	91.7
Bill Landrum, Pit	26	29	89.7
Jay Howell, LA	28	32	87.5
Todd Worrell, StL	20	23	87.0
Jeff Russell, Tex	38	44	86.4
Dave Smith, Hou	25	29	86.2
Dennis Eckersley, Oak	33	39	84.6
Lee Smith, Bos	25	30	83.3
Tom Henke, Tor	20	24	83.3
Craig Lefferts, SF	20	24	83.3

A glance at this list shows some famous names conspicuously missing. The "epic" trade of Randy Myers for John Franco, to use a good example, turns out to be a deal involving the eleventh (Myers) and fifteenth (Franco) best pitchers in save percentage last year. A total of 28 pitchers had at least 20 save opportunities in 1989, and among those bringing up the rear were Doug Jones (20th at 78.1%), Mitch Williams (21st, 76.6%), Steve Bedrosian (23rd, 74.2%), Jeff Reardon (24th, 73.8%) and Dave Righetti (25th, 73.5%). Among other things, one has to wonder why the Red Sox are so excited to be replacing Lee Smith with Reardon.

Fans who follow the Cubs day by day won't be too surprised that Mitch Williams was the major league leader in blown saves last year, with 11. But Mitch wasn't alone in having his ups and downs during '89. Two of the worst performances in converting save opportunities belonged to two heralded young pitchers. Rob Dibble of the Reds blew six saves in '89 while recording only two, and Tom Gordon of the Royals converted only one of seven chances. On the other hand, the "much maligned" Willie Hernandez was a nifty 15-for-17 last year. And Lee Guetterman, who managed the neat trick of being almost invisible while laboring in baseball's biggest market, was a perfect 13-for-13 for the Yankees.

The major league average in converting save opportunities last year was 71.1 percent, so even those down on the list weren't really doing an horrendous job. Many of the blown saves belonged to pitchers who were given only a few chances, then quickly moved out of the role.

A complete listing for this category can be found on page 299.

WHO ARE THE TOUGHEST PITCHERS TO HIT?

Memo to the American League: he's slipping. Back in 1972, when he was 25 and could still throw hard, Nolan Ryan held his American League opponents to a .171 batting average. Seventeen years later, they celebrated his return to the Junior Circuit by tattooing him at a mighty .187 clip. At this rate of progress, approximately one point a year, the AL will catch up to Ryan sometime around the year 2060.

It's hard to put Ryan's 1989 season in perspective, because there's really no one to compare him with except Nolan Ryan. But we'll try. To start, Ryan's .187 opponents' average tied him with three others for the thirteenth lowest one-season average ever. The lowest one season opponent BA among ERA qualifiers belongs to Luis Tiant, who held the AL to a .168 mark in 1968. But the league average in '68 was only .230, so Tiant was 62 points under the norm. Ryan last year, at 42, was 74 points below the league average of .261. We could only find one case in modern baseball history that topped it: Tommy Byrne of the '49 Yanks was 80 points below his league average (.183 to .263). Byrne, one of the wildest pitchers in history, averaged 8.2 walks per nine innings in '49 and was nowhere near as effective as Ryan, who walked 3.7. In terms of stifling opposing batsmen, only a handful of seasons compare with Ryan's '89.

Here are the major league leaders in opponents' batting average in 1989 — or should we say, here are Nolan Ryan and nine humans?

Pitcher, Team	AB	H	Opponent Batting Average
Nolan Ryan, Tex	867	162	.187
Jose DeLeon, StL	878	173	.197
Sid Fernandez, Mets	794	157	.198
Tom Gordon, KC	582	122	.210
John Smoltz, Atl	756	160	.212
Scott Garrelts, SF	704	149	.212
Mike Scott, Hou	848	180	.212
Ken Howell, Phi	722	155	.215
Jim Deshaies, Hou	829	180	.217
Tim Belcher, LA	838	182	.217
Bret Saberhagen, KC	961	209	.217

(Minimum: 500 opponent at bats)

It's no surprise that this is a group of power pitchers, guys who can simply overpower a hitter. Rob Dibble, generally considered to be the hardest thrower among current hurlers, didn't qualify for this title (only 352 opponent at bats), but Dibble held his opponents to an even lower average than Ryan, .176. Though both ERA leaders (Garrelts and Saberhagen) made the list, some pretty good hurlers like Orel Hershiser (.240), Bert Blyleven (.248) and Dave Stewart (.264) didn't. Often pitchers who top this list are inconsistent; in particular, they tend to have control problems. The list includes some hurlers, who are, rightly or wrongly, thought to be underachievers. Included in that group would be DeLeon, Fernandez and Howell. But there's no denying the overall quality of the group, starting with Ryan.

Far removed from Nolan and company are the pitchers who yielded the *highest* opponent batting averages last year:

Pitcher, Team	AB	H	Opponent Batting Average
Dave Schmidt, Bal	632	196	.310
Charlie Leibrandt, KC	644	196	.304
Don August, Mil	579	175	.302
Bruce Ruffin, Phi	505	152	.301
Jerry Reuss, WSox-Mil	570	171	.300
Mike Smithson, Bos	573	170	.297
Richard Dotson, Yanks-WSox	615	181	.294
Shane Rawley, Min	569	167	.293
Mike Witt, Cal	864	252	.292
Andy Hawkins, Yanks	820	238	.290

With the notable exception of Mike Witt, who has fallen on hard times, these hurlers tend to be junkballers who have to rely on finesse to get by. Even at their best, they're going to give up a good number of hits. But not this many, if they want to last in the majors. The *lowest* ERA among this group was Ruffin's 4.44, and none of the ten had a winning record. Hawkins somehow went 15-15 with a 4.80 ERA, and August was 12-12, 5.31. Overall this group had an 83-123 won-lost record, and half the pitchers had ERAs over 5.00. Guys like Schmidt, Leibrandt and Reuss will be fighting for their major league lives in 1990. They'll battle to escape the fate of Tommy John, who exited the majors last year after yielding a truly awesome .336 opponents' average (87 for 259).

A complete listing for this category can be found on page 300.

WHO HAS THE BEST STARTING STAFF IN BASEBALL? THE BEST RELIEF STAFF?

In an age of intense specialization, it makes sense to examine pitching staffs as two separate units — starters and relievers. Looked at from that perspective, the A's relievers were the best corps in baseball last year, while the Yankees' starters were the worst. That makes the Rickey Henderson trade all the more interesting. Last summer the Yanks, desperate for pitching help, sent Henderson to Oakland for a package that included Eric Plunk and Greg Cadaret, integral parts of the major leagues' best relief corps. The Yanks seemed to reason that a good pitcher was a good pitcher, and soon moved both Plunk and Cadaret into their weak starting rotation.

However, the move didn't work; while Oakland quickly found bullpen replacements for Plunk and Cadaret, both struggled as starters in New York. These days it's probably easier to find a good reliever than a good starter. With deep bullpens the norm, a hurler with one or two strong pitches can be very effective for an inning or two. But move such a pitcher into a starting role, where the hitters get three or four looks at his stuff, and those limitations are more easily exposed. A comparison of each team's starting and relief corps last year shows that 24 of the 26 teams got better ERAs out of their bullpens. While relievers have a built-in ERA advantage, since they often come in during the middle of an inning, the difference is nonetheless significant.

BEST GROUPS	ERA
Athletics Relievers	2.63
Dodgers Relievers	2.75
Angels Relievers	2.89
Cubs Relievers	2.90
Mets Relievers	2.96

WORST GROUPS	ERA
Yankees Starters	4.87
Tigers Starters	4.55
White Sox Starters	4.54
Tigers Relievers	4.51
Twins Relievers	4.39

The teams with the biggest differences in ERA between their starters and relievers were:

Team	Starters	Relievers	Difference
Yankees	4.87	3.80	1.07
Red Sox	4.29	3.46	.83
White Sox	4.54	3.73	.81
Cubs	3.67	2.90	.77
Astros	3.91	3.16	.75

With such a huge difference between their starters and relievers, you might suspect that the Yankees would go to their bullpen whenever possible. But that wasn't the case; while the Red Sox, White Sox, Astros, Phillies and Giants all used their relief corps in more than 500 innings, the Yanks used theirs in only 445. It seems that Dallas Green was convinced that his starters would get better if he kept leaving them out there. Obviously, he was wrong, as well as out of a job.

A complete listing for this category can be found on page 301.

WHICH RELIEVERS HAVE THE BEST ENDURANCE?

Even in an age of specialization, there's plenty of use for a reliever who can go several innings without losing effectiveness. Such a pitcher can bail out a weary staff or salvage a game on a night when the starter doesn't have it. A good way to measure endurance is by number of pitches thrown. An inning's work is approximately 15 pitches, so after 30 offerings a hurler is usually in or nearing his third inning of work — a breaking point for many relievers.

The firemen who top our list each met two criteria: they held batters during each 15-pitch interval to less than the major league average (.254), and they each faced at least fifty hitters after throwing more than 30 pitches. We rank them by opponents' batting average, and the number of batters each pitcher faced after 30 pitches. Rather than a top five, we show you the top six, since the sixth pitcher, David Wells, was both unusually effective and durable:

	After the 30th Pitch	
Pitcher, Team	Opponent BA	Batters Faced
Drew Hall, Tex	.157	58
Les Lancaster, Cubs	.173	58
Greg Harris, Phi-Bos	.184	95
Jerry Reed, Sea	.195	96
Calvin Schiraldi, Cubs-SD	.196	113
David Wells, Tor	.202	94

You may not know much about Drew Hall, a former number one draft choice who's been considered a big disappointment. But at 27 Hall has pitched only 137 major league innings, and 1989 was by far his best year. Hall's problem has been control, but he's clearly improving.

The other leaders are not exactly the biggest names in baseball, either. One has some pity for Calvin Schiraldi, who failed both as a starter and (in the harsh glow of a national spotlight) as a closer; now he's a great long man, but the cameras are turned away. The problem with Schiraldi and the others is not that they didn't pitch well; it's that middle relief is a thankless job, with no saves and few wins even for the best. David Wells' rescue work, in particular, was a vital factor in Toronto's division title, and he and the others definitely deserve more recognition.

There are other pitchers who were used in long stints last year, but not always wisely. The following pitchers shared a common trait — they were effective for an inning or two, but then broke down after being asked to do too much:

	Pitches 1 to 30	After the 30th Pitch	
Pitcher, Team	Opponent BA	Opponent BA	Batters Faced
Tom McCarthy, WSox	.256	.320	103
Rob Murphy, Bos	.242	.320	55
Jeff Brantley, SF	.263	.304	77
Mike Henneman, Det	.263	.289	56
Frank Williams, Det	.247	.283	61

You can see that, with these hurlers, more turned out to be less. Mike Henneman, weakened by arm problems, was a particularly good example. For his first 15 pitches, Henneman held opponents to a .206 average . . . but then he struggled. His teammate Frank Williams showed a similar pattern — .232 average on his first 15 pitches, then .265 second 15, finally .283 afterward.

Rob Murphy of the Red Sox is clearly a closer being misused as a setup man. Murphy garnered nine saves last year, a career high, but he also worked 105 relief innings, and that was evidently too many. Murphy held opponents to a .220 mark for his first 15 pitches, then went up to .275 and finally .320. With Boston having signed Jeff Reardon, Murphy is slated for the same role in 1990. The evidence says it's a role he's not well-suited for.

Here are 1989 stats for some other pitchers who "stayed too long at the Fair," as Barbra Streisand once put it (minimum 20 plate appearances in each situation):

	Opponent Batting Average		
Pitcher, Team	Pitches 1-15	Pitches 16-30	Pitches 31+
Gene Nelson, Oak	.198	.164	.262
Danny Darwin, Hou	.199	.212	.258
Ken Dayley, StL	.209	.225	.375
Frank DiPino, StL	.207	.232	.316

If baseball were like football, pitching staffs would have about 15 members, and all these fellows could specialize in going one or two innings. Aren't you glad things are like they are?

A complete listing for this category can be found on page 302.

WHAT IS FIRST BATTER EFFICIENCY?

Relief pitchers are like guys in a singles bar: if they don't make a good first impression, the whole night could be lost. Since a reliever often enters with men on base, retiring the first batter faced is crucial to success. The following pitchers were the major league leaders in first batter efficiency during 1989:

First Batter Efficiency

Pitcher, Team	AB	H	Opponent Batting Average
Gene Nelson, Oak	44	4	.091
Greg W. Harris, SD	45	5	.111
Bob Kipper, Pit	48	6	.125
Calvin Schiraldi, Cubs-SD	46	6	.130
Ken Dayley, StL	61	8	.131
Jeff Reardon, Min	60	8	.133
Steve Bedrosian, Phi-SF	57	8	.140
Gregg Olson, Bal	56	8	.143
Randy Myers, Mets	58	9	.155
Rick Honeycutt, Oak	57	9	.158

(Minimum: 40 relief appearances)

You'll notice something right away about this list: the top five pitchers, and six of the top ten, are middle relievers. That not only points up the importance of the middle men, but underscores how baseball has changed. Until the very recent past, ace relievers usually entered the game with men on base, because a starter was expected to last until he got into real trouble. Legendary firemen like Firpo Marberry in the twenties and Joe Page in the late forties would come in as early as the third inning if the starter didn't have it. (The late Billy Martin, who broke in as a player when Casey Stengel still had Page, brought in his ace, Sparky Lyle, in the fourth inning of a crucial game of the '77 playoffs. As Casey would put it, you could look it up.)

That sort of usage pretty much stopped as the game became more specialized, but even in the sixties and seventies, iron men such as Dick Radatz and Mike Marshall would routinely come in as soon as the seventh. These days clubs worry more about their closers' arms, and since Bruce Sutter, it's been traditional for the ace to be reserved for the ninth, or the eighth when necessary. And more often than not, the closer will start the inning. It's the setup men who tend to come in with men on base, so their first batter efficiency is even more important than the closers'. Successful closers like Tom Henke, Mike Schooler and Doug Jones all racked up big save totals while having batting averages over .300 against first batters last year.

For the most part, relievers were remarkably efficient against first batters last year. As a group, their opponents' average against first batters was a measly .245, significantly below the overall major league average of .254. Those who decry the batting averages of modern hitters should remember that, in the old days, the hitters would be teeing off on a tired starter in the late innings. They would definitely not have to handle someone like Cincinnati's Rob Dibble, who struck out 28 of the 74 first batters he faced last year.

The following pitchers were remarkably *inefficient* against first batters last year, logging the highest opponents' batting averages:

Pitcher, Team	AB	H	Opponent Batting Average
Dennis Lamp, Bos	38	16	.421
Chuck Crim, Mil	69	26	.377
Tim Birtsas, Cin	36	13	.361
Bob Stanley, Bos	40	14	.350
Dennis Powell, Sea	35	12	.343

These figures should be kept in mind when evaluating the '89 seasons of Lamp and Crim. Both had ERAs under 3.00, but their value was compromised by their first batter problems.

Though they didn't have enough appearances to make the preceding list, the following pitchers had so much trouble against first batters that we feel compelled to show your their stats:

Pitcher, Team	AB	H	Opponent Batting Average
Paul Kilgus, Cubs	11	8	.727
Tim Stoddard, Cle	13	8	.615 (.923 SLG)
Steve Frey, Mon	19	11	.579 (3 HR)

Tim Stoddard's career is now apparently over. We wish Kilgus and Frey better success in this unmerciful game during 1990.

A complete listing for this category can be found on page 303.

HOW MUCH REST IS BEST?

In the heat of the pennant race last year, both the Orioles and the Cubs experimented with a four-man starting rotation — something that used to be the norm in baseball, but is now a rarity. As the above chart shows, the experiment worked for the Orioles, thanks to the brilliant efforts of Jeff Ballard and Bob Milacki. Overall, Baltimore starters were 16-11 on three days rest, only 29-33 on four. But for the Cubs, the switch to a four man rotation flopped, as the club ERA was a full run higher on short rest. While the move was widely criticized in Chicago, it really didn't hurt the ballclub much. In fact, Cub starters had an 11-5 record on three days rest.

	ERA				
ORIOLES	**3 DAYS**	**4 DAYS**	**CUBS**	**3 DAYS**	**4 DAYS**
Jeff Ballard	2.24	3.93	Rick Sutcliffe	3.98	3.78
Bob Milacki	2.50	3.90	Mike Bielecki	4.42	2.82
Dave Johnson	4.05	5.00	Greg Maddux	4.69	2.63
TEAM TOTAL	3.68	4.37	TEAM TOTAL	4.47	3.40
Major Leagues	3.85	3.78			

In addition to the Cubs and Orioles, four other teams started their pitchers at least twenty times on three days rest. As was the case with the Baltimore and Chicago, the results were mixed:

Royals	GS	W-L	ERA	IP/start
3 days rest	35	14-13	4.00	5.98
4 days rest	87	36-29	3.53	6.59

Comment: This move looks like it backfired, but that was mainly due to the failure of rookie Tom Gordon to adapt to short rest. Gordon was 5-3, 3.00 on four days rest, a disastrous 0-4, 10.59 in five starts on shorter rest. But Bret Saberhagen was a brilliant 5-2, 1.25 in eight starts on short rest, while Mark Gubicza held his own with 3-1, 3.23.

Athletics	GS	W-L	ERA	IP/start
3 days rest	22	16-3	1.98	6.83
4 days rest	93	45-27	3.45	6.42

Comment: The A's were by far the most successful team that used their pitchers on three days rest with any consistency. Mike Moore was 5-1, 1.24 in six starts, Storm Davis 6-0, 2.76 in seven starts, Bob Welch 3-1, 1.84 in five starts and Dave Stewart 2-1, 2.10 in four starts. Perhaps the secret was that Oakland was careful not to overuse the four man rotation — but whatever the case, no other club had nearly this much success.

Reds	GS	W-L	ERA	IP/start
3 days rest	32	10-15	3.90	6.64
4 days rest	86	25-36	3.90	6.01

Comment: Pete Rose loved the four man rotation, using it for half the season in 1985 and much of the season in 1986. At times it worked well, especially for Tom Browning, who was 15-3 on short rest in 1985 and 5-3, 2.88 in ten starts last year. But none of the other Reds starters were effective on three days rest in '89. Rick Mahler was 2-6, 4.77 in ten starts on short rest, but 5-5, 3.33 when given one more day off.

Cardinals	GS	W-L	ERA	IP/start
3 days rest	31	6-13	3.64	5.74
4 days rest	96	38-33	3.39	6.44

Comment: Like the Cubs and Orioles, the Cardinals moved to a four-man rotation out of desperation when they couldn't find five solid starters. It didn't work except in the case of Jose DeLeon, who had a 1.87 ERA (but only one win) in five starts on three days rest. Cardinal pitchers were more effective on both four and five days rest.

Two other clubs utilized the four man rotation sparingly, but with interesting results. Met starters were 8-2 with a sizzling 2.21 ERA in 13 starts on short rest; David Cone was 4-0, 1.21. The Giants used their starters 19 times on short rest, but the result was a mediocre 4.11 ERA; on four days rest, Giant starters had a 3.37 ERA. Rick Reuschel, however, had a 1.29 ERA in four starts on short rest.

The results, overall, show that switching to a four-man rotation helped some clubs but hurt others. Except for the A's, there was a wide variance from pitcher to pitcher on most clubs. The A's and Mets results suggest that using short rest from time to time can be very effective. But in an era when starting pitchers are expected to go all out from their first pitch, no starter and no club has shown more than periodic effectiveness when used in a four-man rotation. The Oriole experiment, however, shows that it's worth a try when a club is strapped for pitching and really has nothing else to lose.

A complete listing for this category can be found on page 304.

WHICH PITCHERS SHOULD NEVER LEAVE HOME?

When the Yankees shocked the baseball world by firing manager Casey Stengel after the 1960 World Series, one of Casey's decisions was a key factor. In the Series Casey had held out his ace, Whitey Ford, until the third game. Stengel's reasoning was that Ford, his ace lefty, was much more effective in Yankee Stadium, and he wanted to reserve Whitey for the Stadium opener. Ford ended up pitching a shutout in the third game, and another shutout in the sixth game at Pittsburgh. But Whitey wasn't available for the seventh contest, and when the Yankees lost it on Bill Mazeroski's memorable homer, Stengel paid the price.

Though his decision cost him, Stengel was right in knowing that some pitchers are better — or worse — in their home park. Lefties like Ford tend to thrive in Yankee Stadium, but southpaws generally suffer in Fenway Park. Sandy Koufax was a great pitcher wherever he worked, but an overpowering hurler when he was working in Dodger Stadium. Ditto for Nolan Ryan in the Astrodome. The following pitchers had the biggest home/road ERA differences in 1989 (minimum 50 IP home and 50 IP road):

ERA Diff.	Better At Home Pitcher, Team	At Home W	L	ERA	On The Road W	L	ERA
- 3.39	Don Robinson, SF	9	4	2.10	3	7	5.49
- 2.86	Dennis Cook, SF-Phi	5	3	2.54	2	5	5.40
- 2.48	Charlie Leibrandt, KC	3	3	3.71	2	8	6.19
- 2.43	Paul Gibson, Det	2	3	3.49	2	5	5.92
- 2.13	Doug Drabek, Pit	8	5	1.85	6	7	3.99
- 2.10	Bob Walk, Pit	7	4	3.28	6	6	5.38
- 2.00	Don Carman, Phi	4	5	4.26	1	10	6.26
- 2.01	Terry Mulholland, SF-Phi	2	3	3.94	2	4	5.95
- 1.95	Chris Bosio, Mil	9	3	2.06	6	7	4.01
- 1.89	David Cone, Mets	8	2	2.61	6	6	4.50

ERA Diff.	Better On The Road Pitcher, Team	At Home W	L	ERA	On The Road W	L	ERA
+ 4.23	Allan Anderson, Min	6	5	6.47	11	5	2.24
+ 2.53	Bob Knepper, Hou-SF	0	7	6.56	7	5	4.04
+ 2.11	Shane Rawley, Min	2	7	6.18	3	5	4.07
+ 2.03	Rick Sutcliffe, Cubs	5	7	4.80	11	4	2.78
+ 1.91	Greg Harris, Phi-Bos	2	1	4.29	2	3	2.38
+ 1.88	Mark Grant, SD	3	1	4.33	5	1	2.45

+ 1.78	Jim Abbott, Cal	5	5	4.84	7	7	3.06
+ 1.75	Mike Boddicker, Bos	7	8	4.89	8	3	3.15
+ 1.55	Mark Langston, Sea-Mon	8	5	3.58	8	9	2.04
+ 1.54	Dave Schmidt, Bal	3	3	6.67	7	10	5.13

There are some dramatic differences here, and looking at the figures, one wonders why a manager would ever want to start Allan Anderson at the Metrodome, or Don Robinson anywhere but at Candlestick Park. (After watching the World Series, one wonders why you'd want to start Don Robinson anywhere. But hey, that was only one game.) The test of any statistic is whether it's consistent over a period of time. Fortunately for us, eight of the twenty starters have worked at least three seasons in the same home park. Two of them have worked six years in the same yard. Here are home/road ERAs for the eight pitchers, going back as far as 1984:

	Sutcliffe		Leibrandt		Carman		Walk	
Year	Home	Road	Home	Road	Home	Road	Home	Road
1984	2.77	2.63	3.50	3.73	—	—	—	—
1985	3.44	3.00	2.56	2.79	1.05	3.09	—	—
1986	4.35	5.00	4.25	3.94	3.90	2.54	3.68	3.81
1987	3.49	3.88	3.28	3.52	4.72	3.76	3.05	3.74
1988	3.19	4.42	2.94	3.39	3.58	5.16	3.12	2.27
1989	4.80	2.78	3.71	6.19	4.26	6.26	3.28	5.38

	Drabek		Cone		Bosio		Schmidt	
Year	Home	Road	Home	Road	Home	Road	Home	Road
1987	3.66	4.05	3.94	3.52	6.23	4.48	3.39	4.47
1988	3.22	2.95	1.29	3.19	2.73	4.01	4.36	2.40
1989	1.85	3.99	2.61	4.50	2.06	4.01	6.67	5.13

None of the eight hurlers has shown an exclusive home (or road) bias. The closest has been Leibrandt, who was better at Royals Stadium during five of his six seasons there. (Unfortunately for him, Charlie doesn't live there any more.) David Cone worked only 99 innings in 1987, his first at Shea, and his severe home/road differences in '88 and '89 bear some watching.

This doesn't mean that home or road biases don't exist for pitchers. Dwight Gooden, to use a good example, has had lower ERAs at Shea Stadium than on the road for five of his six seasons, with more than a run difference for five of them. But pitchers' biases tend to be less consistent than hitters' for two reasons: they don't work in all that many games either at home or on the road, and the mix of opponents they face varies a lot more for them than it does for hitters. We still think Casey should have started Ford in the first game of that '60 Series . . . but we can understand his reasoning.

A complete listing for this category can be found on page 305.

WHICH PITCHERS MAKE THE LEAST OF THEIR INHERITANCE?

Coming into the middle of an inning with the bases loaded and no outs, all a reliever is asked to do is retire the side with a "minimum amount of damage." For years, people have argued that a fireman could come in during just such a situation, allow all three runners to score, and still escape with no damage to his own ERA. Fortunately we have a new tool, the "inherited runners" stat, to find out which relievers have been most — and least — effective at preventing previous pitchers' runners from scoring. Here are the five best and five worst pitchers in that category during 1989. And note, for what it's worth, that all of the top five throw lefthanded.

BEST	Inherited runners	Inherited runners scored	PERCENTAGE*	WORST			
Bob McClure	50	7	14.0%	Tim Crews	31	17	54.8%
Steve Wilson	51	8	15.7%	Brian Holton	30	16	53.3%
Ken Dayley	60	10	16.7%	Greg Harris	42	21	50.0%
Tony Fossas	55	10	18.2%	Don Pall	47	23	48.9%
Randy Myers	54	10	18.5%	Tom Gordon	33	16	48.5%
*Minimum 30 inherited runners.				Major Leagues	6049	2016	33.3%

One interesting fact you may notice from scanning this list is that only one of the ten pitchers — Randy Myers — is a closer, or late man. Over the last few years, it's become more and more common for the closer to come in to start an inning, usually the ninth, rather than in the middle of a jam.

That conserves the closer's arm to wrap up saves, but it also makes the middle and set-up relievers even more important. If they can't prevent their inherited runners from scoring, the closer may not even get into the game.

You can see the difference in how modern relievers are both used and perceived by examining the work of Kansas City's Tom Gordon. Back in the forties or fifties, Gordon's raw stats — a 17-9 record, 3.64 ERA, 153 strikeouts and only 122 hits allowed in 163 innings — would have been enough to easily wrap up the Rookie of the Year Award. But the voters realized that a lot of Gordon's wins occurred during games in which he came in, allowed the tying run to score, and then snapped up the win for himself. The inherited runner stats show that Gordon's work wasn't nearly as good as it seemed at first glance.

A complete listing for this category can be found on page 306.

IS THE QUALITY START A QUALITY STAT?

The problem with new statistics, Bill James once said, is that people expect them to be perfect. No one complains that a pitcher can get a "win" for giving up nine earned runs in five innings if his team happens to score 10, or a "loss" if he works 12 innings and loses 1-0. No one complains that "hits" mean nothing because a batter can get one on a 10-foot dribbler. And no one complains that the "stolen base" is meaningless because Ernie Lombardi swiped eight in his major league career.

Yet people jump all over the "quality start" because a pitcher can get one by working six innings and allowing three earned runs. We know that quality is in the eye of the beholder, and perhaps that particular word should be replaced. But we like the QS for a simple reason: there's an extremely high correlation between quality starts and winning the game. Last year, for instance, National League pitchers had a winning percentage of .708 when they made a quality start; in the American League, where quality starts are more important because the scores are higher, the winning percentage in QS was .745. If that doesn't impress you, we add that those winning percentages include games where *both* pitchers made quality starts. In games where one pitcher made a quality start but the other didn't, the National League winning percentage was .937 (356-24); the American League percentage was .968 (458-15). Is that good enough for you?

Having established the stat's credibility, here are the major league leaders in quality starts — and the five worst pitchers — in each league last year (minimum 25 starts):

Quality Starts - Best Percentages

National League				American League			
Pitcher, Team	Starts	Quality Starts	%	Pitcher, Team	Starts	Quality Starts	%
McGrane, StL	33	28	84.8	Saberhagen, KC	35	30	85.7
Hershiser, LA	33	27	81.8	Blyleven, Cal	33	25	75.8
Hurst, SD	33	26	78.8	C.Finley, Cal	29	21	72.4
P.Perez, Mon	28	22	78.6	Black, Cle	32	22	68.8
Smiley, Pit	28	22	78.6	Clemens, Bos	35	24	68.6
B.Smith, Mon	32	25	78.1	Stewart, Oak	36	24	66.7
Langston, Mon	24	18	75.0	Bosio, Mil	33	22	66.7
Whitson, SD	33	24	72.7	Bankhead, Sea	33	22	66.7
Darling, Mets	33	24	72.7	McCaskill, Cal	32	21	65.6
Garrelts, SF	29	21	72.4	Candiotti, Cle	31	20	64.5
Smoltz, Atl	29	21	72.4				

Quality Starts - Worst Percentages

National League

Player, Team	Starts	Quality Starts	%
Lilliquist, Atl	30	12	40.0
P. Smith, Atl	27	12	44.4
Knepper, Hou-SF	26	12	46.2
Rasmussen, SD	33	16	48.5
Clancy, Hou	26	13	50.0
D. Robinson, SF	32	16	50.0

American League

Players, Team	Starts	Quality Starts	%
Schmidt, Bal	26	7	26.9
B. Witt, Tex	31	11	35.5
Rawley, Min	25	9	36.0
Leibrandt, KC	27	10	37.0
Reuss, WSox-Mil	26	10	38.5

What the stat does is quite simple: it measures consistent good effort. When pitchers like Joe McGrane or Bret Saberhagen took the hill last year, the odds were better than four to one that they were going to pitch well enough to keep their teams in the game, with an outstanding chance to win. Whereas when Dave Schmidt was working, the Orioles had to figure they'd need both a lot of pitchers and a lot of runs in order to win.

You can see the one weakness of the stat from the presence of the three Montreal pitchers — Langston (12-9), Smith (10-11) and Perez (9-13) — all of whom suffered from the Expos' lack of a reliable bullpen. But the Montreal Three's talents were definitely in demand over the winter. And the leaders' lists sure look like quality to us.

By the way, the definition of a quality start is any game where the starting pitcher goes at least six innings and allows three or less earned runs.

A complete listing for this category can be found on page 307.

WHICH LEFTY RELIEVERS ARE TOUGHEST AGAINST LEFTHANDED HITTERS?

The moral of this story might be the title of a country-and-western song: "Mamas, Don't Let Your Babies Grow Up to Be Righties." Lefthanded relievers are so valued that they often fashion long careers even when they aren't particularly successful. Hurlers like Jerry Don Gleaton (4.72 career ERA), Paul Mirabella (4.51) and Dan Schatzeder (3.80) keep finding jobs for one basic reason: they're lefthanded.

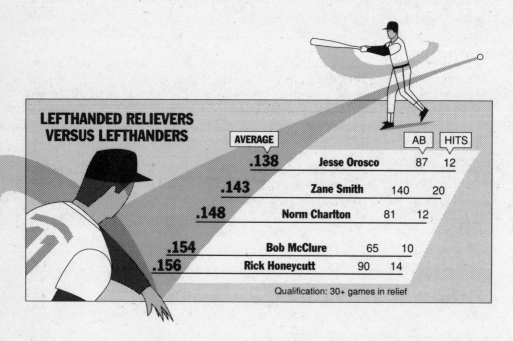

LEFTHANDED RELIEVERS VERSUS LEFTHANDERS

AVERAGE		AB	HITS
.138	Jesse Orosco	87	12
.143	Zane Smith	140	20
.148	Norm Charlton	81	12
.154	Bob McClure	65	10
.156	Rick Honeycutt	90	14

Qualification: 30+ games in relief

The pitchers on the chart have a lot more going for them than mere lefthandedness. As the illustration shows, all five were deadly against lefthanded hitters in '89, and that's the main function of a southpaw relief specialist. But all of these pitchers faced many more righties than lefties last year, and for the most part, they were effective against righthanded hitters as well:

	Vs. Righthanded Batters			
Reliever	AB	H	HR	BA
Orosco	186	42	7	.226
Z. Smith	419	121	6	.286
Charlton	259	55	5	.212

McClure	229	29	1	.244
Honeycutt	181	42	4	.232
Totals vs. RHB	1,164	289	23	.248
Totals vs. LHB	463	68	3	.147

These lefty specialists usually come into a game during the middle innings. They'll face one or two lefthanded hitters to begin with, often with men on base. That's why an ability to handle lefties is so crucial to them. But ordinarily they'll stay in the game after that and face a mix of hitters from both sides, so they need to hold their own against righties. Except for Smith this group was able to do that, though they were obviously nowhere near as effective as they were versus lefties.

Since the above group was so effective against lefties, one might wonder why they're not used more in late-inning situations. The answer is that effectiveness vs. righties is even more important for closers than it is for middlemen. Look at the figures for the seven southpaws who recorded at least 20 saves in 1989:

Reliever	Vs. Lefthanded Batters				Vs. Righthanded Batters			
	AB	H	HR	BA	AB	H	HR	BA
Mark Davis (44)	46	11	2	.239	284	55	4	.194
Mitch Williams (36)	71	18	0	.254	227	53	6	.233
Dan Pleasac (33)	47	11	1	.240	174	36	5	.207
John Franco (32)	50	10	0	.200	249	67	3	.269
Dave Righetti (25)	62	17	1	.274	202	56	2	.277
Randy Myers (24)	73	12	2	.164	228	50	2	.219
Craig Lefferts (20)	85	17	2	.200	314	76	9	.242
Totals	434	96	8	.221	1,678	393	31	.234

Unlike the middlemen, the closers are nearly as effective against righties as they are against lefties. Indeed, the top three had lower opponents' batting averages versus righties. And effectiveness against righthanders is crucial to them because the closers face a much higher ratio of righthanded hitters to lefthanders (3.9 to 1) than the middlemen do (2.5 to 1). Any closer — left or right — who has trouble against righthanded hitters will soon be out of a job.

A complete listing for this category can be found on page 308.

WHICH PITCHERS PERFORM BEST AGAINST THE TOP HITTERS?

We've already shown you the list of players who were the top hitters against baseball's toughest pitchers last year. You'll remember that the list consisted of mostly-predictable names (Mark Grace, Will Clark, Tony Gwynn, Kevin Mitchell, to name four). But there was one big surprise: the leader, Phil Bradley. All in all, it was a very worthy list. Now let's reverse the procedure and see which pitchers perform best against the toughest hitters. The hitters we chose — the top fifteen in runs created per game in each league — are super-tough. Overall these guys batted .295, had a .484 slugging average and a .364 on base percentage. Any pitcher who could handle these hitters was doing quite a job.

So who was the man among men who stopped those sluggers better than anyone? Was it Roger Clemens, Orel Hershiser, Bret Saberhagen? Was it Arnold Schwartzenegger or Sylvester Stallone? Was it Batman? No, it was none of the above. It was Paul Kilgus.

Paul Kilgus? *The* Paul Kilgus?

Yes, the same Paul Kilgus who was a nifty 6-10 with a 4.39 ERA for the division-winning Cubs last year. (Imagine what he could have done for a team which scored some runs.) The same Paul Kilgus who "held" opponents to a .283 batting average last year. The same Paul Kilgus whom the Cubs traded to Toronto in exchange for that other Cy Young Award winner, Jose Nunez; surely the deal was page one news in your home town, as it was in ours. Paul Kilgus.

Before you throw up your hands and decide this study is bogus, let's show you the whole list. Here are the pitchers who performed best against the top hitters last year:

Pitcher, Team	AB	H	HR	RBI	AVG	OBA	SLG
Paul Kilgus, Cubs	74	12	0	6	.162	.311	.216
Jose DeLeon, StL	109	18	4	12	.165	.270	.321
Sid Fernandez, Mets	97	17	6	13	.175	.236	.402
Chuck Finley, Cal	78	14	3	8	.179	.235	.308
Mark Langston, Sea-Mon	95	18	3	7	.189	.267	.337
Chris Bosio, Mil	96	19	2	11	.198	.257	.260
Bobby Ojeda, Mets	101	20	2	11	.198	.328	.287
Scott Bankhead, Sea	95	19	2	8	.200	.287	.316
Ken Howell, Phi	97	21	3	15	.216	.328	.381
Greg Swindell, Cle	73	16	3	7	.219	.310	.425

Now that's better, isn't it? Except for Kilgus, we've got a list of pretty tough pitchers here. There doesn't seem to be a lot in common among them. There are pure power pitchers (DeLeon, Fernandez) and pure finesse pitchers (Kilgus, Ojeda). The one interesting fact is that six of the ten are lefties, including four of the top five.

But while the list is worthy, it doesn't quite glitter with the sort of All Star names we had on the other list, the one of top hitters against the toughest pitchers. The big names were farther down this list: Saberhagen .248, Clemens .250, Hershiser .282, Mike Moore .284, Mike Scott .290. Bert Blyleven, one of last year's top pitchers, was tattooed by the best hitters for a .368 mark.

Is there a reason why the cream doesn't quite rise to the top of this list, as it did with the other? The only thing we can think of is that for a hitter going up against a top pitcher, the hurler is the hitter's major personal challenge for the day; hitting that guy is the focus of his attention from the time he gets to the ballpark. Whereas a top pitcher has to be concerned about getting out *every* hitter, not just the best ones, when he's working. Psychologically, the two situations are much different . . . but even so, there are some very fine pitchers on our list.

The following five pitchers had the worst success against the best hitters last year:

Pitcher, Team	AB	H	HR	RBI	AVG	OBA	SLG
Todd Stottlemyre, Tor	63	26	2	12	.413	.507	.698
Mike Witt, Cal	105	42	3	17	.400	.468	.571
Ken Hill, StL	80	31	1	13	.387	.605	.550
Kevin Gross, Phi	96	37	8	26	.385	.427	.792
Melido Perez, WSox	97	37	9	23	.381	.439	.763

There are no all stars on this list, but it's not the dregs of pitching society, either. If you had to guess which pitcher will help the Blue Jays most this year, Todd Stottlemyre or Kilgus, our hunch is that you'd have to pick Stottlemyre.

A complete listing for this category can be found on page 309.

WHICH PITCHERS ARE VICTIMIZED MOST BY THEIR OWN BULLPENS?

In the modern era, clubs are routinely using three or more pitchers per game — even when they win. These days an earned run average is not just dependent on a pitcher's own work. Often he'll leave the game with runners on base, and his ERA will shoot up if his relievers allow those runners to score. We call the runners passed on to the subsequent reliever "bequeathed runners." These same runners are called "inherited runners," when referred to from the standpoint of the reliever. Then we compute a "runs scored ERA" based on the number of bequeathed runners who ultimately score. This figure is not exact, since it includes both earned and unearned runs, but it's very close. The higher the runs scored ERA, the more that pitcher was victimized by his bullpen. The following pitchers had the highest runs scored ERAs in 1989 (81 or more IP):

Pitcher, Team	GS/GR	Regular ERA	Runners left	Runners scored	Run Scored "ERA"
Pete Harnisch, Bal	17/1	4.62	30	17	1.48
Mike Henneman, Det	0/60	3.70	30	14	1.40
Steve Rosenberg, WSox	38/21	4.94	41	22	1.39
Steve Wilson, Cubs	8/45	4.20	45	13	1.37
Don Carman, Phi	20/29	5.24	36	21	1.27
Brian Holton, Bal	12/27	4.02	31	15	1.16
Rich Yett, Cle	12/20	5.00	37	12	1.09
Mike Dunne, Pit-Sea	18/18	5.60	21	12	1.08
Larry McWilliams, Phi-KC	16/24	4.11	40	17	1.06
Terry Leach, Mets-KC	3/37	4.17	18	11	1.04
Major League Average					**0.48**

You'll notice that all but one of the pitchers had a regular ERA of over 4.00. But since the major league average for runs scored ERA was 0.48, these pitchers' bullpens were responsible in part for the poor figures; with only average bullpen work, for instance, Harnisch's 4.62 ERA would have been a full run lower. The other notable thing about the group is that it consists primarily of middle relievers and swing men. Middle relievers often leave a game for a pitcher who throws from the other side. Thus their regular ERAs are more dependent on subsequent relievers than any other group of pitchers, and are more apt to be deceptive.

Since there were no qualifiers for the ERA title in the first group, let's examine the leaders among pitchers who worked at least 162 innings:

Pitcher, Team	GS/GR	Regular ERA	Runners left	Runners scored	Run Scored "ERA"
Jim Abbott, Cal	29/0	3.92	28	15	0.74
Kevin Gross, Mon	31/0	4.38	25	16	0.72
Bobby Witt, Tex	31/0	5.14	32	14	0.65
Bob Walk, Pit	31/2	4.41	23	14	0.64
Andy Hawkins, Yanks	34/0	4.80	35	14	0.61
Melido Perez, WSox	31/0	5.01	30	12	0.59
Tom Glavine, Atl	29/0	3.68	20	12	0.58
Mike Boddicker, Bos	34/0	4.00	39	13	0.55
Derek Lilliquist, Atl	30/2	3.97	34	10	0.54
Greg Swindell, Cle	28/0	3.37	21	11	0.54

The most obvious thing about this group is that the runs scored ERAs are lower, and closer to the major league average. There were some clunkers in the group — "Gross" has a name that aptly fits — but some fine pitchers as well. Abbott, especially, pitched much better than his ERA would indicate. The Angels are high on him, and with good reason.

Finally, let's look at the elite starters, the five pitchers with the lowest ERAs in 162 or more innings last year:

Pitcher, Team	GS/GR	Regular ERA	Runners left	Runners scored	Run Scored "ERA"
Bret Saberhagen, KC	35/1	2.16	8	2	0.07
Scott Garrelts, KC	29/1	2.28	14	4	0.19
Orel Hershiser, KC	33/2	2.31	4	2	0.07
Chuck Finley, Cal	29/0	2.57	22	5	0.23
Mike Moore, Oak	35/0	2.61	20	5	0.19

The best pitchers have minuscule runs scored ERAs. But that is partly due to the fact that they seldom leave a game with runners on base. There are a couple of reasons why. First, these pitchers don't get into many jams. And when they do, their managers are apt to let them try to work out of trouble themselves. In particular, Tommy Lasorda had so much confidence in Hershiser that Orel left only four runners to his bullpen all season long. The only regular starters given comparable treatment were Mike Scott (5 runners left to relievers), Saberhagen (8) and Bruce Hurst (9).

A complete listing for this category can be found on page 310.

WHAT HAPPENS AFTER A HOME RUN?

Tradition says that, after a home run, the next hitter finds himself at risk. It's assumed that he's likely to hear some chin music, so the hit by pitch rate should go up; the pitcher is likely to be angry and throwing harder than before, so the strikeout rate should go up; and the pitcher's apt to be a bit wild, so the base on balls rate should go up as well. All in all, the next hitter should be in for an interesting experience.

We wondered whether the conventional wisdom about what happens after a HR was true. Since there were over 3,000 home runs hit in 1989, we had a decent database to work with. Here is a comparison of what happened in 1989 at bats, first overall and then after a home run:

Here's the breakdown by league (all figures per 100 plate appearances):

	Avg	Slg	OBA	HR	HBP	BB*	SO
AL Overall	.261	.384	.326	1.99	0.56	7.75	14.3
AL After HR	.249	.372	.323	2.19	1.12	8.81	16.9
NL Overall	.246	.365	.312	1.85	0.43	7.31	15.4
NL After HR	.237	.356	.303	2.09	0.67	7.96	16.8

*unintentional walks

There are certainly some interesting differences here. We find so many, in fact, that we'll go through them, one by one:

1. Hitters who come up after a home run have a significantly lower batting average.

2. The home run rate goes up by about 10 percent.

3. The next batter is definitely in increased danger of getting hit by a pitch. The hit batsmen rate doubles in the American League — this should help dispel notions that the AL is a wimp league — and goes up over fifty percent in the National League.

4. The base on balls rate (for unintentional walks — no one gives a hitter an intentional walk after a home run) decidedly goes up. It rises more in the American League (14%) than it does in the National (9%), but either way it goes up a significant amount.

5. The strikeout rate rises — 18 percent in the American League, 9 percent in the National.

What does this all mean? It definitely means that the nature of the next plate appearance is changed. This isn't surprising; allowing a home run is something of a traumatic event for a pitcher, and one should expect that he'd have a discernable reaction. The reaction is normal — he becomes more aggressive. The pitcher apparently throws harder, resulting in both increased strikeouts and walks. With his adrenaline flowing and his concentration sharpened, he's much harder to hit for average. If the manager went out to the mound during the appearance after a homer, he might say something like, "Gee, you're beautiful when you're mad."

There are other consequences. The pitcher becomes wilder, and not afraid to "throw inside." The batter should be prepared to hang loose, especially if he's an American League hitter. The chances of getting hit by a pitch increase dramatically — this is the biggest single change. But because the pitcher is angry, he's liable to groove another one occasionally, so the hitter's chances of a home run go up.

Often in studying the "conventional wisdom," we find that the old baseball homilies simply don't hold up. But in the plate appearance after a home run, they do. The pitcher's reaction is primal and totally emotional. For one at bat, at least, the game returns to the law of the jungle.

WHO ARE THE TOUGHEST (AND EASIEST) PITCHERS TO STEAL ON?

In an era of high stolen base totals, controlling the running game can be a crucial factor in the makeup of a successful pitcher. If you don't believe that, study the list of 1989's leading hurlers in the category of fewest steals per nine innings (minimum 162 IP). There are some well-known names here, though, curiously, nine of the top ten are righthanded (only Key is lefty):

Pitcher, Team	SB	CS	Pickoffs	SB Percent	SB per 9 innings
Kirk McCaskill, Cal	5	5	1	50.0	0.21
Mike Moore, Oak	7	10	2	41.2	0.26
Kevin Brown, Tex	6	5	2	54.5	0.28
Mark Gubicza, KC	9	8	0	52.9	0.32
Ed Whitson, SD	8	5	0	61.5	0.32
Andy Hawkins, Yanks	8	11	0	42.1	0.35
Walt Terrell, SD-Yanks	8	3	0	72.7	0.35
Jimmy Key, Tor	9	4	2	69.2	0.38
Dave Stewart, Oak	11	8	0	57.9	0.38
Orel Hershiser, LA	11	8	0	57.9	0.39

The list includes such heavies as Mike Moore, Dave Stewart and Orel Hershiser, and the overall depth of talent is most impressive. Of the ten, six won 15 or more games, while only two had losing records. The average among the group was 15.2 wins, 12.3 losses and a fine 3.29 ERA. For the most part, these are veterans (Kevin Brown, a rookie, was the lone exception) who don't pick a lot of guys off, but have the savvy to keep runners close. A couple of them (Terrell, Key) allowed decent stolen base percentages, but their ability to hold runners was so good that few players were tempted to run.

It's interesting to speculate why there aren't more lefties on the list. Maury Wills always used to argue that righties were tougher for him to get a good jump on, because he couldn't see what they were doing with their hands. Perhaps he's right. But these days, the crafty lefthander with the slick move to first — the Whitey Ford/Tommy John type — seems to be something of an endangered species. Modern hurlers who seem to fit that mold, like Teddy Higuera and Fernando Valenzuela, are not especially good at controlling the running game. Others like Sid Fernandez and Frank Viola, are good, but not quite in the top group. To be fair, there are a couple of lefty relievers who had outstanding records at limiting stolen bases last year. Mark Davis allowed only one successful steal in 92.2 innings (0.10 per nine), and John Franco only two in 82.2 (0.22).

As the top ten list suggests, a high pickoff total does not necessarily stop runners from stealing. A total of seven pitchers had four or more pickoffs last year: Doug Drabek 8, Mitch Williams 6, Lance McCullers 5, and 4 each from Mark Langston, Bruce Hurst, Randy Johnson and Brian Dubois. Dubois, a young Tiger southpaw, got his four pickoffs in only 36 innings of work. Williams, Hurst and Dubois had good steals-per-nine innings averages, but Langston and Drabek were only so-so; Drabek gave up 24 steals in 33 attempts, a bad ratio. The other two were even worse. McCullers allowed 11 steals in 12 attempts, and Johnson had the second-highest steals-per-nine average among pitchers who saw significant action. It seems that runners were so eager to run on Lance and Randy that they sometimes got hung out to dry.

Johnson's figures might make you curious about the *worst* starters at controlling the running game. Neither of the top two worked 162 innings, but both allowed so many steals that they would have made the leaders list anyway. These are the five worst players, allowing the most stolen bases per nine innings in the major leagues:

Pitcher, Team	SB	CS	Pickoffs	SB Percent	SB per 9 innings
Dwight Gooden, Mets	30	6	0	83.3	2.28
Randy Johnson, Mon-Sea	32	5	4	86.5	1.79
Mike Scott, Hou	39	2	0	95.1	1.53
Kevin Gross, Mon	34	13	1	72.3	1.52
John Dopson, Bos	28	5	0	84.8	1.49

There are a couple of great pitchers on this list; clearly neither Gooden or Scott pays much attention to baserunners, preferring instead to overpower the hitters with their high leg kicks. Nolan Ryan, who allowed 36 steals in 42 attempts (1.35 per nine), has the same philosophy. It simply isn't true, however, that being a great righthanded fastballer automatically means that the basestealers will run wild. Roger Clemens, probably the pitcher most similar to Gooden and Ryan, allowed only 0.68 steals per nine innings last year. Clemens permitted only 19 steals in 36 attempts, despite the handicap of a weak-throwing catching staff.

Roger's teammate John Dopson has to be the most messed up pitcher in baseball when it comes to trying to hold runners. Along with 28 steals in 33 attempts, Dopson committed the ludicrous total of 15 balks. In 1988, the Year of the Balk, Dopson had only one.

A complete listing for this category can be found on page 311.

DO PITCHERS HAVE TROUBLE AFTER A HIGH PITCH OUTING?

Once expected to go nine innings, starting pitchers are now simply instructed to go all out for as long as they can. Usually the manager will go to the bullpen in the late innings, but if the starter is still pitching well — or if the manager doesn't trust his relievers — he might end up throwing 120 pitches or more. Some of the game's workhorses frequently work these high pitch outings, then come back to start again four days later.

A lot of people question giving a pitcher this kind of workload. Craig Wright feels that overworking a young arm, in particular, is courting disaster in the long run. But what of the short term? Is a pitcher less effective in the start after a high pitch outing? Does an early knockout give his arm a chance to rest and make him more effective the next time out? Do some managers continually ask their starters to go too long? We've gathered some data to shed light on this subject.

Let's begin by restricting the study to starts after no more than four days rest. If pitchers have been overworked, their arms will probably not be fully recovered by then. Here is a "before and after" chart for each league based on all 1989 starts; the structure is based on the number of pitches the starter threw in his previous start, then the results of the subsequent start:

American League
(starts after 0-4 days rest)

# Pitches Previous Start	Starts	Won-Lost	W/L %	ERA	Avg IP
100 or less	666	242-239	.503	3.97	6.0
more than 100	619	257-230	.528	3.89	6.7
110 or less	894	328-322	.505	3.93	6.0
more than 110	391	171-147	.538	3.94	6.7
120 or less	1076	409-387	.514	3.94	6.3
more than 120	209	90-82	.523	3.89	6.7
130 or less	1211	467-440	.515	3.93	6.3
more than 130	74	32-29	.525	4.00	6.7
140 or less	1265	491-461	.516	3.94	6.3
more than 140	20	8-8	.500	3.82	7.0
150 or less	1278	497-464	.517	3.94	6.3
more than 150	7	2-5	.286	3.52	6.7
League Total	1285	499-469	.515	3.93	6.3

National League
(starts after 0-4 days rest)

# Pitches Previous Start	Starts	Won-Lost	W/L %	ERA	Avg IP
100 or less	678	230-259	.470	3.60	6.3
more than 100	495	186-182	.505	3.50	6.3
110 or less	881	309-333	.481	3.62	6.3
more than 110	292	107-108	.498	3.38	6.7
120 or less	1050	377-387	.493	3.51	6.3
more than 120	123	39-54	.419	3.96	6.3
130 or less	1130	402-423	.487	3.52	6.3
more than 130	43	14-18	.438	4.47	6.0
140 or less	1164	411-437	.485	3.55	6.3
more than 140	9	5-4	.556	4.04	7.0
150 or less	1170	415-439	.486	3.55	6.3
more than 150	3	1-2	.333	3.86	7.7
League Total	1173	416-441	.485	3.55	6.3

The most notable factor in these charts is the difference between the leagues. Even after adjusting for the fact that the American League plays more total games, AL pitchers make more long distance starts. This would figure; National League pitchers are often pinch-hit for in the late innings, while an American League starter can keep going as long as he's effective. The surprise, though, is that AL starters stay effective longer. National League starters lose effectiveness markedly in the outing following a 120-pitch start, while American League starters don't show a loss of effectiveness until after a 130-start effort. Even then it's only a slight dip, and AL pitchers were actually *more* effective in their handful of starts after throwing 140 or 150 pitches. You could speculate all day about why this is so. The number of starts from 130 pitches and up is pretty low, so it could be a statistical fluke. But the data, even at 120 pitches, shows clearly that American League pitchers had more resilience. Maybe because they're used to going longer?

One thing the data from both leagues agrees on is that getting knocked out early doesn't make a starter more effective the next time out. Pitchers in both leagues were less effective, not more, after an outing in which they'd thrown 100 pitches or less.

The Red Sox, with Roger Clemens, and the Rangers, with Nolan Ryan among others, each had 14 games where the starter threw more than 130 pitches. But while Red Sox starters had a 3.39 ERA in the outing after a

130-pitch start, Rangers starters had a 4.21 mark. The Braves and Pirates, by contrast, didn't have even one 130 pitch start from their pitching staffs.

WHOSE HEATER IS THE HOTTEST?

It used to be that pitchers with great fastballs were always pegged for the starting rotation. As recently as the fifties, relief aces still tended to be grizzled ex-starters who relied on finesse (Jim Konstanty, Johnny Sain) or younger hurlers who threw trick pitches (Hoyt Wilhelm, Elroy Face). The big flamethrowers like Herb Score and Bob Turley, meanwhile, were almost always used in the starting rotation. Even pitchers who had great fastballs but not a lot of success, like Mickey McDermott and Vinegar Bend Mizell, were never tried as relief aces. And when two of the rare relievers who really *could* throw hard — Don Mossi and Ray Narleski of the old Indians — began to struggle a bit, they were quickly moved into the rotation. About the only major exception was the Yankees' Ryne Duren, a fireballer who had only a brief career as the Yankees' closer.

How times have changed. These days young flamethrowers are often groomed for relief roles from the start of their careers. The chart below shows the results: last year only one starter, Nolan Ryan, placed among the top ten in strikeouts per nine innings. While it's true that relievers have the advantage of being able to cut loose without having to pace themselves, the difference is significant.

One can easily surmise that if the fifties were happening today, pitchers like Mizell and McDermott might well have developed into ace firemen. Even the legendary Steve Dalkowski, the man who averaged almost two strikeouts and two walks an inning in his minor league career, might have reached the majors in a less pressurized middle relief role, and so might other hurlers with exceptional, but narrowly defined, skills. Whole careers might have been salvaged.

A complete listing for this category can be found on page 312.

	Strikeouts	Innings pitched	Strikeouts per 9 innings pitched
Rob Dibble	141	99.0	12.8
Tom Henke	116	89.0	11.7
Nolan Ryan	301	239.1	11.3
Duane Ward	122	114.2	9.6
Gregg Olson	90	85.0	9.5
Randy Myers	88	84.1	9.4
Norm Charlton	98	95.1	9.3
Jeff Montgomery	94	92.0	9.2
Rob Murphy	107	105.0	9.2
Mark Davis	92	92.2	8.9
ML Average			5.6

Minimum 81 innings pitched.

WHO THROWS TO FIRST?

We've shown in another essay that pitchers' throws to first are far from a waste of time. They keep the runner closer to the bag and give the catcher an increased chance of throwing out the runner. One would think, then, that pitchers who throw to first a lot would automatically be tough to steal on. Our list of pitchers who made the most pickoff throws per nine innings (minimum 81 innings) shows that it ain't necessarily so:

Pitcher, Team	Pickoff Throws per 9 innings	Total Pickoff Throws	Stolen Bases per 9 innings
Mike Dunne, Pit-Sea	14.7	163	0.90
Jim Deshaies, Hou	14.2	355	1.08
Pete Smith, Atl	13.8	217	1.08
Charlie Hough, Tex	13.7	277	1.29
Rick Rhoden, Hou	12.1	130	1.68
Danny Darwin, Hou	12.0	163	0.74
Mitch Williams, Cubs	11.4	103	0.44
Bob Knepper, Hou-SF	10.9	200	0.93
John Cerutti, Tor	10.9	249	0.53
Tom Candiotti, Cle	10.8	247	1.05

The major league average last year was 0.74 steals per nine innings. Eight of the ten leaders in pickoff throws had steal rates higher than that, and Rick Rhoden's was more than twice as high. You can instantly see that throwing to first doesn't necessarily stop a runner from stealing; all it can do is reduce his chances. Four of the pickoff leaders worked for Houston, and the Astros had a young catcher, Craig Biggio, who had enormous difficulties throwing anyone out. All the pickoff throws — almost certainly on orders from manager Art Howe — undoubtedly helped Biggio. But they couldn't make a bad thrower (at least at this point of his career) into a good one. Two of the other leaders are Charlie Hough and Tom Candiotti. Both are knuckleballers who have good moves to first. But a knuckler takes so long to get to the plate that the pitcher is easy prey for base stealers. All he can do is try to cut his losses, and that's why both flutterballers throw to first so often. Undoubtedly, it helps a little.

A look at the major league pitchers who made the *fewest* pickoff throws per nine innings underscores the point that there's no direct relationship between simply throwing to first and eliminating the running game:

Pitcher, Team	Pickoff Throws per 9 innings	Total Pickoff Throws	Stolen Bases per 9 innings
Jose DeLeon, StL	0.4	11	0.48
Larry McWilliams, Phi-KC	0.5	8	0.35
Pascual Perez, Mon	0.5	10	0.73
Juan Berenguer, Min	0.7	8	1.36
Chuck Finley, Cal	0.9	20	0.77

The two leaders in fewest pickoff throws actually had stolen base rates much lower than the major league average. Both have good moves to first, and of course it helps to have Tony Pena, Steve Lake or Bob Boone behind the plate. The number three man, Pascual Perez, doesn't have good-throwing catchers, but he does have a herky-jerky motion that is difficult for runners to read. Pickoff tosses probably wouldn't do much to help Juan Berenguer, a fastballer with a high leg kick. But they probably would aid Chuck Finley, a southpaw who's already pretty tough to run against.

Can we learn anything from this? Certainly that there's a limit to the effectiveness of pickoff throws. A weak-armed catcher or a pitcher with a high leg kick or a slow delivery can short-circuit all the pickoff throws in the world. They help . . . but there's a limit to the amount they do.

An added benefit of pickoff throws is that they seem to distract the hitter, just as stolen base attempts do. Last year major league batters hit only .209 during plate appearances when the pitcher made a throw to first. That didn't help Mike Dunne (opponents' BA .310), and not throwing to first didn't seem to hamper Jose Deleon (.197). But who knows how much sooner Mike would have been done without all those pickoff tosses? After looking at the .209 batting average, our own Dick Cramer suggested that pitchers toss to first even when there's no one on base. If you see that strategy in a major league game this year, you'll know whose idea it was.

A complete listing for this category can be found on page 313.

WHICH PITCHERS THROW THE MOST DOUBLE PLAY GROUNDERS?

The double play is often called the "pitcher's best friend" because one pitch can get a hurler out of a jam. One might conclude that the best hurlers would automatically throw a lot of DP grounders . . . but the relationship is not nearly that simple. For one thing, a weak pitcher will have more runners on base than a good one, and thus more chances for twin killings. A better system is to rank pitchers by DPs per opportunity (situations with a runner on first and less than out), and that's the way we do it. But even using that system shows some surprising names at the top:

Pitchers with Highest GDP Frequency

American League	Opp.	GDP	GDP per Opp.
Tom McCarthy, WSox	69	17	.258
Jeff Russell, Tex	56	13	.232
Billy Swift, Sea	130	26	.200
Lee Guetterman, Yanks	93	18	.194
Eric King, WSox	131	25	.191
Kirk McCaskill, Cal	170	32	.188
Mark Thurmond, Bal	85	16	.188
Walt Terrell, Yanks	75	14	.186
Scott Bailes, Cle	99	17	.172
Chuck Crim, Mil	117	20	.171

National League	Opp.	GDP	GDP per Opp.
Atlee Hammaker, SF	71	13	.183
Mike Morgan, LA	100	17	.170
Mark Grant, SD	90	15	.167
Frank DiPino, StL	67	11	.164
Jay Howell, LA	56	9	.161
Orel Hershiser, LA	192	29	.151
Rick Horton, StL	73	11	.151
Bryn Smith, Mon	133	20	.150
Dennis Martinez, Mon	143	21	.147
Joe Magrane, StL	166	24	.145

(Minimum 50 opportunities)

We divide the leaders lists by leagues because American League teams put more runners on base, and thus get more opportunities (last year AL players grounded into 1.62 DPs per game, NL only 1.26). There are certainly some outstanding hurlers among the leaders, like Hershiser, Howell and Magrane, but just as many Tom McCarthys and Billy Swifts. The reason is that groundball pitchers tend to be finesse hurlers. For the most part, they don't strike out a lot of batters and give up an above average number of hits per inning. These are ordinarily not pitchers who are going to blow hitters away. Throwing DP grounders is one of the skills they need to survive . . . but often there are corresponding weaknesses.

This opposite extreme is represented by the pitchers who never — or hardly ever — throw a DP grounder. This is also a mixed bag: a few big names and some "who he?" types:

Pitchers with Lowest GDP Frequency

American League	Opp.	GDP	GDP per Opp.
Lance McCullers, Yanks	71	0	.000
Bryan Harvey, Cal	54	0	.000
Eric Hetzel, Bos	52	0	.000
Frank Wills, Tor	70	2	.029
Nolan Ryan, Tex	132	4	.030

National League	Opp.	GDP	GDP per Opp.
Scott Scudder, Cin	76	2	.026
Norm Charlton, Cin	73	2	.027
Randy Myers, Mets	71	2	.028
Mitch Williams, Cubs	93	3	.032
Kevin Gross, Mon	138	5	.036

As would figure, this group is primarily composed of strikeout pitchers: four of the ten averaged over a K an inning, and McCullers just missed. Even Hetzel and Wills, who didn't have high strikeout ratios in '89, have had good ratios during most of their careers (majors or minors). For the most part these hurlers work high in the strike zone, and give up more flyballs than grounders.

An ability to throw DP grounders is a useful skill. But if you're managing in a fantasy league this year, here's a hint: pick Nolan Ryan before you pick Tom McCarthy.

A complete listing for this category can be found on page 314.

WHICH PITCHERS ARE THE BEST "LONG DISTANCE RUNNERS"?

If pitchers participated in track meets, you'd have some "sprinters," who give it all they've got for as long as they can, and some "long distance runners," who pace themselves and then come on at the finish. If a pitching staff is full of sprinters, then there'd better be a good bullpen behind them. If a staff has a few long-distance runners, a manager often has to decide how long to stick with a starter who's struggling early in the game.

	ERA		
SPRINTERS	INNINGS 1-6	INNINGS 7+	
Pascual Perez	2.55	6.81	+4.26
Walt Terrell	4.08	7.16	+3.08
Bob Walk	3.93	6.97	+3.04
Mike Witt	4.12	6.69	+2.57
Tim Leary	3.14	5.63	+2.49

LONG-DISTANCE			
Frank Viola	4.17	1.45	−2.72
Bobby Witt	5.56	3.06	−2.50
Tom Browning	3.74	1.79	−1.95
Ken Howell	3.70	1.88	−1.82
Jeff Ballard	3.70	1.91	−1.79

Minimum 162 innings pitched.

The above chart shows the starters (minimum 162 innings) with the biggest ERA increases and decreases in innings seven and up. One thing that seems clear is that George Steinbrenner really loves those sprinters. Last year the Yanks had not only Terrell, but ace trackmen Dave LaPoint (11.05 ERA in innings seven-plus) and Tommy John (15.95 ERA). That group is gone from the Bronx rotation, so George went out and got Leary and Perez to take their places.

Those were the pitchers with the biggest increases or decreases; you might wonder which starters had the best ERAs, period, in the late innings. Here they are:

			Innings 7+	
Pitcher, Team	Starts	CG	IP	ERA
Bruce Hurst, SD	33	10	54.2	1.32
Orel Hershiser, LA	33	8	60.2	1.34
Frank Viola, Min-Mets	36	9	49.2	1.45
Greg Maddux, Cubs	35	7	40.2	1.58
Tom Browning, Cin	37	9	45.1	1.79
Mark Gubicza, KC	36	8	54.1	1.82
Ken Howell, Phi	32	1	28.2	1.88
Jeff Ballard, Bal	35	4	33.0	1.91
Kirk McCaskill, Cal	32	6	36.2	1.96
Bryn Smith, Mon	32	3	31.2	1.99

These pitchers had lower late-inning ERAs than all but the best bullpenners, so it made sense to keep them in the game as long as possible. Thus Howell, Ballard and Smith were probably used too conservatively; they might have been kept around a bit longer, at least until they began to show more signs of weakening.

Hershiser's 60.2 innings of work were the most by any starter in innings seven-plus last year. The only other starters to log more than fifty innings from the seventh on were Hurst, Gubicza Bret Saberhagen, Roger Clemens, Nolan Ryan and Dave Stewart — a fairly high-powered, and highly paid, group of pitching talent. Here's how the other workhorses fared in the late innings last year:

	Innings 1-6		Innings 7+		ERA Change
Pitcher, Team	IP	ERA	IP	ERA	
Bret Saberhagen, KC	205.0	1.93	57.1	2.98	+1.05
Roger Clemens, Bos	200.0	3.06	53.1	3.38	+0.32
Nolan Ryan, Tex	188.2	3.29	50.2	2.84	−0.45
Dave Stewart, Oak	207.0	3.22	50.2	3.73	+0.51

The amazing Ryan, at age 42, actually got better in the late innings. But despite Saberhagen's overall 2.16 ERA and Cy Young Award, it looks like the Royals were leaving him in the game a little too long. Hitters batted .211 with seven homers in 743 at bats during Saberhagen's first six innings. But from the seventh on, they hit .239 with six homers in only 218 at bats. There's nothing wrong with those figures, and you can't knock the overall results. But Saberhagen is not exactly built like Roger

Clemens, and after six years he's yet to have two winning seasons in a row. As Craig Wright has suggested, a little caution in the use of his valuable right arm might be a very good idea.

A complete listing for this category can be found on page 315.

IV. QUESTIONS ON DEFENSE

WHICH CATCHERS THROW OUT THE MOST BASERUNNERS?

In the quaint world of Official Baseball Statistics, they still don't count the number of stolen bases allowed by each catcher. Of course they don't, because Joe Garagiola used to tell us that runners were really stealing on the pitcher. But of course, they don't count stolen bases off pitchers, either . . . because everyone knows they're really stealing off the catcher. If this confuses you, they'll give you an even better argument: all these new-fangled statistics are a dangerous cancer which are ruining the poetry of the game.

We're not poets, and we beg to differ. We agree that there are a lot of stupid statistics out there, but two of them most certainly are *not* the number of steals allowed by each pitcher and catcher. Our job is to log the data accurately; then, in a leap of faith, we present the numbers so the reader can decide if any truth can be found. So, at the risk of seeming subversive, here are some numbers the Lords of Baseball don't want you to see — the top ten catchers last year in throwing out runners (minimum 700 innings caught):

Catcher, Team	SB	CS	CS %	SB per 9 innings	Pickoffs
Damon Berryhill, Cubs	36	29	44.6	.42	0
Bob Boone, KC	60	44	42.3	.50	1
Dave Valle, Sea	48	34	41.5	.55	1
Benito Santiago, SD	46	32	41.0	.38	14
Terry Steinbach, Oak	38	26	40.6	.42	3
Mike Scioscia, LA	73	47	39.2	.62	1
Don Slaught, Yanks	52	33	38.8	.57	0
Terry Kennedy, SF	61	36	37.1	.63	0
Jeff Reed, Cin	84	46	35.4	.98	1
Mike Heath, Det	78	42	35.0	.75	0

While Damon Berryhill threw out the highest percentage of runners, the notion that Benito Santiago is the best throwing catcher in baseball gets no quarrel from us. Santiago allowed the fewest number of steals per nine innings, meaning that he controlled the running game better than anyone. And Benito had the wondrous total of 14 pickoffs — 9 more than the number two man, Charlie O'Brien of the Brewers.

The other leaders include some old standbys (Boone, Scioscia, Heath) and some solid younger players (Valle, Steinbach, Reed). Kennedy and Slaught are the big surprises; each improved his percentage a lot from '88 to '89 (Kennedy threw out 28 percent in 1988, Slaught only 22 percent). Kennedy and Slaught were undoubtedly helped by pitching staffs — and managers — who stressed the importance of holding baserunners. This might lead one to conclude that runners really do steal on the pitcher. That's true to an extent; on some clubs all the catchers did well, notably the Braves, Yankees and Giants, while all the Mets and Red Sox catchers did poorly. Some managers preach short leg kicks and holding runners; others like Davey Johnson like the pitcher to concentrate on the hitter. A catcher can be helped or hindered to a great extent by such decisions.

But on other clubs, the differences between catchers becomes obvious. Seattle's Valle, to use a good example, ranked among the major league leaders by throwing out 41 percent of his would-be stealers. But his teammate Scott Bradley threw out only 20 percent, one of the lowest figures in baseball. To cite another case, the Rangers had three catchers who all worked at least 300 innings. Jim Sundberg threw out 38 percent, Gino Petralli 28 percent, Chad Kreuter 18 percent. Kreuter wasn't helped by his frequent role as Nolan Ryan's designated catcher — Ryan is one of the easiest pitchers in baseball to steal on — but even so, he's obviously no Jim Sundberg. On the Phillies, Steve Lake threw out an outstanding 49 percent, his teammate Darren Daulton an average 33 percent. Clearly the role of the catcher is greater than a lot of people are willing to admit.

Though they didn't play enough to qualify for the rankings, a few other catchers displayed exceptional skill at throwing out runners. Steve Lake's percentage of 49.1 percent was the highest of any catcher who saw significant action. Ron Karkovice of the White Sox and Rick Dempsey of the Dodgers each threw out 25 of 51 runners, or 49.0 percent; Karkovice is now generally regarded as the best-throwing catcher in the American League. Jody Davis's .169 batting average made him about as welcome in Atlanta as General Sherman, but Davis, helped by his pitching staff, threw out an impressive 41 percent of all attempted stealers. Jody's teammate Bruce Benedict had a satisfying final season, at least on defense, by also throwing out 41 percent.

A complete listing for this category can be found on page 316.

WHO LED THE LEAGUE IN FUMBLES?

One of Shakespeare's livelier plays, *The Comedy of Errors,* has long been a nationwide hit via superstation WTBS in Atlanta. For years the Braves wowed viewers with Rafael Ramirez, the master of shortstop disaster: five straight years of 30-plus miscues. Ramirez has given way to Andres Thomas, but after two straight 29-error campaigns from Andres, TBS fans have hardly noticed the difference. Knowing what we've come to know and love, Ted Turner gave us 53 games of third baseman Ron Gant (.887 fielding average) during the crucial spring ratings period last year. And how about that John Smoltz? Last year the fumble-fingered Braves pitcher managed to make more errors in 66 chances than Blue Jay shortstop Tony Fernandez committed in 741.

Errors are not just indigenous to Atlanta, of course. For one thing, Ramirez has moved on to Houston, and Raffy hasn't changed a bit: 30 errors once again last year. As our first annual "Hands of Stone/Soft Hands" comparison shows, they're booting 'em (and snaring 'em) in all corners of North America:

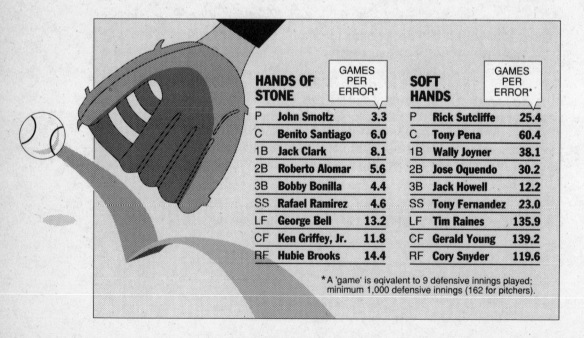

	HANDS OF STONE	GAMES PER ERROR*		SOFT HANDS	GAMES PER ERROR*
P	John Smoltz	3.3	P	Rick Sutcliffe	25.4
C	Benito Santiago	6.0	C	Tony Pena	60.4
1B	Jack Clark	8.1	1B	Wally Joyner	38.1
2B	Roberto Alomar	5.6	2B	Jose Oquendo	30.2
3B	Bobby Bonilla	4.4	3B	Jack Howell	12.2
SS	Rafael Ramirez	4.6	SS	Tony Fernandez	23.0
LF	George Bell	13.2	LF	Tim Raines	135.9
CF	Ken Griffey, Jr.	11.8	CF	Gerald Young	139.2
RF	Hubie Brooks	14.4	RF	Cory Snyder	119.6

*A 'game' is eqivalent to 9 defensive innings played; minimum 1,000 defensive innings (162 for pitchers).

By the way, you'll notice that we use games per error instead of fielding percentage. Games per error is kind of neat, in that it lets a fan know, in more understandable terms (games played), how rare it is to see an error. Compare George Bell and Tim Raines in left field. Bell made an error every 13 games last season while Tim's one error translates into one error for every 136 games. Fielding percentages would tell you that Bell had a .963 percentage to Raines' .996.

We don't know about you, but after years of watching America's Team on the superstation, guys like Tony Fernandez and Jose Oquendo seem downright boring. Give us two-fisted fielders like the Pirates' Bobby Bonilla any day ... even if you have to play him out of position to achieve the desired effect. Or second basemen like Roberto Alomar, who roams far and wide to grab the ball — and then throws it into the dugout.

For true-blue Braves connoisseurs, 1989 was a disappointing year all around. Ron Gant, alas, didn't appear in enough games to boot out (sorry) Bonilla at third; the same goes for Gerald Perry, who was off to a promising start at first base (nine errors in only 72 games) before his unfortunate injury. And Andres Thomas, despite considerable promise, has yet to unseat the master, Ramirez, at shortstop. But it must break Atlanta's heart that they couldn't swing a deal for Benito Santiago. With 20 errors last year, does Benito wear a Gold Glove, or a Golden (boxing) Glove?

A complete listing for this category can be found on page 317.

CAN CATCHERS HELP A PITCHER'S ERA?

The concept of "catchers' ERA" has been around for a few years now. Bill James was the first to popularize the idea, and STATS' own Craig Wright gave it a big boost in his excellent book, *The Diamond Appraised*. The concept is simple: it compiles a pitching staff's ERA under each catcher. Sometimes the ERAs are similar, but often a staff will perform significantly better under a catcher who is a good handler of pitchers. Carlton Fisk is probably the best example of a catcher who has gotten consistently better performances out of his pitchers than his catching partners do.

To be sure, the concept is not perfect. The same catchers on a team may work under a different mix of starting pitchers, weighing the odds in one receiver's favor. (Wright, in fact, has come up with a system for eliminating any usage bias on a particular team.) It's also true that a catcher is helped in the comparison by having an inept handler of pitchers as a teammate, or hurt by having a good one. But the basic idea is sound, particularly when studied over a period of years. The following is a list of the catchers who produced the greatest benefit in ERAs for their pitching staffs last year, in comparison with their catching teammates. And, honestly, the fact that STATS is located in the Chicago area has nothing to do with the results:

Catcher, Team	Staff ERA when catching	Staff ERA with others catching	Difference
Damon Berryhill, Cubs	2.88	4.01	1.13
Carlton Fisk, White Sox	3.80	4.72	0.92
Craig Biggio, Hou	3.42	4.25	0.83
Brian Harper, Min	3.95	4.66	0.71
Mike LaValliere, Pit	3.22	3.87	0.65
Rich Gedman, Bos	3.67	4.28	0.61
Matt Nokes, Det	4.10	4.70	0.60
Chad Kreuter, Tex	3.56	4.12	0.56
Bob Melvin, Bal	3.73	4.22	0.49
Gary Carter, Mets	2.97	3.41	0.44

(Note: minimum 40 games as starter)

You can instantly see why Damon Berryhill is such a highly regarded young receiver. Berryhill has already demonstrated that he's one of the best-throwing catchers in baseball . . . that's assuming, of course, that he recovers from his rotator cuff injury. And his stats show an excellent ability to get the most out of a pitching staff, particularly for a 26-year old. Rick Wrona and Joe Girardi, the other Cub catchers, produced ERAs of 3.17 and 4.36, respectively, from their starters.

Fisk's performance is old hat by now. Last year was the sixth straight season that Carlton has produced a better ERA from his pitchers than the other White Sox catchers did. Fisk's edge was helped in '89 by the growing pains of the Sox' number two receiver, Ron Karkovice. Karkovice has one of the greatest throwing arms in baseball, and he improved markedly as a hitter last year (from .174 to .264). But the Sox ERA with Karko behind the plate was only 4.75; the whole staff improved noticeably when Fisk returned from an early-season injury. Karkovice's struggles demonstrate that there's more than good mechanics and a strong throwing arm in the makeup of a good catcher.

The number three man, Craig Biggio, is another young receiver trying to assert himself. Biggio is already a fine hitter and a terrific baserunner . . . though he won't be a terrific baserunner for long if he keeps squatting down for 120 games a year. The stats show that Biggio can take charge of a pitching staff — the ERA with the Astros' number two man, Alex Trevino, was 4.46. Biggio's problem is the opposite of Karkovice's: he needs to improve his throwing (only 17 percent thrown out last year, and 140 stolen bases allowed, highest in the majors) to become a good all-around catcher.

Among the other leaders, there are a few surprises. The Twins seem happy with Brian Harper, a catcher several other teams tried shifting to other positions; given his handling of pitchers and decent throwing stats, it's possible Harper is simply a late bloomer. Mike Lavalliere continues to show why he's a highly regarded catcher, and Matt Nokes and Bob Melvin are solid young receivers; Nokes's defensive improvement over the last two years has been substantial. Chad Kreuter struggled with both his hitting and throwing, but his handling of pitchers is excellent; his ERA stats were helped by his status as Nolan Ryan's designated catcher, but the fact that he was good enough for Nolan Ryan says something by itself. Rich Gedman's good figures may reflect Rick Cerone's ineptitude more than anything else.

A few famous names are missing from our list. Mike Scioscia, usually excellent in this category, suffered only by the outstanding performance of his substitute, Rick Dempsey (2.34). Bob Boone's sub, Mike MacFarlane, also did a fine job, as did Tony Pena's; there was nothing wrong last year with the work of either Boone or Pena. Terry Steinbach's pitchers had a 2.91 ERA, and he just missed the leaders list. Benito Santiago wasn't close; handling pitchers continues to be a weakness in Benito's game, though San Diego sources say he's improving.

A complete listing for this category can be found on page 318.

WHICH INFIELDERS HAVE THE BEST RANGE?

People have been battling over fielding statistics ever since baseball was invented. Fielding averages are deceptive, it's been said, because some fielders make errors on balls that others couldn't reach. So Bill James invented the "range factor," which was based on chances accepted divided by games played. That was a big improvement, and helped identify fielders who'd been either overrated or overlooked. But range factor, though it took fielding statistics out of the stone ages, still had weaknesses. One of them involved the use of games played. A game played might consist of a single inning, and the range factor of even a solid fielder could be unfairly reduced, especially if he was often used as a defensive replacement.

Since we keep track of innings played on defense, we can eliminate that weakness. When we calculate range factor, we use total chances — putouts, assists, and errors — per nine innings. Some might question including errors, but our position is that an error comes on a ball reached, and we're measuring range here, not accuracy; for accuracy we have fielding average.

Using innings is an improvement, but there is still a major bias in range factors based on the composition of a team's pitching staff. In 1989, St. Louis pitchers allowed 2,261 groundballs while the Mets pitching staff only allowed 1,730. That's over 500 more grounders, a whopping 31 percent more groundballs allowed by Cardinal pitchers. You better believe that the range factors of Mets infielders tend to be understated while Cardinal infielders tend to be overstated.

How do we overcome this pitching staff bias? For every major league game last year STATS charted the direction of every batted ball — grounders, flies, hits, outs . . . everything. Our computer database stores all this information. With that information, we've developed a new defensive statistic called the Zone Rating. The zone rating only counts batted balls hit in the zone of the defensive fielder. For example, the shortstop is only responsible for balls hit in his zone — the area about 50 feet wide around the normal shortstop position. To calculate the zone rating, we take the actual number of outs recorded on balls hit to the fielder divided by the balls hit in his zone to get Outs per Balls Hit in Zone. By using outs recorded we give credit for the quick release needed for a double play since that counts as two outs. We also give credit for outs recorded on balls hit outside a fielder's zone. If a shortstop ranges to the right of second and throws the batter out at first, we give him credit for that play even though it's technically outside of his zone.

Zone ratings eliminate a groundball or flyball pitching staff bias. It also eliminates some of the luck factor (i.e. more or less batted balls hit towards a given infielder based on chance). It's hard to believe that Ozzie Smith really is 14th and Kevin Elster 16th out of 19 major league shortstops with 1,000 innings in 1989, as range factors would indicate. Our zone ratings put Ozzie Smith seventh (second in the NL) while Kevin Elster moves up to the middle of the pack at number nine (fourth in the NL).

But before we actually give you any of these numbers, we should point out one more thing. No matter how many numbers you look at in the world of fielding statistics, you'll never be able to eliminate the importance of subjective impressions based on watching players. The wizardry of Ozzie Smith, the cannon-arm of Shawon Dunston, the grace of Ryne Sandberg will never be fully appreciated by the numbers. In our opinion, visual observation should still count for at least 50 percent in determining a player's overall defensive abilities.

Without further ado, here are the numbers. We'll give you both range factors and zone ratings for the top five at each position (minimum 1,000 defensive innings in 1989). We also include the player with the *worst* numbers:

Second Base

	Range Factors				Zone Ratings		
Player, Team	P+A	E	TC/9 inn.	Player, Team	Balls in Zone	Outs	Outs per Ball in Zone
Top Five – Range				**Top Five – Zone**			
Reynolds, Sea	817	17	5.78	Thompson, SF	643	637	.991
Oquendo, StL	846	5	5.63	Oquendo, StL	680	657	.966
Whitaker, Det	720	11	5.58	Sax, Yanks	691	667	.965
White, KC	645	10	5.56	Liriano, Tor	544	518	.952
Alomar, SD	813	28	5.41	Whitaker, Det	620	585	.944
Worst				**Worst**			
Jefferies, Mets	477	12	4.37	Doran, Hou	620	554	.894

You can see why it's called a *range* factor, and not one for sure-handedness. Both Reynolds and Alomar roam far and wide, but commit errors more than they should. Gold Glove voters thought highly enough of Reynolds to reward him for each of the last two years; we agree that they knew what they were talking about. But Robbie Thompson doesn't get the recognition he deserves. And where was the other Gold Glove winner, Ryne Sandberg? Farther down the list, at 5.15 range factor and .925 zone rating. We won't criticize Ryno, an outstanding player . . .

but National League Gold Glove winner of the future may well be the 26-year-old Jose Oquendo, who has demonstrated both sure-handedness and outstanding range since being given a regular job at second.

By the way, you may have noticed that the zone ratings appear to look a little like fielding averages. That makes sense and makes the zone ratings a nice complement to traditional fielding averages.

Here are the leaders at third base:

Third Base

Range Factors				Zone Ratings			
Player, Team	P+A	E	TC/9 inn.	Player, Team	Balls in Zone	Outs	Outs per Ball in Zone
Top Five – Range				**Top Five – Zone**			
Gruber, Tor	377	22	3.44	Gaetti, Min	364	330	.907
Pendleton, StL	505	15	3.37	Caminiti, Hou	458	414	.904
Bonilla, Pit	455	35	3.19	Buechele, Tex	358	321	.897
J. Howell, Cal	417	11	3.18	Boggs, Bos	362	322	.890
Gaetti, Min	355	10	3.11	Wallach, Mon	405	356	.879
Worst				**Worst**			
H. Johnson, Mets	243	24	2.11	H. Johnson, Mets	289	229	.792

Probably the biggest shocker on the range factor list is the presence of Bobby Bonilla. We don't argue that Bonilla is a great fielder; we do feel he has good range. Clearly he's not a solid third baseman, but he does have some defensive attributes at this position. Bonilla turned 31 double plays last year, tops in the major leagues. The always improving play of Wade Boggs also begins to show itself on the zone rating list.

The trailer at this position for both ratings, Howard Johnson, was probably hurt a bit by a hard-throwing pitching staffs which was tough to pull. But Johnson's fielding average was .910, while Bonilla's was .929; Johnson participated in 0.12 double plays per nine innings, Bonilla in 0.20. Which one of these was the "horrible" fielder?

Here are the range leaders ar shortstop:

Shortstop

Range Factors				Zone Ratings		
Player, Team	P+A	E	TC/9 inn.	Player, Team	Balls in Zone	Outs	Outs per Ball in Zone

Player, Team	P+A	E	TC/9 inn.	Player, Team	Balls in Zone	Outs	Outs per Ball in Zone
Top Five – Range				**Top Five – Zone**			
Guillen, WSox	784	22	5.41	C. Ripken, Bal	827	793	.959
Fermin, Cle	759	26	5.39	Templeton, SD	628	597	.951
Fernandez, Tor	735	6	5.37	Trammell, Det	608	576	.947
Espinoza, NYY	708	22	5.36	Fernandez, Tor	739	697	.943
Trammell, Det	584	9	5.28	Guillen, WSox	821	772	.940
Worst				**Worst**			
Ramirez, Hou	515	30	3.99	Ramirez, Hou	636	546	.858

Ozzie Guillen's splendid play has been obscured by playing for the lowly White Sox, a team a lot of Chicagoans haven't even heard of. The heady play of Cal Ripken comes to the fore in the zone ratings. The surprise here is that most of both sets of leaders play on American League teams.

Rafael Ramirez has no range, commits a million errors, and can't hit, either. He must have a lot of "intangibles," because everything he touches (or doesn't touch) is hurting his team. Howard Johnson played 179.1 innings at short, and had the lowest range factor of anyone who appeared in more than fifteen games. However, if there's anyone whose statistics are biased by groundball/flyball pitchers, it's Howard Johnson. *By design,* the other Johnson on the Mets, Dave, would only play HoJo at short when his flyball pitchers were pitching. Sid Fernandez actually went a full nine inning game last year without an assist being credited — only the second time that's *ever* been done. That's why HoJo's range factor is so low. As if out to prove Dave Johnson wrong about playing him only sparingly at short, HoJo fielded 1.000 and had a slightly above average zone rating of .930!

Now we present first basemen. Range factors don't really make sense for first basemen because of all their putouts, but zone ratings work quite well. They only count balls actually hit towards them, not those hit to other infielders.

First Base Zone Ratings

Player, Team	Balls in Zone	Outs	Outs per Ball in Zone
Top Five			
W. Clark, SF	350	320	.914
Joyner, Cal	292	265	.908
Mattingly, Yanks	306	274	.895
McGwire, Oak	280	250	.893
McGriff, Tor	287	256	.892
Worst			
Guerrero, LA	326	243	.745

Two things stand out from this chart. The guys with the excellent defensive reputations are at the top: Will Clark, Wally Joyner and Don Mattingly. This is as it should be. The surprise is not that Pedro Guerrero is at the bottom, but that his zone rating is so low. The top first basemen are turning outs at a 90 percent clip, while Guerrero gets 15 less outs per 100 balls hit in his direction.

Finally the STATS Gold Gloves for infielders:

- **First Base** — AL, Don Mattingly (3rd in zone rating). NL, Will Clark (1st in zone).

- **Second Base** — AL, Harold Reynolds (1st in range factor). Ryne Sandberg (remember what we said about observation!)

- **Third Base** — AL, Gary Gaetti (1st in zone; 5th in range). NL, Tim Wallach (5th in zone)

- **Shortstop** — AL, Ozzie Guillen (1st in range; 5th in zone). NL, Ozzie Smith (2nd in NL zone rating).

A complete listing for this category can be found on pages 319-320.

WHICH OUTFIELDERS ARE THE TOUGHEST TO RUN ON?

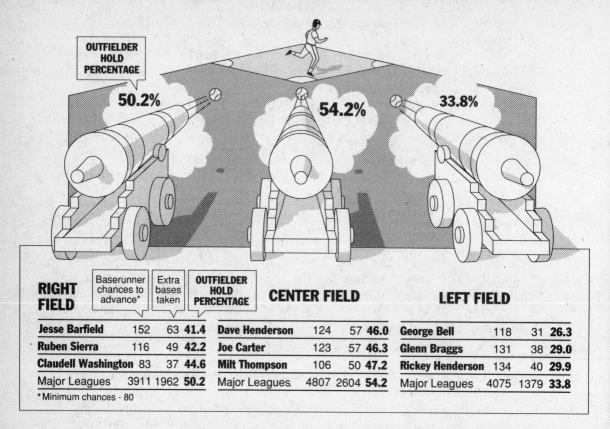

RIGHT FIELD	Baserunner chances to advance*	Extra bases taken	OUTFIELDER HOLD PERCENTAGE	CENTER FIELD				LEFT FIELD			
Jesse Barfield	152	63	**41.4**	Dave Henderson	124	57	**46.0**	George Bell	118	31	**26.3**
Ruben Sierra	116	49	**42.2**	Joe Carter	123	57	**46.3**	Glenn Braggs	131	38	**29.0**
Claudell Washington	83	37	**44.6**	Milt Thompson	106	50	**47.2**	Rickey Henderson	134	40	**29.9**
Major Leagues	3911	1962	**50.2**	Major Leagues	4807	2604	**54.2**	Major Leagues	4075	1379	**33.8**

*Minimum chances - 80

We often hear that Jesse Barfield has a cannon in right field. People say that runners won't take chances on Barfield or other strong-armed outfielders like Ruben Sierra. Impressive words, but up to now, we've never had any real data to measure whether the statements are true or not.

Enter STATS. With our advanced database, we're able to track where every ball is hit during the major league season. When there are one or more runners on base and a hit lands in an outfielder's area, we charge the fielder with a "baserunner chance to advance." The fielder's task is to limit the advancement, so we charge the outfielder with an "extra base taken" each time a runner makes a two base advance on a single, or scores all the way from first on a double. We divide the extra bases taken by the number of chances, and come up with an "outfielder hold percentage" for each player. The lower the percentage, the more effective the outfielder. The major league leaders by position are shown in the chart at the top of the page.

It is indeed true that runners are less likely to take an extra base against the likes of Barfield or Sierra. But they're also likely to hold up against George Bell and Rickey Henderson, which might be a bit of a surprise. One thing the data points out is that it isn't only the strength of the outfielder's arm which stops runners from advancing. Runners will also hold up against a fielder who can get to the ball quickly and unload it in a flash, as Rickey does. The other side of the coin is represented by Hubie Brooks, the worst regular outfielder in the majors last year at preventing runners from advancing. Brooks has a strong arm, but that doesn't help him because he lacks the quick reactions and instincts of a good outfielder.

A good arm is important in limiting advancement, however. It's particularly important in right field, where the throw is longest. For the most part, the right fielders who are considered to have the best throwing arms — Barfield, Sierra, Cory Snyder, Tom Brunansky, Andre Dawson, Glenn Wilson — rate at the top of this category. The cannon-arm types are a little less likely to dominate in center and left fields, where the throws are shorter and the ability to get rid of the ball quickly becomes more important. Since left fielders have much shorter throws to make, they are far more successful in stopping runners from advancing than fielders at the other two positions.

You'll note from the chart that eight of the nine leaders come from American League teams. This probably isn't because American League outfielders are superior. More likely, it's because AL parks tend to be smaller that their National League counterparts. American League parks are also primarily grass fields, and on grass an outfielder can charge the ball much more easily. (Seven of the nine leaders played their home games on grass.) NL outfielders, playing on bigger fields that usually have an artificial surface, are forced to play deeper. That gives runners a better opportunity to advance.

For the record, here are the National League leaders at each position:

Left field—Billy Hatcher 30.4%, Chris James 30.5, Barry Bonds 31.3.
Center field—Thompson, Brett Butler 48.3%, John Shelby 48.4.
Right field—Tom Brunansky 45.5%, Andre Dawson 46.8, Paul O'Neill 47.1.

A complete listing for this category can be found on page 321.

WHO ARE THE PRIME PIVOT MEN?

Of all a second baseman's skills, the ability to turn a double play has always been surprisingly overlooked. Frank White of the Royals, to use a good example, has won eight Gold Gloves in tribute to his grace and exceptional range. And yet White has never led the American League in double plays. Ryne Sandberg of the Cubs has won seven consecutive Gold Gloves and is generally considered to be one of the best defensive second sackers of all time. And yet Sandberg, too, has never led the National League in DPs.

None of this is meant to criticize White or Sandberg or to say their reputations are undeserved. Leading a league in DPs can sometimes be a function of playing behind a groundball pitching staff or on a team that simply allows a lot of runners on base. But we feel the good double play pivot men should be recognized, and we've developed a simple method for rating their abilities. We count all double play opportunities — none or one out, with the second sacker having already recorded one out on a toss from another fielder. Then we measure how many times he turned the play into a DP. We don't consider 4-6-3 DPs, or 4-3 DPs, or double plays on liners; we're only evaluating the pivot here. We also know the system isn't perfect. Many times the ball is hit slowly, and one out is all that's possible. And some second sackers are blessed with a shortstop who can get him the ball quickly, thus increasing his chances of completing the DP. But it's a start. Here are the 1989 leaders in percentage of DPs turned (minimum 20 DPs completed):

Player, Team	DP Opp.	DP	% Turned
Scott Fletcher, Tex-WSox	36	27	75.0
Willie Randolph, LA	59	43	72.9
Jody Reed, Bos	45	31	68.9
Al Newman, Min	35	24	68.6
Jeff Treadway, Atl	72	49	68.1
Johnny Ray, Cal	89	59	66.3
Steve Lyons, WSox	48	31	64.6
Jim Gantner, Mil	79	49	62.0
Billy Ripken, Bal	76	47	61.8
Rene Gonzalez, Bal	37	23	62.1

Scott Fletcher, the leader, may be a surprise to some. He was only shifted to second after his trade to the White Sox, so not many people saw him in action. We in Chicago did, and we can tell you he was outstanding at the pivot; he's also blessed by working with Ozzie Guillen, who has an extremely quick release after he fields a ball. Willie Randolph, the number two man, has always been known for his excellent work on the DP; it's probably Randolph's greatest skill. Among the others, Treadway, Gantner and Ripken all have reputations as fine pivot men. Johnny Ray is considered a poor fielder, but mostly because of his lack of range; his ability on the DP has been one of his strengths. Reed, Newman and Gonzalez are former shortstops, and ex-shortstops often turn into fine pivot men. Steve Lyons, a newcomer at the position in '89, did a surprisingly fine job. Like Fletcher, he was certainly helped by working with Ozzie Guillen.

After looking at this list, you may still be skeptical that we're really measuring a pivot man's strength. But when you look at our list of the worst performers at this exercise, you may be a little more reassured:

Player, Team	DP Opp.	DP	% Turned
Julio Franco, Tex	70	33	47.1
Gregg Jefferies, Mets	41	20	48.8
Tony Phillips, Oak	41	20	48.8
Jerry Browne, Cle	81	40	49.4
Tom Foley, Mon	46	23	50.0

You could say one thing about the two trailers in turning the DP: they're not playing the position because of their gloves. Franco, a converted shortstop, was in his first year at the position, and he wasn't helped by the fact that he had to work with a variety of shortstops. He may get better, but word is that he's already being considered for another position change, this time to first base. Gregg Jefferies was also new to the position, and while he was game enough, no one who watched him work would say he wasn't struggling on the pivot. The other three are also known much more for their bats than their gloves.

In case you're wondering, second sackers like Sandberg, White, Harold Reynolds and Jose Lind all ranked in the 55 to 60 percent range — good, but not quite at the top in this category. Jose Oquendo, at 61.3 percent, just missed the leaders. Ron Oester, generally considered one of the better pivot men, was in the 55 percent range. Oester, like Franco, wasn't helped by having to work with several different shortstops.

A complete listing for this category can be found on page 322.

WHICH CATCHERS ARE BEST AT BLOCKING PITCHES?

A catcher's duties include everything from coddling pitchers to blocking off the plate when Bo Jackson is barrelling home from third. It's a dirty job, and not one for the faint of heart. Some can handle the responsibility fearlessly; others get so overwhelmed that they have trouble even throwing the ball back to the pitcher.

One of the catcher's nastiest, but most essential skills, is his ability to keep wayward pitches from rolling to the backstop. Even just knocking down a pitch in the dirt is often enough to keep a runner from advancing. There's an elementary way to measure this skill: count the number passed balls and wild pitches allowed by each receiver, and then rate them by the number of games caught per miscue. Some might think it unfair to blame the catcher for a wild pitch, which is supposed to be the pitcher's "fault." We disagree. Anyone who watches even a handful of games knows that the difference between a wild pitch and a passed ball is often negligible, and left to the arbitrary decision of an official scorer. Anyway, we want to learn which catchers are good at preventing even difficult pitches from getting away. That said, here are the top catchers at blocking pitches in 1989, rated by the number of nine-inning games per miscue (minimum 500 innings caught):

Catcher, Team	Innings Caught	WP	PB	Games per Miscue
Bob Melvin, Bal	633.0	9	1	7.0
Charlie O'Brien, Mil	527.0	8	1	6.5
Brian Harper, Min	756.2	13	5	4.7
Rich Gedman, Bos	661.1	11	6	4.3
Terry Kennedy, SF	870.0	23	2	3.9
Dave Valle, Sea	783.1	17	6	3.8
Nelson Santovenia, Mon	737.2	18	4	3.7
Don Slaught, Yanks	827.0	21	4	3.7
Mike Heath, Det	937.1	27	2	3.6
Tony Pena, StL	1086.1	31	5	3.4

One noticeable thing is that there are many more wild pitches than passed balls — about four times as many in 1989. These receivers are good at avoiding both, particularly Melvin and O'Brien. Dave Valle and Brian Harper were charged with a decent number of passed balls, but both made up for that by their excellence in preventing wild pitches.

The following catchers were the *worst* in this category during 1989:

Catcher, Team	Innings Caught	WP	PB	Games per Miscue
Chad Kreuter, Tex	528.0	27	21	1.2
Darren Daulton, Phi	965.1	60	5	1.7
Terry Steinbach, Oak	823.0	48	9	1.6
Tim Laudner, Min	500.1	27	2	1.9
Junior Ortiz, Pit	594.1	22	9	2.1

One criticism of this stat is that some catchers are forced to deal with very difficult pitching staffs — knuckleballers, forkballers, fastballers whose velocity is better than their aim. Catching Charlie Hough, Bobby Witt and Nolan Ryan didn't help Chad Kreuter; ditto for Ken Howell's effect on Darren Daulton, or the Oakland forkballers on Terry Steinbach. But if you think this stat has no validity, look at a comparison of receivers on the same teams, and notice the differences:

Catcher, Team	Innings Caught	WP	PB	Games per Miscue
Bob Melvin, Bal	633.0	9	1	7.0
Mickey Tettleton, Bal	646.2	23	3	2.8
Charlie O'Brien, Mil	527.0	8	1	6.5
B.J. Surhoff, Mil	899.1	27	10	2.7
Brian Harper, Min	500.2	13	5	4.7
Tim Laudner, Min	756.2	27	2	1.9
Joe Oliver, Cin	347.0	3	1	9.6
Bo Diaz, Cin	318.0	5	2	5.1
Jeff Reed, Cin	770.1	30	5	2.5

All of these receivers caught at least 300 innings, enough to give us a fair sample. None, as far a we know, were burdened by having to work with an especially tricky pitcher while the other catcher or catchers got a break. But in about the same number of innings, Tettleton's pitchers were charged with two and half times the number of wild pitches as Melvin's were. Jeff Reed's pitchers threw a wild pitch every 26 innings; but when teammates Bo Diaz and Joe Oliver were working, they threw only one every 83. We hardly think those are just coincidences.

A complete listing for this category can be found on page 323.

WHICH PARKS PRODUCE THE MOST ERRORS?

One of the biggest changes in modern baseball has been the influx of artificial turf. Though plastic grass has been accused of evils ranging from increasing injuries to artificially inflating batting averages, one thing is certain: it reduces errors. We rated the ballparks for errors in the same way we rated them for foulouts. We compared the total number of errors committed in each team's home games (by both the home club and the visitors) with the number committed in the team's road games (again by both clubs). We then divide the home total by the road and round off that figure to the nearest one percent. A park factor of 100 would denote a neutral park. A factor above 100 denotes that the park increases errors; under 100 parks decrease them. We took two readings: one for total errors, and one for groundball errors only. The second is obviously more park dependent, since a fielder can throw a ball away anywhere. Anyway, here are the two charts of park factors, based on data from 1987-'89:

Home and Road Errors — 1987 to 1989

Team	All Errors			Team	Ground Ball Errors		
	Home Games	Road Games	Park Factor		Home Games	Road Games	Park Factor
Cubs	447	337	133	Cubs	238	154	155
Brewers	401	347	116	Brewers	186	153	122
Braves	415	371	112	Pirates	220	182	121
Indians	376	340	111	Yankees	186	161	116
Pirates	401	367	109	Red Sox	165	144	115
Yankees	352	332	106	Mets	189	166	114
Orioles	330	319	103	Braves	204	179	114
Red Sox	346	337	103	Giants	190	175	109
White Sox	389	378	103	Orioles	153	143	107
Giants	388	379	102	Indians	158	147	107
Tigers	370	366	101	Rangers	183	172	106
Expos	384	379	101	White Sox	195	189	103
Rangers	372	373	100	Royals	159	159	100
Dodgers	397	401	99	Dodgers	187	188	99
Mariners	354	362	98	Astros	182	188	97
Royals	326	335	97	Twins	159	166	96
Mets	376	390	96	Tigers	159	170	94
Cardinals	352	376	94	Angels	141	154	92
A's	353	375	94	Blue Jays	149	162	92
Padres	385	414	93	Expos	171	186	92
Twins	319	349	91	Cardinals	153	181	85

Home and Road Errors — 1987 to 1989

	All Errors				Ground Ball Errors		
Team	Home Games	Road Games	Park Factor	Team	Home Games	Road Games	Park Factor
Angels	336	368	91	Mariners	148	180	82
Reds	337	378	89	Reds	138	175	79
Astros	350	393	89	Phillies	141	181	78
Blue Jays	336	380	88	A's	138	179	77
Phillies	327	373	88	Padres	139	197	71

The most obvious thing about the charts is the grass/turf difference. Eleven of the top twelve parks in the groundball chart are grass fields. The sixteen grass fields have a park factor of 106 in the second chart; the ten turf fields have a factor of 96. This is true despite the fact that the worn carpet in Pittsburgh has a factor of 121 (the only turf field over 100), while the two least error-prone fields, Oakland and San Diego, are grass fields.

The big surprise in the charts is the high rating of Chicago's Wrigley Field. Some parks' high ratings may be due a little to strict official scoring, but that's not true of Wrigley. Most of the same official scorers who record Cub games also do White Sox games, and the Comiskey rating is only a little above average. The high Wrigley rating underscores the brilliance of Ryne Sandberg, who sets records for fewest errors while playing on the most difficult infield in the majors.

Among the grass field teams, the groundskeeper and the texture of the infield seem to play a crucial role. The Dodger Stadium infield, once renowned as a rockpile, has been redone in recent years and has now become a neutral field as far as errors are concerned. Wrigley and Milwaukee's County Stadium seem to be headed in the other direction. Last year the Cubs and their opponents committed 75 groundball errors at Wrigley, only 48 in Cub road games. The Brewers and their opponents made 84 groundball errors in Milwaukee, only 55 on the road. Let's get out those rakes and hoses, fellows!

WHICH FIRST BASEMEN RECORD THE MOST 3-6-3 DOUBLE PLAYS?

In evaluating first basemen, one of the first things brought up is the ability to turn the 3-6-3 double play. It's one of the most difficult — and rarest — plays in baseball. Indeed, only 270 hard-way DPs have been turned over the last three years, about one for every 40 games.

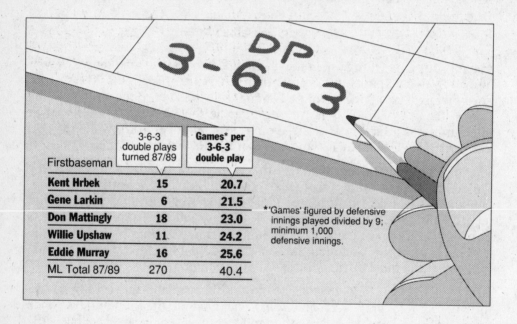

Firstbaseman	3-6-3 double plays turned 87/89	Games* per 3-6-3 double play
Kent Hrbek	15	20.7
Gene Larkin	6	21.5
Don Mattingly	18	23.0
Willie Upshaw	11	24.2
Eddie Murray	16	25.6
ML Total 87/89	270	40.4

*'Games' figured by defensive innings played divided by 9; minimum 1,000 defensive innings.

It's ironic that, for a play deemed easier for lefthanded throwers, the two most proficient first baseman at the 3-6-3 are righthanded throwers — Kent Hrbek and Gene Larkin of the Twins. Indeed, four of the top six are righties. The chart above shows the 3-6-3 leaders for the period 1987-89.

Hrbek and Larkin might have been surprises, but not Don Mattingly and Eddie Murray, the leaders in total 3-6-3 DPs with 18 and 16. Each knows how to set up quickly, fire the ball to second while avoiding the runner who's headed there from first, and then get back to first for the return throw. It's a complicated maneuver, and one that's not easy to master. Some first sackers, even some good ones, never quite become adept at it.

One requisite for turning 3-6-3 DPs seems to be a good throwing arm. Mattingly started his career as an outfielder, as did Willie Upshaw, and Larkin frequently plays right field for the Twins. The number six man on the leaders list is the Mets' Dave Magadan, who's used to making the long throw from third base. Magadan ranks ahead of even his slick-fielding former teammate, Keith Hernandez, in terms of games per 3-6-3 DP. While no one would claim that Magadan is a better defensive first baseman than Hernandez, Dave appears to have the skills that turning the hard-way DP requires. (Hernandez is no slouch at it, either.) On the other hand, someone like Steve Garvey, who was moved to first because of his wild throwing, never could master the 3-6-3.

One thing these statistics should do is enhance the defensive reputation of Kent Hrbek. People in Minnesota have been arguing for years that Hrbek — who appears at first glance to be just a big, lumbering hulk — is in fact quite a good glove man. The study supports that position, though one should point out that the 3-6-3 DP is such a rare play that the ability to turn it should not be a large factor in evaluating first sackers. Garvey could justifiably be considered an excellent first baseman, despite an inability to turn this play. Even with that caveat, the stats certainly increase the defensive reputation of Hrbek, and give more credence to the supporters of Mattingly. But what can you say about Gerald Perry, who managed only one 3-6-3 double play in three years and nearly 3,000 innings of action?

A complete listing for this category can be found on page 324.

WHICH OUTFIELDERS HAVE THE BEST RANGE?

We've studied infielders' range, using range factors and zone ratings as our tools. Now let's do the same for outfielders. One error we can correct, at long last, is to stop lumping the stats for left, center and right fielders in one pile. That way we can rate the players against the competition at their individual positions. We'd like to say that makes us revolutionary. But the truth is that, for a few years around 1910, the official league averages did the very same thing. Then that logical distinction mysteriously disappeared, never to return on an official basis. Even the modern-day Gold Glove award goes to three "outfielders," regardless of whether they play left, center or right. Last year five of the six Gold Gloves went to center fielders. That makes about as much sense as awarding the four infield Gold Gloves to Ozzie Smith, Tony Fernandez, Ryne Sandberg and Ozzie Guillen.

So we'll begin by studying each outfield position separately and hope that credit goes to some deserving, but overlooked, players. Here are the range leaders for left field, based on total chances per nine innings (minimum 1,000 innings); we add the worst qualifier at the position:

Left Field

Range Factors				Zone Ratings		
Player, Team	P+A	E	TC/9 inn.	Player, Team	Balls in Zone	Outs	Outs per Ball in Zone

Player, Team	P+A	E	TC/9 inn.	Player, Team	Balls in Zone	Outs	Outs per Ball in Zone
Top Five – Range				**Top Five – Zone**			
Bonds, Pit	377	6	2.58	R. Henderson, Yanks-Oak	385	325	.844
R. Henderson, Yanks-Oak	343	4	2.46	Coleman, StL	271	228	.841
McReynolds, Mets	317	10	2.35	L. Smith, Atl	344	285	.828
L. Smith, Atl	293	2	2.32	Braggs, Mil	303	249	.822
Braggs, Mil	259	7	2.27	Bell, Tor	313	257	.821
Worst				**Worst**			
Greenwell, Bos	231	8	1.75	Mitchell, SF	389	289	.743

The key to good outfield range is speed. All the left field leaders except George Bell stole at least 15 bases, and the worst SB success rate among them (aside from Bell again) was 68 percent. They have weaknesses, to be sure; Henderson is known for his weak throwing arm, and Smith didn't get his nickname, "Skates," because he was a graceful flychaser. But they can go get 'em. Bonds's 364 putouts were more than a lot of center fielders record.

The trailer at range factor, Mike Greenwell, is hurt by the left field wall at Fenway. A lot of balls that would be outs elsewhere turn into Green Monster hits. His zone rating gets hurt by the wall also, but he slips ahead of Kevin Mitchell.

The leaders in center field were:

Center Field

Range Factors				Zone Ratings			
Player, Team	P+A	E	TC/9 inn.	Player, Team	Balls in Zone	Outs	Outs per Ball in Zone
Top Five – Range				**Top Five – Zone**			
Puckett, Min	452	4	3.09	D.White, Cal	498	447	.898
Young, Hou	426	1	3.07	D.Henderson, Oak	482	417	.865
Butler, SF	419	6	2.96	Gallagher, WSox	431	371	.861
Van Slyke, Pit	346	4	2.96	Dykstra, Mets-Phi	391	336	.859
D.White, Cal	436	5	2.91	E.Davis, Cin	372	313	.841
Worst				**Worst**			
Shelby, LA	227	2	2.49	Van Slyke, Pit	468	363	.776

Devon White won his second straight Gold Glove in '89 and his zone rating backs up the voters. His range factor was also solid. The surprise on this list is Andy Van Slyke. He shows up fourth in range factor and also won a second straight Gold Glove. But his zone rating was the worst among center fielders with 1,000 innings. How does that happen? The answer is that Pirate pitchers allowed the most flyballs in the National League last year. Van Slyke's range factor is good because there were a lot of balls heading into the Pittsburgh outfield in '89. You can see that in Barry Bonds' range figure also. But when it comes down to looking only at the balls hit into Van Slyke's area (plus any that he tracked down outside his zone), Andy simply didn't reach as many as other center fielders. It's probably that Andy's nagging knee injury cut down a bit on his range. But it's also probable that Andy is still an excellent outfielder, and that there were more balls hit on the fringes of his zone than for other outfielders.

Here are the leaders in right field:

Right Field

	Range Factors				Zone Ratings		
Player, Team	P+A	E	TC/9 inn.	Player, Team	Balls in Zone	Outs	Outs per Ball in Zone
Top Five – Range				**Top Five – Zone**			
Snyder, Cle	312	1	2.62	Sierra, Tex	362	309	.854
Barfield, Tor-Yanks	318	7	2.47	Barfield, Tor-Yanks	362	299	.826
Deer, Mil	276	8	2.41	Brunansky, StL	316	260	.823
Strawberry, Mets	276	8	2.33	Snyder, Cle	344	283	.823
Dawson, Cubs	231	3	2.25	Deer, Mil	328	264	.805
Worst				**Worst**			
Brooks, Mon	241	9	1.93	Brooks, Mon	296	231	.780

Jesse Barfield and Cory Snyder are known for their great throwing arms; they also possess great range. Barfield has won two Gold Gloves, but Snyder is one player who clearly suffers from the fact that voters simply choose three "outfielders." White, Puckett and Pettis, the American League winners, were all worthy, but it's unfair to neglect a worthy candidate like Cory, who's never going to make 400 putouts playing right field. Ruben Sierra is the guy to watch for in this group. He has Gold Glove written in his future.

The STATS Gold Gloves for the outfield — which of course would be made from solid gold — would have gone to (the envelope, please):

National League — Barry Bonds LF, Eric Davis CF, Andre Dawson RF.

American League — Rickey Henderson LF, Devon White CF, Jesse Barfield RF.

But nobody asked us.

A complete listing for this category can be found on pages 325-326.

About STATS Inc.

It all starts with the system. The STATS scoring method, which includes pitch-by-pitch and the direction, distance, and velocity of each ball hit into play, yields an immense amount of information. Sure, we have all the statistics you're used to seeing, but where other statistics sources quit, STATS is just getting started.

Then, there is the network. We get our game reports via computer so that they are timely. Statistics are checked, rechecked, and are updated and available daily.

Analysis comes next. STATS constantly searches for new ways to use this wealth of information to open windows into the workings of Baseball. Accurate numbers, intelligent computer programming, and a large dose of imagination all help coax the most valuable information from its elusive cover.

Finally, distribution!

STATS has served Major League teams for 10 years now including the World Champion Oakland A's, the New York Yankees and the Chicago White Sox. *Sports Illustrated* and *The Sporting News* regularly feature STATS, Inc., as do *The New York Post, The St. Petersburg Times,* and many other national and regional publications. We provide statistics for *Earl Weaver Baseball, Rotisserie Baseball, The Los Angeles Times'* Dugout Derby, and other baseball games and fantasy leagues all over the country.

For the baseball fan, STATS publishes monthly and year-end reports on each Major League team. We offer a host of year-end statistical breakdowns on paper or disk that cover hitting, pitching, catching, baserunning, throwing, and more. STATS also produces custom reports on request.

Computer users with modems can access the STATS computer for information with *STATS Online*. If you own a computer with a modem, there is no other source with the scope of baseball information that STATS can offer.

STATS and Bill James enjoy an on-going affiliation that has produced several baseball products including *STATS 1990 Major League Handbook* and *Bill James Fantasy Baseball*, a game designed by Bill which allows you to own and manage your own team and compete with other team owners around the country.

Keep an eye out for other exciting future projects.

It is STATS, Inc.'s purpose to make the best possible Baseball information available to all Baseball interests: fans, players, teams, or media. Write to:

STATS, Inc.
7250 North Cicero
Lincolnwood, IL 60646

... or call us at 1-708-676-3322. We can send you a STATS brochure, a free *Bill James Fantasy Baseball* information kit, and/or information on *STATS Online*.

To maintain its information, STATS hires scorers around the country to cover games. If you are interested in applying for a scorer's position, please write or call STATS.

Finally, look for *The Scouting Report: 1990* in your bookstores this year! It features scouting reports on over 700 players for the 1990 season.

APPENDIX

Welcome to the Appendix!

Or, rather, welcome to the appendices! There are 88 of them in the following section, each corresponding to an essay in the main portion of this book. For essays where the complete data was presented, no appendix is provided.

Each appendix is keyed twice. The "Title" key serves as a reminder as to what data you're looking at (with 101 different topics, it should help). The "Page" key refers you to the page where you'll find the appropriate essay.

We've made every effort to present the data logically. For some items, that means presenting the whole ball game (sorry); for others it means presenting the data on a "Per Game," "Per At Bat," or percentage basis. In general, we've attempted to give you all the data which we used for the essay — and then some.

Each appendix is accompanied by a descriptive label, telling you how the data has been organized, and, if it is a listing of players, which players have been included in the list. Most of the lists with players have been listed alphabetically, to help you find your favorite players (one of the fun parts of a book like this).

When this book was in its planning stages, some 18 months ago, we had four main goals in mind: 1) interesting questions, 2) a lively, entertaining presentation, 3) illustrative graphics, and 4) a complete appendix for each question. We feel we've accomplished the first three goals 100 percent. Regarding the fourth, you'll notice that there are "qualifications" in many of the appendices. We had to use these qualifications in order to keep the appendix from bursting the seams of this book. We weren't quite at 100 percent in terms of completeness, but in most cases, listing players down to one at bat would be rather meaningless. We're confident in saying that these appendices are the most complete statistical breakdowns of a baseball season ever compiled!

The team abbreviation following a player's name refers to the team with which he finished the season. Here are the abbreviations:

American League Teams		National League Teams	
Bal	Baltimore Orioles	Atl	Atlanta Braves
Bos	Boston Red Sox	ChN	Chicago Cubs
Cal	California Angels	Cin	Cincinnati Reds
ChA	Chicago White Sox	Hou	Houston Astros
Cle	Cleveland Indians	LA	Los Angeles Dodgers
Det	Detroit Tigers	Mon	Montreal Expos
KC	Kansas City Royals	NYN	New York Mets
Mil	Milwaukee Brewers	Phi	Philadelphia Phillies
Min	Minnesota Twins	Pit	Pittsburgh Pirates
NYA	New York Yankees	StL	St. Louis Cardinals
Oak	Oakland Athletics	SD	San Diego Padres
Sea	Seattle Mariners	SF	San Francisco Giants
Tex	Texas Rangers		
Tor	Toronto Blue Jays		

Enjoy the season. See you in the bleachers!

DO BASE STEALERS HAVE AN ADVANTAGE ON ARTIFICIAL TURF? (p. 4)

Both Leagues — Listed Alphbetically
(players with 25 or more stolen base attempts)

Player, Team	Grass			Turf		
	SB	CS	SB%	SB	CS	SB%
Alomar R, SD	21	13	61.8	21	4	84.0
Bonds, Pit	5	6	45.5	27	4	87.1
Bradley P, Bal	19	5	79.2	1	1	50.0
Burks, Bos	17	4	81.0	4	1	80.0
Butler, SF	24	11	68.6	7	5	58.3
Coleman, StL	14	1	93.3	51	9	85.0
Davis E, Cin	2	3	40.0	19	4	82.6
Devereaux, Bal	19	10	65.5	3	1	75.0
Doran, Hou	6	0	100.0	16	3	84.2
Dunston, ChN	12	10	54.5	7	1	87.5
Dykstra, Phi	13	3	81.3	17	9	65.4
Eisenreich, KC	14	2	87.5	13	6	68.4
Espy, Tex	40	19	67.8	5	1	83.3
Felder, Mil	19	4	82.6	7	1	87.5
Felix, Tor	8	6	57.1	10	6	62.5
Fernandez T, Tor	8	2	80.0	14	4	77.8
Gantner, Mil	18	5	78.3	2	1	66.7
Gladden, Min	12	2	85.7	11	5	68.8
Guillen, ChA	32	14	69.6	4	3	57.1
Gwynn T, SD	25	11	69.4	15	5	75.0
Hatcher B, Pit	4	1	80.0	20	6	76.9
Hayes V, Phi	6	5	54.5	22	2	91.7
Henderson R, Oak	63	10	86.3	14	4	77.8
Jackson B, KC	13	5	72.2	13	4	76.5
Jefferies, NYN	11	6	64.7	10	0	100.0
Johnson H, NYN	25	5	83.3	16	3	84.2
Kelly, NYA	28	7	80.0	7	5	58.3
Lansford, Oak	29	11	72.5	8	4	66.7
Martinez Da, Mon	9	3	75.0	14	1	93.3
McDowell O, Atl	21	12	63.6	6	3	66.7
Molitor, Mil	23	9	71.9	4	2	66.7
Moseby, Tor	9	5	64.3	15	2	88.2
Newman A, Min	11	3	78.6	14	9	60.9
Nixon O, Mon	11	3	78.6	26	9	74.3
O'Neill, Cin	3	2	60.0	17	3	85.0
Pettis, Det	39	12	76.5	4	3	57.1
Polonia, NYA	22	7	75.9	0	1	0.0
Raines, Mon	9	3	75.0	32	6	84.2
Redus, Pit	6	1	85.7	19	5	79.2
Reynolds H, Sea	9	8	52.9	16	10	61.5
Reynolds RJ, Pit	2	1	66.7	20	4	83.3
Roberts Bip, SD	13	9	59.1	8	2	80.0
Samuel, NYN	23	9	71.9	19	3	86.4
Sax S, NYA	37	15	71.2	6	2	75.0
Seitzer, KC	3	2	60.0	14	6	70.0
Smith Lo, Atl	19	9	67.9	6	3	66.7
Smith O, StL	3	2	60.0	26	5	83.9
Surhoff BJ, Mil	13	10	56.5	1	2	33.3
Thompson M, StL	6	5	54.5	21	3	87.5
Walton, ChN	15	4	78.9	9	3	75.0
White D, Cal	38	13	74.5	6	3	66.7
Wilson W, KC	9	4	69.2	15	2	88.2
Young G, Hou	10	8	55.6	24	17	58.5

HOW DO RUNS SCORE? (p. 6)

Team by Team Totals — 1989

American League

Team	Single	Double	Triple	Homerun	Sac Fly	Error	Misc	Total
Baltimore	230	90	20	209	47	73	39	708
Pct	32	13	3	30	7	10	6	100
Boston	264	131	23	183	58	73	42	774
Pct	34	17	3	24	8	9	5	100
California	225	86	22	211	46	55	24	669
Pct	34	13	3	32	7	8	4	100
Chicago	262	112	27	157	51	60	24	693
Pct	38	16	4	23	7	9	4	100
Cleveland	186	80	15	196	41	51	35	604
Pct	31	13	2	32	7	8	6	100
Detroit	205	80	12	176	44	66	34	617
Pct	33	13	2	29	7	11	6	100
Kansas City	264	96	22	158	51	60	39	690
Pct	38	14	3	23	7	9	6	100
Milwaukee	243	97	19	192	54	67	35	707
Pct	34	14	3	27	7	10	5	100
Minnesota	250	100	24	198	58	75	35	740
Pct	34	14	3	27	8	10	5	100
New York	262	89	11	201	49	59	27	698
Pct	38	13	2	29	7	9	4	100
Oakland	239	91	18	202	62	68	32	712
Pct	34	13	3	28	9	10	5	100
Seattle	210	113	15	210	52	68	26	694
Pct	30	16	2	30	8	10	4	100
Texas	242	114	25	185	40	58	31	695
Pct	35	16	4	27	6	8	5	100
Toronto	223	101	19	237	53	67	31	731
Pct	31	14	3	32	7	9	4	100
Totals	3305	1380	272	2715	706	900	454	9732
Pct	34	14	3	28	7	9	5	100

National League

Team	Single	Double	Triple	Homerun	Sac Fly	Error	Misc	Total
Atlanta	195	84	18	185	42	32	28	584
Pct	33	14	3	32	7	6	5	100
Chicago	240	102	32	182	50	61	35	702
Pct	34	15	5	26	7	9	5	100
Cincinnati	164	103	25	211	49	52	28	632
Pct	26	16	4	33	8	8	4	100
Houston	228	103	22	155	44	66	29	647
Pct	35	16	3	24	7	10	5	100
Los Angeles	170	101	7	153	41	46	36	554
Pct	31	18	1	28	7	8	7	100
Montreal	201	109	19	165	46	62	30	632
Pct	32	17	3	26	7	10	5	100
New York	212	110	11	215	48	62	25	683
Pct	31	16	2	31	7	9	4	100
Philadelphia	208	70	25	203	42	50	31	629
Pct	33	11	4	32	7	8	5	100
Pittsburgh	214	108	36	137	51	66	25	637
Pct	34	17	6	22	8	10	4	100
St. Louis	240	119	28	116	43	54	32	632
Pct	38	19	4	18	7	9	5	100
San Diego	186	82	23	213	41	70	27	642
Pct	29	13	4	33	6	11	4	100
San Francisco	186	117	30	233	39	58	36	699
Pct	27	17	4	33	6	8	5	100
Total	2444	1208	276	2168	536	679	362	7673
Pct	32	16	4	28	7	9	5	100

Percentages may not total to 100 due to rounding.

WHICH UMPIRES ARE OFFENSIVE? (p. 10)

Home Plate Umpires — Listed Alphabetically

American League Umpires: 1989

Umpire	Yr	G	Avg	Slg	R per 9	K per 9	BB* per 9
Barnett, Larry	21	35	.258	.395	8.3	11.3	6.5
Brinkman, Joe	17	38	.264	.401	9.1	11.6	6.4
Cedarstrom,	1	1	.186	.339	3.2	14.8	6.4
Clark, Al	14	36	.255	.367	7.8	10.5	6.3
Coble, Drew	8	39	.258	.372	8.6	11.3	5.9
Cooney, Terry	15	35	.251	.367	8.5	10.5	5.2
Cousins, Derryl	11	39	.258	.382	8.8	11.4	7.5
Craft, Terry	1	6	.269	.377	8.8	8.8	6.8
Denkinger, Don	21	32	.247	.375	7.9	11.1	6.8
Evans, Jim	18	40	.269	.385	8.8	11.0	5.6
Ford, Dale	14	38	.276	.405	9.7	10.7	5.3
Garcia, Rich	15	39	.272	.403	9.0	10.6	5.9
Hendry, Ted	12	35	.249	.359	9.2	11.5	6.5
Hirschbeck, John	7	38	.245	.367	8.0	11.7	5.2
Johnson, Mark	7	36	.248	.374	7.6	10.6	5.0
Joyce, Jim	1	27	.269	.406	9.7	10.6	7.0
Kaiser, Ken	13	31	.279	.401	8.9	11.5	5.7
Kosc, Greg	14	34	.248	.355	8.3	11.2	5.5
McClelland, Tim	8	37	.258	.388	8.1	11.0	5.4
McCoy, Larry	19	35	.254	.371	8.4	12.1	4.8
McKean, Jim	16	38	.280	.399	9.2	10.6	5.6
Merrill, Derwood	13	37	.254	.368	8.3	10.4	5.5
Meriwether, Chuck	1	8	.256	.371	7.6	8.4	7.2
Morrison, Dan	8	35	.273	.417	10.6	10.7	7.3
Palermo, Steve	13	38	.248	.368	7.9	11.8	5.5
Phillips, Dave	19	34	.269	.390	8.6	10.1	5.9
Reed, Rick	8	36	.272	.392	9.9	10.0	6.2
Reilly, Mike	13	34	.253	.367	7.7	10.6	5.7
Roe, Rocky	10	37	.262	.401	9.4	10.8	6.9
Scott, Dale	4	24	.256	.375	8.1	11.8	5.9
Shulock, John	11	37	.257	.374	8.5	10.7	6.7
Tschida, Tim	4	25	.281	.412	9.7	11.3	5.7
Voltaggio, Vic	13	36	.262	.391	8.3	11.0	5.8
Welke, Tim	6	35	.258	.381	9.2	11.2	5.8
Young, Larry	5	28	.265	.382	8.4	10.9	5.6

National League Umpires: 1989

Umpire	Yr	G	Avg	Slg	R per 9	K per 9	BB* per 9
Bonin, Greg	4	37	.234	.350	6.5	11.8	4.3
Brocklander, Fred	11	36	.253	.361	7.3	11.4	4.8
Crawford, Jerry	13	37	.234	.357	7.7	12.5	5.8
Darling, Gary	2	36	.251	.381	8.6	12.3	6.5
Davidson, Bob	8	39	.237	.353	7.2	12.8	4.6
Davis, Gerry	6	34	.253	.358	8.0	10.8	5.7
DeMuth, Dana	6	37	.283	.417	10.6	11.8	6.5
Engel, Bob	24	37	.239	.385	8.1	11.6	5.5
Froemming, Bruce	19	38	.242	.362	7.5	10.5	7.1
Gregg, Eric	13	37	.259	.390	9.4	11.8	5.9
Hallion, Tom	4	27	.252	.381	8.4	12.1	6.4
Harvey, Doug	28	37	.245	.361	7.6	11.6	5.3
Hirschbeck, Mark	2	25	.237	.350	7.1	11.5	4.8
Hohn, Bill	1	24	.247	.378	8.1	11.4	5.8
Kibler, John	25	35	.245	.340	7.2	11.0	5.6
Layne, Jerry	1	21	.222	.317	6.5	11.1	5.4
Marsh, Randy	8	37	.240	.355	8.2	11.8	6.0
McSherry, John	19	40	.245	.364	7.0	10.3	6.0
Montague, Ed	14	35	.243	.354	7.8	12.5	5.5
Pulli, Frank	18	36	.252	.369	8.4	11.2	5.8
Quick, Jim	14	35	.236	.352	7.4	12.0	5.4
Rehliford, Cahrlie	1	5	.277	.440	8.8	11.3	6.6
Rennert, Dutch	16	36	.256	.386	8.3	11.6	5.4
Rippley, Steve	7	35	.254	.376	9.0	12.2	5.9
Runge, Paul	16	34	.258	.388	8.1	10.8	5.1
Tata, Terry	17	39	.254	.384	9.1	12.9	5.1
Wendelstedt, Harry	24	32	.252	.356	7.5	12.1	5.0
West, Joe	12	37	.226	.336	6.9	12.3	5.0
Williams, Charlie	9	31	.230	.329	6.5	10.3	4.6
Winter, Mike	4	4	.213	.310	7.2	10.8	5.9

*Unintentional Walks

HOW DO TEAMS PERFORM IN THE LATE INNINGS OF CLOSE GAMES? (p. 12)

Team Batting and Pitching — Late and Close Situations, 1989

American League Batting

Team	Avg	OBP	Slg	AB	H	2B	3B	HR	RBI	BB	K
Baltimore	.243	.333	.358	754	183	35	2	16	97	103	150
Boston	.269	.350	.387	895	241	46	4	17	111	110	145
California	.222	.291	.308	878	195	24	3	15	76	85	197
Chicago	.265	.327	.358	933	247	54	3	9	103	87	178
Cleveland	.216	.302	.312	927	200	31	2	18	89	108	204
Detroit	.215	.303	.307	944	203	26	5	17	96	114	202
Kansas City	.280	.360	.390	836	234	37	2	17	111	104	151
Milwaukee	.255	.321	.355	754	192	34	3	12	84	73	137
Minnesota	.287	.340	.431	828	238	35	6	24	118	64	125
New York	.271	.341	.392	827	224	32	4	20	114	88	160
Oakland	.237	.313	.351	792	188	26	5	18	94	87	145
Seattle	.236	.296	.351	883	208	26	2	24	93	71	195
Texas	.257	.322	.371	778	200	35	3	16	94	77	154
Toronto	.255	.333	.368	938	239	37	6	19	118	109	178

National League Batting

Team	Avg	OBP	Slg	AB	H	2B	3B	HR	RBI	BB	K
Atlanta	.217	.275	.312	1002	217	29	5	19	96	78	224
Chicago	.239	.299	.334	842	201	30	4	14	79	75	159
Cincinnati	.242	.323	.359	891	216	42	4	18	110	107	159
Houston	.233	.304	.345	1012	236	38	3	23	115	103	181
Los Angeles	.222	.294	.295	1064	236	32	5	12	76	108	201
Montreal	.250	.325	.363	1043	261	45	5	21	122	115	196
New York	.230	.304	.372	873	201	41	1	27	88	90	147
Philadelphia	.240	.319	.344	905	217	31	6	17	102	105	162
Pittsburgh	.230	.314	.334	1041	239	42	11	15	96	127	203
St. Louis	.257	.331	.344	871	224	36	8	8	96	98	141
San Diego	.259	.331	.353	853	221	24	4	16	106	94	162
San Francisco	.254	.331	.381	834	212	35	7	19	99	95	189

American League Pitching

Team	Avg	OBP	Slg	AB	H	2B	3B	HR	RBI	BB	K
Baltimore	.234	.323	.339	821	192	34	5	14	84	106	122
Boston	.248	.321	.353	870	216	29	1	20	105	91	204
California	.233	.318	.332	929	216	32	3	18	102	115	177
Chicago	.253	.329	.390	825	209	27	7	24	100	88	118
Cleveland	.250	.298	.369	979	245	41	6	21	109	69	183
Detroit	.272	.364	.397	769	209	34	4	18	99	108	134
Kansas City	.225	.298	.311	951	214	36	5	12	90	95	218
Milwaukee	.275	.329	.389	732	201	24	3	18	90	63	109
Minnesota	.260	.318	.367	747	194	30	1	16	108	63	125
New York	.296	.362	.431	780	231	41	2	20	108	80	128
Oakland	.219	.285	.311	884	194	29	2	16	90	84	180
Seattle	.273	.356	.370	874	239	41	2	13	102	111	179
Texas	.238	.327	.356	794	189	39	2	17	97	99	191
Toronto	.240	.313	.339	1012	243	41	7	15	114	108	253

National League Pitching

Team	Avg	OBP	Slg	AB	H	2B	3B	HR	RBI	BB	K
Atlanta	.261	.326	.373	962	251	39	6	19	124	94	195
Chicago	.237	.321	.345	985	233	32	6	21	106	123	193
Cincinnati	.232	.313	.327	914	212	39	3	14	100	106	236
Houston	.214	.280	.291	982	210	20	7	14	83	91	192
Los Angeles	.238	.310	.332	1067	254	47	7	13	93	112	209
Montreal	.262	.325	.376	997	261	37	7	21	110	94	176
New York	.234	.304	.334	941	220	32	4	18	93	94	214
Philadelphia	.228	.319	.327	734	167	23	4	14	79	96	132
Pittsburgh	.239	.312	.361	1092	261	52	6	23	123	116	167
St. Louis	.233	.309	.339	908	212	43	7	13	100	97	150
San Diego	.225	.290	.329	978	220	29	2	23	92	85	191
San Francisco	.233	.302	.335	920	214	38	4	16	90	94	147

DO HITTERS SPEND MOST OF THEIR TIME JUST STANDING AROUND? (p. 16)

The tables below shows how hitters react to pitches thrown based on the count.

Listed by League — all teams

American League

Count	Total	Ball	Taken Strike	Swing-ing Strike	Foul	In Play
0-0	86647	37480	22023	5033	9813	12298
Percent	100	43	25	6	11	14
0-1	36557	16192	3929	3416	5781	7239
Percent	100	44	11	9	16	20
0-2	15678	7873	668	1644	2550	2943
Percent	100	50	4	11	16	19
1-0	37111	13052	7954	2780	5735	7590
Percent	100	35	21	8	16	20
1-1	32482	11995	3564	3285	6050	7588
Percent	100	37	11	10	19	23
1-2	26145	9626	1142	3264	5521	6592
Percent	100	37	4	13	21	25
2-0	12994	4271	3199	799	1971	2754
Percent	100	33	25	6	15	21
2-1	17868	5205	1887	1653	3885	5238
Percent	100	29	11	9	22	29
2-2	22413	6519	931	2768	5497	6698
Percent	100	29	4	12	25	30
3-0	4235	1625	2271	46	110	183
Percent	100	38	54	1	3	4
3-1	7597	2213	1135	520	1540	2189
Percent	100	29	15	7	20	29
3-2	13351	3013	549	1388	3625	4776
Percent	100	23	4	10	27	36

Note: Percentages may not add to 100 due to rounding

National League

Count	Total	Ball	Taken Strike	Swing-ing Strike	Foul	In Play
0-0	74249	31367	18088	4933	8748	11113
Percent	100	42	24	7	12	15
0-1	31359	13152	3237	3284	5303	6383
Percent	100	42	10	11	17	20
0-2	14255	6593	740	1709	2479	2734
Percent	100	46	5	12	17	19
1-0	31005	10854	6179	2477	4983	6512
Percent	100	35	20	8	16	21
1-1	26626	9231	2915	2867	5184	6429
Percent	100	35	11	11	19	24
1-2	22280	7862	1080	2982	4856	5500
Percent	100	35	5	13	22	25
2-0	10746	3552	2768	671	1606	2149
Percent	100	33	26	6	15	20
2-1	14198	4086	1412	1356	3258	4086
Percent	100	29	10	10	23	29
2-2	18383	5147	851	2354	4611	5420
Percent	100	28	5	13	25	29
3-0	3549	1440	1699	71	144	195
Percent	100	41	48	2	4	5
3-1	5968	1752	924	387	1188	1717
Percent	100	29	16	6	20	29
3-2	10654	2369	442	1173	2966	3704
Percent	100	22	4	11	28	35

WHICH TEAMS BUNT MOST IN THE EARLY INNINGS? (p. 18)

1989 Team Bunting by Inning
Sac Hits with #9 hitter/ Sac Hits without #9 hitter

American League

Team	1	2	3	4	5	6	7	8	9	10+
Baltimore	3/3	6/3	10/6	8/5	10/6	9/4	8/5	4/2	5/3	0/0
Boston	5/5	2/2	4/3	4/3	7/4	6/6	6/4	6/5	5/3	7/4
California	7/7	0/0	8/5	3/2	6/5	4/4	8/7	4/2	8/6	6/6
Chicago	11/11	3/2	6/4	9/8	12/7	7/5	13/10	12/11	12/10	0/0
Cleveland	11/11	3/2	8/5	1/0	12/11	6/6	8/5	10/8	10/6	3/3
Detroit	2/2	0/0	3/3	2/1	2/1	3/3	9/8	4/4	7/6	3/1
Kansas City	0/0	6/5	3/2	2/1	0/0	3/3	10/8	8/3	3/3	7/7
Milwaukee	4/4	3/3	8/7	2/1	10/7	5/4	8/7	7/7	2/1	2/2
Minnesota	4/4	2/2	5/4	5/4	6/5	5/2	12/9	10/10	1/1	1/1
New York	4/4	4/4	6/5	9/8	4/4	5/4	13/10	8/7	3/3	2/1
Oakland	3/3	4/3	6/1	0/0	3/1	7/4	6/2	3/3	1/1	3/3
Seattle	0/0	2/2	3/1	3/1	4/2	4/3	4/2	10/6	3/1	2/1
Texas	5/5	3/3	7/5	3/1	10/6	9/9	12/9	8/8	4/2	2/2
Toronto	2/2	2/2	5/3	1/1	6/5	2/1	4/3	2/2	2/2	4/3

National League

Team	1	2	3	4	5	6	7	8	9	10+
Atlanta	3/3	4/1	13/1	8/1	7/0	11/9	7/5	7/5	4/4	1/1
Chicago	3/3	13/2	12/4	4/2	11/4	9/3	11/5	4/3	7/5	6/5
Cincinnati	4/4	7/0	8/1	9/2	7/0	6/3	7/6	5/5	5/4	6/6
Houston	2/2	4/2	11/1	8/2	14/2	8/4	9/5	10/7	9/9	8/7
Los Angeles	2/1	9/0	11/1	5/2	16/4	9/5	10/6	10/8	6/4	5/5
Montreal	3/3	8/2	8/1	8/2	11/0	5/2	6/2	4/3	9/7	9/9
New York	0/0	6/1	10/1	3/0	13/4	4/2	11/3	4/4	2/2	3/2
Philadelphia	2/2	9/1	8/0	5/1	7/0	6/2	9/6	5/4	4/3	2/2
Pittsburgh	6/6	11/4	10/2	5/1	9/5	5/2	10/4	16/9	6/6	5/5
St. Louis	4/4	9/2	17/3	4/1	9/0	6/3	9/4	7/5	8/5	5/4
San Diego	14/14	7/0	11/2	6/3	11/4	5/3	9/6	10/10	16/14	6/6
San Francisco	1/1	9/2	12/7	11/3	11/5	10/7	11/8	11/9	4/4	2/2

What were the fastest games in the majors last year? (p. 23)

Average game time based on starting pitcher is shown below.

Both Leagues — Listed Alphabetically (pitchers with 10 or more starts)

Pitcher, Team	GS	Time	Pitcher, Team	GS	Time	Pitcher, Team	GS	Time
Abbott, Cal	29	2:55	Gordon, KC	16	2:41	Portugal, Hou	15	2:41
Aguilera, Min	11	2:46	Gross K, Mon	31	3:01	Power, StL	15	2:48
Alexander, Det	33	3:00	Gubicza, KC	36	2:52	Rasmussen D, SD	33	2:46
Anderson A, Min	33	2:41	Hanson, Sea	17	2:36	Rawley, Min	25	2:48
Aquino, KC	16	2:39	Harnisch, Bal	17	2:59	Reuschel, SF	32	2:36
August, Mil	25	2:49	Hawkins, NYA	34	2:49	Reuss, Mil	26	2:46
Bailes, Cle	11	2:28	Heaton, Pit	18	2:39	Rhoden, Hou	17	3:06
Ballard, Bal	35	3:08	Hershiser, LA	33	2:50	Rijo, Cin	19	2:54
Bankhead,, Sea	33	2:54	Hetzel, Bos	11	2:58	Ritz, Det	12	2:52
Bannister F, KC	14	2:49	Hibbard, ChA	23	2:58	Robinson D, SF	33	2:47
Bautista, Bal	10	2:52	Higuera, Mil	22	2:42	Robinson JD, Pit	19	2:58
Belcher, LA	30	2:49	Hill K, StL	33	2:51	Robinson JM, Det	16	3:01
Benes, SD	10	2:45	Hillegas, ChA	13	2:58	Robinson R, Cin	15	2:57
Bielecki, ChN	33	2:49	Holman B, Sea	25	2:42	Rosenberg, ChA	21	2:54
Black, Cle	32	2:45	Holton, Bal	12	3:05	Ruffin, Phi	23	2:45
Blyleven, Cal	33	2:45	Hough, Tex	30	2:57	Ryan, Tex	32	3:01
Boddicker, Bos	34	2:54	Howell K, Phi	32	2:45	Saberhagen, KC	35	2:43
Bosio, Mil	33	2:50	Hurst, SD	33	2:46	Sanderson, ChN	23	2:51
Boyd, Bos	10	2:59	Jackson Dan, Cin	20	2:39	Schmidt D, Bal	26	2:52
Brown Kev, Tex	28	2:58	Jeffcoat, Tex	22	2:51	Scott M, Hou	32	2:41
Browning, Cin	37	2:25	John, NYA	10	2:51	Scudder, Cin	17	2:44
Cadaret, NYA	13	2:47	Johnson D, Bal	14	2:53	Show, SD	16	2:43
Candiotti, Cle	31	2:37	Johnson R, Sea	28	2:54	Smiley, Pit	28	2:43
Carman, Phi	20	2:50	Key, Tor	33	2:49	Smith B, Mon	32	2:49
Cary, NYA	11	2:53	Kilgus, ChN	23	2:40	Smith P, Atl	27	2:47
Cerutti, Tor	31	2:53	King E, ChA	25	3:10	Smith Roy, Min	26	2:46
Clancy, Hou	26	2:48	Knepper, SF	26	3:08	Smith Z, Mon	17	2:36
Clary, Atl	17	2:43	Kramer, Pit	15	2:43	Smithson, Bos	19	2:53
Clemens, Bos	35	2:58	LaCoss, SF	18	2:55	Smoltz, Atl	29	2:40
Clutterbuck, Mil	11	2:50	Langston, Mon	34	2:46	Stewart D, Oak	36	2:44
Cone, NYN	33	2:53	LaPoint, NYA	20	2:54	Stieb, Tor	33	2:56
Cook D, Phi	18	2:50	Leary, Cin	31	2:53	Stottlemyre, Tor	18	2:51
Darling, NYN	33	2:46	Leibrandt, KC	27	2:51	Sutcliffe, ChN	34	2:56
Davis Storm, Oak	31	2:46	Lilliquist, Atl	30	2:43	Swift, Sea	16	2:52
DeLeon J, StL	36	2:41	Maddux G, ChN	35	2:43	Swindell, Cle	28	2:46
Deshaies, Hou	34	2:47	Magrane, StL	33	2:41	Tanana, Det	33	2:50
Dopson, Bos	28	2:59	Mahler R, Cin	31	2:35	Terrell, NYA	32	2:40
Dotson, ChA	26	2:59	Martinez De, Mon	33	3:00	Terry, StL	24	2:52
Downs, SF	15	2:41	Martinez R, LA	15	2:51	Valenzuela, LA	31	2:56
Drabek, Pit	34	2:46	McCaskill, Cal	32	2:53	Viola, NYN	36	2:44
Dunne, Sea	18	2:52	McWilliams, KC	21	2:39	Walk, Pit	31	2:55
Dyer, Min	12	2:40	Milacki, Bal	36	3:05	Welch, Oak	33	2:52
Farrell, Cle	31	2:52	Moore M, Oak	35	2:54	Wetteland, LA	12	2:44
Fernandez S, NYN	32	3:00	Morgan M, LA	19	2:34	Whitson, SD	33	2:34
Filer, Mil	13	2:37	Morris Jk, Det	24	2:50	Witt B, Tex	31	3:05
Finley C, Cal	29	2:46	Moyer, Tex	15	2:55	Witt M, Cal	33	2:52
Flanagan, Tor	30	2:54	Mulholland, Phi	18	2:47	Yett, Cle	12	2:49
Forsch B, Hou	15	3:08	Navarro, Mil	17	2:47	Youmans, Phi	10	2:52
Gardner W, Bos	16	3:00	Nichols Rod, Cle	11	2:39	Young C, Oak	20	2:47
Garrelts, SF	29	2:47	Ojeda, NYN	31	2:44	Zavaras, Sea	10	2:45
Gibson P, Det	13	3:03	Parker C, NYA	17	2:56			
Glavine, Atl	29	2:43	Perez M, ChA	31	2:49			
Gooden, NYN	17	2:57	Perez P, Mon	28	2:54			

WHAT ARE BASEBALL'S MOST AND LEAST COMMON PLAYS? (p. 32)

Number of Plays by League — Listed by Frequency of Plays

American League		National League	
Event	Number	Event	Number
Ground Out	17,264	Ground Out	15,164
Single	14,497	Single	11,530
Strikeout	12,256	Strikeout	11,308
Fly Out	12,132	Fly Out	10,088
Walk	6,684	Walk	5,398
Pop Out	3,733	Pop Out	3,491
Line Out	3,609	Line Out	2,963
Double	3,404	Double	2,903
Force Out	2,303	Force Out	1,883
Ground DP	1,835	Foul Pop Out	1,599
Foul Pop Out	1,745	Stolen Base	1,372
Home Run	1,718	Home Run	1,365
Stolen Base	1,393	Ground DP	1,209
One Base Error	854	Intentl BB	853
Caught Stealing	718	Sacrifice Hit	843
Sacrifice Fly	696	One Base Error	770
Sacrific Hit	679	Caught Stealing	697
Wild Pitch	667	Wild Pitch	553
Intentl Walk	593	Sacrifice Fly	530
Advance on Error	563	Advance on Error	513
Hit by Pitch	483	Triple	411
Triple	457	Out Advancing	324
Out Advancing	418	Hit by Pitch	318
Bunt Out	275	Bunt Out	240
Foul Fly Out	250	Balk	239
Advance on Throw	242	Foul Fly Out	230
Passed Ball	184	Advance on Throw	218
Line Drive DP	183	Line Drive DP	179
Balk	168	Passed Ball	134
Double Steal	150	Two Base Error	118
Two Base Error	131	Double Steal	116
Bunt Fly Out	98	Pickoff	104
Pickoff	90	Bunt Fly Out	95
Bunt Force Out	69	Bunt Force Out	77
Fly DP	66	Error on Pickoff	65
Reached on Failed FC	51	Fly DP	46
Error on Pickoff	49	SB + Error	41
SB + Error	44	Reached on Failed FC	39
Error on Foul Fly	37	Reached on K+Wild Pitch	36
1B/SacBunt+Err	29	1B/SacBunt+Err	34
Advance-No Play	28	Error on Foul Fly	27
Reached on K+Wild Pitch	28	Advance-No Play	24
Reached SacBunt+FC	9	Reached SacBunt+FC	22
Three Base Error	13	GDP on Bunt	19
Batter Out on Obstruction	12	Batter Out on Obstruction	18
Reached on K+Passed Ball	11	CS + Error	18
Catcher's Interference	9	Runner Out on Obstruction	11
GDP on Bunt	9	Three Base Error	11
CS + Error	8	Reached on K+Passed Bal	8
SF+Error	8	Catcher's Interference	8
Runner Out on Obstruction	3	SF+Error	6
Bunt Fly DP	3	Single - Ball Hits Runner	6
Single - Ball Hits Runner	2	Bunt Fly DP	6
Line Triple Play	1	Line Triple Play	3
Reached First on K+Error	1	Reached First on K+Error	2

How Rare is a Two Strike Homer? (p. 35)

Batters and Pitchers — Listed Separately
(16 or more total home runs hit or given up)

Batters

Player, Team	2-s HR	Tot HR	%
Baines, Tex	5	16	31.3
Balboni, NYA	7	17	41.2
Barfield Je, NYA	8	23	34.8
Bell Geo, Tor	3	18	16.7
Benzinger, Cin	6	17	35.3
Bonds, Pit	1	19	5.3
Bonilla B, Pit	10	24	41.7
Brunansky, StL	10	20	50.0
Buechele, Tex	2	16	12.5
Canseco, Oak	7	17	41.2
Carter J, Cle	13	35	37.1
Clark Jk, SD	8	26	30.8
Clark W, SF	9	23	39.1
Davis A, Sea	6	21	28.6
Davis C, Cal	5	22	22.7
Davis E, Cin	11	34	32.4
Davis G, Hou	6	34	17.6
Dawson, ChN	4	21	19.0
Deer, Mil	8	26	30.8
Esasky, Bos	6	30	20.0
Evans Dw, Bos	3	20	15.0
Gaetti, Min	7	19	36.8
Galarraga, Mon	5	23	21.7
Griffey Jr, Sea	4	16	25.0
Gruber, Tor	5	18	27.8
Guerrero, StL	4	17	23.5
Hall M, NYA	3	17	17.6
Hayes V, Phi	4	26	15.4
Howell Jk, Cal	3	20	15.0
Hrbek, Min	5	25	20.0
Incaviglia, Tex	5	21	23.8
Jackson B, KC	12	32	37.5
Johnson H, NYN	15	36	41.7
Joyner, Cal	4	16	25.0
Leonard J, Sea	2	24	8.3
Mattingly, NYA	6	23	26.1
McGriff F, Tor	9	36	25.0
McGwire, Oak	6	33	18.2
McReynolds, NYN	4	22	18.2
Mitchell K, SF	7	47	14.9
Murphy Dl, Atl	5	20	25.0
Murray E, LA	6	20	30.0
Parker D, Oak	4	22	18.2
Parrish Ln, Cal	6	17	35.3
Ripken C, Bal	5	21	23.8
Sandberg, ChN	8	30	26.7
Santiago, SD	5	16	31.3
Sierra, Tex	4	29	13.8
Smith Lo, Atl	2	21	9.5
Snyder C, Cle	4	18	22.2
Strawberry, NYN	10	29	34.5
Tartabull, KC	9	18	50.0
Tettleton, Bal	8	26	30.8
Whitaker, Det	7	28	25.0
Williams MD, SF	3	18	16.7
Yount, Mil	7	21	33.3

Pitchers

Pitcher, Team	2-s HR	Tot HR	%
Alexander, Det	7	28	25.0
August, Mil	3	17	17.6
Ballard, Bal	4	16	25.0
Bankhead, Sea	2	19	10.5
Bautista, Bal	5	17	29.4
Belcher, LA	8	20	40.0
Bielecki, ChN	7	16	43.8
Boddicker, Bos	3	19	15.8
Bosio, Mil	2	16	12.5
Browning, Cin	10	31	32.3
Carman, Phi	8	21	38.1
Cerutti, Tor	2	19	10.5
Clemens, Bos	8	20	40.0
Cone, NYN	4	20	20.0
Cook D, Phi	7	18	38.9
Darling, NYN	3	19	15.8
Davis Storm, Oak	4	19	21.1
DeLeon J, StL	4	16	25.0
Dotson, ChA	2	16	12.5
Drabek, Pit	10	21	47.6
Fernandez S, NYN	4	21	19.0
Glavine, Atl	7	20	35.0
Gross K, Mon	4	20	20.0
Hawkins, NYA	5	23	21.7
Hough, Tex	10	28	35.7
Hurst, SD	5	16	31.3
Key, Tor	5	18	27.8
Knepper, SF	7	16	43.8
Langston, Mon	3	16	18.8
Leary, Cin	5	17	29.4
Lilliquist, Atl	6	16	37.5
Martinez De, Mon	6	21	28.6
McCaskill, Cal	4	16	25.0
Milacki, Bal	5	21	23.8
Morris Jk, Det	5	23	21.7
Ojeda, NYN	7	16	43.8
Perez M, ChA	6	23	26.1
Rasmussen D, SD	1	18	5.6
Rawley, Min	2	19	10.5
Reuschel, SF	3	18	16.7
Reuss, Mil	8	19	42.1
Robinson D, SF	6	22	27.3
Ryan, Tex	7	17	41.2
Sanderson, ChN	3	16	18.8
Schmidt D, Bal	6	24	25.0
Scott M, Hou	6	23	26.1
Smiley, Pit	3	22	13.6
Smith B, Mon	3	16	18.8
Smith Roy, Min	7	22	31.8
Smithson, Bos	5	21	23.8
Stewart D, Oak	7	23	30.4
Sutcliffe, ChN	5	18	27.8
Swindell, Cle	4	16	25.0
Tanana, Det	4	21	19.0
Terrell, NYA	5	23	21.7
Viola, NYN	3	22	13.6
Whitson, SD	4	22	18.2
Witt M, Cal	9	26	34.6

WHICH TEAMS HAVE THE BEST BENCH PLAYERS? (p. 38)

Starters and Bench Players by Team, 1989

American League

Team Group	Avg	OBP	Slg	AB	R	H	HR	RBI
Baltimore Starters	.257	.341	.402	3742	515	960	105	458
Baltimore Bench	.241	.292	.326	1698	193	409	24	201
Boston Starters	.288	.368	.432	3637	528	1049	89	522
Boston Bench	.257	.321	.349	2029	246	522	19	194
California Starters	.262	.320	.397	4490	555	1176	123	516
California Bench	.233	.269	.338	1055	114	246	22	108
Chicago Starters	.273	.327	.387	3800	468	1038	65	466
Chicago Bench	.267	.331	.374	1704	225	455	29	195
Cleveland Starters	.251	.318	.370	4110	474	1030	97	417
Cleveland Bench	.229	.288	.349	1353	130	310	30	150
Detroit Starters	.253	.335	.369	3534	432	893	81	375
Detroit Bench	.222	.283	.319	1898	185	422	35	189
Kansas City Starters	.267	.342	.388	3679	462	983	79	471
Kansas City Bench	.248	.302	.341	1796	227	445	22	182
Milwaukee Starters	.271	.333	.403	3772	511	1021	94	464
Milwaukee Bench	.232	.284	.335	1701	195	394	32	196
Minnesota Starters	.287	.338	.427	3729	505	1071	96	498
Minnesota Bench	.254	.328	.350	1851	235	471	21	193
New York Starters	.275	.340	.398	3775	481	1038	84	456
New York Bench	.257	.310	.377	1683	217	432	46	201
Oakland Starters	.270	.344	.404	3968	530	1072	112	535
Oakland Bench	.236	.294	.320	1448	181	342	15	124
Seattle Starters	.263	.327	.393	4154	526	1092	104	498
Seattle Bench	.239	.297	.356	1358	168	325	30	155
Texas Starters	.266	.331	.410	3799	511	1012	98	493
Texas Bench	.254	.316	.359	1659	184	421	24	161
Toronto Starters	.264	.331	.417	4275	585	1129	122	557
Toronto Bench	.245	.296	.335	1306	146	320	20	128

National League (excluding pitchers)

Team Group	Avg	OBP	Slg	AB	R	H	HR	RBI
Atlanta Starters	.251	.314	.379	3036	347	761	82	346
Atlanta Bench	.226	.291	.335	2096	211	474	45	180
Chicago Starters	.282	.340	.430	3563	483	1004	99	473
Chicago Bench	.248	.308	.350	1582	202	393	24	160
Cincinnati Starters	.267	.332	.411	2975	354	793	88	383
Cincinnati Bench	.232	.293	.342	2221	260	516	39	189
Houston Starters	.247	.319	.359	3935	494	972	74	442
Houston Bench	.236	.301	.339	1231	138	291	20	135
Los Angeles Starters	.245	.314	.350	3580	366	878	65	335
Los Angeles Bench	.252	.317	.353	1537	171	387	24	157
Montreal Starters	.261	.337	.392	3681	441	962	80	430
Montreal Bench	.235	.303	.329	1451	169	341	20	138
New York Starters	.256	.323	.422	3500	470	897	119	470
New York Bench	.244	.311	.347	1604	186	391	25	144
Philadelphia Starters	.265	.332	.398	3359	406	890	80	394
Philadelphia Bench	.228	.308	.340	1770	209	403	43	191
Pittsburgh Starters	.255	.327	.394	3360	441	856	72	376
Pittsburgh Bench	.233	.305	.326	1808	185	421	22	181
St. Louis Starters	.273	.339	.386	4420	541	1207	63	507
St. Louis Bench	.231	.288	.320	707	73	163	7	64
San Diego Starters	.272	.340	.396	3163	383	860	73	375
San Diego Bench	.241	.311	.364	1882	233	453	45	209
San Francisco Starters	.268	.342	.425	3727	530	998	109	467
San Francisco Bench	.228	.275	.345	1371	145	312	29	162

ARE PITCHERS' THROWS TO FIRST A WASTE OF TIME?
(p. 40)

Both Leagues—Listed Alphabetically
(25 or more stolen base attempts)

Runner, Team	No Throws Made			Throws Made		
	SB	CS	%	SB	CS	%
Alomar R, SD	16	4	80	19	11	63
Bonds, Pit	10	3	77	15	6	71
Bradley P, Bal	5	2	71	7	3	70
Burks, Bos	8	0	100	12	4	75
Butler, SF	11	0	100	18	15	55
Coleman, StL	25	3	89	23	5	82
Davis E, Cin	10	2	83	6	5	55
Devereaux, Bal	11	2	85	6	6	50
Doran, Hou	5	1	83	16	2	89
Dunston, ChN	10	2	83	4	5	44
Dykstra, Phi	13	6	68	12	6	67
Eisenreich, KC	10	3	77	10	4	71
Espy, Tex	12	2	86	26	15	63
Felder, Mil	7	0	100	13	4	76
Felix, Tor	9	5	64	8	6	57
Fernandez T, Tor	9	2	82	10	2	83
Gantner, Mil	14	3	82	2	2	50
Gladden, Min	9	2	82	10	3	77
Guillen, ChA	18	8	69	16	7	70
Gwynn T, SD	22	5	81	10	11	48
Hatcher B, Pit	6	1	86	13	4	76
Hayes V, Phi	16	4	80	9	2	82
Henderson R, Oak	33	2	94	19	6	76
Jackson B, KC	3	2	60	19	5	79
Jefferies, NYN	11	2	85	8	4	67
Johnson H, NYN	24	3	89	14	3	82
Kelly, NYA	10	3	77	23	8	74
Lansford, Oak	14	6	70	10	8	56
Martinez Da, Mon	10	2	83	6	1	86
McDowell O, Atl	7	3	70	19	11	63
Molitor, Mil	13	2	87	8	5	62
Moseby, Tor	11	2	85	12	5	71
Newman A, Min	11	1	92	10	10	50
Nixon O, Mon	10	2	83	18	6	75
O'Neill, Cin	13	3	81	5	0	100
Pettis, Det	17	0	100	19	15	56
Polonia, NYA	5	4	56	14	3	82
Raines, Mon	18	0	100	11	7	61
Redus, Pit	12	4	75	7	1	88
Reynolds H, Sea	14	3	82	7	13	35
Reynolds RJ, Pit	9	1	90	8	3	73
Roberts Bip, SD	8	4	67	12	6	67
Samuel, NYN	23	4	85	18	8	69
Sax S, NYA	20	2	91	12	8	60
Seitzer, KC	11	2	85	3	6	33
Smith Lo, Atl	15	2	88	10	10	50
Smith O, StL	15	0	100	11	5	69
Surhoff BJ, Mil	9	5	64	1	5	17
Thompson M, StL	13	2	87	12	6	67
Walton, ChN	9	3	75	9	2	82
White D, Cal	13	3	81	18	13	58
Wilson W, KC	10	2	83	11	4	73
Young G, Hou	11	10	52	15	14	52

Note: Steals of third or home and back ends of double steals not included.

DO GROUNDBALL HITTERS DO BETTER AGAINST FLYBALL PITCHERS? (p. 42)

Batter Type vs. Pitcher Type — 1987 to 1989

1989

Batter—Pitcher	AB	H	2b	3b	HR	RBI	W+HBP	SO	SF	Ave	OBA	Slg
GbB vs. GbP	14028	3705	557	86	127	1352	979	1881	88	.264	.310	.343
AvB vs. GbP	22378	5936	997	144	443	2743	1757	3198	216	.265	.316	.382
FbB vs. GbP	8101	2147	383	44	254	1146	680	1458	87	.265	.319	.417
GbB vs. AvP	18847	5033	788	137	191	1723	1417	2632	135	.267	.316	.354
AvB vs. AvP	32291	8221	1467	185	752	3701	2210	5296	293	.255	.300	.381
FbB vs. AvP	11506	2824	547	67	420	1611	913	2262	132	.245	.298	.414
GbB vs. FbP	9471	2449	415	70	128	918	711	1464	68	.259	.308	.358
AvB vs. FbP	15919	4005	786	98	494	1960	1385	2739	144	.252	.309	.406
FbB vs. FbP	6044	1382	280	26	256	858	566	1251	69	.229	.292	.411

1988

Batter—Pitcher	AB	H	2b	3b	HR	RBI	W+HBP	SO	SF	Ave	OBA	Slg
GbB vs. GbP	10437	2697	430	59	91	994	970	1485	62	.258	.320	.337
AvB vs. GbP	17801	4702	802	120	309	2059	1598	2387	142	.264	.322	.375
FbB vs. GbP	10494	2787	510	46	270	1365	994	1587	101	.266	.326	.400
GbB vs. AvP	15762	4164	655	102	203	1539	1309	2283	122	.264	.318	.357
AvB vs. AvP	30537	7869	1393	187	689	3451	2496	4746	284	.258	.311	.383
FbB vs. AvP	17955	4661	833	106	640	2399	1876	3078	194	.260	.326	.425
GbB vs. FbP	8351	2193	387	53	127	842	780	1328	57	.263	.324	.367
AvB vs. FbP	16716	4140	807	110	443	1983	1413	2966	168	.248	.303	.389
FbB vs. FbP	10187	2449	471	48	394	1360	1037	1985	118	.240	.307	.412

1987

Batter—Pitcher	AB	H	2b	3b	HR	RBI	W+HBP	SO	SF	Ave	OBA	Slg
GbB vs. GbP	9909	2718	419	76	128	1067	1017	1333	60	.274	.340	.371
AvB vs. GbP	19953	5471	921	133	491	2640	2006	2915	113	.274	.339	.408
FbB vs. GbP	9742	2656	497	64	373	1511	1070	1507	98	.273	.342	.452
GbB vs. AvP	14110	3823	632	145	223	1553	1493	2219	98	.271	.339	.384
AvB vs. AvP	30672	8008	1497	159	1021	4074	3395	5425	257	.261	.332	.420
FbB vs. AvP	15950	4081	831	87	702	2289	1841	3029	133	.256	.330	.451
GbB vs. FbP	9029	2446	427	76	198	987	948	1385	57	.271	.338	.401
AvB vs. FbP	19833	5192	965	115	774	2726	2072	3540	184	.262	.329	.439
FbB vs. FbP	10615	2537	516	35	528	1620	1221	2209	98	.239	.315	.443

HOW DOES TEMPERATURE AFFECT OFFENSIVE PRODUCTION? (p. 46)

Both Leagues — 1987 through 1989

Category	Temperature: <60	60-69	70-79	80-89	90+
Games in Sample	548	767	1,383	827	348
Batting Average	.248	.253	.259	.263	.263
On Base Average	.318	.320	.323	.328	.329
Slugging Average	.366	.385	.391	.403	.402
At Bats	36,380	51,721	93,829	56,851	23,640
Runs per Game	8.0	8.5	8.6	9.1	9.1
Hits per Game	16.4	17.1	17.6	18.1	17.9
Homeruns per Game	1.40	1.65	1.69	1.85	1.83
Walks per Game	6.8	6.5	6.3	6.5	6.5
Strikeouts per Game	11.4	11.6	11.3	11.1	11.4
Stolen Bases per Game	1.6	1.5	1.6	1.6	1.7
Errors per Game	1.6	1.6	1.5	1.5	1.6

WHICH TEAMS PERFORM BEST WITH RUNNERS IN SCORING POSITION? (p. 48)

Listed Alphabetically by Team

American League—Batting with Runners in Scoring Position

Team	Avg	OBP	Slg	AB	H	2B	3B	HR	RBI	BB	K
Baltimore	.261	.356	.389	1371	358	52	11	34	519	219	227
Boston	.281	.365	.404	1571	441	87	11	28	591	230	228
California	.261	.328	.376	1286	336	48	9	27	461	143	249
Chicago	.276	.342	.384	1418	391	66	9	23	538	163	249
Cleveland	.228	.321	.330	1305	297	53	6	23	413	189	273
Detroit	.240	.324	.331	1308	314	44	6	21	422	175	232
Kansas City	.267	.352	.378	1412	377	54	11	27	541	203	230
Milwaukee	.283	.351	.407	1320	373	59	9	29	520	155	193
Minnesota	.259	.333	.385	1444	374	68	9	32	564	178	234
New York	.270	.347	.370	1391	375	59	4	24	504	185	215
Oakland	.264	.340	.375	1329	351	50	7	28	504	175	234
Seattle	.257	.328	.375	1301	335	62	8	25	491	150	232
Texas	.266	.337	.387	1344	357	65	10	26	505	153	262
Toronto	.260	.337	.394	1433	373	69	7	36	528	182	266

National League—Batting with Runners in Scoring Position

Team	Avg	OBP	Slg	AB	H	2B	3B	HR	RBI	BB	K
Atlanta	.257	.349	.373	1094	281	48	8	21	375	169	205
Chicago	.277	.359	.385	1269	351	64	13	16	477	183	214
Cincinnati	.253	.355	.411	1184	300	59	10	36	439	206	249
Houston	.257	.349	.368	1287	331	60	11	20	455	199	210
Los Angeles	.231	.331	.350	1145	265	54	5	24	383	187	186
Montreal	.261	.370	.386	1266	331	68	9	24	447	235	225
New York	.251	.342	.383	1275	320	68	5	30	457	192	244
Philadelphia	.250	.338	.374	1261	315	41	14	29	444	182	221
Pittsburgh	.261	.363	.386	1245	325	62	21	17	435	220	211
St. Louis	.273	.355	.396	1339	365	76	16	19	488	187	221
San Diego	.241	.336	.384	1266	305	47	10	38	463	201	242
San Francisco	.257	.358	.418	1226	315	65	9	38	474	200	246

American League—Pitching with Runners in Scoring Position

Team	Avg	OBP	Slg	AB	H	2B	3B	HR	RBI	BB	K
Baltimore	.265	.350	.382	1366	362	55	6	31	494	194	202
Boston	.268	.343	.378	1401	376	55	9	27	529	178	269
California	.232	.309	.316	1239	288	37	3	20	417	155	253
Chicago	.266	.326	.392	1455	387	57	14	33	536	153	220
Cleveland	.254	.321	.363	1340	341	58	11	22	484	149	238
Detroit	.277	.377	.408	1428	395	60	13	34	592	257	242
Kansas City	.254	.325	.359	1372	348	72	8	19	483	159	253
Milwaukee	.254	.325	.380	1348	343	40	9	37	495	159	223
Minnesota	.273	.340	.405	1447	395	87	7	30	538	158	229
New York	.307	.386	.448	1396	429	64	9	38	585	190	199
Oakland	.230	.319	.320	1256	289	52	5	17	410	176	232
Seattle	.264	.351	.384	1441	380	77	8	27	526	204	254
Texas	.260	.353	.356	1399	364	57	4	23	511	217	296
Toronto	.264	.331	.384	1347	355	65	11	25	501	151	214

National League—Pitching with Runners in Scoring Position

Team	Avg	OBP	Slg	AB	H	2B	3B	HR	RBI	BB	K
Atlanta	.252	.332	.367	1331	336	65	9	23	483	176	256
Chicago	.239	.333	.346	1314	314	52	13	21	442	202	254
Cincinnati	.258	.353	.371	1340	346	56	4	29	492	217	280
Houston	.252	.348	.359	1449	365	72	13	19	478	227	277
Los Angeles	.222	.323	.338	1258	279	60	7	24	398	196	286
Montreal	.239	.328	.375	1326	317	56	20	28	454	192	297
New York	.236	.331	.363	1270	300	47	15	28	429	194	299
Philadelphia	.271	.377	.400	1419	385	84	9	27	529	255	252
Pittsburgh	.259	.352	.390	1462	379	63	13	34	510	220	230
St. Louis	.260	.349	.386	1350	351	72	16	22	456	202	216
San Diego	.250	.340	.380	1210	303	54	8	29	424	184	225
San Francisco	.240	.317	.383	1234	296	56	8	35	435	156	201

DOES THE PURPOSE PASS PAY OFF? (p. 51)

The table below shows how each player performed after the batter prior to him was intentionally passed.

Both Leagues — Listed by Most Plate Appearances
(players with 6 or more plate appearances after an intentional walk)

Player, Team	PA	AB	H	HR	RBI	AVG	Player, Team	PA	AB	H	HR	RBI	AVG
Lind, Pit	19	18	4	0	4	.222	Joyner, Cal	7	7	2	0	1	.286
James C, Phi-SD	16	16	4	0	6	.250	Moseby, Tor	7	7	1	0	1	.221
Clark Jk, SD	15	12	5	2	11	.417	Grace, ChN	7	5	1	0	3	.200
McReynolds, NYN	15	12	4	0	8	.333	Fitzgerald Mk, Mon	7	5	1	0	3	.200
Worthington, Bal	13	13	9	0	10	.692	O'Brien, Cle	7	6	1	0	2	.167
Wilson G, Pit-Hou	13	11	2	0	4	.182	McGwire, Oak	7	6	1	0	3	.167
Leonard, Sea	13	12	0	0	1	.000	Barrett M, Bos	7	7	1	0	1	.143
Hamilton, LA	12	11	5	1	11	.455	DeLeon J, StL	7	7	1	0	1	.143
Marshall, LA	12	11	3	0	4	.273	Murphy Da, Atl	7	7	0	0	0	.000
Mitchell K, SF	11	10	3	1	5	.300	Scisocia, LA	6	6	3	1	5	.500
Maldonado, SF	11	10	3	0	3	.300	Braggs, Mil	6	6	3	0	4	.500
Reed, Bos	11	7	2	0	4	.286	Bradley, Bal	6	4	2	0	6	.500
Brunansky, StL	10	9	2	0	2	.222	Belle, Cle	6	5	2	1	8	.400
Jackson B, KC	10	9	1	0	2	.111	Redus, Pit	6	5	2	1	5	.400
Williams MD, SF	10	10	1	0	1	.100	Thomas, Atl	6	6	2	0	2	.333
O'Neill, Cin	9	6	3	0	7	.500	Jordan, Phi	6	6	2	0	2	.333
Ramirez, Hou	9	6	1	0	3	.167	Hernandez K, NYN	6	6	2	0	3	.333
Law V, CHN	9	6	1	0	5	.167	Carter J, Cle	6	5	1	0	1	.243
Brooks, Mon	9	6	1	0	3	.167	Harper, Min	6	5	1	1	4	.200
Gross K, Mon	9	9	1	0	1	.111	Quinones R, Pit	6	5	1	0	3	.200
Phelps, NYA-Oak	8	6	4	0	7	.667	Snyder, Cle	6	6	1	0	2	.167
Henderson D, Oak	8	8	3	0	5	.375	Anderosn K, Cal	6	6	1	0	1	.167
Valle, Sea	8	8	3	0	5	.375	Gallagher, CHA	6	6	1	0	1	.167
Santovenia, Mon	8	7	2	0	4	.286	Wallach, Mon	6	6	1	1	5	.167
Fermin, Cle	8	8	2	0	1	.250	Magrane, StL	6	5	0	0	1	.000
Tartabull, KC	8	5	1	0	4	.200	Jacoby, Cle	6	5	0	0	2	.000
Bonds, Pit	8	5	1	0	3	.200	Balboni, NYA	6	6	0	0	0	.000
Bielecki, ChN	8	7	1	0	1	.143	McClendon, ChN	6	5	0	0	1	.000
Hall, NYA	7	6	3	0	4	.500	Lyons B, NYN	6	5	0	0	1	.000
Eisenereich, KC	7	6	3	0	5	.500	Evans Da, Atl	6	5	0	0	1	.000
Oliver, Cin	7	7	3	0	5	.429							
Armas, Cal	7	7	3	1	6	.429							
Barfield, Tor-NYA	7	5	2	0	4	.400							
Kruk, SD-Phi	7	5	2	0	3	.400							
Martinez Crm, SD	7	6	2	0	5	.333							
Jackson Dar, ChN-SD	7	7	2	0	2	.286							

DOES RUNNING AGGRESSIVELY MEAN MORE RUNS? (p. 54)

1989 Team by Team Data

American League

Team	Runs Scored Rank	Base-running Rank	Extra Bases Taken	Opportunities	%	Outs on the Bases
Baltimore	5	9	455	1085	41.9	29
Boston	1	14	505	1303	38.8	24
California	12	6	460	1048	43.9	27
Chicago	10	8	504	1174	42.9	45
Cleveland	14	13	408	994	41.0	21
Detroit	13	4	463	1048	44.2	26
Kansas City	11	11	480	1153	41.6	25
Milwaukee	6	5	471	1070	44.0	25
Minnesota	2	3	530	1185	44.7	35
New York	7	12	477	1151	41.4	30
Oakland	4	1	507	1098	46.2	27
Seattle	9	10	451	1082	41.7	37
Texas	8	2	465	1011	46.0	31
Toronto	3	7	460	1063	43.3	38

National League

Team	Runs Scored Rank	Base-running Rank	Extra Bases Taken	Opportunities	%	Outs on the Bases
Atlanta	11	12	383	925	41.4	21
Chicago	1	2	505	1076	46.9	35
Cincinnati	7	7	402	921	43.6	26
Houston	4	5	463	1052	44.0	25
Los Angeles	12	8	439	1010	43.5	32
Montreal	7	9	441	1016	43.4	29
New York	3	3	454	1003	45.3	38
Philadelphia	10	10	416	966	43.1	19
Pittsburgh	6	1	494	990	49.9	23
St. Louis	7	11	459	1095	41.9	35
San Diego	5	6	437	1000	43.7	30
San Francisco	2	4	422	950	44.4	22

How Do Teams Perform vs. Lefties and Righties?
(p. 56)

American League—Batting Vs. LHP

Team	Avg	OBP	Slg	HR	W-L
Baltimore	.242	.317	.376	42	27-20
Boston	.279	.345	.396	28	21-21
California	.247	.299	.370	49	25-25
Chicago	.273	.326	.373	26	23-36
Cleveland	.246	.307	.370	68	22-27
Detroit	.258	.326	.378	40	23-27
Kansas City	.273	.348	.382	76	29-20
Milwaukee	.284	.342	.424	39	33-16
Minnesota	.288	.341	.422	34	23-23
New York	.298	.362	.427	42	30-28
Oakland	.266	.335	.389	33	32-14
Seattle	.259	.314	.392	38	20-17
Texas	.266	.323	.418	42	26-19
Toronto	.257	.317	.369	36	27-25

American League—Pitching Vs. LHB

Team	Avg	OBP	Slg	HR
Baltimore	.269	.332	.391	52
Boston	.271	.339	.388	57
California	.258	.311	.368	44
Chicago	.270	.346	.422	60
Cleveland	.247	.312	.354	39
Detroit	.280	.360	.429	60
Kansas City	.249	.311	.345	33
Milwaukee	.261	.318	.373	50
Minnesota	.284	.350	.428	45
New York	.296	.365	.462	62
Oakland	.226	.300	.320	35
Seattle	.262	.333	.387	49
Texas	.224	.318	.333	48
Toronto	.261	.338	.373	29

National League—Batting Vs. LHP

Team	Avg	OBP	Slg	HR	W-L
Atlanta	.231	.302	.336	35	20-38
Chicago	.282	.346	.424	41	31-17
Cincinnati	.241	.309	.364	45	20-26
Houston	.257	.327	.375	31	27-21
Los Angeles	.234	.301	.327	28	31-30
Montreal	.272	.339	.410	43	27-18
New York	.246	.313	.377	51	33-27
Philadelphia	.250	.319	.359	39	23-37
Pittsburgh	.245	.319	.360	27	21-30
St. Louis	.253	.314	.361	30	25-23
San Diego	.267	.340	.387	32	27-19
San Francisco	.248	.320	.391	49	36-20

National League—Pitching Vs. LHB

Team	Avg	OBP	Slg	HR
Atlanta	.242	.316	.341	35
Chicago	.259	.332	.374	45
Cincinnati	.268	.340	.391	42
Houston	.263	.331	.381	46
Los Angeles	.246	.317	.341	41
Montreal	.243	.311	.363	52
New York	.242	.314	.359	37
Philadelphia	.249	.339	.380	39
Pittsburgh	.247	.324	.347	33
St. Louis	.255	.329	.363	33
San Diego	.254	.322	.382	52
San Francisco	.257	.323	.371	47

American League—Batting Vs. RHP

Team	Avg	OBP	Slg	HR	W-L
Baltimore	.256	.331	.380	87	60-55
Boston	.277	.354	.405	80	62-58
California	.262	.317	.395	96	66-46
Chicago	.270	.329	.388	68	46-56
Cleveland	.245	.312	.363	89	51-62
Detroit	.234	.314	.338	76	36-76
Kansas City	.256	.321	.369	72	63-50
Milwaukee	.249	.309	.366	87	48-65
Minnesota	.271	.331	.393	83	57-59
New York	.255	.316	.373	88	44-59
Oakland	.259	.330	.378	94	67-49
Seattle	.256	.322	.380	96	53-72
Texas	.261	.328	.384	80	57-60
Toronto	.261	.327	.411	106	62-48

American League—Pitching Vs. RHB

Team	Avg	OBP	Slg	HR
Baltimore	.274	.330	.405	82
Boston	.252	.318	.378	74
California	.250	.313	.355	69
Chicago	.268	.328	.403	84
Cleveland	.262	.314	.380	68
Detroit	.270	.346	.405	90
Kansas City	.263	.317	.372	53
Milwaukee	.267	.324	.384	79
Minnesota	.262	.322	.397	94
New York	.273	.333	.408	88
Oakland	.249	.309	.370	68
Seattle	.257	.328	.380	65
Texas	.249	.328	.370	71
Toronto	.253	.307	.373	70

National League—Batting Vs. RHP

Team	Avg	OBP	Slg	HR	W-L
Atlanta	.236	.296	.356	93	44-59
Chicago	.252	.309	.372	83	62-52
Cincinnati	.250	.310	.374	83	55-61
Houston	.232	.299	.334	66	59-55
Los Angeles	.244	.309	.346	61	46-53
Montreal	.236	.311	.341	57	54-63
New York	.246	.310	.389	96	54-48
Philadelphia	.239	.311	.366	84	44-58
Pittsburgh	.239	.306	.359	68	53-58
St. Louis	.261	.326	.365	43	61-43
San Diego	.244	.310	.361	88	62-54
San Francisco	.250	.314	.389	92	56-50

National League—Pitching Vs. RHB

Team	Avg	OBP	Slg	HR
Atlanta	.256	.304	.384	79
Chicago	.242	.303	.356	61
Cincinnati	.245	.312	.367	83
Houston	.234	.303	.346	59
Los Angeles	.229	.291	.337	54
Montreal	.247	.312	.369	68
New York	.225	.292	.342	78
Philadelphia	.264	.332	.400	88
Pittsburgh	.248	.308	.383	88
St. Louis	.234	.287	.354	51
San Diego	.245	.301	.373	81
San Francisco	.231	.287	.359	73

WHICH TEAMS RUN LATE? (p. 58)

1989 Team Base Stealing by Inning
Stolen Bases/Stolen Base Attempts

American League

Team	1	2	3	4	5	6	7	8	9	10+
Baltimore	23/31	8/15	14/21	8/16	12/19	16/23	21/25	9/12	5/7	2/4
Boston	8/14	2/5	11/15	3/10	4/5	8/14	3/6	14/18	3/4	0/0
California	12/16	3/8	14/22	12/17	13/17	13/18	11/13	8/13	0/0	3/5
Chicago	12/17	12/20	16/24	13/20	12/19	7/14	11/16	9/11	1/4	4/4
Cleveland	14/17	6/12	13/20	12/17	14/20	1/8	5/12	6/15	2/2	1/2
Detroit	22/33	6/15	15/20	10/17	9/12	17/22	6/10	3/6	13/14	2/4
Kansas City	28/40	18/25	19/26	22/28	22/28	14/20	10/12	7/8	8/9	6/9
Milwaukee	24/37	21/30	18/24	20/24	13/20	18/24	19/26	19/27	12/13	1/2
Minnesota	25/32	4/13	26/37	12/14	20/26	4/9	12/17	6/12	2/3	0/1
New York	23/36	4/15	27/33	14/21	13/22	14/17	20/25	10/11	10/14	2/3
Oakland	34/44	8/16	16/23	14/19	12/21	21/28	19/23	21/24	8/10	4/4
Seattle	14/24	10/16	4/10	9/20	18/25	4/6	9/15	8/13	5/5	0/2
Texas	16/28	12/20	10/19	10/13	15/23	12/15	5/7	12/14	4/6	5/5
Toronto	22/30	17/34	15/19	20/27	12/20	19/22	10/11	18/26	6/6	5/7

National League

Team	1	2	3	4	5	6	7	8	9	10+
Atlanta	20/34	4/10	11/19	10/18	7/13	7/12	9/9	8/11	3/5	4/6
Chicago	31/41	7/14	29/41	16/21	10/16	15/20	12/15	10/12	5/10	1/3
Cincinnati	25/41	6/15	14/24	14/20	13/19	14/20	8/17	9/14	18/20	7/9
Houston	23/38	10/14	16/23	24/26	13/20	14/18	18/26	13/22	11/16	2/3
Los Angeles	14/24	4/12	11/19	11/18	10/14	8/14	8/12	11/14	0/2	4/6
Montreal	24/34	11/19	14/20	14/22	19/31	14/21	20/28	16/20	21/24	7/11
New York	30/35	14/19	24/32	12/18	17/23	15/25	18/22	16/22	10/11	2/4
Philadelphia	23/27	12/17	9/16	12/18	13/20	14/20	12/19	8/14	1/2	2/3
Pittsburgh	30/39	7/22	17/25	26/34	17/28	19/25	15/18	12/16	7/10	5/7
St. Louis	34/42	7/12	24/31	9/17	12/16	19/24	18/22	18/28	10/12	4/5
San Diego	29/43	15/22	13/20	13/18	17/22	12/24	13/21	13/18	5/8	6/7
San Francisco	14/15	12/23	17/21	13/19	5/17	8/12	8/14	7/10	1/6	2/4

WHICH IS THE BEST DIVISION IN BASEBALL? (p. 60)

1989 Inter-divisional Records — Listed by Winning Percentage

American League

East vs. West

Team	W	L	Pct
Blue Jays	43	41	.512
Orioles	42	42	.500
Yankees	40	43	.482
Indians	40	44	.476
Red Sox	39	45	.464
Brewers	37	47	.440
Tigers	32	52	.381
TOTAL	273	314	.465

West vs. East

Team	W	L	Pct
Athletics	53	31	.631
Angels	50	34	.595
Twins	46	38	.548
Royals	45	39	.536
Mariners	41	43	.488
Rangers	41	43	.488
White Sox	38	45	.458
TOTAL	314	273	.535

National League

East vs. West

Team	W	L	Pct
Cardinals	42	30	.583
Cubs	40	32	.556
Expos	39	33	.542
Mets	39	33	.542
Pirates	31	41	.431
Phillies	27	45	.375
TOTALS	218	214	.505

West vs. East

Team	W	L	Pct
Giants	42	30	.583
Astros	40	32	.556
Padres	39	33	.542
Dodgers	33	39	.458
Reds	32	40	.444
Braves	28	44	.389
TOTALS	214	218	.495

DOES ARTIFICIAL TURF PRODUCE MORE GROUNDBALL HITS? (p. 62)

Groundball Results, 1989

America League

Team	Home Games			Road Games			Diff
	No. of Grounders	Ground Hits	% Ground Hits	No. of Grounders	Ground Hits	% Ground Hits	
Baltimore	2070	468	22.6	2031	457	22.5	+0.1
Boston	2150	472	22.0	2098	523	24.9	-2.9
California	2048	449	21.9	1967	432	22.0	-0.1
Chicago	2052	461	22.5	1995	507	25.4	-2.9
Cleveland	1976	424	21.5	2051	432	21.1	+0.4
Detroit	1953	370	18.9	2059	471	22.9	-4.0
Kansas City	2114	518	24.5	2052	467	22.8	+1.7
Milwaukee	2097	452	21.6	2171	466	21.5	+0.1
Minnesota	2019	486	24.1	2056	425	20.7	+3.4
New York	2127	536	25.2	2106	470	22.3	+2.9
Oakland	1944	419	21.6	1979	422	21.3	+0.3
Seattle	2098	494	23.5	2061	438	21.3	+2.2
Texas	1981	465	23.5	1991	454	22.8	+0.7
Toronto	2034	399	19.6	2046	449	21.9	-2.3

National League

Team	No. of Grounders	Ground Hits	% Ground Hits	No. of Grounders	Ground Hits	% Ground Hits	Diff
Atlanta	1973	429	21.7	1943	468	24.1	-2.4
Chicago	2201	517	23.5	2074	487	23.5	0.0
Cincinnati	2026	499	24.6	1968	405	20.6	+4.0
Houston	2121	489	23.1	2025	429	21.2	+1.9
Los Angeles	1997	451	22.6	1993	460	23.1	-0.5
Montreal	2119	479	22.6	2016	430	21.3	+1.3
New York	1718	402	23.4	1910	417	21.8	+1.6
Philadelphia	2012	463	23.0	2176	480	22.1	+0.9
Pittsburgh	2100	440	21.0	2171	508	23.4	-2.4
St. Louis	2267	486	21.4	2151	512	23.8	-2.4
San Diego	2029	458	22.6	2113	485	23.0	-0.4
San Francisco	1921	369	19.2	1944	401	20.6	-1.4

WHAT ARE THE BEST HITTERS' COUNTS? (p. 64)

Both Leagues Combined (pitchers hitting excluded)

At the Count

Count	Avg	OBP*	Slg	AB	H	2B	3B	HR	SH	SF	HBP	BB*	IBB	K
0-0 count	.313	.313	.470	21313	6661	1190	145	622	533	246	199	0	1113	0
0-1 Count	.304	.307	.440	12861	3904	684	80	303	208	138	126	0	20	0
0-2 Count	.161	.168	.224	9602	1543	243	35	99	12	57	97	0	0	4225
1-0 Count	.307	.305	.465	13418	4113	706	110	398	169	159	37	0	50	0
1-1 Count	.305	.306	.449	13462	4105	735	101	333	130	132	79	0	16	0
1-2 Count	.172	.177	.237	19680	3383	522	64	208	10	98	130	0	0	7903
2-0 Count	.324	.322	.508	4752	1539	298	43	164	33	63	15	0	80	0
2-1 Count	.311	.310	.474	9073	2818	486	75	281	57	80	22	0	20	0
2-2 Count	.191	.193	.272	18408	3514	596	81	242	4	99	57	0	0	6576
3-0 Count	.372	.927	.631	358	133	23	5	20	0	14	0	2905	109	0
3-1 Count	.332	.664	.534	3828	1270	246	39	150	17	44	5	3880	32	0
3-2 Count	.225	.458	.340	11676	2628	469	78	240	0	88	16	5098	6	3403

*Excluding Intentional Walks

After the Count

Count	Avg	OBP	Slg	AB	H	2B	3B	HR	SH	SF	HBP	BB	IW	K
After (0-1)	.229	.269	.331	61135	14015	2401	321	1068	317	440	384	3103	219	14594
After (0-2)	.177	.206	.249	22580	3998	648	102	255	14	123	157	702	16	9120
After (1-0)	.267	.372	.400	56052	14945	2608	390	1370	323	532	271	9412	411	7601
After (1-1)	.236	.301	.347	51984	12277	2135	278	1030	188	378	271	4706	54	11189
After (1-2)	.185	.230	.262	34475	6365	1055	143	438	10	189	204	1897	6	13004
After (2-0)	.285	.491	.436	16367	4668	836	141	452	61	174	53	6717	170	1901
After (2-1)	.254	.382	.384	25768	6554	1146	172	617	69	198	79	5371	40	4596
After (2-2)	.201	.294	.291	26254	5276	919	135	396	4	164	117	3423	9	8934
After (3-0)	.291	.729	.449	2868	835	142	27	86	9	35	11	4721	59	363
After (3-1)	.278	.579	.437	7705	2144	393	63	235	17	66	23	5570	15	1064
After (3-2)	.225	.459	.340	11712	2634	470	78	240	0	87	44	5095	3	3402

Note: In the first chart, intentional walks are counted from the point they became intentional.

WHICH PLAYERS TURNED IN THE BEST MONTHLY PERFORMANCES OF 1989? (p. 66)

Monthly League Batting and Pitching Averages — 1989

American League Batting

Month	Avg	OBP	Slg	AB	R	H	2B	3B	HR	RBI	BB	K	SB/CS
April	.255	.324	.378	11152	1420	2848	508	61	244	1317	1100	1771	272/126
May	.264	.330	.391	12651	1637	3344	578	84	287	1534	1230	1931	255/127
June	.269	.331	.388	13188	1715	3543	563	64	295	1601	1217	1935	251/118
July	.263	.330	.389	12490	1635	3285	543	71	298	1538	1214	2002	258/116
August	.257	.319	.382	14075	1693	3620	624	101	312	1595	1239	2368	288/107
September	.256	.323	.375	12973	1587	3325	560	73	276	1478	1243	2196	253/126
October	.238	.290	.347	475	45	113	28	3	6	40	34	93	10/ 6

National League Batting

Month	Avg	OBP	Slg	AB	R	H	2B	3B	HR	RBI	BB	K	SB/CS
April	.243	.310	.360	9498	1112	2309	437	57	185	1027	916	1549	230/101
May	.239	.308	.343	10793	1163	2578	458	66	179	1074	1056	1842	296/154
June	.253	.321	.375	11220	1334	2835	508	85	231	1247	1122	1875	264/122
July	.247	.313	.366	10867	1296	2689	493	57	228	1196	1011	1893	237/129
August	.247	.312	.377	11688	1395	2884	497	70	294	1286	1087	1973	241/106
September	.249	.312	.369	11332	1340	2823	488	74	242	1266	1030	2149	252/103
October	.232	.282	.337	419	33	97	22	2	6	30	29	73	9/ 0

American League Pitching

Month	G	Saves	ERA	Innings	Runs	ER	BB	K	HB	WP	BK
April	330	82	3.87	2946.2	1420	1268	1100	1771	78	98	35
May	374	96	4.09	3305.2	1637	1503	1230	1931	73	133	30
June	382	108	4.01	3415.2	1715	1522	1217	1935	75	99	39
July	368	88	4.06	3273.0	1635	1477	1214	2002	83	94	19
August	418	113	3.67	3706.0	1693	1510	1239	2368	89	135	26
September	380	90	3.72	3407.2	1587	1407	1243	2196	84	134	18
October	14	5	2.92	126.1	45	41	34	93	1	2	1

National League Pitching

Month	G	Saves	ERA	Innings	Runs	ER	BB	K	HB	WP	BK
April	284	78	3.45	2533.0	1112	970	916	1549	45	88	60
May	320	82	3.13	2908.1	1163	1012	1056	1842	57	100	42
June	328	83	3.67	2978.1	1334	1214	1122	1875	48	92	41
July	324	85	3.56	2890.1	1296	1142	1011	1893	61	88	45
August	342	76	3.62	3122.0	1395	1256	1087	1973	57	106	32
September	336	80	3.61	2990.0	1340	1198	1030	2149	49	112	18
October	12	3	2.41	112.0	33	30	29	73	1	3	1

DO SACRIFICES SACRIFICE TOO MUCH? (p. 68)

Analysis of Bunting Effectivenes — 1987 to 1989 Bunting Data

American League

	# of Innings	Runs Scored	Runs per Inning	# Innings with Runs	% of Innings with Runs
0 Out; Men on 1st ONLY; #9 Hitter NOT Up					
Innings with successful SH	907	627	.691	358	.395
Innings with failed SH	140	71	.507	44	.314
Innings—SH not attempted	11883	10040	.845	4830	.406
0 Out; Men on 1st ONLY; #9 Hitter Up					
Innings with successful SH	314	238	.758	134	.427
Innings with failed SH	58	39	.672	19	.328
Innings—SH not attempted	1099	965	.878	439	.399
0 Out; Men on 1st & 2nd; #9 Hitter NOT Up					
Innings with successful SH	400	640	1.600	263	.658
Innings with failed SH	82	86	1.049	36	.439
Innings—SH not attempted	2774	3784	1.364	1575	568
0 Out; Men on 1st & 2nd; #9 Hitter Up					
Innings with successful SH	79	128	1.620	52	.658
Innings with failed SH	23	45	1.957	15	.652
Innings—SH not attempted	210	312	1.486	112	.533

National League

	# of Innings	Runs Scored	Runs per Inning	# Innings with Runs	% of Innings with Runs
0 Out; Men on 1st ONLY; #9 Hitter NOT Up					
Innings with successful SH	743	524	.705	298	.401
Innings with failed SH	110	49	.445	27	.245
Innings—SH not attempted	9675	7450	.770	3765	.389
0 Out; Men on 1st ONLY; #9 Hitter Up					
Innings with successful SH	584	437	.748	236	.404
Innings with failed SH	84	31	.369	17	.202
Innings—SH not attempted	588	455	.774	234	.398
0 Out; Men on 1st & 2nd; #9 Hitter NOT Up					
Innings with successful SH	234	350	1.496	149	.637
Innings with failed SH	50	51	1.020	24	.480
Innings—SH not attempted	2086	2650	1.270	1127	.540
0 Out; Men on 1st & 2nd; #9 Hitter Up					
Innings with successful SH	88	131	1.489	57	.648
Innings with failed SH	40	23	.575	11	.275
Innings—SH not attempted	166	187	1.127	83	.500

Notes: Successful SH includes bunt singles. All runs in inning count, so lead-off HR's will be counted too.

WHICH TEAMS SHOWED THE MOST IMPROVEMENT DURING THE SECOND HALF OF 1989? (p. 70)

Records by Half — 1989

American League East
April-June

Baltimore	43-33	.566
New York	38-39	.494
Boston	36-39	.480
Toronto	37-41	.474
Milwaukee	37-42	.468
Cleveland	36-41	.468
Detroit	30-46	.395

American League East
July-October

Toronto	52-32	.619
Boston	47-40	.540
Milwaukee	44-39	.530
Baltimore	44-42	.512
Cleveland	37-48	.435
New York	36-48	.429
Detroit	29-57	.337

American League West
April-June

Oakland	47-32	.595
California	45-31	.592
Kansas City	44-33	.571
Texas	43-35	.551
Minnesota	40-39	.506
Seattle	37-42	.468
Chicago	30-50	.375

American League West
July-October

Oakland	52-31	.627
Kansas City	48-37	.565
California	46-40	.535
Minnesota	40-43	.482
Chicago	39-42	.481
Texas	40-44	.476
Seattle	36-47	.434

National League East
April-June

Montreal	44-35	.557
New York	40-35	.533
Chicago	41-37	.526
St. Louis	38-37	.507
Pittsburgh	33-41	.446
Philadelphia	27-48	.360

National League East
July-October

Chicago	52-32	.619
St. Louis	48-39	.552
New York	47-40	.540
Pittsburgh	41-47	.466
Philadelphia	40-47	.460
Montreal	37-46	.446

National League West
April-June

San Francisco	47-32	.595
Houston	45-34	.570
Cincinnati	41-37	.526
San Diego	39-41	.488
Los Angeles	37-41	.474
Atlanta	32-46	.410

National League West
July-October

San Diego	50-32	.610
San Francisco	45-38	.542
Houston	41-42	.494
Los Angeles	40-42	.488
Cincinnati	34-50	.405
Atlanta	31-51	.378

WHEN ARE TWO OUTS BETTER THAN ONE? (p. 74)

The table below shows the runs scored by outs for every team, along with the percentage of total runs at each out.

Team Totals — Listed Alphabetically by Team

American League

Team	Runs	0 Out	%	1 Out	%	2 Out	%
Baltimore	708	120	17	239	34	349	49
Boston	774	126	16	291	38	357	46
California	669	128	19	214	32	327	49
Chicago	693	127	18	265	38	301	43
Cleveland	604	114	19	230	38	260	43
Detroit	617	115	19	202	33	300	48
Kansas City	690	122	18	261	38	307	44
Milwaukee	707	108	15	268	38	331	47
Minnesota	740	133	18	284	38	323	44
New York	698	113	16	265	38	320	46
Oakland	712	163	23	230	32	319	45
Seattle	694	102	15	259	37	333	48
Texas	695	109	16	270	39	316	45
Toronto	731	159	22	258	35	314	43

National League

Team	Runs	0 Out	%	1 Out	%	2 Out	%
Atlanta	584	94	16	205	35	285	49
Chicago	702	123	18	231	33	348	49
Cincinnati	632	95	15	234	37	303	48
Houston	647	103	16	228	35	316	49
Los Angeles	554	91	16	190	34	273	49
Montreal	632	108	17	223	35	301	48
New York	683	145	21	232	34	306	45
Philadelphia	629	120	19	217	35	292	46
Pittsburgh	637	99	16	245	38	293	46
St. Louis	632	105	17	202	32	325	51
San Diego	642	167	26	218	34	257	40
San Francisco	699	124	18	264	38	311	44

WHEN DO GOOD TEAMS SCORE? (p. 76)

Team Run Scoring by Inning

American League

Team	Total Runs	1	2	3	4	5	6	7	8	9	10+
Baltimore	708	104	66	82	103	71	78	91	53	48	12
Boston	774	127	82	101	88	78	97	69	73	41	18
California	669	71	57	95	85	80	92	62	57	62	8
Chicago	693	80	87	88	84	63	68	67	93	56	7
Cleveland	604	91	61	74	55	81	59	70	69	41	3
Detroit	617	82	64	77	86	57	67	54	67	57	6
Kansas City	690	86	79	76	64	76	91	75	77	44	22
Milwaukee	707	72	72	96	83	76	87	81	76	58	6
Minnesota	704	87	74	75	66	96	72	99	105	55	11
New York	698	93	52	85	79	91	92	73	82	45	6
Oakland	712	98	60	103	73	88	77	72	84	48	9
Seattle	694	89	71	95	81	79	84	72	71	43	9
Texas	695	106	56	72	90	93	82	66	68	48	14
Toronto	731	94	73	72	89	86	66	80	73	70	28

National League

Team	Total Runs	1	2	3	4	5	6	7	8	9	10+
Atlanta	584	85	46	71	49	70	77	54	88	41	3
Chicago	702	114	68	103	85	76	95	49	51	49	12
Cincinnati	632	92	51	66	65	52	85	72	65	64	20
Houston	647	83	82	62	67	75	66	84	52	62	14
Los Angeles	554	73	65	54	58	61	81	59	44	46	13
Montreal	632	83	73	55	83	78	58	67	66	53	16
New York	683	76	70	107	64	102	76	59	60	54	15
Philadelphia	629	98	60	63	89	63	67	59	73	44	13
Pittsburgh	637	108	62	58	98	56	58	82	65	35	15
St. Louis	632	71	42	99	69	55	95	76	71	38	16
San Diego	642	72	51	72	73	104	72	70	78	32	18
San Francisco	699	103	68	107	68	73	87	80	61	41	11

WHICH HITTERS SWING AND MISS MOST OFTEN? (p. 80)

The table below shows swings missed (Sw) as a percent of total pitches the player swung at. (Pit). Example: Bo Jackson missed 38.6% of all pitches he swung at.

Both Leagues — Listed Alphabetically (450 or more plate appearances)

Player, Team	Sw	Pit	%	Player, Team	Sw	Pit	%	Player, Team	Sw	Pit	%
Alomar R, SD	155	1176	13.2	Guerrero, StL	251	1177	21.3	Reynolds H, Sea	64	959	6.7
Baines, Tex	165	925	17.8	Guillen, ChA	125	1109	11.4	Ripken C, Bal	157	1140	13.8
Barfield Je, NYA	315	1049	30.0	Gwynn T, SD	70	974	7.2	Samuel, NYN	321	1138	28.2
Bell Geo, Tor	163	1081	15.1	Hamilton J, LA	223	1022	21.8	Sandberg, ChN	192	1031	18.6
Benzinger, Cin	255	1201	21.2	Hatcher B, Pit	150	892	16.8	Santiago, SD	193	899	21.5
Biggio, Hou	125	790	15.8	Hayes V, Phi	178	1017	17.5	Sax S, NYA	98	1113	8.8
Blauser, Atl	196	847	23.1	Henderson D, Oak	295	1186	24.9	Scioscia, LA	67	702	9.5
Boggs W, Bos	59	1101	5.4	Henderson R, Oak	97	891	10.9	Seitzer, KC	116	1137	10.2
Bonds, Pit	151	1058	14.3	Herr, Phi	121	1026	11.8	Sierra, Tex	211	1145	18.4
Bonilla B, Pit	223	1198	18.6	Howell Jk, Cal	267	963	27.7	Smith Lo, Atl	269	1106	24.3
Boone, KC	61	629	9.7	Incaviglia, Tex	335	943	35.5	Smith O, StL	63	1018	6.2
Bradley P, Bal	229	1166	19.6	Jackson B, KC	452	1170	38.6	Snyder C, Cle	321	1008	31.8
Braggs, Mil	251	981	25.6	Jacoby, Cle	182	992	18.3	Steinbach, Oak	157	837	18.8
Brett, KC	146	861	17.0	James C, SD	157	875	17.9	Stillwell, KC	111	779	14.2
Brooks, Mon	241	1071	22.5	James D, Cle	100	781	12.8	Strawberry, NYN	230	956	24.1
Browne J, Cle	137	1091	12.6	Jefferies, NYN	101	930	10.9	Surhoff BJ, Mil	52	647	8.0
Brunansky, StL	227	1044	21.7	Johnson H, NYN	256	1206	21.2	Tartabull, KC	318	956	33.3
Buechele, Tex	198	895	22.1	Jordan, Phi	175	958	18.3	Templeton, SD	171	1005	17.0
Butler, SF	89	1108	8.0	Joyner, Cal	156	1124	13.9	Tettleton, Bal	196	747	26.2
Calderon, ChA	229	1255	18.2	Kelly, NYA	235	931	25.2	Thomas A, Atl	165	953	17.3
Caminiti, Hou	181	1091	16.6	Lansford, Oak	59	888	6.6	Thompson M, StL	147	999	14.7
Carter J, Cle	298	1372	21.7	Larkin G, Min	116	795	14.6	Thompson Ro, SF	281	1105	25.4
Clark Jk, SD	321	999	32.1	Law V, ChN	153	812	18.8	Thon, Phi	176	760	23.2
Clark W, SF	280	1299	21.6	Lemon, Det	130	773	16.8	Trammell, Det	87	761	11.4
Coleman, StL	170	1050	16.2	Leonard J, Sea	335	1209	27.7	Treadway, Atl	76	827	9.2
Coles, Sea	129	934	13.8	Lind, Pit	109	1036	10.5	Uribe, SF	153	821	18.6
Davis A, Sea	91	812	11.2	Liriano, Tor	94	679	13.8	Van Slyke, Pit	168	904	18.6
Davis C, Cal	290	1111	26.1	Lyons S, ChA	158	884	17.9	Wallach, Mon	232	1136	20.4
Davis E, Cin	271	938	28.9	Mattingly, NYA	88	1031	8.5	Walton, ChN	145	856	16.9
Davis G, Hou	299	1208	24.8	McDowell O, Atl	152	915	16.6	Washington C, Cal	198	803	24.7
Dawson, ChN	196	837	23.4	McGriff F, Tor	268	1052	25.5				
Deer, Mil	326	1039	31.4	McGwire, Oak	204	950	21.5	Whitaker, Det	122	925	13.2
Doran, Hou	139	948	14.7	McReynolds, NYN	174	986	17.6	White D, Cal	361	1318	27.4
Downing, Cal	179	1021	17.5	Mitchell K, SF	269	1111	24.2	White F, KC	137	812	16.9
Dunston, ChN	190	944	20.1	Molitor, Mil	163	1231	13.2	Wilson G, Hou	152	891	17.1
Dykstra, Phi	82	901	9.1	Moreland, Bal	89	709	12.6	Wilson M, Tor	218	1009	21.6
Eisenreich, KC	98	822	11.9	Moseby, Tor	204	969	21.1	Worthington, Bal	194	955	20.3
Elster, NYN	159	844	18.8	Murphy Dl, Atl	348	1188	29.3	Young G, Hou	73	873	8.4
Esasky, Bos	285	1145	24.9	Murray E, LA	260	1273	20.4	Yount, Mil	169	1151	14.6
Espinoza, NYA	120	919	13.1	Newman A, Min	97	744	13.0				
Espy, Tex	167	929	18.0	O'Brien P, Cle	93	890	10.4				
Evans Dw, Bos	168	920	18.3	O'Neill, Cin	141	781	18.1				
Felix, Tor	196	812	24.1	Oquendo, StL	116	979	11.8				
Fermin, Cle	48	892	5.4	Owen S, Mon	86	760	11.3				
Fernandez T, Tor	117	1028	11.4	Palmeiro, Tex	98	957	10.2				
Fletcher S, ChA	94	897	10.5	Parker D, Oak	276	1141	24.2				
Franco Ju, Tex	143	955	15.0	Parrish Ln, Cal	243	888	27.4				
Gaetti, Min	260	1079	24.1	Pena T, StL	90	752	12.0				
Gagne, Min	187	902	20.7	Pendleton, StL	210	1212	17.3				
Galarraga, Mon	325	1192	27.3	Pettis, Det	191	888	21.5				
Gallagher, ChA	128	1106	11.6	Phillips, Oak	132	854	15.5				
Gantner, Mil	92	733	12.6	Polonia, NYA	96	833	11.5				
Gladden, Min	114	797	14.3	Puckett, Min	181	1123	16.1				
Grace, ChN	74	857	8.6	Raines, Mon	98	938	10.4				
Greenwell, Bos	116	1001	11.6	Ramirez R, Hou	143	939	15.2				
Griffey Jr, Sea	180	891	20.2	Randolph, LA	74	847	8.7				
Griffin Alf, LA	130	925	14.1	Ray, Cal	78	971	8.0				
Gruber, Tor	195	1076	18.1	Reed Jd, Bos	66	847	7.8				

WHO CAN POP IN THE CLUTCH? (p. 82)

Both Leagues — Listed Alphabetically
(85 or more plate appearances in the late innings of close games)

Player, Team	Avg	AB	H	HR	RBI	Player, Team	Avg	AB	H	HR	RBI
Alomar R, SD	.319	94	30	1	7	Jordan, Phi	.310	87	27	2	19
Baines, Tex	.224	76	17	3	9	Joyner, Cal	.247	97	24	2	12
Barfield Je, NYA	.133	75	10	3	11	Kelly, NYA	.329	79	26	2	10
Bell Geo, Tor	.330	97	32	3	20	Lansford, Oak	.280	82	23	0	5
Benzinger, Cin	.167	96	16	2	12	Lemon, Det	.203	79	16	0	7
Biggio, Hou	.311	90	28	3	19	Leonard J, Sea	.233	90	21	3	11
Blauser, Atl	.260	100	26	2	11	Lind, Pit	.215	107	23	0	5
Boggs W, Bos	.276	98	27	1	7	Liriano, Tor	.235	85	20	0	13
Bonds, Pit	.214	98	21	1	8	Lyons S, ChA	.301	83	25	1	12
Bonilla B, Pit	.220	123	27	5	15	Mattingly, NYA	.303	89	27	4	21
Brooks, Mon	.278	97	27	3	14	McDowell O, Atl	.237	76	18	2	7
Browne J, Cle	.299	97	29	1	4	McGriff F, Tor	.292	89	26	4	15
Brunansky, StL	.209	86	18	3	14	McReynolds, NYN	.313	99	31	5	9
Butler, SF	.293	92	27	1	9	Mitchell K, SF	.303	76	23	6	15
Calderon, ChA	.300	100	30	1	14	Moseby, Tor	.239	88	21	1	8
Caminiti, Hou	.210	119	25	3	9	Murphy Dl, Atl	.253	95	24	3	18
Carter J, Cle	.185	108	20	5	15	Murray E, LA	.198	111	22	4	10
Clark Jk, SD	.221	77	17	6	24	O'Brien P, Cle	.186	86	16	0	7
Clark W, SF	.300	90	27	5	20	O'Neill, Cin	.284	74	21	0	8
Coleman, StL	.209	91	19	0	5	Oquendo, StL	.308	91	28	0	4
Coles, Sea	.289	83	24	3	10	Owen S, Mon	.231	91	21	3	10
Davis A, Sea	.208	77	16	3	16	Parker D, Oak	.182	77	14	3	7
Davis C, Cal	.184	87	16	2	4	Parrish Ln, Cal	.218	78	17	2	5
Davis E, Cin	.325	80	26	8	26	Pendleton, StL	.227	97	22	2	9
Davis G, Hou	.252	111	28	7	17	Pettis, Det	.265	68	18	0	9
Doran, Hou	.189	95	18	3	7	Phillips, Oak	.233	73	17	1	9
Downing, Cal	.299	87	26	3	10	Puckett, Min	.352	91	32	3	16
Dykstra, Phi	.253	87	22	0	5	Raines, Mon	.340	97	33	1	15
Elster, NYN	.256	78	20	1	5	Ramirez R, Hou	.255	98	25	1	15
Esasky, Bos	.303	89	27	5	16	Randolph, LA	.248	101	25	1	10
Evans Dw, Bos	.283	92	26	1	16	Ray, Cal	.200	75	15	0	10
Fermin, Cle	.273	66	18	0	4	Reed Jd, Bos	.260	73	19	0	9
Fernandez T, Tor	.256	82	21	1	7	Reynolds H, Sea	.351	77	27	0	6
Fletcher S, ChA	.202	84	17	0	6	Reynolds RJ, Pit	.291	86	25	0	7
Gaetti, Min	.232	82	19	6	15	Ripken C, Bal	.241	87	21	5	14
Galarraga, Mon	.237	118	28	6	17	Sandberg, ChN	.277	94	26	4	10
Gallagher, ChA	.194	98	19	0	5	Santiago, SD	.226	84	19	1	10
Grace, ChN	.348	69	24	3	9	Sax S, NYA	.315	92	29	1	12
Greenwell, Bos	.364	77	28	2	9	Scioscia, LA	.244	78	19	1	4
Griffin Alf, LA	.221	104	23	0	4	Seitzer, KC	.318	85	27	1	11
Gruber, Tor	.284	81	23	2	12	Sierra, Tex	.310	84	26	4	16
Guerrero, StL	.282	85	24	2	23	Smith O, StL	.361	83	30	0	8
Guillen, ChA	.300	110	33	0	12	Snyder C, Cle	.141	99	14	0	3
Gwynn T, SD	.351	94	33	0	13	Strawberry, NYN	.134	82	11	3	8
Hamilton J, LA	.252	115	29	0	7	Templeton, SD	.200	90	18	0	4
Hatcher B, Pit	.198	81	16	1	6	Thomas A, Atl	.271	107	29	4	11
Hayes V, Phi	.225	89	20	4	9	Thompson M, StL	.294	85	25	0	8
Heath, Det	.294	85	25	5	12	Thompson Ro, SF	.233	86	20	3	10
Henderson D, Oak	.253	79	20	4	16	Trammell, Det	.301	73	22	1	9
Henderson R, Oak	.256	78	20	2	11	Treadway, Atl	.255	94	24	2	9
Herr, Phi	.260	100	26	1	12	Van Slyke, Pit	.198	96	19	1	10
Howell Jk, Cal	.259	85	22	4	10	Wallach, Mon	.263	99	26	3	16
Jackson B, KC	.241	83	20	5	11	Whitaker, Det	.220	82	18	7	21
Jacoby, Cle	.264	91	24	3	14	White D, Cal	.212	85	18	0	4
James C, SD	.215	79	17	2	11	Wilson G, Hou	.322	87	28	2	15
James D, Cle	.237	76	18	0	7	Wilson M, Tor	.207	87	18	0	6
Jefferies, NYN	.165	79	13	0	4	Young G, Hou	.216	97	21	0	6
Johnson H, NYN	.250	84	21	5	12	Yount, Mil	.337	83	28	0	17

WHAT IS THE AVERAGE OFFENSIVE PERFORMANCE FROM EACH POSITION? (p. 84)

By League — Per 600 Plate Appearances

American League

Position	Avg	OBA	SLG	AB	H	2B	3B	HR	RBI	BB	K
As c	.249	.310	.360	538	134	22	2	11	62	46	88
As 1b	.269	.350	.430	524	141	25	2	18	77	65	73
As 2b	.273	.336	.363	531	145	24	3	6	54	51	61
As 3b	.263	.330	.380	536	141	24	3	11	54	51	86
As ss	.247	.299	.334	543	134	22	4	6	49	39	70
As lf	.266	.329	.402	539	143	23	4	14	70	49	90
As cf	.264	.327	.386	539	142	23	5	11	58	49	95
As rf	.266	.327	.416	541	144	24	4	16	72	49	103
As dh	.256	.322	.392	536	137	26	2	15	70	53	95

National League

Position	Avg	OBA	SLG	AB	H	2B	3B	HR	RBI	BB	K
As c	.236	.299	.335	541	127	22	2	9	57	47	81
As 1b	.271	.354	.429	523	141	26	3	17	75	67	91
As 2b	.261	.326	.366	535	140	23	4	8	48	51	70
As 3b	.251	.312	.392	541	136	29	4	14	63	49	86
As ss	.249	.300	.348	546	136	24	4	8	52	41	76
As lf	.268	.347	.420	527	141	26	5	15	64	63	84
As cf	.251	.313	.352	541	136	22	4	8	49	48	90
As rf	.257	.326	.409	535	138	26	3	16	70	55	96
As p	.139	.177	.177	521	72	11	1	2	27	23	181

WHICH HITTERS PERFORM BEST AGAINST THE TOP PITCHERS? (p. 86)

Top American League pitchers (top 10 in ERA and top five in saves): Saberhagen KC, Finley Cal, Moore Oak, Blyleven Cal, McCaskill Cal, Bosio Mil, Welch Oak, Gubicza KC, Cerutti Tor, Candiotti Cle, Russell Tex, Thigpen Chi, Schooler Sea, Plesac Mil, Eckersley Oak

Top National League pitchers: Garrelts SF, Hershiser LA, Langston Mon, Whitson SD, Hurst SD, Drabek Pit, Smiley Pit, Belcher LA, Fernandez NY, Smith Mon, Davis SD, Williams Chi, Franco Cin, Burke Mon, Howell LA

Batters in Both Leagues — Listed Alphabetically
(70 or more at bats against the top pitchers)

Player, Team	AB	H	HR	RBI	Avg	Player, Team	AB	H	HR	RBI	Avg
Alomar R, SD	76	15	1	3	.197	Johnson H, NYN	100	27	8	18	.270
Benzinger, Cin	97	29	4	11	.299	Jordan, Phi	85	17	1	5	.200
Biggio, Hou	70	16	1	7	.229	Lansford, Oak	85	26	0	6	.306
Blauser, Atl	79	18	1	9	.228	Law V, ChN	73	14	0	4	.192
Boggs W, Bos	85	18	0	3	.212	Leonard J, Sea	84	18	2	7	.214
Bonds, Pit	76	16	1	5	.211	Lind, Pit	77	15	0	2	.195
Bonilla B, Pit	79	17	2	9	.215	Mattingly, NYA	74	20	2	9	.270
Bradley P, Bal	81	34	1	8	.420	McDowell O, Atl	82	21	3	5	.256
Braggs, Mil	73	19	3	6	.260	McReynolds, NYN	90	25	3	3	.278
Browne J, Cle	95	22	1	5	.232	Mitchell K, SF	75	25	9	18	.333
Brunansky, StL	72	16	2	9	.222	Molitor, Mil	85	28	0	6	.329
Bush, Min	72	17	2	7	.236	Murphy Dl, Atl	95	19	3	7	.200
Butler, SF	81	24	1	3	.296	Murray E, LA	87	23	3	7	.264
Calderon, ChA	81	23	2	9	.284	Newman A, Min	70	16	0	4	.229
Caminiti, Hou	91	15	2	6	.165	O'Brien P, Cle	79	16	1	7	.203
Carter J, Cle	99	28	5	16	.283	O'Neill, Cin	71	19	2	12	.268
Clark W, SF	78	29	3	18	.372	Oquendo, StL	82	21	0	6	.256
Coleman, StL	76	22	0	4	.289	Parker D, Oak	80	16	2	6	.200
Coles, Sea	73	16	3	12	.219	Pendleton, StL	78	20	2	5	.256
Davis A, Sea	70	20	1	4	.286	Puckett, Min	100	29	2	11	.290
Davis E, Cin	78	17	2	6	.218	Raines, Mon	74	21	1	5	.284
Davis G, Hou	95	18	6	11	.189	Ramirez R, Hou	83	21	0	5	.253
Dawson, ChN	87	24	7	14	.276	Randolph, LA	88	18	0	5	.205
Deer, Mil	70	19	8	17	.271	Reed Jd, Bos	72	16	0	4	.222
Dunston, ChN	71	24	0	4	.338	Reynolds H, Sea	80	25	0	5	.313
Elster, NYN	85	21	2	12	.247	Ripken C, Bal	93	19	1	10	.204
Esasky, Bos	74	19	4	13	.257	Samuel, NYN	111	24	1	8	.216
Fernandez T, Tor	71	18	2	7	.254	Sandberg, ChN	109	29	5	8	.266
Gaetti, Min	70	19	2	6	.271	Sax S, NYA	74	23	0	7	.311
Gallagher, ChA	74	20	1	5	.270	Seitzer, KC	75	18	0	1	.240
Gladden, Min	70	20	1	4	.286	Sierra, Tex	76	18	2	7	.237
Grace, ChN	78	30	3	15	.385	Smith Lo, Atl	77	19	5	13	.247
Greenwell, Bos	77	25	0	12	.325	Smith O, StL	84	19	0	8	.226
Griffin Alf, LA	87	28	0	8	.322	Strawberry, NYN	80	13	2	10	.162
Guerrero, StL	76	18	3	10	.237	Thomas A, Atl	92	15	2	6	.163
Guillen, ChA	76	20	0	8	.263	Thompson M, StL	70	16	1	10	.229
Gwynn T, SD	74	26	1	8	.351	Thompson Ro, SF	82	17	3	5	.207
Hamilton J, LA	90	16	2	4	.178	Wallach, Mon	70	14	1	6	.200
Hayes V, Phi	89	23	3	6	.258	Walton, ChN	92	23	1	11	.250
Henderson D, Oak	75	18	1	9	.240	Whitaker, Det	79	27	5	17	.342
Henderson R, Oak	81	23	3	9	.284	Worthington, Bal	80	16	2	7	.200
Herr, Phi	92	23	1	7	.250	Young G, Hou	83	24	0	5	.289
Jacoby, Cle	72	17	1	8	.236	Yount, Mil	83	23	4	9	.277
James C, SD	90	21	3	13	.233						
Jefferies, NYN	80	20	2	7	.250						

WHO ARE THE MAJOR LEAGUE LEADERS IN GO-AHEAD RBIS? (p. 88)

Both Leagues — Listed Alphabetically (50 total RBI or more)

Player, Team	Go-ahead RBI	Tot RBI	%	GW RBI
Alomar R, SD	11	56	19.6	7
Baines, Tex	21	72	29.2	12
Balboni, NYA	18	59	30.5	5
Barfield Je, NYA	11	67	16.4	5
Bell Geo, Tor	30	104	28.8	16
Benzinger, Cin	17	76	22.4	9
Biggio, Hou	11	60	18.3	8
Boggs W, Bos	8	54	14.8	4
Bonds, Pit	8	58	13.8	2
Bonilla B, Pit	24	86	27.9	18
Bradley P, Bal	12	55	21.8	3
Braggs, Mil	14	66	21.2	7
Brett, KC	14	80	17.5	6
Briley, Sea	11	52	21.2	7
Brock, Mil	7	52	13.5	5
Brooks, Mon	24	70	34.3	14
Brunansky, StL	11	85	12.9	6
Buechele, Tex	12	59	20.3	5
Burks, Bos	18	61	29.5	12
Bush, Min	13	54	24.1	10
Calderon, ChA	25	87	28.7	10
Caminiti, Hou	20	72	27.8	11
Canseco, Oak	14	57	24.6	8
Carter J, Cle	29	105	27.6	14
Clark Jk, SD	23	94	24.5	13
Clark W, SF	39	111	35.1	20
Coles, Sea	11	59	18.6	6
Davis A, Sea	25	95	26.3	14
Davis C, Cal	27	90	30.0	17
Davis E, Cin	22	101	21.8	12
Davis G, Hou	18	89	20.2	7
Dawson, ChN	25	77	32.5	14
Deer, Mil	11	65	16.9	4
Doran, Hou	22	58	37.9	12
Downing, Cal	14	59	23.7	7
Dunston, ChN	12	60	20.0	7
Eisenreich, KC	17	59	28.8	10
Elster, NYN	18	55	32.7	8
Esasky, Bos	16	108	14.8	7
Evans Dw, Bos	13	100	13.0	9
Fernandez T, Tor	14	64	21.9	9
Fisk, ChA	17	68	25.0	9
Franco Ju, Tex	14	92	15.2	7
Gaetti, Min	12	75	16.0	5
Galarraga, Mon	20	85	23.5	11
Grace, ChN	26	79	32.9	11
Greenwell, Bos	24	95	25.3	8
Griffey Jr, Sea	18	61	29.5	10
Gruber, Tor	20	73	27.4	11
Guerrero, StL	40	117	34.2	19
Guillen, ChA	12	54	22.2	7
Gwynn T, SD	25	62	40.3	12
Hall M, NYA	13	58	22.4	6
Hamilton J, LA	9	56	16.1	4
Harper B, Min	12	57	21.1	5
Hatcher B, Pit	11	51	21.6	4
Hayes V, Phi	15	78	19.2	5
Henderson D, Oak	24	80	30.0	14
Henderson R, Oak	13	57	22.8	8
Howell Jk, Cal	8	52	15.4	5
Hrbek, Min	20	84	23.8	10
Incaviglia, Tex	17	81	21.0	13
Jackson B, KC	26	105	24.8	12
Jacoby, Cle	17	64	26.6	11
James C, SD	18	65	27.7	12
Jefferies, NYN	14	56	25.0	5
Johnson H, NYN	24	101	23.8	14
Jordan, Phi	20	75	26.7	6
Joyner, Cal	20	79	25.3	13
Lansford, Oak	13	52	25.0	8
Leonard J, Sea	24	93	25.8	9
Liriano, Tor	8	53	15.1	5
Lyons S, ChA	8	50	16.0	5
Manrique, Tex	12	52	23.1	7
Mattingly, NYA	31	113	27.4	15
McGriff F, Tor	18	92	19.6	11
McGwire, Oak	24	95	25.3	13
McReynolds, NYN	25	85	29.4	18
Mitchell K, SF	36	125	28.8	18
Molitor, Mil	21	56	37.5	13
Murphy Dl, Atl	16	84	19.0	11
Murray E, LA	26	88	29.5	11
O'Brien P, Cle	17	55	30.9	4
O'Neill, Cin	11	74	14.9	6
Orsulak, Bal	14	55	25.5	8
Palmeiro, Tex	26	64	40.6	12
Parker D, Oak	22	97	22.7	10
Parrish Ln, Cal	13	50	26.0	3
Pendleton, StL	17	74	23.0	11
Puckett, Min	28	85	32.9	13
Raines, Mon	10	60	16.7	8
Ramirez R, Hou	14	54	25.9	10
Ray, Cal	19	62	30.6	12
Ripken C, Bal	28	93	30.1	14
Sandberg, ChN	18	76	23.7	8
Santiago, SD	15	62	24.2	9
Sax S, NYA	13	63	20.6	7
Sierra, Tex	25	119	21.0	14
Smith Dw, ChN	13	52	25.0	7
Smith Lo, Atl	19	79	24.1	9
Smith O, StL	11	50	22.0	8
Snyder C, Cle	16	59	27.1	8
Stillwell, KC	8	54	14.8	2
Strawberry, NYN	18	77	23.4	5
Surhoff BJ, Mil	8	55	14.5	5
Tartabull, KC	19	62	30.6	12
Tettleton, Bal	15	65	23.1	10
Thomas A, Atl	7	57	12.3	5
Thompson M, StL	20	68	29.4	14
Thompson Ro, SF	10	50	20.0	5
Thon, Phi	15	60	25.0	8
Van Slyke, Pit	14	53	26.4	3
Wallach, Mon	17	77	22.1	5
Whitaker, Det	30	85	35.3	10
White D, Cal	13	56	23.2	5
Whitt, Tor	10	53	18.9	6
Williams MD, SF	5	50	10.0	3
Wilson G, Hou	14	64	21.9	5
Worthington, Bal	12	70	17.1	7
Yount, Mil	22	103	21.4	12

WHICH HITTERS ARE AT HOME ON THE ROAD? (p. 90)

Both Leagues — Listed Alphabetically (502 or more plate appearances)

Player, Team	Hm Rd Diff	Player, Team	Hm Rd Diff	Player, Team	Hm Rd Diff
Alomar R, SD	.329 .267 .062	Greenwell, Bos	.325 .291 .034	Raines, Mon	.271 .301 -.030
Baines, Tex	.296 .322 -.026	Griffey Jr, Sea	.261 .266 -.004	Ramirez R, Hou	.246 .245 .001
Barfield Je, NYA	.241 .227 .014	Griffin Alf, LA	.252 .242 .010	Randolph, LA	.305 .261 .043
Bell Geo, Tor	.306 .289 .017	Gruber, Tor	.295 .285 .010	Ray, Cal	.265 .313 -.048
Benzinger, Cin	.278 .214 .063	Guerrero, StL	.288 .332 -.044	Reed Jd, Bos	.300 .276 .024
Biggio, Hou	.233 .281 -.048	Guillen, ChA	.240 .266 -.026	Reynolds H, Sea	.300 .301 -.001
Blauser, Atl	.249 .291 -.042	Gwynn T, SD	.326 .345 -.019	Ripken C, Bal	.247 .266 -.020
Boggs W, Bos	.377 .287 .090	Hamilton J, LA	.232 .256 -.024	Samuel, NYN	.230 .240 -.009
Bonds, Pit	.204 .290 -.086	Hatcher B, Pit	.234 .228 .006	Sandberg, ChN	.297 .284 .013
Bonilla B, Pit	.311 .253 .058	Hayes V, Phi	.249 .269 -.020	Sax S, NYA	.324 .306 .018
Bradley P, Bal	.286 .269 .017	Henderson D, Oak	.280 .221 .060	Seitzer, KC	.311 .252 .059
Braggs, Mil	.211 .289 -.078	Henderson R, Oak	.289 .260 .028	Sierra, Tex	.317 .295 .022
Brett, KC	.275 .289 -.014	Herr, Phi	.285 .289 -.003	Smith Lo, Atl	.358 .277 .081
Brooks, Mon	.288 .248 .040	Howell Jk, Cal	.236 .221 .015	Smith O, StL	.253 .294 -.041
Browne J, Cle	.332 .262 .070	Jackson B, KC	.234 .277 -.043	Snyder C, Cle	.207 .222 -.015
Brunansky, StL	.232 .246 -.014	Jacoby, Cle	.266 .277 -.011	Stillwell, KC	.226 .293 -.067
Buechele, Tex	.225 .243 -.019	James C, SD	.267 .224 .042	Strawberry, NYN	.272 .183 .090
Butler, SF	.304 .262 .042	Jefferies, NYN	.287 .232 .054	Tartabull, KC	.280 .256 .025
Calderon, ChA	.248 .318 -.070	Johnson H, NYN	.290 .285 .005	Templeton, SD	.259 .251 .008
Caminiti, Hou	.256 .253 .003	Jordan, Phi	.274 .296 -.021	Thomas A, Atl	.195 .228 -.033
Carter J, Cle	.243 .242 .001	Joyner, Cal	.273 .290 -.017	Thompson M, StL	.303 .277 .025
Clark Jk, SD	.232 .250 -.018	Lansford, Oak	.309 .360 -.051	Thompson Ro, SF	.266 .215 .051
Clark W, SF	.325 .341 -.016	Larkin G, Min	.259 .275 -.016	Trammell, Det	.250 .235 .015
Coleman, StL	.260 .248 .012	Leonard J, Sea	.260 .250 .010	Treadway, Atl	.261 .293 -.032
Coles, Sea	.286 .224 .062	Lind, Pit	.220 .245 -.025	Van Slyke, Pit	.213 .258 -.045
Davis A, Sea	.365 .245 .120	Mattingly, NYA	.334 .271 .064	Wallach, Mon	.318 .237 .081
Davis C, Cal	.248 .294 -.046	McDowell O, Atl	.289 .247 .041	Walton, ChN	.303 .283 .020
Davis E, Cin	.289 .275 .014	McGriff F, Tor	.282 .255 .027	Whitaker, Det	.264 .241 .023
Davis G, Hou	.317 .221 .096	McGwire, Oak	.232 .230 .002	White D, Cal	.243 .248 -.005
Deer, Mil	.201 .220 -.019	McReynolds, NYN	.266 .277 -.010	Wilson M, Tor	.223 .279 -.056
Doran, Hou	.252 .187 .065	Mitchell K, SF	.298 .285 .013	Worthington, Bal	.262 .232 .029
Downing, Cal	.296 .272 .024	Molitor, Mil	.328 .304 .024	Young G, Hou	.247 .218 .029
Dunston, ChN	.307 .252 .055	Moseby, Tor	.180 .254 -.073	Yount, Mil	.307 .328 -.021
Dykstra, Phi	.252 .224 .028	Murphy Dl, Atl	.257 .201 .056		
Eisenreich, KC	.307 .279 .028	Murray E, LA	.253 .242 .012		
Elster, NYN	.226 .238 -.012	Newman A, Min	.259 .248 .011		
Esasky, Bos	.300 .253 .048	O'Brien P, Cle	.287 .235 .052		
Espinoza, NYA	.299 .267 .032	Oquendo, StL	.301 .282 .019		
Espy, Tex	.272 .242 .030	Owen S, Mon	.274 .199 .074		
Evans Dw, Bos	.273 .295 -.022	Palmeiro, Tex	.259 .291 -.032		
Fermin, Cle	.226 .249 -.023	Parker D, Oak	.279 .249 .030		
Fernandez T, Tor	.239 .273 -.034	Pendleton, StL	.271 .258 .013		
Fletcher S, ChA	.256 .250 .006	Pettis, Det	.265 .248 .017		
Franco Ju, Tex	.356 .278 .078	Phillips, Oak	.271 .253 .018		
Gaetti, Min	.249 .253 -.004	Puckett, Min	.390 .283 .107		
Galarraga, Mon	.241 .273 -.031				
Gallagher, ChA	.270 .263 .007				
Grace, ChN	.337 .290 .048				

WHICH PLAYERS CREATE THE MOST RUNS? (p. 93)

In the chart below, the abbreviations are: RC - runs created and Off Win % - offensive winning percentage.

Both Leagues — Listed Alphabetically (502 or more plate appearances)

Player, Team	RC	Off Win %	Player, Team	RC	Off Win %	Player, Team	RC	Off Win %
Alomar R, SD	84.7	.583	Gruber, Tor	77.3	.584	Sandberg, ChN	108.7	.735
Baines, Tex	92.0	.708	Guerrero, StL	108.7	.757	Sax S, NYA	91.1	.573
Barfield Je, NYA	78.5	.584	Guillen, ChA	49.4	.290	Seitzer, KC	84.8	.569
Bell Geo, Tor	89.2	.592	Gwynn T, SD	101.4	.707	Sierra, Tex	121.6	.735
Benzinger, Cin	70.0	.481	Hamilton J, LA	54.9	.428	Smith Lo, Atl	112.9	.824
Biggio, Hou	64.6	.615	Hatcher B, Pit	43.6	.372	Smith O, StL	76.2	.560
Blauser, Atl	62.0	.590	Hayes V, Phi	103.1	.737	Snyder C, Cle	41.3	.292
Boggs W, Bos	122.2	.746	Henderson D, Oak	69.4	.474	Stillwell, KC	59.6	.522
Bonds, Pit	92.3	.655	Henderson R, Oak	109.9	.731	Strawberry, NYN	72.0	.627
Bonilla B, Pit	107.6	.714	Herr, Phi	73.5	.585	Tartabull, KC	73.6	.651
Bradley P, Bal	86.8	.628	Howell Jk, Cal	59.6	.492	Templeton, SD	46.5	.386
Braggs, Mil	58.5	.439	Jackson B, KC	77.2	.588	Thomas A, Atl	35.0	.212
Brett, KC	70.9	.606	Jacoby, Cle	74.5	.571	Thompson M, StL	73.3	.600
Brooks, Mon	64.7	.514	James C, SD	44.9	.378	Thompson Ro, SF	74.8	.584
Browne J, Cle	90.1	.611	Jefferies, NYN	61.0	.514	Trammell, Det	49.9	.433
Brunansky, StL	69.5	.530	Johnson H, NYN	127.0	.807	Treadway, Atl	56.4	.530
Buechele, Tex	49.6	.379	Jordan, Phi	62.4	.528	Van Slyke, Pit	54.8	.487
Butler, SF	78.1	.573	Joyner, Cal	82.4	.568	Wallach, Mon	76.7	.578
Calderon, ChA	87.1	.572	Lansford, Oak	88.2	.650	Walton, ChN	64.0	.603
Caminiti, Hou	70.1	.530	Larkin G, Min	60.1	.534	Whitaker, Det	91.3	.672
Carter J, Cle	89.0	.545	Leonard J, Sea	72.3	.508	White D, Cal	64.8	.384
Clark Jk, SD	95.3	.765	Lind, Pit	48.8	.330	Wilson M, NYN	17.4	.255
Clark W, SF	136.4	.839	Mattingly, NYA	104.2	.665	Wilson M, Tor	27.7	.491
Coleman, StL	69.6	.537	McDowell O, Cle	22.8	.341	Worthington, Bal	65.3	.526
Coles, Sea	54.2	.394	McDowell O, Atl	48.5	.722	Young G, Hou	51.2	.376
Davis A, Sea	109.0	.776	McGriff F, Tor	120.8	.760	Yount, Mil	125.3	.764
Davis C, Cal	80.1	.570	McGwire, Oak	76.4	.576			
Davis E, Cin	91.9	.748	McReynolds, NYN	80.0	.631			
Davis G, Hou	102.2	.715	Mitchell K, SF	135.8	.843			
Deer, Mil	59.4	.483	Molitor, Mil	106.0	.681			
Doran, Hou	54.4	.448	Moseby, Tor	57.7	.435			
Downing, Cal	82.7	.626	Murphy Dl, Atl	63.4	.464			
Dunston, ChN	58.8	.545	Murray E, LA	84.4	.604			
Dykstra, Phi	61.9	.505	Newman A, Min	51.9	.447			
Eisenreich, KC	73.4	.623	O'Brien P, Cle	77.2	.563			
Elster, NYN	44.9	.393	Oquendo, StL	81.0	.629			
Esasky, Bos	99.8	.690	Owen S, Mon	52.7	.510			
Espinoza, NYA	47.8	.356	Palmeiro, Tex	73.6	.537			
Espy, Tex	52.2	.418	Parker D, Oak	68.3	.492			
Evans Dw, Bos	100.1	.713	Pendleton, StL	71.8	.516			
Fermin, Cle	39.6	.259	Pettis, Det	58.4	.501			
Fernandez T, Tor	66.1	.457	Phillips, Oak	52.9	.447			
Fletcher S, ChA	60.0	.427	Puckett, Min	106.9	.690			
Franco Ju, Tex	95.2	.680	Raines, Mon	95.6	.737			
Gaetti, Min	55.8	.439	Ramirez R, Hou	49.4	.390			
Galarraga, Mon	80.8	.607	Randolph, LA	69.7	.565			
Gallagher, ChA	61.7	.401	Ray, Cal	62.1	.475			
Grace, ChN	96.7	.757	Reed Jd, Bos	80.9	.609			
Greenwell, Bos	90.9	.639	Reynolds H, Sea	83.5	.569			
Griffey Jr, Sea	64.9	.575	Ripken C, Bal	78.9	.486			
Griffin Alf, LA	45.3	.370	Samuel, NYN	58.1	.461			

WHO ARE THE MOST CONSISTENT GROUNDBALL HITTERS IN BASEBALL — AND WHO ARE THE BEST FLYBALL HITTERS? (p. 96)

In the table below, Grd stands for total groundballs hit during the season (both hits and outs). Fly includes all flyballs hit (both hits and outs). G/F is the the groundball flyball ratio (groundballs divided by flyballs).

Listed Alphabetically by league (502 or more plate appearances)

American League

Player, Team	Grd	Fly	G/F
Baines, Tex	205	113	1.81
Barfield Je, NYA	162	139	1.17
Bell Geo, Tor	196	238	0.82
Boggs W, Bos	291	140	2.08
Bradley P, Bal	231	117	1.97
Braggs, Mil	195	136	1.43
Brett, KC	184	151	1.22
Browne J, Cle	244	169	1.44
Buechele, Tex	168	129	1.30
Calderon, ChA	229	180	1.27
Carter J, Cle	155	277	0.56
Coles, Sea	187	182	1.03
Davis A, Sea	169	179	0.94
Davis C, Cal	216	149	1.45
Deer, Mil	101	144	0.70
Downing, Cal	182	180	1.01
Eisenreich, KC	195	165	1.18
Esasky, Bos	173	180	0.96
Espinoza, NYA	206	108	1.91
Espy, Tex	175	97	1.80
Evans Dw, Bos	167	181	0.92
Fermin, Cle	296	71	4.17
Fernandez T, Tor	219	187	1.17
Fletcher S, ChA	250	130	1.92
Franco Ju, Tex	218	146	1.49
Gaetti, Min	177	156	1.13
Gallagher, ChA	234	172	1.36
Gladden, Min	191	138	1.38
Greenwell, Bos	249	162	1.54
Griffey Jr, Sea	161	124	1.30
Gruber, Tor	198	176	1.13
Guillen, ChA	271	160	1.69
Henderson D, Oak	157	190	0.83
Henderson R, Oak	194	171	1.13
Howell Jk, Cal	136	136	1.00
Jackson B, KC	143	134	1.07
Jacoby, Cle	186	153	1.22
Joyner, Cal	186	241	0.77
Lansford, Oak	256	133	1.92
Larkin G, Min	174	129	1.35
Leonard J, Sea	165	185	0.89
Mattingly, NYA	229	224	1.02
McGriff F, Tor	174	155	1.12
McGwire, Oak	128	193	0.66
Molitor, Mil	251	170	1.48
Moseby, Tor	165	155	1.06
Newman A, Min	206	102	2.02
O'Brien P, Cle	220	182	1.21
Palmeiro, Tex	221	159	1.39
Parker D, Oak	211	166	1.27
Pettis, Det	179	74	2.42
Phillips, Oak	190	118	1.61
Puckett, Min	314	139	2.26
Ray, Cal	187	182	1.03
Reed Jd, Bos	205	167	1.23
Reynolds H, Sea	276	157	1.76
Ripken C, Bal	261	208	1.25
Sax S, NYA	383	96	3.99
Seitzer, KC	274	157	1.75
Sierra, Tex	224	197	1.14
Snyder C, Cle	139	138	1.01
Stillwell, KC	158	146	1.08
Tartabull, KC	136	115	1.18
Trammell, Det	169	142	1.19
Whitaker, Det	161	198	0.81
White D, Cal	224	161	1.39
Wilson M, Tor	217	107	2.03
Worthington, Bal	176	124	1.42
Yount, Mil	236	191	1.24

National League

Player, Team	Grd	Fly	G/F
Alomar R, SD	280	158	1.77
Benzinger, Cin	221	196	1.13
Biggio, Hou	177	127	1.39
Blauser, Atl	143	136	1.05
Bonds, Pit	194	188	1.03
Bonilla B, Pit	226	203	1.11
Brooks, Mon	182	156	1.17
Brunansky, StL	152	221	0.69
Butler, SF	242	150	1.61
Caminiti, Hou	208	173	1.20
Clark Jk, SD	115	130	0.88
Clark W, SF	166	187	0.89
Coleman, StL	239	124	1.93
Davis E, Cin	154	131	1.18
Davis G, Hou	183	192	0.95
Doran, Hou	188	176	1.07
Dunston, ChN	180	135	1.33
Dykstra, Phi	197	164	1.20
Elster, NYN	160	138	1.16
Galarraga, Mon	212	120	1.77
Grace, ChN	222	134	1.66
Griffin Alf, LA	218	127	1.72
Guerrero, StL	201	180	1.12
Gwynn T, SD	304	145	2.10
Hamilton J, LA	195	189	1.03
Hatcher B, Pit	206	135	1.53
Hayes V, Phi	183	166	1.10
Herr, Phi	237	136	1.74
James C, SD	190	139	1.37
Jefferies, NYN	204	124	1.65
Johnson H, NYN	128	202	0.63
Jordan, Phi	210	157	1.34
Lind, Pit	265	160	1.66
McDowell O, Atl	170	154	1.10
McReynolds, NYN	156	196	0.80
Mitchell K, SF	140	198	0.71
Murphy Dl, Atl	198	168	1.18
Murray E, LA	212	207	1.02
Oquendo, StL	201	175	1.15
Owen S, Mon	166	151	1.10
Pendleton, StL	245	175	1.40
Raines, Mon	212	148	1.43
Ramirez R, Hou	222	157	1.41
Randolph, LA	233	151	1.54
Samuel, NYN	200	119	1.68
Sandberg, ChN	252	172	1.47
Smith Lo, Atl	126	157	0.80
Smith O, StL	269	167	1.61
Strawberry, NYN	133	135	0.99
Templeton, SD	211	122	1.73
Thomas A, Atl	225	185	1.22
Thompson M, StL	250	103	2.43
Thompson Ro, SF	146	175	0.83
Treadway, Atl	180	151	1.19
Van Slyke, Pit	156	139	1.12
Wallach, Mon	210	183	1.15
Walton, ChN	199	97	2.05
Young G, Hou	225	155	1.45

WHICH PLAYERS HOMER TO THE OPPOSITE FIELD MOST OFTEN? (p. 98)

The table below shows the percentage of home runs hit to the opposite field for each player. Op stands for the number of opposite field home runs.

Both Leagues — Listed Alphabetically (eight or more total home runs)

Player, Team	Op	HR	%	Player, Team	Op	HR	%	Player, Team	Op	HR	%
Armas, Cal	2	11	18	Franco Ju, Tex	5	13	38	Moseby, Tor	0	11	0
Baines, Tex	6	16	38	Gaetti, Min	3	19	16	Murphy Dl, Atl	5	20	25
Balboni, NYA	0	17	0	Gagne, Min	1	9	11	Murphy Dw, Phi	1	9	11
Barfield Je, NYA	1	23	4	Galarraga, Mon	4	23	17	Murray E, LA	0	20	0
Bell Geo, Tor	0	18	0	Gant, Atl	0	9	0	Nokes, Det	0	9	0
Benzinger, Cin	2	17	12	Geren, NYA	0	9	0	O'Brien P, Cle	0	12	0
Biggio, Hou	1	13	8	Gibson K, LA	1	9	11	O'Neill, Cin	1	15	7
Blauser, Atl	0	12	0	Gladden, Min	0	8	0	Palmeiro, Tex	0	8	0
Bonds, Pit	3	19	16	Grace, ChN	3	13	23	Parker D, Oak	0	22	0
Bonilla B, Pit	1	24	4	Greenwell, Bos	0	14	0	Parrish Ln, Cal	4	17	24
Bradley P, Bal	5	11	45	Griffey, Cin	0	8	0	Pasqua, ChA	1	11	9
Braggs, Mil	0	15	0	Griffey Jr, Sea	2	16	13	Pendleton, StL	2	13	15
Brett, KC	2	12	17	Gruber, Tor	1	18	6	Presley, Sea	0	12	0
Briley, Sea	0	13	0	Guerrero, StL	2	17	12	Puckett, Min	2	9	22
Brock, Mil	0	12	0	Hall M, NYA	1	17	6	Quinones L, Cin	0	12	0
Brooks, Mon	1	14	7	Hamilton J, LA	0	12	0	Raines, Mon	1	9	11
Brunansky, StL	5	20	25	Harper B, Min	0	8	0	Ready, Phi	1	8	13
Buechele, Tex	2	16	13	Hayes C, Phi	1	8	13	Ripken C, Bal	0	21	0
Buhner, Sea	2	9	22	Hayes V, Phi	1	26	4	Salazar L, ChN	0	9	0
Burks, Bos	0	12	0	Heath, Det	2	10	20	Samuel, NYN	1	11	9
Bush, Min	0	14	0	Henderson D, Oak	1	15	7	Sandberg, ChN	2	30	7
Calderon, ChA	4	14	29	Henderson R, Oak	0	12	0	Santiago, SD	3	16	19
Caminiti, Hou	0	10	0	Howell Jk, Cal	6	20	30	Scioscia, LA	0	10	0
Canseco, Oak	2	17	12	Hrbek, Min	5	25	20	Sierra, Tex	3	29	10
Carter J, Cle	3	35	9	Incaviglia, Tex	7	21	33	Smith Dw, ChN	3	9	33
Castillo C, Min	1	8	13	Jackson B, KC	16	32	50	Smith Lo, Atl	2	21	10
Clark D, Cle	2	8	25	Jacoby, Cle	1	13	8	Snyder C, Cle	1	18	6
Clark Jk, SD	5	26	19	James C, SD	2	13	15	Strawberry, NYN	6	29	21
Clark W, SF	5	23	22	Jefferies, NYN	0	12	0	Tartabull, KC	4	18	22
Coles, Sea	0	10	0	Johnson H, NYN	1	36	3	Tettleton, Bal	7	26	27
Cotto, Sea	0	9	0	Jordan, Phi	1	12	8	Thomas A, Atl	1	13	8
Daulton, Phi	1	8	13	Joyner, Cal	4	16	25	Thompson Ro, SF	1	13	8
Davis A, Sea	0	21	0	Kelly, NYA	3	9	33	Thon, Phi	1	15	7
Davis C, Cal	5	22	23	Kittle, ChA	3	11	27	Treadway, Atl	1	8	13
Davis E, Cin	5	34	15	Komminsk, Cle	0	8	0	Van Slyke, Pit	0	9	0
Davis G, Hou	3	34	9	Kruk, Phi	6	8	75	Wallach, Mon	1	13	8
Dawson, ChN	0	21	0	Kunkel, Tex	1	8	13	Ward G, Det	3	9	33
Deer, Mil	2	26	8	Leonard J, Sea	2	24	8	Washington C, Cal	0	13	0
Devereaux, Bal	0	8	0	Lynn, Det	1	11	9	Whitaker, Det	0	28	0
Doran, Hou	0	8	0	Maldonado, SF	0	9	0	White D, Cal	2	12	17
Downing, Cal	2	14	14	Marshall, LA	1	11	9	Whitt, Tor	0	11	0
Dunston, ChN	1	9	11	Mattingly, NYA	1	23	4	Williams MD, SF	2	18	11
Eisenreich, KC	0	9	0	McClendon, ChN	0	12	0	Wilson G, Hou	1	11	9
Elster, NYN	0	10	0	McDowell O, Atl	0	10	0	Worthington, Bal	2	15	13
Esasky, Bos	3	30	10	McGriff F, Tor	10	36	28	Yount, Mil	10	21	48
Evans Da, Atl	0	11	0	McGwire, Oak	4	33	12				
Evans Dw, Bos	0	20	0	McReynolds, NYN	0	22	0				
Felix, Tor	2	9	22	Milligan, Bal	4	12	33				
Fernandez T, Tor	1	11	9	Mitchell K, SF	6	47	13				
Fisk, ChA	0	13	0	Molitor, Mil	1	11	9				

WHO ARE THE BEST LEADOFF HITTERS IN BASEBALL?
(p. 100)

Both Leagues — Listed Alphabetically
(players with 100 plate appearances batting leadoff)

Player, Team	OBA	AB	R	H	BB	HB	SB
Alomar R, SD	.348	164	20	49	12	1	11
Anderson B, Bal	.330	241	38	52	38	3	16
Backman, Min	.287	94	9	22	7	0	0
Boggs W, Bos	.414	497	85	155	86	4	2
Bonds, Pit	.353	426	75	108	67	1	21
Bradley P, Bal	.360	172	20	52	12	4	8
Browne J, Cle	.385	456	67	138	61	1	13
Butler, SF	.347	590	99	166	58	3	30
Coleman, StL	.319	551	93	141	50	2	64
Dascenzo, ChN	.230	134	19	22	12	0	6
Dernier, Phi	.225	104	15	18	7	0	2
Devereaux, Bal	.324	186	24	48	17	2	13
Downing, Cal	.353	216	25	62	19	4	0
Duncan, Cin	.265	139	21	31	5	3	4
Dykstra, Phi	.312	482	57	113	54	2	27
Eisenreich, KC	.349	99	16	30	7	0	8
Espy, Tex	.301	439	57	107	35	2	40
Felder, Mil	.328	111	19	29	11	0	7
Felix, Tor	.332	307	52	85	25	2	14
Gallagher, ChA	.309	340	43	88	23	2	0
Gant, Atl	.214	160	18	29	7	0	7
Gladden, Min	.310	184	23	51	8	2	10
Griffin Alf, LA	.283	291	35	69	19	0	6
Guillen, ChA	.271	214	25	53	7	0	15
Harris L, LA	.248	101	10	22	4	0	3
Hatcher B, Pit	.292	277	38	65	21	2	13
Henderson R, Oak	.411	539	112	147	126	3	76
Jefferies, NYN	.380	165	30	56	12	0	7
Johnson L, ChA	.345	132	20	37	13	0	13
Martinez Da, Mon	.338	215	31	63	15	0	12
McDowell O, Atl	.333	433	77	117	40	1	22
Molitor, Mil	.366	475	63	140	53	4	19
Moseby, Tor	.310	272	36	59	33	4	14
Newman A, Min	.317	321	47	78	35	1	22
Nixon O, Mon	.304	167	20	34	24	0	17
Pettis, Det	.373	436	75	111	82	0	40
Polonia, NYA	.314	199	26	56	10	0	12
Raines, Mon	.399	244	35	71	44	2	23
Randolph, LA	.335	165	19	38	25	2	3
Reed Jd, Bos	.365	148	28	43	17	1	3
Reynolds H, Sea	.357	592	82	178	51	3	24
Roberts Bip, SD	.388	294	69	88	43	1	17
Sabo, Cin	.355	138	22	41	12	1	4
Samuel, NYN	.287	230	36	54	14	3	17
Sax S, NYA	.366	364	49	118	25	1	25
Schofield, Cal	.350	108	22	28	14	1	2
Seitzer, KC	.376	139	19	38	21	3	5
Smith Lo, Atl	.414	113	20	35	18	2	5
Stillwell, KC	.354	147	20	45	10	1	5
Walton, ChN	.334	475	64	139	26	6	24
Washington C, Cal	.328	216	26	61	15	0	9
White D, Cal	.266	104	14	24	5	0	10
Williams K, Det	.211	110	12	21	3	0	5
Wilson M, Tor	.280	180	19	46	5	1	3
Wilson W, KC	.304	235	31	59	20	0	15
Winningham, Cin	.340	136	23	37	14	0	9
Young G, Hou	.308	289	38	62	38	2	14

TO WHOM DOES THE GREEN MONSTER BECKON? (p. 102)

The chart below shows the number of flyouts for each player that would have been hits in Fenway over the last two years (1988-1989).

Both Leagues — Listed by Most Would-be Hits
(players with four or more would-be hits)

Player, Team	Fenway Hits	Player, Team	Fenway Hits	Player, Team	Fenway Hits	Player, Team	Fenway Hits
McReynolds, NYN	20	Gant, Atl	8	Nixon O, Mon	6	Daulton, Phi	4
Brett, KC	16	Gwynn T, SD	8	Parker D, Oak	6	Davis Mike, LA	4
Sabo, Cin	15	Hamilton J, LA	8	Pena T, StL	6	Dawson, ChN	4
Davis C, Cal	14	McGwire, Oak	8	Seitzer, KC	6	Evans Dw, Bos	4
Howell Jk, Cal	14	Pasqua, ChA	8	Stillwell, KC	6	Francona, Mil	4
Baines, Tex	13	Pendleton, StL	8	Wallach, Mon	6	Hatcher M, LA	4
Joyner, Cal	13	Ready, Phi	8	Worthington, Bal	6	Heath, Det	4
Ripken C, Bal	13	Reed Jd, Bos	8	Yount, Mil	6	Henderson D, Oak	4
Balboni, NYA	12	Thomas A, Atl	8	Aldrete, Mon	5	Hudler, Mon	4
Biggio, Hou	12	Benedict, Atl	7	Armas, Cal	5	Javier, Oak	4
Boggs W, Bos	12	Brock, Mil	7	Bell B, Tex	5	Kunkel, Tex	4
Daniels, LA	12	Clark W, SF	7	Brantley M, Sea	5	Liriano, Tor	4
Mitchell K, SF	12	Dunston, ChN	7	Brookens, NYA	5	Lombardozzi, Hou	4
Ramirez R, Hou	12	Dykstra, Phi	7	Buhner, Sea	5	Lyons Bar, NYN	4
Benzinger, Cin	11	Eisenreich, KC	7	Davis Jody, Atl	5	Manrique, Tex	4
Brunansky, StL	11	Elster, NYN	7	Deer, Mil	5	McDowell O, Atl	4
Davis A, Sea	11	Gallagher, ChA	7	Diaz B, Cin	5	Melvin, Bal	4
Downing, Cal	11	Hatcher B, Pit	7	Fernandez T, Tor	5	Nokes, Det	4
Kruk, Phi	11	Jackson Dar, SD	7	Franco Ju, Tex	5	Oquendo, StL	4
Magadan, NYN	11	James C, SD	7	Gallego, Oak	5	Palmeiro, Tex	4
Ray, Cal	11	Johnson H, NYN	7	Gibson K, LA	5	Phelps, Oak	4
Schmidt M, Phi	11	Larkin B, Cin	7	Grace, ChN	5	Presley, Sea	4
Tartabull, KC	11	Moseby, Tor	7	Greenwell, Bos	5	Quinones L, Cin	4
Bonds, Pit	10	Murphy Dl, Atl	7	Guillen, ChA	5	Quinones R, Pit	4
Canseco, Oak	10	Perry G, Atl	7	Hall M, NYA	5	Reed Jf, Cin	4
Carter G, NYN	10	Reynolds RJ, Pit	7	Herr, Phi	5	Reynolds H, Sea	4
Carter J, Cle	10	Sandberg, ChN	7	Hrbek, Min	5	Santiago, SD	4
Lansford, Oak	10	Schu, Det	7	Jacoby, Cle	5	Santovenia, Mon	4
Schofield, Cal	10	Shelby, LA	7	Jefferies, NYN	5	Scioscia, LA	4
Strawberry, NYN	10	Slaught, NYA	7	Leach R, Tex	5	Sheets, Bal	4
Teufel, NYN	10	Smith O, StL	7	Leonard J, Sea	5	Steinbach, Oak	4
Van Slyke, Pit	10	Templeton, SD	7	Lynn, Det	5	Thompson M, StL	4
Barrett M, Bos	9	Tettleton, Bal	7	Moreland, Bal	5	Webster M, ChN	4
Bass K, Hou	9	Thompson Ro, SF	7	Murray E, LA	5	Williams MD, SF	4
Brooks, Mon	9	Trammell, Det	7	Randolph, LA	5	Wilson M, Tor	4
Doran, Hou	9	Whitaker, Det	7	Ripken B, Bal	5		
Fisk, ChA	9	White D, Cal	7	Snyder C, Cle	5		
Gaetti, Min	9	White F, KC	7	Tabler, KC	5		
McGriff F, Tor	9	Whitt, Tor	7	Ward G, Det	5		
O'Neill, Cin	9	Boone, KC	6	Washington C, Cal	5		
Oberkfell, SF	9	Burks, Bos	6	Backman, Min	4		
Raines, Mon	9	Caminiti, Hou	6	Berryhill, ChN	4		
Sierra, Tex	9	Coleman, StL	6	Blauser, Atl	4		
Alomar R, SD	8	Coles, Sea	6	Boston, ChA	4		
Barfield Je, NYA	8	Gantner, Mil	6	Buckner, KC	4		
Bell Geo, Tor	8	Griffey, Cin	6	Buechele, Tex	4		
Bonilla B, Pit	8	Gruber, Tor	6	Clark D, Cle	4		
Davis G, Hou	8	James D, Cle	6	Clark Jk, SD	4		
Fletcher S, ChA	8	Lyons S, ChA	6	Darling, NYN	4		

WHO ARE BASEBALL'S MOST (AND LEAST) AGGRESSIVE BASERUNNERS? (p. 104)

Both Leagues — Listed Alphabetically
(40 or more opportunities to advance as a baserunner)

Player, Team	Opp	XB	%
Alomar R, SD	53	35	66.0
Baines, Tex	56	28	50.0
Barfield Je, NYA	50	26	52.0
Benzinger, Cin	55	22	40.0
Boggs W, Bos	83	35	42.2
Bonds, Pit	50	29	58.0
Bonilla B, Pit	52	33	63.5
Bradley P, Bal	47	34	72.3
Braggs, Mil	47	27	57.4
Brooks, Mon	40	16	40.0
Browne J, Cle	44	22	50.0
Brunansky, StL	43	18	41.9
Burks, Bos	43	24	55.8
Butler, SF	46	32	69.6
Calderon, ChA	48	24	50.0
Caminiti, Hou	49	36	73.5
Clark W, SF	55	27	49.1
Coleman, StL	43	25	58.1
Davis A, Sea	62	13	21.0
Davis C, Cal	47	27	57.4
Davis G, Hou	41	20	48.8
Deer, Mil	41	20	48.8
Downing, Cal	57	19	33.3
Esasky, Bos	53	17	32.1
Espinoza, NYA	42	21	50.0
Espy, Tex	40	26	65.0
Evans Dw, Bos	71	32	45.1
Fermin, Cle	45	24	53.3
Fernandez T, Tor	41	21	51.2
Fletcher S, ChA	64	38	59.4
Franco Ju, Tex	44	31	70.5
Gaetti, Min	45	23	51.1
Galarraga, Mon	41	19	46.3
Gallagher, ChA	66	38	57.6
Gantner, Mil	46	18	39.1
Gladden, Min	46	27	58.7
Grace, ChN	44	28	63.6
Greenwell, Bos	54	23	42.6
Griffey Jr, Sea	41	24	58.5
Gruber, Tor	48	26	54.2
Guerrero, StL	42	14	33.3
Gwynn T, SD	53	30	56.6
Hayes V, Phi	43	24	55.8
Henderson D, Oak	49	29	59.2
Henderson R, Oak	64	40	62.5
Herr, Phi	57	22	38.6
Jacoby, Cle	41	15	36.6
Jefferies, NYN	49	26	53.1
Johnson H, NYN	46	30	65.2
Jordan, Phi	42	21	50.0
Joyner, Cal	62	35	56.5
Kelly, NYA	41	27	65.9
Lansford, Oak	61	37	60.7
Larkin G, Min	42	21	50.0
Lyons S, ChA	43	21	48.8
Martinez Crl, ChA	42	15	35.7
Mattingly, NYA	51	26	51.0
McDowell O, Atl	43	30	69.8
McGriff F, Tor	44	17	38.6
McGwire, Oak	46	13	28.3
McReynolds, NYN	42	25	59.5
Molitor, Mil	62	26	41.9
Murphy Dl, Atl	44	18	40.9
Murray E, LA	40	10	25.0
Newman A, Min	46	26	56.5
O'Brien P, Cle	49	27	55.1
Oquendo, StL	57	27	47.4
Orsulak, Bal	41	21	51.2
Palmeiro, Tex	68	34	50.0
Pendleton, StL	57	33	57.9
Pettis, Det	41	32	78.0
Phillips, Oak	40	24	60.0
Polonia, NYA	42	35	83.3
Puckett, Min	51	28	54.9
Randolph, LA	59	35	59.3
Ray, Cal	46	26	56.5
Reed Jd, Bos	67	36	53.7
Reynolds H, Sea	56	31	55.4
Ripken C, Bal	46	30	65.2
Roberts Bip, SD	48	34	70.8
Sandberg, ChN	66	38	57.6
Sax S, NYA	62	36	58.1
Seitzer, KC	61	37	60.7
Sierra, Tex	56	31	55.4
Smith Lo, Atl	40	27	67.5
Smith O, StL	57	36	63.2
Tartabull, KC	40	16	40.0
Tettleton, Bal	43	24	55.8
Thompson M, StL	40	30	75.0
Treadway, Atl	43	20	46.5
Vizquel, Sea	40	20	50.0
Wallach, Mon	43	19	44.2
Whitaker, Det	55	28	50.9
White D, Cal	42	30	71.4
Young G, Hou	40	25	62.5
Yount, Mil	56	32	57.1

WHICH HITTERS ARE EASIEST TO DOUBLE UP? (p. 106)

Both Leagues — Listed Alphabetically (81 or more GDP opportunites)

Batter, Team	Opp	DP	DP %	Batter, Team	Opp	DP	DP %	Batter, Team	Opp	DP	DP %
Alomar R, SD	124	10	8.1	Greenwell, Bos	169	21	12.4	Palmeiro, Tex	127	18	14.2
Baines, Tex	127	15	11.8	Griffey Jr, Sea	94	4	4.3	Parker D, Oak	112	21	18.8
Barfield Je, NYA	110	8	7.3	Gruber, Tor	100	13	13.0	Parrish Ln, Cal	100	10	10.0
Bell Geo, Tor	113	18	15.9	Guerrero, StL	113	17	15.0	Pena T, StL	94	19	20.2
Benzinger, Cin	105	5	4.8	Guillen, ChA	120	8	6.7	Pendleton, StL	143	16	11.2
Biggio, Hou	99	7	7.1	Gwynn T, SD	147	12	8.2	Pettis, Det	85	14	16.5
Blauser, Atl	89	7	7.9	Hamilton J, LA	111	10	9.0	Phillips, Oak	98	17	17.3
Boggs W, Bos	122	19	15.6	Hayes V, Phi	139	7	5.0	Puckett, Min	168	21	12.5
Bonds, Pit	84	8	9.5	Heath, Det	82	18	22.0	Raines, Mon	89	8	9.0
Bonilla B, Pit	109	10	9.2	Heep, Bos	90	13	14.4	Ramirez R, Hou	87	8	9.2
Boone, KC	95	16	16.8	Henderson D, Oak	123	13	10.6	Randolph, LA	88	10	11.4
Bradley P, Bal	88	12	13.6	Henderson R, Oak	81	8	9.9	Ray, Cal	105	14	13.3
Braggs, Mil	122	13	10.7	Herr, Phi	98	9	9.2	Reed Jd, Bos	117	12	10.3
Brett, KC	133	18	13.5	Howell Jk, Cal	103	8	7.8	Reynolds H, Sea	95	4	4.2
Briley, Sea	87	9	10.3	Hrbek, Min	97	6	6.2	Reynolds RJ, Pit	87	13	14.9
Brooks, Mon	113	15	13.3	Incaviglia, Tex	110	12	10.9	Ripken C, Bal	142	22	15.5
Browne J, Cle	116	9	7.8	Jackson B, KC	115	10	8.7	Samuel, NYN	90	7	7.8
Brunansky, StL	130	11	8.5	Jacoby, Cle	112	15	13.4	Sandberg, ChN	128	9	7.0
Buechele, Tex	93	21	22.6	James C, SD	114	20	17.5	Santiago, SD	93	9	9.7
Burks, Bos	107	8	7.5	James D, Cle	92	9	9.8	Sax S, NYA	99	19	19.2
Bush, Min	86	16	18.6	Jefferies, NYN	94	16	17.0	Seitzer, KC	127	16	12.6
Butler, SF	82	4	4.9	Johnson H, NYN	127	4	3.1	Sheffield, Mil	85	4	4.7
Calderon, ChA	160	20	12.5	Jordan, Phi	132	19	14.4	Sierra, Tex	152	7	4.6
Caminiti, Hou	113	8	7.1	Joyner, Cal	115	15	13.0	Smith Lo, Atl	100	7	7.0
Carter J, Cle	148	6	4.1	Kelly, NYA	93	9	9.7	Smith O, StL	107	10	9.3
Clark Jk, SD	120	10	8.3	Lansford, Oak	132	21	15.9	Snyder C, Cle	103	11	10.7
Clark W, SF	141	6	4.3	Larkin G, Min	104	13	12.5	Steinbach, Oak	85	14	16.5
Coles, Sea	106	13	12.3	Law V, ChN	90	10	11.1	Stillwell, KC	93	3	3.2
Davis A, Sea	122	15	12.3	Lemon, Det	86	7	8.1	Strawberry, NYN	81	4	4.9
Davis C, Cal	133	21	15.8	Leonard J, Sea	145	12	8.3	Surhoff BJ, Mil	87	8	9.2
Davis E, Cin	114	15	13.2	Lind, Pit	122	13	10.7	Tartabull, KC	92	12	13.0
Davis G, Hou	96	9	9.4	Liriano, Tor	104	10	9.6	Templeton, SD	115	15	13.0
Dawson, ChN	85	16	18.8	Lynn, Det	91	5	5.5	Tettleton, Bal	98	8	8.2
Deer, Mil	103	8	7.8	Lyons S, ChA	100	3	3.0	Thomas A, Atl	96	17	17.7
Doran, Hou	100	8	8.0	Marshall, LA	84	8	9.5	Thompson M, StL	112	12	10.7
Downing, Cal	96	6	6.3	Martinez Crl, ChA	87	14	16.1	Thompson Ro, SF	107	6	5.6
Dunston, ChN	91	7	7.7	Mattingly, NYA	151	15	9.9	Thon, Phi	84	6	7.1
Eisenreich, KC	98	8	8.2	McDowell O, Atl	95	3	3.2	Trammell, Det	104	9	8.7
Elster, NYN	97	13	13.4	McGriff F, Tor	118	14	11.9	Treadway, Atl	81	9	11.1
Esasky, Bos	136	11	8.1	McGwire, Oak	123	23	18.7	Uribe, SF	92	7	7.6
Espinoza, NYA	120	14	11.7	McReynolds, NYN	85	8	9.4	Van Slyke, Pit	104	13	12.5
Evans Dw, Bos	145	16	11.0	Milligan, Bal	99	12	12.1	Wallach, Mon	134	21	15.7
Fermin, Cle	117	15	12.8	Mitchell K, SF	142	6	4.2	Whitaker, Det	117	7	6.0
Fernandez T, Tor	110	9	8.2	Molitor, Mil	98	11	11.2	White D, Cal	144	11	7.6
Fisk, ChA	91	15	16.5	Moreland, Bal	86	21	24.4	White F, KC	86	7	8.1
Fletcher S, ChA	88	12	13.6	Moseby, Tor	95	7	7.4	Whitt, Tor	83	10	12.0
Franco Ju, Tex	110	27	24.5	Murphy Dl, Atl	124	15	12.1	Worthington, Bal	113	10	8.8
Gaetti, Min	120	12	10.0	Murray E, LA	123	12	9.8	Yount, Mil	128	9	7.0
Gagne, Min	99	10	10.1	O'Brien P, Cle	93	10	10.8				
Galarraga, Mon	127	12	9.4	O'Neill, Cin	86	7	8.1				
Gallagher, ChA	81	9	11.1	Oquendo, StL	110	12	10.9				
Gladden, Min	84	6	7.1	Orsulak, Bal	94	9	9.6				
Grace, ChN	119	12	10.1	Owen S, Mon	88	11	12.5				

WHICH BATTERS HAVE THE BIGGEST DAY/NIGHT DIFFERENCES? (p. 108)

Listed Alphabetically by League
(150 plate appearances in the day and 300 plate appearances at night)

American League

Player, Team	Day	Night	Diff
Baines, Tex	.405	.277	.128
Barfield Je, NYA	.195	.253	-.058
Bell Geo, Tor	.245	.321	-.076
Boggs W, Bos	.336	.327	.010
Braggs, Mil	.201	.273	-.072
Browne J, Cle	.291	.303	-.012
Calderon, ChA	.282	.288	-.006
Carter J, Cle	.225	.251	-.026
Davis A, Sea	.371	.281	.090
Deer, Mil	.221	.204	.017
Downing, Cal	.239	.298	-.059
Esasky, Bos	.266	.282	-.016
Espinoza, NYA	.258	.293	-.034
Evans Dw, Bos	.219	.320	-.102
Fermin, Cle	.253	.230	.023
Fernandez T, Tor	.271	.251	.020
Gaetti, Min	.267	.242	.025
Gagne, Min	.282	.267	.014
Gallagher, ChA	.250	.273	-.023
Gladden, Min	.257	.312	-.055
Greenwell, Bos	.322	.301	.021
Gruber, Tor	.259	.305	-.046
Guillen, ChA	.270	.247	.023
Henderson D, Oak	.273	.237	.036
Henderson R, Oak	.297	.263	.034
Jacoby, Cle	.236	.290	-.054
James D, Cle	.365	.248	.117
Joyner, Cal	.315	.272	.043
Lansford, Oak	.364	.320	.044
Larkin G, Min	.306	.247	.059
Leonard J, Sea	.211	.269	-.058
Liriano, Tor	.275	.257	.018
Lyons S, ChA	.286	.255	.031
Mattingly, NYA	.333	.288	.045
McGriff F, Tor	.242	.282	-.040
McGwire, Oak	.268	.208	.059
Molitor, Mil	.340	.303	.037
Moseby, Tor	.223	.220	.003
Newman A, Min	.289	.237	.052
O'Brien P, Cle	.266	.257	.010
Parker D, Oak	.269	.261	.008
Phillips, Oak	.271	.256	.015
Puckett, Min	.359	.330	.029
Reed Jd, Bos	.312	.277	.035
Reynolds H, Sea	.284	.305	-.021
Ripken C, Bal	.247	.260	-.013
Sax S, NYA	.266	.337	-.071
Seitzer, KC	.316	.271	.045
Snyder C, Cle	.176	.233	-.057
Steinbach, Oak	.287	.265	.023
Surhoff BJ, Mil	.268	.238	.030
Trammell, Det	.283	.224	.059
Whitaker, Det	.284	.237	.047
White D, Cal	.248	.244	.004
Wilson M, Tor	.220	.266	-.046
Yount, Mil	.356	.298	.058

National League

Player, Team	Day	Night	Diff
Alomar R, SD	.295	.296	-.001
Benzinger, Cin	.226	.254	-.028
Biggio, Hou	.275	.248	.027
Bonds, Pit	.260	.242	.018
Bonilla B, Pit	.280	.281	-.001
Brooks, Mon	.268	.267	.001
Brunansky, StL	.230	.244	-.014
Butler, SF	.255	.300	-.045
Caminiti, Hou	.288	.239	.049
Clark W, SF	.356	.318	.038
Coleman, StL	.270	.246	.024
Davis E, Cin	.242	.300	-.059
Davis G, Hou	.230	.286	-.057
Doran, Hou	.185	.233	-.048
Dykstra, Phi	.224	.242	-.018
Elster, NYN	.251	.220	.032
Galarraga, Mon	.231	.266	-.035
Griffin Alf, LA	.236	.252	-.016
Guerrero, StL	.333	.300	.034
Gwynn T, SD	.365	.325	.040
Hamilton J, LA	.253	.241	.012
Hatcher B, Pit	.261	.219	.042
Hayes V, Phi	.293	.247	.046
Herr, Phi	.302	.282	.020
Jefferies, NYN	.253	.261	-.008
Johnson H, NYN	.305	.279	.026
Jordan, Phi	.273	.290	-.017
Lind, Pit	.203	.246	-.043
McDowell O, Atl	.247	.274	-.027
McReynolds, NYN	.255	.280	-.025
Mitchell K, SF	.283	.296	-.013
Murphy Dl, Atl	.262	.217	.045
Murray E, LA	.239	.251	-.012
O'Neill, Cin	.234	.296	-.062
Oquendo, StL	.246	.313	-.067
Pendleton, StL	.305	.246	.059
Raines, Mon	.292	.284	.008
Ramirez R, Hou	.279	.229	.050
Randolph, LA	.299	.277	.022
Samuel, NYN	.201	.248	-.047
Sandberg, ChN	.319	.257	.062
Smith O, StL	.328	.249	.078
Strawberry, NYN	.258	.208	.050
Templeton, SD	.227	.266	-.039
Thompson M, StL	.251	.309	-.058
Thompson Ro, SF	.220	.257	-.037
Van Slyke, Pit	.266	.224	.043
Wallach, Mon	.270	.281	-.011
Wilson G, Hou	.255	.272	-.017
Young G, Hou	.257	.221	.036

WHICH HITTERS HAVE THE BEST STRIKEOUT TO WALK RATIOS? (p. 111)

Both Leagues — Listed Alphabetically (502 or more plate appearances)

Player, Team	K	BB	K/BB	Player, Team	K	BB	K/BB	Player, Team	K	BB	K/BB
Alomar R, SD	76	53	1.43	Franco Ju, Tex	69	66	1.05	Owen S, Mon	44	76	0.58
Baines, Tex	79	73	1.08	Gaetti, Min	87	25	3.48	Palmeiro, Tex	48	63	0.76
Barfield Je, NYA	150	87	1.72	Galarraga, Mon	158	48	3.29	Parker D, Oak	91	38	2.39
Bell Geo, Tor	60	33	1.82	Gallagher, ChA	79	46	1.72	Pendleton, StL	81	44	1.84
Benzinger, Cin	120	44	2.73	Grace, ChN	42	80	0.52	Pettis, Det	106	84	1.26
Biggio, Hou	64	49	1.31	Greenwell, Bos	44	56	0.79	Phillips, Oak	66	58	1.14
Blauser, Atl	101	38	2.66	Griffey Jr, Sea	83	44	1.89	Puckett, Min	59	41	1.44
Boggs W, Bos	51	107	0.48	Griffin Alf, LA	57	29	1.97	Raines, Mon	48	93	0.52
Bonds, Pit	93	93	1.00	Gruber, Tor	60	30	2.00	Ramirez R, Hou	64	29	2.21
Bonilla B, Pit	93	76	1.22	Guerrero, StL	84	79	1.06	Randolph, LA	51	71	0.72
Bradley P, Bal	103	70	1.47	Guillen, ChA	48	15	3.20	Ray, Cal	30	36	0.83
Braggs, Mil	111	42	2.64	Gwynn T, SD	30	56	0.54	Reed Jd, Bos	44	73	0.60
Brett, KC	47	59	0.80	Hamilton J, LA	71	20	3.55	Reynolds H, Sea	45	55	0.82
Brooks, Mon	108	39	2.77	Hatcher B, Pit	62	30	2.07	Ripken C, Bal	72	57	1.26
Browne J, Cle	64	68	0.94	Hayes V, Phi	103	101	1.02	Samuel, NYN	120	42	2.86
Brunansky, StL	107	59	1.81	Henderson D, Oak	131	54	2.43	Sandberg, ChN	85	59	1.44
Buechele, Tex	107	36	2.97	Henderson R, Oak	68	126	0.54	Sax S, NYA	44	52	0.85
Butler, SF	69	59	1.17	Herr, Phi	63	54	1.17	Seitzer, KC	76	102	0.75
Calderon, ChA	94	43	2.19	Howell Jk, Cal	125	52	2.40	Sierra, Tex	82	43	1.91
Caminiti, Hou	93	51	1.82	Jackson B, KC	172	39	4.41	Smith Lo, Atl	95	76	1.25
Carter J, Cle	112	39	2.87	Jacoby, Cle	90	62	1.45	Smith O, StL	37	55	0.67
Clark Jk, SD	145	132	1.10	James C, SD	68	26	2.62	Snyder C, Cle	134	23	5.83
Clark W, SF	103	74	1.39	Jefferies, NYN	46	39	1.18	Stillwell, KC	64	42	1.52
Coleman, StL	90	50	1.80	Johnson H, NYN	126	77	1.64	Strawberry, NYN	105	61	1.72
Coles, Sea	61	27	2.26	Jordan, Phi	62	23	2.70	Tartabull, KC	123	69	1.78
Davis A, Sea	49	101	0.49	Joyner, Cal	58	46	1.26	Templeton, SD	80	23	3.48
Davis C, Cal	109	61	1.79	Lansford, Oak	25	51	0.49	Thomas A, Atl	62	12	5.17
Davis E, Cin	116	68	1.71	Larkin G, Min	57	54	1.06	Thompson M, StL	91	39	2.33
Davis G, Hou	123	69	1.78	Leonard J, Sea	125	38	3.29	Thompson Ro, SF	133	51	2.61
Deer, Mil	158	60	2.63	Lind, Pit	64	39	1.64	Trammell, Det	45	45	1.00
Doran, Hou	63	59	1.07	Mattingly, NYA	30	51	0.59	Treadway, Atl	38	30	1.27
Downing, Cal	87	56	1.55	McDowell O, Atl	73	52	1.40	Van Slyke, Pit	100	47	2.13
Dunston, ChN	86	30	2.87	McGriff F, Tor	132	119	1.11	Wallach, Mon	81	58	1.40
Dykstra, Phi	53	60	0.88	McGwire, Oak	94	83	1.13	Walton, ChN	77	27	2.85
Eisenreich, KC	44	37	1.19	McReynolds, NYN	74	46	1.61	Whitaker, Det	59	89	0.66
Elster, NYN	77	34	2.26	Mitchell K, SF	115	87	1.32	White D, Cal	129	31	4.16
Esasky, Bos	117	66	1.77	Molitor, Mil	67	64	1.05	Wilson M, Tor	84	13	6.46
Espinoza, NYA	60	14	4.29	Moseby, Tor	101	56	1.80	Worthington, Bal	114	61	1.87
Espy, Tex	99	38	2.61	Murphy Dl, Atl	142	65	2.18	Young G, Hou	60	74	0.81
Evans Dw, Bos	84	99	0.85	Murray E, LA	85	87	0.98	Yount, Mil	71	63	1.13
Fermin, Cle	27	41	0.66	Newman A, Min	46	59	0.78				
Fernandez T, Tor	51	29	1.76	O'Brien P, Cle	48	83	0.58				
Fletcher S, ChA	60	64	0.94	Oquendo, StL	59	79	0.75				

WHO WERE THE HOTTEST (AND COLDEST) SECOND-HALF HITTERS LAST YEAR? (p. 114)

Batting Averages by Half Season

Both Leagues — Listed Alphabetically (502 or more plate appearances)

Player, Team	1st	2nd	Diff
Alomar R, SD	.256	.337	.081
Baines, Tex	.316	.302	-.014
Barfield Je, NYA	.226	.241	.015
Bell Geo, Tor	.269	.322	.053
Benzinger, Cin	.246	.245	-.001
Biggio, Hou	.265	.252	-.013
Blauser, Atl	.250	.282	.032
Boggs W, Bos	.325	.334	.009
Bonds, Pit	.240	.257	.017
Bonilla B, Pit	.281	.280	-.001
Bradley P, Bal	.279	.275	-.004
Braggs, Mil	.265	.223	-.043
Brett, KC	.231	.309	.078
Brooks, Mon	.277	.258	-.019
Browne J, Cle	.300	.299	-.001
Brunansky, StL	.244	.235	-.010
Buechele, Tex	.240	.228	-.012
Butler, SF	.299	.269	-.031
Calderon, ChA	.282	.290	.008
Caminiti, Hou	.251	.259	.008
Carter J, Cle	.254	.232	-.022
Clark Jk, SD	.219	.266	.047
Clark W, SF	.342	.326	-.016
Coleman, StL	.264	.244	-.020
Coles, Sea	.257	.248	-.009
Davis A, Sea	.322	.292	-.030
Davis C, Cal	.255	.285	.030
Davis E, Cin	.293	.273	-.020
Davis G, Hou	.256	.282	.026
Deer, Mil	.227	.183	-.044
Doran, Hou	.272	.141	-.130
Downing, Cal	.310	.254	-.056
Dunston, ChN	.225	.313	.089
Dykstra, Phi	.281	.210	-.071
Eisenreich, KC	.297	.289	-.009
Elster, NYN	.213	.246	.033
Esasky, Bos	.258	.292	.034
Espinoza, NYA	.267	.294	.027
Espy, Tex	.252	.263	.011
Evans Dw, Bos	.291	.279	-.012
Fermin, Cle	.254	.221	-.033
Fernandez T, Tor	.262	.252	-.010
Fletcher S, ChA	.255	.251	-.004
Franco Ju, Tex	.339	.290	-.049
Gaetti, Min	.266	.227	-.040
Galarraga, Mon	.258	.256	-.002
Gallagher, ChA	.303	.221	-.082
Grace, ChN	.316	.312	-.004
Greenwell, Bos	.300	.316	.016
Griffey Jr, Sea	.284	.239	-.045
Griffin Alf, LA	.277	.227	-.050
Gruber, Tor	.317	.261	-.056
Guerrero, StL	.302	.318	.017
Guillen, ChA	.239	.271	.032
Gwynn T, SD	.361	.309	-.052
Hamilton J, LA	.234	.253	.019
Hatcher B, Pit	.231	.231	.000
Hayes V, Phi	.270	.249	-.021
Henderson D, Oak	.250	.251	.001
Henderson R, Oak	.262	.285	.022
Herr, Phi	.284	.290	.007
Howell Jk, Cal	.238	.219	-.019
Jackson B, KC	.268	.243	-.025
Jacoby, Cle	.262	.281	.020
James C, SD	.201	.282	.081
Jefferies, NYN	.221	.289	.068
Johnson H, NYN	.290	.285	-.005
Jordan, Phi	.261	.301	.041
Joyner, Cal	.286	.278	-.008
Lansford, Oak	.340	.332	-.008
Larkin G, Min	.237	.294	.057
Leonard J, Sea	.270	.239	-.030
Lind, Pit	.239	.225	-.014
Mattingly, NYA	.306	.299	-.007
McDowell O, Atl	.216	.307	.091
McGriff F, Tor	.280	.257	-.023
McGwire, Oak	.245	.218	-.026
McReynolds, NYN	.283	.261	-.022
Mitchell K, SF	.290	.292	.003
Molitor, Mil	.307	.323	.017
Moseby, Tor	.202	.238	.036
Murphy Dl, Atl	.249	.205	-.044
Murray E, LA	.237	.257	.020
Newman A, Min	.251	.255	.004
O'Brien P, Cle	.285	.236	-.049
Oquendo, StL	.252	.326	.074
Owen S, Mon	.238	.229	-.009
Palmeiro, Tex	.315	.230	-.085
Parker D, Oak	.273	.255	-.017
Pendleton, StL	.231	.294	.063
Pettis, Det	.238	.266	.028
Phillips, Oak	.281	.245	-.036
Puckett, Min	.333	.344	.010
Raines, Mon	.292	.280	-.012
Ramirez R, Hou	.258	.233	-.026
Randolph, LA	.297	.267	-.030
Ray, Cal	.281	.295	.014
Reed Jd, Bos	.268	.307	.039
Reynolds H, Sea	.290	.310	.020
Ripken C, Bal	.282	.234	-.049
Samuel, NYN	.244	.228	-.016
Sandberg, ChN	.268	.310	.042
Sax S, NYA	.331	.300	-.032
Seitzer, KC	.287	.276	-.011
Sierra, Tex	.335	.278	-.058
Smith Lo, Atl	.325	.308	-.017
Smith O, StL	.290	.260	-.030
Snyder C, Cle	.232	.191	-.040
Stillwell, KC	.257	.266	.009
Strawberry, NYN	.224	.225	.001
Tartabull, KC	.262	.273	.011
Templeton, SD	.254	.256	.002
Thomas A, Atl	.242	.180	-.062
Thompson M, StL	.294	.287	-.007
Thompson Ro, SF	.275	.205	-.069
Trammell, Det	.265	.224	-.040
Treadway, Atl	.292	.262	-.031
Van Slyke, Pit	.276	.211	-.065
Wallach, Mon	.263	.291	.028
Walton, ChN	.285	.297	.012
Whitaker, Det	.264	.238	-.026
White D, Cal	.268	.224	-.044
Wilson M, Tor	.206	.283	.077
Worthington, Bal	.233	.261	.027
Young G, Hou	.229	.237	.009
Yount, Mil	.301	.333	.032

WHAT WOULD AN AVERAGE MAJOR LEAGUE LINEUP LOOK LIKE? (p. 116)

1989 Composite League Statistics — Per 600 Plate Appearances

American League

Lineup Position	Avg	OBA	Slg	AB	R	H	2B	3B	HR	RBI	BB	K	SB
Batting #1	.269	.341	.361	531	77	143	22	5	6	42	57	75	27
Batting #2	.265	.325	.358	536	71	142	22	4	7	51	46	68	14
Batting #3	.287	.354	.443	534	75	153	28	3	17	84	55	67	9
Batting #4	.266	.334	.433	534	74	142	25	3	19	84	55	89	7
Batting #5	.263	.332	.407	536	68	141	24	3	16	70	54	94	7
Batting #6	.262	.326	.409	539	65	141	24	3	16	70	50	100	8
Batting #7	.244	.309	.365	538	57	131	23	3	12	62	50	95	6
Batting #8	.246	.306	.346	540	57	133	23	2	9	56	45	96	7
Batting #9	.238	.295	.322	539	62	128	20	3	6	51	42	92	12

National League

Lineup Position	Avg	OBA	Slg	AB	R	H	2B	3B	HR	RBI	BB	K	SB
Batting #1	.254	.323	.358	536	79	136	23	5	8	41	53	74	28
Batting #2	.261	.323	.368	537	71	140	24	3	9	48	48	77	17
Batting #3	.278	.349	.424	530	75	147	25	4	15	71	58	88	19
Batting #4	.266	.349	.453	523	73	139	26	3	22	85	67	95	9
Batting #5	.248	.307	.387	544	63	135	27	4	14	70	47	88	10
Batting #6	.250	.317	.374	538	57	134	26	3	12	60	53	87	10
Batting #7	.247	.303	.354	544	49	134	23	3	10	60	44	88	6
Batting #8	.233	.301	.321	537	50	125	23	3	6	50	51	85	6
Batting #9	.168	.218	.222	525	36	88	13	2	4	34	33	157	3

WHO ARE THE LEADERS IN SECONDARY AVERAGE? (p. 118)

Both Leagues — Listed Alphabetically (350 or more plate appearances)

Player, Team	Sec. Avg	Player, Team	Sec. Avg	Player, Team	Sec. Avg	Player, Team	Sec. Avg
Allanson, Cle	.133	Fermin, Cle	.112	Liriano, Tor	.237	Sax S, NYA	.192
Alomar R, SD	.205	Fernandez T, Tor	.211	Lynn, Det	.263	Scioscia, LA	.235
Baines, Tex	.295	Fisk, ChA	.280	Lyons S, ChA	.160	Seitzer, KC	.241
Barfield Je, NYA	.347	Fletcher S, ChA	.178	Magadan, NYN	.241	Sheffield, Mil	.174
Barrett M, Bos	.167	Foley T, Mon	.235	Maldonado, SF	.261	Shelby, LA	.128
Bell Geo, Tor	.217	Franco Ju, Tex	.299	Manrique, Tex	.146	Sierra, Tex	.314
Benzinger, Cin	.199	Gaetti, Min	.211	Marshall, LA	.228	Slaught, NYA	.206
Bergman, Det	.203	Gagne, Min	.204	Martinez Crl, ChA	.174	Smith Dw, ChN	.274
Berryhill, ChN	.135	Galarraga, Mon	.273	Martinez Da, Mon	.235	Smith Lo, Atl	.402
Biggio, Hou	.296	Gallagher, ChA	.123	Mattingly, NYA	.260	Smith O, StL	.218
Blauser, Atl	.230	Gallego, Oak	.179	McDowell O, Atl	.249	Snyder C, Cle	.194
Boggs W, Bos	.285	Gantner, Mil	.144	McGriff F, Tor	.477	Spiers, Mil	.162
Bonds, Pit	.376	Gladden, Min	.200	McGwire, Oak	.406	Steinbach, Oak	.143
Bonilla B, Pit	.333	Grace, ChN	.314	McReynolds, NYN	.277	Stillwell, KC	.216
Boone, KC	.173	Greenwell, Bos	.246	Milligan, Bal	.403	Strawberry, NYN	.384
Bradley P, Bal	.294	Griffey Jr, Sea	.273	Mitchell K, SF	.503	Surhoff BJ, Mil	.154
Braggs, Mil	.228	Griffin Alf, LA	.125	Molitor, Mil	.254	Tabler, KC	.144
Brett, KC	.300	Gruber, Tor	.222	Moreland, Bal	.165	Tartabull, KC	.333
Briley, Sea	.289	Guerrero, StL	.309	Moseby, Tor	.273	Templeton, SD	.140
Brock, Mil	.268	Guillen, ChA	.122	Murphy Dl, Atl	.247	Tettleton, Bal	.431
Brooks, Mon	.199	Gwynn T, SD	.220	Murray E, LA	.308	Thomas A, Atl	.125
Browne J, Cle	.217	Hall M, NYA	.224	Newman A, Min	.211	Thompson M, StL	.209
Brunansky, StL	.270	Hamilton J, LA	.170	O'Brien P, Cle	.265	Thompson Ro, SF	.271
Buechele, Tex	.222	Harper B, Min	.153	O'Neill, Cin	.313	Thon, Phi	.246
Burks, Bos	.298	Harris L, LA	.137	Oquendo, StL	.219	Trammell, Det	.209
Bush, Min	.286	Hatcher B, Pit	.175	Orsulak, Bal	.246	Treadway, Atl	.167
Butler, SF	.195	Hayes V, Phi	.428	Owen S, Mon	.275	Uribe, SF	.135
Calderon, ChA	.230	Heath, Det	.202	Pagliarulo, SD	.208	Valle, Sea	.209
Caminiti, Hou	.207	Heep, Bos	.188	Palmeiro, Tex	.213	Van Slyke, Pit	.256
Carter J, Cle	.295	Henderson D, Oak	.228	Parker D, Oak	.237	Vizquel, Sea	.106
Clark Jk, SD	.516	Henderson R, Oak	.475	Parrish Ln, Cal	.247	Wallach, Mon	.236
Clark W, SF	.347	Herr, Phi	.178	Pena T, StL	.165	Walton, ChN	.185
Coleman, StL	.266	Howell Jk, Cal	.287	Pendleton, StL	.204	Washington C, Cal	.239
Coles, Sea	.159	Hrbek, Min	.395	Pettis, Det	.304	Whitaker, Det	.391
Daulton, Phi	.253	Incaviglia, Tex	.283	Phillips, Oak	.204	White D, Cal	.219
Davis A, Sea	.392	Jackson B, KC	.348	Polonia, NYA	.178	White F, KC	.146
Davis C, Cal	.279	Jacoby, Cle	.258	Presley, Sea	.203	Whitt, Tor	.291
Davis E, Cin	.437	James C, SD	.185	Puckett, Min	.202	Wilson G, Hou	.231
Davis G, Hou	.346	James D, Cle	.186	Puhl, Hou	.223	Wilson M, Tor	.133
Dawson, ChN	.315	Jefferies, NYN	.240	Quinones L, Cin	.235	Wilson W, KC	.222
Deer, Mil	.335	Johnson H, NYN	.464	Raines, Mon	.373	Worthington, Bal	.258
Devereaux, Bal	.233	Jordan, Phi	.168	Ramirez R, Hou	.136	Wynne, ChN	.164
Doran, Hou	.258	Joyner, Cal	.218	Randolph, LA	.175	Young G, Hou	.199
Downing, Cal	.230	Kelly, NYA	.261	Ray, Cal	.143	Yount, Mil	.322
Dunston, ChN	.206	Kennedy, SF	.177	Reed Jd, Bos	.242		
Dykstra, Phi	.272	Kruk, Phi	.269	Reynolds H, Sea	.170		
Eisenreich, KC	.274	Lansford, Oak	.201	Reynolds RJ, Pit	.245		
Elster, NYN	.205	Larkin B, Cin	.182	Ripken B, Bal	.132		
Esasky, Bos	.339	Larkin G, Min	.229	Ripken C, Bal	.234		
Espinoza, NYA	.078	Law V, ChN	.213	Roberts Bip, SD	.301		
Espy, Tex	.206	Lemon, Det	.208	Samuel, NYN	.235		
Evans Dw, Bos	.369	Leonard J, Sea	.242	Sandberg, ChN	.320		
Felix, Tor	.231	Lind, Pit	.149	Santiago, SD	.219		

WHO ARE THE BEST RBI MEN WITH RUNNERS IN SCORING POSITION? (p. 120)

Both Leagues — Listed Alphabetically (125 or more RBI opportunities)

Player, Team	BI	Op	%
Baines, Tex	46	177	26.0
Balboni, NYA	30	140	21.4
Barfield Je, NYA	32	204	15.7
Bell Geo, Tor	78	225	34.7
Benzinger, Cin	51	231	22.1
Bergman, Det	27	132	20.5
Biggio, Hou	39	171	22.8
Boggs W, Bos	44	202	21.8
Bonds, Pit	31	158	19.6
Bonilla B, Pit	51	215	23.7
Boone, KC	38	146	26.0
Bradley P, Bal	39	198	19.7
Braggs, Mil	44	179	24.6
Brett, KC	58	200	29.0
Briley, Sea	30	125	24.0
Brock, Mil	33	149	22.1
Brooks, Mon	51	201	25.4
Browne J, Cle	37	176	21.0
Brunansky, StL	51	221	23.1
Buechele, Tex	32	159	20.1
Burks, Bos	42	168	25.0
Bush, Min	30	133	22.6
Butler, SF	31	142	21.8
Calderon, ChA	59	214	27.6
Caminiti, Hou	57	223	25.6
Carter J, Cle	56	244	23.0
Clark Jk, SD	53	244	21.7
Clark W, SF	67	206	32.5
Coleman, StL	26	164	15.9
Coles, Sea	40	171	23.4
Daulton, Phi	30	134	22.4
Davis A, Sea	57	204	27.9
Davis C, Cal	58	204	28.4
Davis E, Cin	48	176	27.3
Davis G, Hou	39	204	19.1
Dawson, ChN	45	183	24.6
Deer, Mil	31	176	17.6
Devereaux, Bal	30	143	21.0
Doran, Hou	40	173	23.1
Downing, Cal	40	172	23.3
Dunston, ChN	45	181	24.9
Eisenreich, KC	40	155	25.8
Elster, NYN	40	167	24.0
Esasky, Bos	60	252	23.8
Espinoza, NYA	38	153	24.8
Espy, Tex	28	138	20.3
Evans Dw, Bos	69	245	28.2
Felix, Tor	33	145	22.8
Fermin, Cle	21	149	14.1
Fernandez T, Tor	45	176	25.6
Fisk, ChA	41	149	27.5
Fitzgerald, Mon	27	132	20.5
Fletcher S, ChA	39	178	21.9
Foley T, Mon	29	134	21.6
Franco Ju, Tex	66	206	32.0
Gaetti, Min	43	180	23.9
Gagne, Min	33	149	22.1
Galarraga, Mon	47	209	22.5
Gallagher, ChA	42	210	20.0
Gantner, Mil	30	130	23.1
Gladden, Min	33	136	24.3
Grace, ChN	54	201	26.9
Greenwell, Bos	70	252	27.8
Griffey Jr, Sea	39	153	25.5
Griffin Alf, LA	26	138	18.8
Gruber, Tor	47	183	25.7
Guerrero, StL	89	248	35.9
Guillen, ChA	49	196	25.0
Gwynn T, SD	53	190	27.9
Hamilton J, LA	37	167	22.2
Harper B, Min	45	150	30.0
Hatcher B, Pit	45	171	26.3
Hayes V, Phi	42	188	22.3
Heep, Bos	40	141	28.4
Henderson D, Oak	55	203	27.1
Henderson R, Oak	37	208	17.8
Herr, Phi	33	149	22.1
Howell Jk, Cal	22	159	13.8
Hrbek, Min	45	152	29.6
Incaviglia, Tex	48	171	28.1
Jackson B, KC	61	208	29.3
Jacoby, Cle	40	168	23.8
James C, SD	45	191	23.6
James D, Cle	27	131	20.6
Jefferies, NYN	40	166	24.1
Johnson H, NYN	52	191	27.2
Jordan, Phi	49	185	26.5
Joyner, Cal	54	214	25.2
Kelly, NYA	34	143	23.8
Kruk, Phi	28	136	20.6
Lansford, Oak	47	189	24.9
Larkin G, Min	36	183	19.7
Law V, ChN	34	160	21.3
Lemon, Det	33	143	23.1
Leonard J, Sea	56	207	27.1
Lind, Pit	41	194	21.1
Liriano, Tor	44	169	26.0
Lynn, Det	29	134	21.6
Lyons S, ChA	43	167	25.7
Magadan, NYN	32	131	24.4
Maldonado, SF	27	137	19.7
Martinez Crl, ChA	25	125	20.0
Martinez Crm, SD	26	138	18.8
Mattingly, NYA	77	239	32.2
McDowell O, Atl	28	140	20.0
McGriff F, Tor	44	211	20.9
McGwire, Oak	47	175	26.9
McReynolds, NYN	50	210	23.8
Milligan, Bal	26	131	19.8
Mitchell K, SF	53	226	23.5
Molitor, Mil	44	164	26.8
Moreland, Bal	29	142	20.4
Moseby, Tor	26	161	16.1
Murphy Dl, Atl	50	219	22.8
Murray E, LA	49	225	21.8
Newman A, Min	33	142	23.2
O'Brien P, Cle	40	217	18.4
O'Neill, Cin	41	157	26.1
Oquendo, StL	43	199	21.6
Orsulak, Bal	42	147	28.6
Owen S, Mon	31	163	19.0
Palmeiro, Tex	48	173	27.7
Parker D, Oak	59	202	29.2
Parrish Ln, Cal	28	150	18.7
Pena T, StL	29	161	18.0
Pendleton, StL	52	195	26.7
Phillips, Oak	35	151	23.2
Polonia, NYA	39	154	25.3
Presley, Sea	21	130	16.2
Puckett, Min	67	233	28.8
Raines, Mon	41	182	22.5
Ramirez R, Hou	40	191	20.9
Randolph, LA	30	146	20.5
Ray, Cal	52	155	33.5
Reed Jd, Bos	35	202	17.3
Reynolds H, Sea	40	153	26.1
Reynolds RJ, Pit	35	142	24.6
Ripken C, Bal	55	229	24.0
Samuel, NYN	33	173	19.1
Sandberg, ChN	34	172	19.8
Santiago, SD	38	183	20.8
Sax S, NYA	55	238	23.1
Scioscia, LA	26	151	17.2
Seitzer, KC	42	215	19.5
Sheffield, Mil	25	126	19.8
Sierra, Tex	72	206	35.0
Slaught, NYA	31	134	23.1
Smith Lo, Atl	50	146	34.2
Smith O, StL	43	197	21.8
Snyder C, Cle	33	151	21.9
Steinbach, Oak	32	141	22.7
Stillwell, KC	42	160	26.3
Strawberry, NYN	37	203	18.2
Surhoff BJ, Mil	42	135	31.1
Tabler, KC	35	160	21.9
Tartabull, KC	35	166	21.1
Templeton, SD	29	147	19.7
Tettleton, Bal	30	164	18.3
Thomas A, Atl	37	163	22.7
Thompson M, StL	57	198	28.8
Thompson Ro, SF	24	169	14.2
Thon, Phi	36	145	24.8
Trammell, Det	34	135	25.2
Treadway, Atl	30	131	22.9
Uribe, SF	28	142	19.7
Van Slyke, Pit	37	150	24.7
Wallach, Mon	52	216	24.1
Whitaker, Det	47	175	26.9
White D, Cal	36	173	20.8
White F, KC	34	135	25.2
Whitt, Tor	30	135	22.2
Wilson G, Hou	46	169	27.2
Wilson M, Tor	29	157	18.5
Wilson W, KC	34	125	27.2
Worthington, Bal	48	182	26.4
Young G, Hou	37	162	22.8
Yount, Mil	68	216	31.5

IS IT BETTER TO PULL OR GO THE OTHER WAY? (p. 122)

The table below shows the percentage of batted balls pulled (Pl) vs. those hit the opposite way (Op) for each batter. The batting side (B) is also shown for each player.

Listed Alphabetically by League
(502 or more plate appearances)

American League

Player, Team	B	Op	Pl
Baines, Tex	L	52	48
Barfield Je, NYA	R	28	72
Bell Geo, Tor	R	39	61
Boggs W, Bos	L	69	31
Bradley P, Bal	R	56	44
Braggs, Mil	R	39	61
Brett, KC	L	40	60
Browne J, Cle	S	52	48
Buechele, Tex	R	39	61
Calderon, ChA	R	50	50
Carter J, Cle	R	36	64
Coles, Sea	R	43	57
Davis A, Sea	L	37	63
Davis C, Cal	S	44	56
Deer, Mil	R	31	69
Downing, Cal	R	32	68
Eisenreich, KC	L	47	53
Esasky, Bos	R	35	65
Espinoza, NYA	R	50	50
Espy, Tex	S	50	50
Evans Dw, Bos	R	38	62
Fermin, Cle	R	60	40
Fernandez T, Tor	S	48	52
Fletcher S, ChA	R	45	55
Franco Ju, Tex	R	48	52
Gaetti, Min	R	33	67
Gallagher, ChA	R	49	51
Gladden, Min	R	36	64
Greenwell, Bos	L	45	55
Griffey Jr, Sea	L	45	55
Gruber, Tor	R	41	59
Guillen, ChA	L	52	48
Henderson D, Oak	R	40	60
Henderson R, Oak	R	44	56
Howell Jk, Cal	L	41	59
Jackson B, KC	R	52	48
Jacoby, Cle	R	39	61
Joyner, Cal	L	38	62
Lansford, Oak	R	43	57
Larkin G, Min	S	35	65
Leonard J, Sea	R	40	60
Mattingly, NYA	L	40	60
McGriff F, Tor	L	34	66
McGwire, Oak	R	36	64
Molitor, Mil	R	46	54
Moseby, Tor	L	49	51
Newman A, Min	S	34	66
O'Brien P, Cle	L	37	63
Palmeiro, Tex	L	36	64
Parker D, Oak	L	42	58
Pettis, Det	S	50	50
Phillips, Oak	S	49	51
Puckett, Min	R	51	49
Ray, Cal	S	45	55
Reed Jd, Bos	R	32	68
Reynolds H, Sea	S	41	59
Ripken C, Bal	R	33	67
Sax S, NYA	R	48	52
Seitzer, KC	R	61	39
Sierra, Tex	S	31	69
Snyder C, Cle	R	29	71
Stillwell, KC	S	45	55
Tartabull, KC	R	37	63
Trammell, Det	R	40	60
Whitaker, Det	L	30	70
White D, Cal	S	39	61
Wilson M, Tor	S	48	52
Worthington, Bal	R	38	62
Yount, Mil	R	42	58

National League

Player, Team	B	Op	Pl
Alomar R, SD	S	46	54
Benzinger, Cin	S	42	58
Biggio, Hou	R	32	68
Blauser, Atl	R	34	66
Bonds, Pit	L	42	58
Bonilla B, Pit	S	32	68
Brooks, Mon	R	43	57
Brunansky, StL	R	36	64
Butler, SF	L	53	47
Caminiti, Hou	S	32	68
Clark Jk, SD	R	28	72
Clark W, SF	L	43	57
Coleman, StL	S	47	53
Davis E, Cin	R	36	64
Davis G, Hou	R	27	73
Doran, Hou	S	36	64
Dunston, ChN	R	48	52
Dykstra, Phi	L	42	58
Elster, NYN	R	44	56
Galarraga, Mon	R	39	61
Grace, ChN	L	45	55
Griffin Alf, LA	S	45	55
Guerrero, StL	R	37	63
Gwynn T, SD	L	54	46
Hamilton J, LA	R	35	65
Hatcher B, Pit	R	39	61
Hayes V, Phi	L	27	73
Herr, Phi	S	47	53
James C, SD	R	40	60
Jefferies, NYN	S	42	58
Johnson H, NYN	S	32	68
Jordan, Phi	R	37	63
Lind, Pit	R	47	53
McDowell O, Atl	L	36	64
McReynolds, NYN	R	35	65
Mitchell K, SF	R	37	63
Murphy Dl, Atl	R	38	62
Murray E, LA	S	36	64
Oquendo, StL	S	43	57
Owen S, Mon	S	36	64
Pendleton, StL	S	50	50
Raines, Mon	S	42	58
Ramirez R, Hou	R	46	54
Randolph, LA	R	50	50
Samuel, NYN	R	41	59
Sandberg, ChN	R	36	64
Smith Lo, Atl	R	39	61
Smith O, StL	S	42	58
Strawberry, NYN	L	38	62
Templeton, SD	S	48	52
Thomas A, Atl	R	39	61
Thompson M, StL	L	52	48
Thompson Ro, SF	R	36	64
Treadway, Atl	L	46	54
Van Slyke, Pit	L	39	61
Wallach, Mon	R	38	62
Walton, ChN	R	36	64
Young G, Hou	S	45	55

WHO LEADS THE LEAGUE IN LOOKING? (p. 124)

Both Leagues — Listed Alphabetically (300 or more plate appearances)

Player, Team	P/PA	Player, Team	P/PA	Player, Team	P/PA	Player, Team	P/PA
Allanson, Cle	3.59	Felder, Mil	3.63	Lind, Pit	3.53	Rivera L, Bos	3.44
Alomar R, SD	3.59	Felix, Tor	3.53	Liriano, Tor	3.48	Roberts Bip, SD	3.94
Anderson B, Bal	4.08	Fermin, Cle	3.20	Lynn, Det	3.73	Romine, Bos	3.46
Backman, Min	3.61	Fernandez T, Tor	3.31	Lyons S, ChA	3.45	Roomes, Cin	3.45
Baines, Tex	3.54	Fisk, ChA	3.59	Magadan, NYN	3.81	Sabo, Cin	3.43
Balboni, NYA	3.71	Fitzgerald, Mon	3.63	Maldonado, SF	3.61	Salazar L, ChN	3.77
Barfield Je, NYA	4.18	Fletcher S, ChA	3.45	Manrique, Tex	3.32	Samuel, NYN	3.81
Barrett M, Bos	3.52	Foley T, Mon	3.42	Marshall, LA	3.35	Sandberg, ChN	3.39
Bass K, Hou	3.57	Franco Ju, Tex	3.64	Martinez Crl, ChA	3.34	Santiago, SD	3.23
Bell Geo, Tor	3.27	Gaetti, Min	3.29	Martinez Crm, SD	3.89	Santovenia, Mon	3.21
Bell Jay, Pit	3.59	Gagne, Min	3.29	Martinez Da, Mon	3.72	Sax S, NYA	3.47
Benzinger, Cin	3.38	Galarraga, Mon	3.68	Mattingly, NYA	3.23	Schofield, Cal	3.77
Bergman, Det	3.80	Gallagher, ChA	3.80	McClendon, ChN	3.66	Scioscia, LA	3.51
Berryhill, ChN	3.27	Gallego, Oak	3.55	McDowell O, Atl	3.52	Seitzer, KC	3.95
Biggio, Hou	3.44	Gantner, Mil	3.00	McGriff F, Tor	3.89	Sheets, Bal	3.54
Blauser, Atl	3.72	Gladden, Min	3.18	McGwire, Oak	3.70	Sheffield, Mil	3.10
Boggs W, Bos	4.15	Grace, ChN	3.36	McReynolds, NYN	3.38	Shelby, LA	3.50
Bonds, Pit	3.72	Greenwell, Bos	3.12	Melvin, Bal	3.35	Sheridan, SF	3.77
Bonilla B, Pit	3.50	Griffey Jr, Sea	3.51	Milligan, Bal	4.23	Sierra, Tex	3.41
Boone, KC	3.42	Griffin Alf, LA	3.23	Mitchell K, SF	3.49	Slaught, NYA	3.20
Bradley P, Bal	3.85	Gruber, Tor	3.12	Molitor, Mil	3.59	Smith Dw, ChN	3.55
Braggs, Mil	3.60	Guerrero, StL	3.55	Moreland, Bal	3.60	Smith Lo, Atl	3.80
Brett, KC	3.32	Guillen, ChA	2.91	Moseby, Tor	3.86	Smith O, StL	3.41
Briley, Sea	3.69	Gwynn T, SD	3.35	Mulliniks, Tor	3.49	Snyder C, Cle	3.38
Brock, Mil	3.67	Hall M, NYA	3.27	Murphy Dl, Atl	3.52	Spiers, Mil	3.23
Brooks, Mon	3.47	Hamilton J, LA	3.02	Murray E, LA	3.47	Steinbach, Oak	3.46
Browne J, Cle	3.56	Harper B, Min	2.95	Newman A, Min	3.40	Stillwell, KC	3.53
Brunansky, StL	3.78	Harris L, LA	3.10	O'Brien P, Cle	3.43	Strawberry, NYN	3.74
Buechele, Tex	3.76	Hatcher B, Pit	3.38	O'Neill, Cin	3.48	Surhoff BJ, Mil	3.15
Burks, Bos	3.65	Hayes C, Phi	3.38	Oester, Cin	3.35	Tabler, KC	3.36
Bush, Min	3.54	Hayes V, Phi	3.88	Oquendo, StL	3.50	Tartabull, KC	3.94
Butler, SF	3.71	Heath, Det	3.56	Orsulak, Bal	3.38	Templeton, SD	3.10
Calderon, ChA	3.38	Heep, Bos	3.51	Owen S, Mon	3.73	Tettleton, Bal	4.05
Caminiti, Hou	3.40	Henderson D, Oak	3.76	Pagliarulo, SD	3.69	Thomas A, Atl	2.98
Carter J, Cle	3.37	Henderson R, Oak	4.10	Palmeiro, Tex	3.54	Thompson M, StL	3.43
Cerone, Bos	3.53	Herr, Phi	3.62	Parker D, Oak	3.36	Thompson Ro, SF	3.68
Clark Jk, SD	3.93	Howell Jk, Cal	3.68	Parrish Ln, Cal	3.66	Thon, Phi	3.24
Clark W, SF	3.54	Hrbek, Min	3.33	Pena T, StL	2.92	Trammell, Det	3.58
Coleman, StL	3.65	Incaviglia, Tex	3.55	Pendleton, StL	3.34	Treadway, Atl	3.04
Coles, Sea	3.47	Jackson B, KC	3.60	Perry G, Atl	3.21	Uribe, SF	3.28
Cotto, Sea	3.13	Jacoby, Cle	3.50	Pettis, Det	4.12	Valle, Sea	3.52
Daulton, Phi	3.72	James C, SD	3.32	Phillips, Oak	3.80	Van Slyke, Pit	3.75
Davis A, Sea	3.72	James D, Cle	3.56	Polonia, NYA	3.33	Vizquel, Sea	3.43
Davis C, Cal	3.38	Javier, Oak	3.55	Presley, Sea	3.51	Wallach, Mon	3.33
Davis E, Cin	3.56	Jefferies, NYN	3.35	Puckett, Min	2.78	Walton, ChN	3.37
Davis G, Hou	3.50	Jeltz, Phi	4.08	Puhl, Hou	3.43	Ward G, Det	3.65
Dawson, ChN	3.30	Johnson H, NYN	3.60	Quinones L, Cin	3.61	Washington C, Cal	3.60
Deer, Mil	3.98	Jordan, Phi	3.08	Raines, Mon	3.54	Webster M, ChN	3.36
Devereaux, Bal	3.87	Joyner, Cal	3.45	Ramirez R, Hou	3.28	Whitaker, Det	3.67
Doran, Hou	3.50	Kelly, NYA	3.79	Randolph, LA	3.59	White D, Cal	3.59
Downing, Cal	4.08	Kennedy, SF	3.29	Ray, Cal	3.43	White F, KC	3.48
Dunston, ChN	3.21	Kruk, Phi	3.51	Ready, Phi	4.03	Whitt, Tor	3.96
Dykstra, Phi	3.57	Kunkel, Tex	3.59	Redus, Pit	3.73	Williams MD, SF	3.42
Eisenreich, KC	2.99	Lansford, Oak	3.15	Reed Jf, Cin	3.57	Wilson G, Hou	3.20
Elster, NYN	3.44	Larkin B, Cin	3.18	Reed Jd, Bos	3.82	Wilson M, Tor	3.49
Esasky, Bos	3.59	Larkin G, Min	3.55	Reynolds H, Sea	3.52	Wilson W, KC	3.87
Espinoza, NYA	2.76	Law V, ChN	3.64	Reynolds RJ, Pit	3.38	Worthington, Bal	4.04
Espy, Tex	3.57	Lee M, Tor	3.37	Riles, SF	3.67	Wynne, ChN	3.22
Evans Da, Atl	4.11	Lemon, Det	3.88	Ripken B, Bal	3.45	Young G, Hou	3.53
Evans Dw, Bos	3.86	Leonard J, Sea	3.51	Ripken C, Bal	3.74	Yount, Mil	3.49

WHY DON'T THEY STEAL THIRD MORE OFTEN? (p. 126)

Both Leagues — Listed Alphabetically (2 or more attempts to steal third)

Player, Team	Stealing Third SB	CS	%	Stealing Second SB	CS	%	Player, Team	Stealing Third SB	CS	%	Stealing Second SB	CS	%
Alomar R, SD	7	1	88	35	15	70	Lind, Pit	2	0	100	13	1	93
Anderson B, Bal	2	1	67	14	3	82	Liriano, Tor	2	0	100	14	7	67
Bass K, Hou	2	0	100	9	4	69	Lyons S, ChA	1	1	50	8	3	73
Biggio, Hou	4	0	100	16	3	84	Marshall, LA	0	2	0	2	3	40
Blankenship L, Oak	2	0	100	3	1	75	Martinez Da, Mon	7	1	88	16	3	84
Bonds, Pit	7	1	88	25	9	74	McDowell O, Atl	1	1	50	26	14	65
Boone, KC	1	1	50	2	1	67	Melvin, Bal	0	2	0	1	2	33
Bradley P, Bal	4	0	100	16	5	76	Milligan, Bal	3	0	100	6	4	60
Braggs, Mil	1	1	50	13	2	87	Molitor, Mil	5	1	83	22	8	73
Bream, Pit	0	2	0	0	2	0	Moses, Min	1	1	50	13	6	68
Briley, Sea	1	2	33	10	3	77	Murray E, LA	2	0	100	5	2	71
Brooks, Mon	0	4	0	6	7	46	Newman A, Min	4	1	80	21	11	66
Brumley, Det	1	1	50	7	3	70	Nixon D, SF	1	1	50	9	2	82
Brunansky, StL	1	1	50	4	7	36	Nixon O, Mon	9	3	75	28	8	78
Butler, SF	2	0	100	29	16	64	O'Neill, Cin	1	1	50	19	3	86
Cangelosi, Pit	2	0	100	9	8	53	Orsulak, Bal	1	1	50	4	1	80
Canseco, Oak	2	0	100	4	3	57	Pecota, KC	2	0	100	3	0	100
Coleman, StL	17	2	89	48	8	86	Perry G, Atl	1	1	50	9	5	64
Cotto, Sea	3	0	100	7	4	64	Pettis, Det	6	0	100	37	15	71
Dascenzo, ChN	2	1	67	4	1	80	Polonia, NYA	2	0	100	20	8	71
Davis E, Cin	4	0	100	17	7	71	Puckett, Min	2	0	100	9	3	75
Devereaux, Bal	5	3	63	17	8	68	Puhl, Hou	0	2	0	9	6	60
Duncan, Cin	2	0	100	7	5	58	Raines, Mon	9	1	90	32	7	82
Dunston, ChN	4	3	57	15	7	68	Ray, Cal	1	1	50	5	2	71
Dykstra, Phi	5	0	100	25	12	68	Redus, Pit	2	1	67	23	5	82
Eisenreich, KC	7	0	100	20	7	74	Reynolds H, Sea	4	1	80	21	17	55
Espy, Tex	7	3	70	38	17	69	Reynolds RJ, Pit	5	1	83	17	4	81
Felder, Mil	5	1	83	21	4	84	Roberts Bip, SD	1	1	50	20	10	67
Felix, Tor	1	1	50	17	11	61	Roomes, Cin	2	2	50	10	5	67
Fernandez T, Tor	1	1	50	21	5	81	Sabo, Cin	3	4	43	11	5	69
Finley S, Bal	3	0	100	14	3	82	Sax S, NYA	11	6	65	32	11	74
Franco Ju, Tex	2	1	67	18	2	90	Smith O, StL	3	1	75	26	6	81
Gaetti, Min	1	1	50	4	1	80	Snyder C, Cle	2	0	100	4	5	44
Gagne, Min	2	1	67	8	3	73	Sosa, ChA	2	0	100	5	5	50
Garcia D, Mon	2	0	100	3	4	43	Spiers, Mil	1	1	50	9	1	90
Gibson K, LA	1	1	50	11	2	85	Strawberry, NYN	1	1	50	10	3	77
Gladden, Min	2	0	100	20	5	80	Surhoff BJ, Mil	3	2	60	11	10	52
Griffey Jr, Sea	4	1	80	12	6	67	Thon, Phi	2	0	100	4	3	57
Griffin Alf, LA	4	0	100	6	6	50	Walton, ChN	1	0	83	19	5	79
Guillen, ChA	2	1	67	34	15	69	Washington C, Cal	5	0	100	8	5	62
Gwynn T, SD	7	0	100	33	16	67	Webster M, ChN	6	0	100	8	2	80
Harris L, LA	1	1	50	13	8	62	Whitaker, Det	1	1	50	5	2	71
Hatcher B, Pit	4	1	80	20	5	80	White D, Cal	11	0	100	32	16	67
Hayes V, Phi	2	0	100	26	6	81	Wilson G, Hou	0	2	0	1	3	25
Henderson D, Oak	1	1	50	7	3	70	Wilson M, Tor	3	0	100	16	5	76
Henderson R, Oak	24	5	83	53	8	87	Wilson W, KC	3	0	100	21	6	78
Hudler, Mon	1	2	33	14	2	88	Winningham, Cin	4	0	100	11	5	69
Jackson B, KC	2	2	50	23	7	77	Yelding, Hou	2	1	67	9	4	69
James C, SD	1	1	50	4	1	80	Young G, Hou	7	1	88	26	24	52
Jefferson, Bal	5	0	100	5	4	56							
Johnson H, NYN	3	1	75	38	6	86							
Johnson L, ChA	3	2	60	13	1	93							
Kelly, NYA	2	0	100	33	12	73							
Lansford, Oak	6	1	86	31	14	69							
Lawless, Tor	2	0	100	10	1	91							

WHO ARE THE BEST BUNTERS IN BASEBALL? (p. 128)

Listed Alphabetically by League (10 or more bunts in play)

American League

Player, Team	In Play	Bunt Hits	Sac Hits	Foul & Miss	%
Anderson B, Bal	15	3	5	6	38.1
Backman, Min	17	8	4	16	36.4
Barrett M, Bos	20	4	15	12	59.4
Browne, Cle	22	4	14	19	43.9
Brumley, Det	11	3	3	9	30.0
Espinoza, NYA	34	4	23	22	48.2
Espy, Tex	29	8	10	25	33.3
Felder, Mil	25	6	7	21	28.3
Felix, Tor	24	11	0	36	18.3
Fermin, Cle	42	1	32	40	40.2
Fernandez T, Tor	10	5	2	7	41.2
Finley S, Bal	17	4	6	13	26.7
Fletcher S, Tex-ChA	24	6	11	18	40.5
Gagne, Min	10	2	7	8	50.0
Gallagher, ChA	32	7	16	42	30.3
Gallego, Oak	15	3	8	17	34.4
Gantner, Mil	13	3	8	10	47.8
Geren, NYA	12	5	6	8	55.0
Gladden, Min	11	2	5	6	38.9
Gonzales, Bal	10	0	6	9	31.6
Guillen, ChA	22	1	11	41	19.1
Javier, Oak	13	4	4	20	24.2
Johnson L, ChA	12	2	2	16	14.3
Karkovice, ChA	20	9	7	11	51.6
Kelly, NYA	15	3	8	21	30.6
Kunkel, Tex	18	4	10	13	45.2
Liriano, Tor	36	7	10	24	28.3
Lyons S, ChA	42	13	12	26	36.8
Manrique, ChA-Tex	20	3	13	24	36.4
Martinez Crl, ChA	10	2	6	4	57.1
Molitor, Mil	12	5	4	19	29.0
Moseby, Tor	16	4	7	11	40.7
Newman, Min	23	6	10	24	34.0
Orsulak, Bal	12	1	7	23	22.9
Petis, Det	23	6	8	13	38.9
Phillips, Oak	13	5	5	20	30.3
Polonia, Oak-NYA	17	4	2	28	13.3
Reed Jd, Bos	15	2	13	8	65.2
Reynolds H, Sea	15	5	3	10	32.0
Ripken B, Bal	24	2	19	23	44.7
Rivera, Bos	10	3	4	9	36.8
Sax, NYA	16	3	8	27	25.6
Schofield, Cal	14	2	11	9	56.5
Seitzer, KC	19	6	4	41	16.7
Spiers, Mil	13	1	4	26	12.8
Surhoff, Mil	11	4	3	8	36.8
Vizquel, Sea	23	4	13	40	27.0
White D, Cal	20	5	7	20	30.0
White F, KC	10	2	5	12	31.8
Wilson W, KC	15	2	6	21	22.2

National League

Player, Team	In Play	Bunt Hits	Sac Hits	Foul & Miss	%
Alomar R, SD	37	7	17	60	24.7
Belcher, LA	11	0	10	15	38.5
Bell Jay, Pit	15	3	10	10	52.0
Bielecki, ChN	14	1	9	19	30.3
Biggio, Hou	26	10	6	51	20.8
Blauser, Atl	16	1	8	13	31.0
Browning, Cin	16	1	14	21	40.5
Butler, SF	49	22	13	66	30.4
Carman, Phi	11	1	7	9	40.0
Clancy, Hou	11	0	7	7	38.8
Coleman, StL	40	19	7	74	22.8
DeLeon J, StL	14	1	9	15	34.5
Deshaies, Hou	12	1	9	15	37.0
Duncan, LA-Cin	10	3	2	10	25.0
Dunston, ChN	18	3	6	18	25.0
Dykstra, NYN-Phi	13	1	5	16	20.7
Fernandez S, NYN	11	0	10	10	50.0
Gonzalez J, LA	10	4	1	7	29.4
Griffin A, LA	29	5	11	29	27.6
Gwynn T, SD	16	4	11	4	75.0
Harris L, Cin-LA	11	3	1	11	18.2
Hatcher B, Hou	11	2	3	20	16.1
Herr, Phi	10	2	6	13	34.8
Hershiser, LA	17	2	10	23	30.0
Howell K, Phi	16	0	10	10	38.5
Leary, LA-Cin	11	0	9	9	45.0
Lind, Pit	18	0	13	19	35.1
Magrane, StL	11	0	8	7	44.4
Martinez Da, Mon	11	0	7	16	25.9
Martinez De, Mon	12	0	9	9	42.9
McDowell O, Cle-Atl	45	16	4	28	27.4
Nixon D, Mon	12	7	0	12	29.2
Nixon O, SF	29	7	2	32	14.8
Ojeda, NYN	11	1	6	7	38.9
Oquendo, StL	10	2	7	4	64.3
Perez P, Mon	11	0	9	13	37.5
Puhl, Hou	11	2	4	14	24.0
Quinones L, Cin	11	1	8	12	39.1
Randolph, LA	13	5	4	25	23.7
Reuschel, SF	20	1	16	15	48.9
Roberts, SD	18	5	6	13	35.5
Salazar L, ChN	10	2	7	22	28.1
Scioscia, LA	10	1	7	8	44.4
Smith B, Mon	11	0	10	11	45.5
Smith Dw, ChN	10	4	4	14	33.3
Smith O, StL	21	5	11	18	46.2
Sutcliffe, ChN	15	1	10	5	55.0
Thompson M, StL	13	6	0	15	21.4
Thompson Ro, SF	24	10	9	18	45.2
Treadway, Atl	16	5	6	18	32.4
Uribe, SF	10	2	6	15	32.0
Valenzuela, LA	10	0	7	3	53.9
Walton, ChN	34	18	2	33	29.9
Webster M, ChN	10	5	3	16	30.8
Winningham, Cin	14	5	3	7	38.1
Young, Hou	16	1	6	25	17.1

WHICH PLAYERS PRODUCE THE MOST RBI PER HOME RUN? (p. 130)

Both Leagues — Listed Alphabetically (10 or more home runs)

Player, Team	HR	RBI	RBI/HR
Armas, Cal	11	16	1.45
Baines, Tex	16	24	1.50
Balboni, NYA	17	30	1.76
Barfield Je, NYA	23	41	1.78
Bell Geo, Tor	18	26	1.44
Benzinger, Cin	17	30	1.76
Biggio, Hou	13	21	1.62
Blauser, Atl	12	13	1.08
Bonds, Pit	19	26	1.37
Bonilla B, Pit	24	31	1.29
Bradley P, Bal	11	13	1.18
Braggs, Mil	15	21	1.40
Brett, KC	12	18	1.50
Briley, Sea	13	18	1.38
Brock, Mil	12	20	1.67
Brooks, Mon	14	23	1.64
Brunansky, StL	20	34	1.70
Buechele, Tex	16	21	1.31
Burks, Bos	12	22	1.83
Bush, Min	14	23	1.64
Calderon, ChA	14	27	1.93
Caminiti, Hou	10	14	1.40
Canseco, Oak	17	28	1.65
Carter J, Cle	35	52	1.49
Clark Jk, SD	26	54	2.08
Clark W, SF	23	43	1.87
Coles, Sea	10	18	1.80
Davis A, Sea	21	35	1.67
Davis C, Cal	22	39	1.77
Davis E, Cin	34	61	1.79
Davis G, Hou	34	49	1.44
Dawson, ChN	21	34	1.62
Deer, Mil	26	41	1.58
Downing, Cal	14	17	1.21
Elster, NYN	10	15	1.50
Esasky, Bos	30	59	1.97
Evans Da, Atl	11	14	1.27
Evans Dw, Bos	20	35	1.75
Fernandez T, Tor	11	19	1.73
Fisk, ChA	13	22	1.69
Franco Ju, Tex	13	21	1.62
Gaetti, Min	19	36	1.89
Galarraga, Mon	23	41	1.78
Grace, ChN	13	21	1.62
Greenwell, Bos	14	18	1.29
Griffey Jr, Sea	16	21	1.31
Gruber, Tor	18	27	1.50
Guerrero, StL	17	31	1.82
Hall M, NYA	17	26	1.53
Hamilton J, LA	12	17	1.42
Hayes V, Phi	26	42	1.62
Heath, Det	10	16	1.60
Henderson D, Oak	15	20	1.33
Henderson R, Oak	12	18	1.50
Howell Jk, Cal	20	30	1.50
Hrbek, Min	25	44	1.76
Incaviglia, Tex	21	38	1.81
Jackson B, KC	32	56	1.75
Jacoby, Cle	13	20	1.54
James C, SD	13	24	1.85
Jefferies, NYN	12	16	1.33
Johnson H, NYN	36	56	1.56
Jordan, Phi	12	20	1.67
Joyner, Cal	16	22	1.38
Kittle, ChA	11	19	1.73
Leonard J, Sea	24	43	1.79
Lynn, Det	11	16	1.45
Marshall, LA	11	19	1.73
Mattingly, NYA	23	35	1.52
McClendon, ChN	12	16	1.33
McDowell O, Atl	10	16	1.60
McGriff F, Tor	36	56	1.56
McGwire, Oak	33	57	1.73
McReynolds, NYN	22	34	1.55
Milligan, Bal	12	22	1.83
Mitchell K, SF	47	75	1.60
Molitor, Mil	11	13	1.18
Moseby, Tor	11	18	1.64
Murphy Dl, Atl	20	42	2.10
Murray E, LA	20	43	2.15
O'Brien P, Cle	12	16	1.33
O'Neill, Cin	15	29	1.93
Parker D, Oak	22	37	1.68
Parrish Ln, Cal	17	24	1.41
Pasqua, ChA	11	16	1.45
Pendleton, StL	13	18	1.38
Presley, Sea	12	16	1.33
Quinones L, Cin	12	15	1.25
Ripken C, Bal	21	38	1.81
Samuel, NYN	11	14	1.27
Sandberg, ChN	30	38	1.27
Santiago, SD	16	27	1.69
Scioscia, LA	10	19	1.90
Sierra, Tex	29	47	1.62
Smith Lo, Atl	21	28	1.33
Snyder C, Cle	18	28	1.56
Strawberry, NYN	29	43	1.48
Tartabull, KC	18	24	1.33
Tettleton, Bal	26	40	1.54
Thomas A, Atl	13	19	1.46
Thompson Ro, SF	13	21	1.62
Thon, Phi	15	27	1.80
Wallach, Mon	13	23	1.77
Washington C, Cal	13	15	1.15
Whitaker, Det	28	43	1.54
White D, Cal	12	17	1.42
Whitt, Tor	11	24	2.18
Williams MD, SF	18	34	1.89
Wilson G, Hou	11	16	1.45
Worthington, Bal	15	22	1.47
Yount, Mil	21	31	1.48

IF LINEOUTS WERE HITS...? (p. 132)

Both Leagues — Listed Alphabetically (502 or more plate appearances)

Player, Team	LO	New Avg	Gain
Alomar R, SD	24	.334	.039
Baines, Tex	25	.358	.050
Barfield Je, NYA	19	.271	.036
Bell Geo, Tor	33	.351	.054
Benzinger, Cin	22	.280	.035
Biggio, Hou	18	.298	.041
Blauser, Atl	18	.309	.039
Boggs W, Bos	43	.399	.069
Bonds, Pit	30	.300	.052
Bonilla B, Pit	23	.318	.037
Bradley P, Bal	27	.327	.050
Braggs, Mil	17	.280	.033
Brett, KC	22	.330	.048
Brooks, Mon	23	.310	.042
Browne J, Cle	26	.343	.043
Brunansky, StL	27	.288	.049
Buechele, Tex	22	.280	.045
Butler, SF	33	.338	.056
Calderon, ChA	32	.338	.051
Caminiti, Hou	35	.315	.060
Carter J, Cle	33	.293	.051
Clark Jk, SD	16	.277	.035
Clark W, SF	20	.367	.034
Coleman, StL	31	.309	.055
Coles, Sea	23	.295	.043
Davis A, Sea	34	.373	.068
Davis C, Cal	17	.302	.030
Davis E, Cin	12	.307	.026
Davis G, Hou	18	.299	.031
Deer, Mil	17	.247	.036
Doran, Hou	31	.280	.061
Downing, Cal	27	.333	.050
Dunston, ChN	10	.299	.021
Dykstra, Phi	25	.286	.049
Eisenreich, KC	19	.333	.040
Elster, NYN	28	.293	.061
Esasky, Bos	19	.310	.034
Espinoza, NYA	30	.342	.060
Espy, Tex	25	.309	.053
Evans Dw, Bos	31	.344	.060
Fermin, Cle	24	.287	.050
Fernandez T, Tor	29	.307	.051
Fletcher S, ChA	29	.306	.053
Franco Ju, Tex	31	.372	.057
Gaetti, Min	15	.281	.030
Galarraga, Mon	22	.295	.038
Gallagher, ChA	27	.311	.045
Grace, ChN	31	.375	.061
Greenwell, Bos	31	.362	.054
Griffey Jr, Sea	27	.323	.059
Griffin Alf, LA	23	.292	.045
Gruber, Tor	30	.345	.055
Guerrero, StL	27	.358	.047
Guillen, ChA	41	.322	.069
Gwynn T, SD	41	.404	.068
Hamilton J, LA	35	.308	.064
Hatcher B, Pit	21	.274	.044
Hayes V, Phi	25	.306	.046
Henderson D, Oak	24	.292	.041
Henderson R, Oak	27	.323	.050
Herr, Phi	50	.376	.089
Howell Jk, Cal	21	.272	.044
Jackson B, KC	16	.287	.031
Jacoby, Cle	25	.320	.048
James C, SD	32	.309	.066
Jefferies, NYN	55	.366	.108
Johnson H, NYN	24	.329	.042
Jordan, Phi	24	.331	.046
Joyner, Cal	25	.324	.042
Lansford, Oak	36	.401	.065
Larkin G, Min	21	.314	.047
Leonard J, Sea	16	.283	.028
Lind, Pit	30	.284	.052
Mattingly, NYA	40	.366	.063
McDowell O, Atl	20	.304	.039
McGriff F, Tor	22	.309	.040
McGwire, Oak	26	.284	.053
McReynolds, NYN	37	.339	.068
Mitchell K, SF	18	.324	.033
Molitor, Mil	34	.371	.055
Moseby, Tor	22	.265	.044
Murphy Dl, Atl	20	.263	.035
Murray E, LA	25	.290	.042
Newman A, Min	20	.298	.045
O'Brien P, Cle	23	.301	.042
Oquendo, StL	36	.356	.065
Owen S, Mon	24	.288	.055
Palmeiro, Tex	39	.345	.070
Parker D, Oak	22	.304	.040
Pendleton, StL	23	.302	.038
Pettis, Det	17	.295	.038
Phillips, Oak	16	.297	.035
Puckett, Min	25	.378	.039
Raines, Mon	30	.344	.058
Ramirez R, Hou	29	.300	.054
Randolph, LA	39	.353	.071
Ray, Cal	39	.362	.074
Reed Jd, Bos	37	.359	.071
Reynolds H, Sea	36	.359	.059
Ripken C, Bal	41	.320	.063
Samuel, NYN	33	.297	.062
Sandberg, ChN	26	.333	.043
Sax S, NYA	36	.370	.055
Seitzer, KC	22	.318	.037
Sierra, Tex	36	.363	.057
Smith Lo, Atl	32	.382	.066
Smith O, StL	30	.324	.051
Snyder C, Cle	18	.252	.037
Stillwell, KC	33	.333	.071
Strawberry, NYN	40	.309	.084
Tartabull, KC	12	.295	.027
Templeton, SD	25	.304	.049
Thomas A, Atl	28	.264	.051
Thompson M, StL	23	.332	.042
Thompson Ro, SF	21	.280	.038
Trammell, Det	34	.318	.076
Treadway, Atl	35	.351	.074
Van Slyke, Pit	25	.290	.053
Wallach, Mon	19	.311	.033
Walton, ChN	17	.328	.036
Whitaker, Det	24	.299	.047
White D, Cal	29	.291	.046
Wilson M, Tor	25	.302	.051
Worthington, Bal	22	.292	.044
Young G, Hou	24	.278	.045
Yount, Mil	28	.363	.046

LO=lineouts

WHO ARE THE BEST CLEANUP HITTERS IN BASEBALL?
(p. 136)

Both Leagues — Listed Alphabetically
(players with 100 plate appearances batting cleanup)

Player, Team	SLG	AB	H	2B	3B	HR	RBI	AB/RBI
Balboni, NYA	.467	210	47	10	1	13	45	4.7
Bell Geo, Tor	.425	424	122	29	1	9	63	6.7
Benzinger, Cin	.384	99	23	6	0	3	10	9.9
Bonilla B, Pit	.491	613	172	37	10	24	85	7.2
Brooks, Mon	.463	281	83	14	0	11	43	6.5
Brunansky, StL	.418	146	32	5	0	8	25	5.8
Calderon, ChA	.409	252	63	11	4	7	36	7.0
Carter J, Cle	.439	228	52	12	3	10	33	6.9
Clark Jk, SD	.479	411	101	19	1	25	87	4.7
Davis E, Cin	.581	179	53	7	1	14	45	4.0
Davis G, Hou	.490	575	153	25	1	34	86	6.7
Dawson, ChN	.475	284	74	12	5	13	50	5.7
Deer, Mil	.427	211	44	8	1	12	27	7.8
Fisk, ChA	.462	182	50	13	0	7	31	5.9
Gaetti, Min	.508	177	53	3	2	10	37	4.8
Grace, ChN	.456	272	85	11	2	8	43	6.3
Greenwell, Bos	.437	577	177	36	0	13	94	6.1
Griffey, Cin	.466	88	21	2	3	4	14	6.3
Guerrero, StL	.441	422	128	32	1	8	76	5.6
Hall M, NYA	.476	246	69	6	0	14	44	5.6
Hrbek, Min	.480	256	67	11	0	15	57	4.5
Jackson B, KC	.487	359	92	9	4	22	81	4.4
Jordan, Phi	.397	257	76	13	2	3	28	9.2
Joyner, Cal	.430	433	123	22	1	13	59	7.3
Kittle, ChA	.627	118	39	8	0	9	30	3.9
Kruk, Phi	.550	131	47	8	4	3	24	5.5
Leonard J, Sea	.407	519	126	20	1	21	82	6.3
Lynn, Det	.413	104	26	5	0	4	17	6.1
Marshall, LA	.444	90	23	8	0	3	16	5.6
McGriff F, Tor	.410	183	44	8	1	7	25	7.3
McGwire, Oak	.467	338	84	14	0	20	66	5.1
McReynolds, NYN	.472	142	43	4	1	6	24	5.9
Mitchell K, SF	.636	541	157	34	6	47	125	4.3
Moreland, Bal	.299	157	39	5	0	1	17	9.2
Murphy Dl, Atl	.357	482	108	16	0	16	72	6.7
Murray E, LA	.385	480	119	25	1	13	71	6.8
O'Brien P, Cle	.332	232	54	8	0	5	24	9.7
O'Neill, Cin	.478	136	43	7	0	5	24	5.7
Parker D, Oak	.367	180	40	8	0	6	26	6.9
Phelps, Oak	.385	104	28	3	0	3	15	6.9
Raines, Mon	.405	259	71	11	1	7	28	9.3
Ripken C, Bal	.390	123	32	10	0	2	16	7.7
Schmidt M, Phi	.372	148	30	7	0	6	28	5.3
Sierra, Tex	.552	585	182	35	14	26	110	5.3
Snyder C, Cle	.377	114	26	2	0	5	15	7.6
Strawberry, NYN	.440	418	88	19	1	25	67	6.2
Tartabull, KC	.461	206	63	11	0	7	33	6.2
Tettleton, Bal	.537	281	79	17	2	17	43	6.5
Trammell, Det	.324	281	69	11	1	3	24	11.7
White D, Cal	.421	95	25	4	4	1	12	7.9
Yount, Mil	.546	273	90	18	4	11	46	5.9

WHO ARE THE LEADERS IN "POWER PERCENTAGE?" (p. 138)

Both Leagues — Listed Alphabetically (350 or more plate appearances)

Player, Team	Pwr %	Player, Team	Pwr %	Player, Team	Pwr %	Player, Team	Pwr %
Allanson, Cle	.062	Fermin, Cle	.023	Liriano, Tor	.112	Sax S, NYA	.072
Alomar R, SD	.080	Fernandez T, Tor	.133	Lynn, Det	.130	Scioscia, LA	.113
Baines, Tex	.156	Fisk, ChA	.181	Lyons S, ChA	.074	Seitzer, KC	.055
Barfield Je, NYA	.180	Fletcher S, ChA	.059	Magadan, NYN	.107	Sheffield, Mil	.090
Barrett M, Bos	.063	Foley T, Mon	.117	Maldonado, SF	.145	Shelby, LA	.046
Bell Geo, Tor	.162	Franco Ju, Tex	.146	Manrique, Tex	.103	Sierra, Tex	.237
Benzinger, Cin	.135	Gaetti, Min	.153	Marshall, LA	.149	Slaught, NYA	.120
Bergman, Det	.094	Gagne, Min	.152	Martinez Crl, ChA	.106	Smith Dw, ChN	.169
Berryhill, ChN	.084	Galarraga, Mon	.177	Martinez Da, Mon	.108	Smith Lo, Atl	.218
Biggio, Hou	.144	Gallagher, ChA	.048	Mattingly, NYA	.174	Smith O, StL	.088
Blauser, Atl	.140	Gallego, Oak	.076	McDowell O, Atl	.125	Snyder C, Cle	.145
Boggs W, Bos	.119	Gantner, Mil	.059	McGriff F, Tor	.256	Spiers, Mil	.078
Bonds, Pit	.178	Gladden, Min	.115	McGwire, Oak	.237	Steinbach, Oak	.079
Bonilla B, Pit	.209	Grace, ChN	.143	McReynolds, NYN	.178	Stillwell, KC	.119
Boone, KC	.049	Greenwell, Bos	.135	Milligan, Bal	.189	Strawberry, NYN	.242
Bradley P, Bal	.139	Griffey Jr, Sea	.156	Mitchell K, SF	.344	Surhoff BJ, Mil	.092
Braggs, Mil	.123	Griffin Alf, LA	.061	Molitor, Mil	.124	Tabler, KC	.049
Brett, KC	.149	Gruber, Tor	.158	Moreland, Bal	.089	Tartabull, KC	.172
Briley, Sea	.175	Guerrero, StL	.167	Moseby, Tor	.127	Templeton, SD	.099
Brock, Mil	.139	Guillen, ChA	.065	Murphy Dl, Atl	.132	Tettleton, Bal	.251
Brooks, Mon	.137	Gwynn T, SD	.088	Murray E, LA	.153	Thomas A, Atl	.103
Browne J, Cle	.090	Hall M, NYA	.166	Newman A, Min	.049	Thompson M, StL	.103
Brunansky, StL	.171	Hamilton J, LA	.133	O'Brien P, Cle	.112	Thompson Ro, SF	.159
Buechele, Tex	.152	Harper B, Min	.125	O'Neill, Cin	.171	Thon, Phi	.163
Burks, Bos	.168	Harris L, LA	.063	Oquendo, StL	.081	Trammell, Det	.091
Bush, Min	.171	Hatcher B, Pit	.077	Orsulak, Bal	.136	Treadway, Atl	.101
Butler, SF	.071	Hayes V, Phi	.202	Owen S, Mon	.098	Uribe, SF	.060
Calderon, ChA	.151	Heath, Det	.126	Pagliarulo, SD	.102	Valle, Sea	.117
Caminiti, Hou	.115	Heep, Bos	.100	Palmeiro, Tex	.098	Van Slyke, Pit	.132
Carter J, Cle	.223	Henderson D, Oak	.130	Parker D, Oak	.168	Vizquel, Sea	.041
Clark Jk, SD	.218	Henderson R, Oak	.126	Parrish Ln, Cal	.150	Wallach, Mon	.141
Clark W, SF	.213	Herr, Phi	.077	Pena T, StL	.078	Walton, ChN	.093
Coleman, StL	.080	Howell Jk, Cal	.184	Pendleton, StL	.126	Washington C, Cal	.156
Coles, Sea	.107	Hrbek, Min	.245	Pettis, Det	.052	Whitaker, Det	.210
Daulton, Phi	.109	Incaviglia, Tex	.216	Phillips, Oak	.086	White D, Cal	.126
Davis A, Sea	.191	Jackson B, KC	.239	Polonia, NYA	.088	White F, KC	.072
Davis C, Cal	.164	Jacoby, Cle	.145	Presley, Sea	.149	Whitt, Tor	.153
Davis E, Cin	.260	James C, SD	.124	Puckett, Min	.126	Wilson G, Hou	.155
Davis G, Hou	.224	James D, Cle	.080	Puhl, Hou	.093	Wilson M, Tor	.078
Dawson, ChN	.224	Jefferies, NYN	.134	Quinones L, Cin	.168	Wilson W, KC	.104
Deer, Mil	.215	Johnson H, NYN	.271	Raines, Mon	.132	Worthington, Bal	.137
Devereaux, Bal	.113	Jordan, Phi	.122	Ramirez R, Hou	.078	Wynne, ChN	.111
Doran, Hou	.105	Joyner, Cal	.138	Randolph, LA	.044	Young G, Hou	.043
Downing, Cal	.131	Kelly, NYA	.116	Ray, Cal	.070	Yount, Mil	.194
Dunston, ChN	.125	Kennedy, SF	.085	Reed Jd, Bos	.105		
Dykstra, Phi	.119	Kruk, Phi	.137	Reynolds H, Sea	.069		
Eisenreich, KC	.156	Lansford, Oak	.069	Reynolds RJ, Pit	.105		
Elster, NYN	.129	Larkin B, Cin	.105	Ripken B, Bal	.066		
Esasky, Bos	.223	Larkin G, Min	.101	Ripken C, Bal	.144		
Espinoza, NYA	.050	Law V, ChN	.120	Roberts Bip, SD	.122		
Espy, Tex	.074	Lemon, Det	.106	Samuel, NYN	.100		
Evans Dw, Bos	.179	Leonard J, Sea	.166	Sandberg, ChN	.206		
Felix, Tor	.137	Lind, Pit	.057	Santiago, SD	.152		

DOES PLATOONING MAKE SENSE? (p. 140)

Both Leagues — Batters vs. Pitchers — 1987 to 1989

1987

Pitcher—Batter	AB	H	2B	3B	HR	RBI	HBP	BB	IW	SO	BA	OBA	SLG
LHP vs. LHB	9768	2411	436	47	242	1275	67	907	19	1980	.247	.313	.375
RHP vs. LHB	30891	8638	1638	203	1148	4352	111	3605	459	4632	.280	.354	.457
LHP vs. RHB	27244	7321	1396	151	973	3620	131	2889	316	4696	.269	.339	.438
RHP vs. RHB	45207	11683	2036	234	1538	6157	410	4005	218	8423	.258	.322	.416
LHP vs. SHB	9437	2534	405	74	211	1108	31	913	76	1390	.269	.333	.394
RHP vs. SHB	18655	4903	823	183	329	2028	85	1974	159	2946	.263	.334	.379

1988

Pitcher—Batter	AB	H	2B	3B	HR	RBI	HBP	BB	IW	SO	BA	OBA	SLG
LHP vs. LHB	8984	2160	373	55	163	1058	81	774	23	1674	.240	.303	.349
RHP vs. LHB	32136	8550	1544	174	777	3756	105	3622	574	4603	.266	.339	.397
LHP vs. RHB	26512	6836	1271	131	710	2999	135	2461	297	4129	.258	.322	.396
RHP vs. RHB	49073	12133	2104	266	1162	5834	475	3736	241	9004	.247	.304	.372
LHP vs. SHB	8157	2068	350	61	130	788	38	653	60	1150	.254	.310	.359
RHP vs. SHB	17706	4497	744	153	238	1784	84	1738	184	2795	.254	.321	.354

1989

Pitcher—Batter	AB	H	2B	3B	HR	RBI	HBP	BB	IW	SO	BA	OBA	SLG
LHP vs. LHB	9074	2176	378	49	147	1084	70	839	21	1646	.240	.307	.341
RHP vs. LHB	30755	8065	1434	181	737	3542	118	3403	528	4378	.262	.336	.393
LHP vs. RHB	27354	7260	1314	160	684	3223	122	2692	358	4310	.265	.331	.400
RHP vs. RHB	47623	11582	1990	217	1098	5595	378	3864	259	9147	.243	.303	.363
LHP vs. SHB	9180	2386	422	71	136	935	39	822	81	1294	.260	.321	.366
RHP vs. SHB	18835	4824	769	190	281	1850	74	1908	201	2875	.256	.325	.362

LHP=Lefthanded Pitcher, RHP=Righthanded Pitcher
LHB=Lefthanded Batter, RHB=Righthanded Batter, SHB=Switch-Hitting Batter

WHAT GOOD IS A FOUL BALL? (p. 142)

By League — Plate appearances with "X" amout of two-strike foul balls

American League

#2-stk Fouls	AB	H	TB	BFP	Times OB	BA	Slg	OBA	#Fouls
0	22516	4135	5769	24286	5791	.184	.256	.238	0
1	7260	1381	2002	8148	2218	.190	.276	.272	8151
2	2261	481	688	2574	784	.213	.304	.305	5148
3	738	157	247	862	276	.213	.335	.320	2586
4	247	46	67	292	87	.186	.271	.298	1168
5	78	19	33	97	37	.244	.423	.381	485
6	25	5	9	37	17	.200	.360	.459	222
7	15	5	9	17	7	.333	.600	.412	119
8	3	1	2	3	1	.333	.667	.333	24
9	1	0	0	2	1	.000	.000	.500	18
10+	1	0	0	1	0	.000	000	.000	13
Total	33145	6230	8826	36319	9219	.188	.266	.254	17934

National League

#2-stk Fouls	AB	H	TB	BFP	Times OB	BA	Slg	OBA	#Fouls
0	19155	3213	4524	20513	4470	.168	.236	.218	0
1	6460	1209	1821	7111	1833	.187	.282	.258	7116
2	1979	405	595	2278	690	.205	.301	.303	4556
3	630	135	218	738	232	.214	.346	.314	2214
4	210	47	66	245	82	.224	.314	.335	980
5	55	13	22	73	30	.236	.400	.411	365
6	19	5	12	20	6	.263	.632	.300	120
7	7	3	4	9	5	.429	.571	.556	63
8	4	1	1	5	1	.250	.250	.200	40
9	3	1	4	4	2	.333	1.333	.500	36
10+	0	0	0	0	0	.000	.000	.000	0
Total	28522	5032	7267	30996	7351	.176	.255	.237	15490

How Important Is A First Pitch Strike? (p. 146)

The first pitch thrown to a batter by each pitcher is divided into three categories in the table below: balls, strikes (including swinging strikes, called strikes and fouls) and balls hit in play. The strike percentage (Strk %) is determined by strikes divded by total first pitches.

Both Leagues — Listed by First Pitch Strike Percentage
(pitchers with 140 or more innings)

Pitcher, Team	Balls	Strks	In Play	Strk %	Pitcher, Team	Balls	Strks	In Play	Strk %
Saberhagen, KC	366	530	132	51.6	Leary, Cin	369	371	134	42.4
Belcher, LA	368	467	113	49.3	Cerutti, Tor	356	365	142	42.3
Cone, NYN	369	437	111	47.7	Finley C, Cal	357	354	126	42.3
Swindell, Cle	293	360	105	47.5	Gordon, KC	327	288	66	42.3
Aguilera, Min	225	285	92	47.3	Boddicker, Bos	406	387	126	42.1
Smithson, Bos	223	302	114	47.3	Martinez De, Mon	399	400	152	42.1
Anderson A, Min	334	397	120	46.7	Gross K, Mon	405	368	102	42.1
Blyleven, Cal	359	456	165	46.5	Terrell, NYA	344	373	170	42.1
Smith B, Mon	329	403	137	46.4	Howell K, Phi	375	351	109	42.0
Perez P, Mon	316	379	123	46.3	Johnson R, Sea	336	302	83	41.9
Moore M, Oak	421	453	110	46.0	Clancy, Hou	288	274	93	41.8
Bankhead, Sea	341	398	130	45.8	Bielecki, ChN	398	369	120	41.6
Dopson, Bos	297	337	103	45.7	Glavine, Atl	327	318	122	41.5
Welch, Oak	354	406	128	45.7	Ballard, Bal	385	382	155	41.4
Hurst, SD	382	457	162	45.7	Rosenberg, ChA	283	257	81	41.4
Ryan, Tex	460	453	81	45.6	Stewart D, Oak	471	450	169	41.3
Key, Tor	346	389	121	45.4	Robinson JD, Pit	285	267	95	41.3
Whitson, SD	337	416	167	45.2	Candiotti, Cle	377	352	126	41.2
Browning, Cin	377	466	189	45.2	Stieb, Tor	390	351	113	41.1
Reuss, Mil	236	281	107	45.0	Flanagan, Tor	321	298	109	40.9
Sanderson, ChN	245	275	91	45.0	Ojeda, NYN	379	340	112	40.9
Smoltz, Atl	356	384	114	45.0	Sutcliffe, ChN	413	383	147	40.6
Scott M, Hou	360	416	150	44.9	Milacki, Bal	456	416	153	40.6
Bosio, Mil	377	437	161	44.8	Mahler R, Cin	396	383	166	40.5
Aquino, KC	232	265	96	44.7	Black, Cle	408	373	141	40.5
Drabek, Pit	405	447	150	44.6	Maddux G, ChN	427	408	177	40.3
Terry, StL	235	277	109	44.6	Lilliquist, Atl	290	292	143	40.3
Farrell, Cle	347	403	154	44.6	Hill K, StL	390	351	133	40.2
Viola, NYN	446	483	156	44.5	Magrane, StL	407	391	181	39.9
Fernandez S, NYN	389	396	105	44.5	Walk, Pit	404	341	110	39.9
Darling, NYN	350	410	166	44.3	Leibrandt, KC	313	286	121	39.7
Smiley, Pit	313	371	155	44.2	Kilgus, ChN	279	255	109	39.7
Smith P, Atl	276	273	69	44.2	Valenzuela, LA	396	340	122	39.6
LaCoss, SF	258	288	106	44.2	Langston, Mon	503	414	129	39.6
Abbott, Cal	328	352	118	44.1	Hawkins, NYA	437	366	123	39.5
Schmidt D, Bal	265	304	121	44.1	Brown Kev, Tex	372	315	111	39.5
Tanana, Det	434	423	104	44.0	Rawley, Min	287	251	101	39.3
Clemens, Bos	471	463	120	43.9	Holman B, Sea	387	329	122	39.3
DeLeon J, StL	425	429	123	43.9	Carman, Phi	333	268	82	39.2
Morris Jk, Det	299	324	124	43.4	Perez M, ChA	382	321	116	39.2
Hershiser, LA	419	457	178	43.4	Reuschel, SF	347	336	180	38.9
Davis Storm, Oak	317	321	104	43.3	Dotson, ChA	315	267	106	38.8
Garrelts, SF	308	333	129	43.2	Hough, Tex	409	312	83	38.8
Smith Roy, Min	309	318	112	43.0	Rasmussen D, SD	370	308	125	38.4
Deshaies, Hou	387	399	146	42.8	August, Mil	304	249	100	38.1
McCaskill, Cal	368	372	129	42.8	Smith Z, Mon	292	243	105	38.0
Robinson D, SF	320	341	136	42.8	Alexander, Det	474	372	138	37.8
Gubicza, KC	424	454	184	42.7	Witt M, Cal	466	354	122	37.6
Morgan M, LA	243	259	106	42.6	Knepper, SF	372	279	98	37.2
Witt B, Tex	381	373	123	42.5	King E, ChA	317	250	106	37.1
Heaton, Pit	248	265	111	42.5	McWilliams, KC	331	249	97	36.8

WHO ARE THE BEST HITTING PITCHERS IN BASEBALL?
(p. 148)

Both Leagues — Listed by Batting Average
(active pitchers with 50 or more career at bats)

Player, Team	Avg	AB	H	HR	RBI
Robinson D, SF	.243	510	124	11	57
McDowell R, Phi	.242	62	15	0	6
Schatzeder, Hou	.239	238	57	5	29
Rhoden, Hou	.238	760	181	9	74
Dayley, StL	.227	75	17	0	2
Leary, Cin	.221	163	36	1	19
Harris GA, Bos	.215	65	14	0	4
Forsch B, Hou	.213	569	121	9	61
Aguilera, Min	.203	138	28	3	11
Fernandez S, NYN	.201	319	64	1	25
Heaton, Pit	.200	130	26	0	10
Maddux G, ChN	.195	231	45	0	11
Valenzuela, LA	.192	738	142	7	61
Hershiser, LA	.192	449	86	0	29
Sutcliffe, ChN	.191	502	96	4	52
Lilliquist, Atl	.190	63	12	0	4
Terry, StL	.190	79	15	2	5
Krukow, SF	.188	621	117	5	49
Mahler R, Cin	.184	532	98	1	35
Gooden, NYN	.183	438	80	2	30
Candelaria, Mon	.174	596	104	1	48
Langston, Mon	.172	64	11	0	3
Cone, NYN	.171	187	32	0	6
Rasmussen D, SD	.170	153	26	0	6
Gott, Pit	.167	66	11	4	5
Acker, Tor	.167	54	9	0	1
Jackson Dan, Cin	.167	126	21	0	10
Glavine, Atl	.161	143	23	0	10
Show, SD	.158	481	76	4	26
Robinson R, Cin	.158	133	21	0	5
Lefferts, SF	.157	70	11	1	2
Reuschel, SF	.156	767	120	2	51
Garrelts, SF	.154	162	25	1	10
Tudor, LA	.154	338	52	0	15
Gross K, Mon	.154	410	63	3	19
Smith Z, Mon	.153	255	39	0	12
Browning, Cin	.150	394	59	0	17
Downs, SF	.149	161	24	0	9
Robinson JD, Pit	.148	149	22	2	10
Darling, NYN	.148	454	67	2	16
Walk, Pit	.147	333	49	0	35
Sebra, Cin	.146	96	14	0	1
Magrane, StL	.145	179	26	3	10
Hill K, StL	.145	62	9	0	3
Puleo, Atl	.144	153	22	1	10
Knepper, SF	.140	684	96	6	45
McWilliams, KC	.140	414	58	0	15
Scott M, Hou	.139	647	90	2	46
Youmans, Phi	.139	173	24	2	13
Kipper, Pit	.138	87	12	0	2
Eckersley, Oak	.133	180	24	3	12
Rijo, Cin	.133	75	10	1	2
Martinez De, Mon	.133	226	30	0	16
Drabek, Pit	.132	212	28	0	12
LaCoss, SF	.131	419	55	2	18
Smith B, Mon	.131	383	50	2	22
Fisher, Pit	.124	105	13	2	10
Ojeda, NYN	.123	212	26	0	3
Darwin, Hou	.123	155	19	1	13
Terrell, NYA	.122	164	20	3	10
Whitson, SD	.122	485	59	0	22
Dravecky, SF	.121	313	38	1	14
Perez P, Mon	.120	342	41	0	15
Hammaker, SF	.119	285	34	0	10
Hawkins, NYA	.117	325	38	0	10
Smoltz, Atl	.114	79	9	1	6
Horton, StL	.113	106	12	0	0
Pena A, LA	.112	170	19	1	6
Price, Bos	.111	171	19	0	5
Smiley, Pit	.111	135	15	0	9
Dunne, Sea	.107	103	11	0	6
Smith P, Atl	.105	105	11	0	3
DiPino, StL	.104	67	7	0	2
Sanderson, ChN	.100	441	44	2	26
Bair, Pit	.098	51	5	1	4
Leach T, KC	.097	72	7	0	3
Belcher, LA	.096	136	13	1	10
Hudson, Det	.095	210	20	0	10
DeLeon J, StL	.095	285	27	0	5
Ruffin, Phi	.092	195	18	0	6
Schiraldi, SD	.092	87	8	1	9
Reardon, Min	.091	55	5	0	2
Power, StL	.089	146	13	1	6
Lancaster, ChN	.087	80	7	0	3
Howell K, Phi	.083	84	7	0	1
Bedrosian, SF	.083	145	12	0	1
Tekulve, Cin	.083	121	10	0	2
Deshaies, Hou	.081	234	19	0	9
Hurst, SD	.071	70	5	0	0
Hesketh, Mon	.071	85	6	0	2
Maddux M, Phi	.069	58	4	0	4
Bielecki, ChN	.052	154	8	0	4
Grant, SD	.051	98	5	0	1
McGaffigan, Mon	.048	126	6	0	5
Carman, Phi	.047	193	9	0	4
Mulholland, Phi	.043	69	3	0	1

DO THEY STILL BRUSH 'EM BACK? (p. 153)

Career leaders in hit batsmen per nine innings pitched are shown below.

Both Leagues — Listed by HB per Nine Innings
(active pitchers with 500 or more career innings pitched)

Pitcher, Team	IP	HB	HB per 9 I	Pitcher, Team	IP	HB	HB per 9 I	Pitcher, Team	IP	HB	HB per 9 I
Smithson, Bos	1356.1	73	.48	Trout, Sea	1501.2	33	.20	Robinson D, SF	1618.2	24	.13
Hough, Tex	2888.0	127	.40	Dotson, ChA	1828.1	40	.20	Sutcliffe, ChN	2109.0	31	.13
Stieb, Tor	2458.1	108	.40	Perez P, Mon	1156.1	25	.19	Bosio, Mil	621.1	9	.13
Guante, Tex	548.1	24	.39	Honeycutt, Oak	1858.0	40	.19	Whitson, SD	1933.1	28	.13
Swift, Sea	540.2	22	.37	Krukow, SF	2190.0	47	.19	Candelaria, Mon	2368.0	34	.13
Acker, Tor	693.2	27	.35	Gott, Pit	748.2	16	.19	Key, Tor	1115.0	16	.13
Gross K, Mon	1306.0	50	.34	Carman, Phi	796.2	17	.19	Pena A, LA	769.0	11	.13
Boddicker, Bos	1574.1	52	.30	Hershiser, LA	1457.0	31	.19	Hurst, SD	1704.0	24	.13
McWilliams, KC	1550.0	51	.30	Schmidt D, Bal	846.2	18	.19	Gooden, NYN	1291.0	18	.13
Young C, Oak	832.0	27	.29	Eckersley, Oak	2555.0	54	.19	Robinson R, Cin	580.2	8	.12
Farr, KC	500.0	16	.29	Smith Z, Mon	901.0	19	.19	Stoddard T, Cle	729.1	10	.12
Harris GA, Bos	791.0	25	.28	Downs, SF	525.0	11	.19	Terrell, NYA	1473.1	20	.12
Magrane, StL	570.1	18	.28	John, NYA	4707.1	98	.19	Witt B, Tex	669.1	9	.12
Young Mt, Oak	730.2	23	.28	Reardon, Min	892.1	18	.18	Minton, Cal	1115.2	15	.12
Blyleven, Cal	4702.1	143	.27	Palmer Dv, Det	1086.0	21	.17	Garrelts, SF	757.2	10	.12
Tanana, Det	3403.2	102	.27	Rijo, Cin	675.0	13	.17	Ojeda, NYN	1364.1	18	.12
Maddux G, ChN	674.0	20	.27	Stewart D, Oak	1560.2	30	.17	McMurtry, Tex	615.2	8	.12
Nelson G, Oak	844.0	25	.27	Robinson JD, Pit	677.2	13	.17	Krueger, Mil	541.1	7	.12
Aguilera, Min	548.2	16	.26	Cerutti, Tor	632.1	12	.17	Righetti, NYA	1083.0	14	.12
McClure, Cal	1058.2	30	.26	Langston, Mon	1374.1	26	.17	Saberhagen, KC	1329.0	17	.12
Show, SD	1497.0	42	.25	McGaffigan, Mon	742.0	14	.17	Leibrandt, KC	1572.2	20	.11
Ryan, Tex	4786.1	133	.25	Bedrosian, SF	910.1	17	.17	Flanagan, Tor	2616.2	33	.11
Leary, Cin	831.1	23	.25	Youmans, Phi	539.0	10	.17	Power, StL	876.1	11	.11
Black, Cle	1260.0	34	.24	Schatzeder, Hou	1241.1	23	.17	Sanderson, ChN	1620.0	20	.11
Russell Jf, Tex	752.2	19	.23	Fisher, Pit	543.2	10	.17	Hammaker, SF	979.2	12	.11
Reuschel, SF	3452.0	87	.23	Moore M, Oak	1698.2	31	.16	Hudson, Det	1007.2	12	.11
Berenguer, Min	963.0	24	.22	Walk, Pit	1099.1	20	.16	Clancy, Hou	2353.0	28	.11
Clemens, Bos	1284.2	32	.22	Rasmussen D, SD	1044.2	19	.16	Howell K, Phi	506.2	6	.11
Candiotti, Cle	964.2	24	.22					Tekulve, Cin	1436.1	17	.11
Moyer, Tex	566.1	14	.22	Morgan M, LA	938.0	17	.16	DiPino, StL	592.0	7	.11
Wegman, Mil	691.0	17	.22	Heaton, Pit	1223.1	22	.16	Boyd, Bos	1016.2	12	.11
Darwin, Hou	1750.2	43	.22	Darling, NYN	1391.2	25	.16	Lefferts, SF	683.2	8	.11
Martinez De, Mon	2485.1	61	.22	Andersen L, Hou	724.0	13	.16	LaPoint, NYA	1324.1	15	.10
Cone, NYN	573.0	14	.22	Atherton, Cle	566.1	10	.16	Deshaies, Hou	738.2	8	.10
Hawkins, NYA	1311.0	32	.22	Knepper, SF	2663.0	46	.16	Morris Jk, Det	2793.2	30	.10
Gubicza, KC	1313.1	32	.22	Howell Jay, LA	579.0	10	.16	Price, Bos	840.2	9	.10
DeLeon J, StL	1234.1	30	.22	McCaskill, Cal	869.0	15	.16	Davis Storm, Oak	1319.0	14	.10
Fernandez S, NYN	1033.0	25	.22	Mahler R, Cin	1750.2	30	.15	Thurmond, Bal	781.0	8	.09
				Smith Dv, Hou	702.0	12	.15	Ruffin, Phi	621.0	6	.09
Witt M, Cal	1945.0	47	.22	Lamp, Bos	1605.1	27	.15	Franco Jn, Cin	528.0	5	.09
Petry, Cal	1829.2	44	.22	LaCoss, SF	1614.2	27	.15	Allen N, Cle	988.1	9	.08
Stanley B, Bos	1708.0	41	.22	Scott M, Hou	1855.1	31	.15	Havens, Det	590.2	5	.08
Hernandez G, Det	1045.0	25	.22	Higuera, Mil	1085.0	18	.15	Smith Le, Bos	836.1	7	.08
				Tudor, LA	1650.2	27	.15	Bair, Pit	883.2	7	.07
Welch, Oak	2274.1	53	.21	Bankhead, Sea	615.2	10	.15	Bielecki, ChN	505.0	4	.07
Davis Mrk, SD	858.1	20	.21	Viola, NYN	1858.0	30	.15	Valenzuela, LA	2144.2	16	.07
Gossage, NYA	1636.0	38	.21	Reuss, Mil	3661.0	59	.15	Tibbs, Bal	805.0	6	.07
Jackson Dan, Cin	1089.0	25	.21	Forsch B, Hou	2795.0	45	.14	Quisenberry, StL	1036.0	7	.06
McDowell R, Phi	525.0	12	.21	Bannister F, KC	2325.2	37	.14	Aase, NYN	1070.2	7	.06
Finley C, Cal	531.0	12	.20	Alexander, Det	3366.1	53	.14	Swindell, Cle	590.1	3	.05
Horton, StL	631.1	14	.20	Browning, Cin	1211.1	19	.14				
Smith B, Mon	1400.1	31	.20	Drabek, Pit	771.2	12	.14				
Puleo, Atl	632.2	14	.20	Dravecky, SF	1062.2	16	.14				
Niedenfuer, Sea	588.0	13	.20	Rhoden, Hou	2593.1	39	.14				
Orosco, Cle	726.1	16	.20	Rawley, Min	1870.2	28	.13				

WHO THROWS GROUNDBALLS? (p. 156)

The table below includes all grounders and flies (not just outs).

Both Leagues — Listed Alphabetically (350 or more balls in play)

Pitcher, Team	Grd	Fly	G/F	Pitcher, Team	Grd	Fly	G/F
Abbott, Cal	311	157	1.98	McCaskill, Cal	292	233	1.25
Alexander, Det	301	295	1.02	McWilliams, KC	228	167	1.37
Anderson A, Min	326	235	1.39	Milacki, Bal	344	284	1.21
Aquino, KC	199	168	1.18	Moore M, Oak	304	251	1.21
August, Mil	243	175	1.39	Morgan M, LA	280	117	2.39
Ballard, Bal	326	246	1.33	Morris Jk, Det	231	173	1.34
Bankhead, Sea	233	286	0.81	Ojeda, NYN	292	180	1.62
Belcher, LA	237	262	0.90	Perez M, ChA	206	218	0.94
Bielecki, ChN	281	252	1.12	Perez P, Mon	337	152	2.22
Black, Cle	340	251	1.35	Rasmussen D, SD	276	220	1.25
Blyleven, Cal	353	257	1.37	Rawley, Min	180	190	0.95
Boddicker, Bos	294	222	1.32	Reuschel, SF	299	241	1.24
Bosio, Mil	331	228	1.45	Reuss, Mil	244	167	1.46
Brown Kev, Tex	391	118	3.31	Robinson D, SF	235	270	0.87
Browning, Cin	258	382	0.68	Robinson JD, Pit	261	126	2.07
Candiotti, Cle	311	186	1.67	Rosenberg, ChA	158	204	0.77
Carman, Phi	173	212	0.82	Ruffin, Phi	267	89	3.00
Cerutti, Tor	310	237	1.31	Ryan, Tex	231	224	1.03
Clancy, Hou	202	165	1.22	Saberhagen, KC	325	313	1.04
Clemens, Bos	326	214	1.52	Sanderson, ChN	162	217	0.75
Cone, NYN	238	231	1.03	Schmidt D, Bal	250	203	1.23
Darling, NYN	258	212	1.22	Scott M, Hou	268	286	0.94
Davis Storm, Oak	233	190	1.23	Smiley, Pit	223	288	0.77
DeLeon J, StL	248	299	0.83	Smith B, Mon	330	192	1.72
Deshaies, Hou	243	302	0.80	Smith P, Atl	204	149	1.37
Dopson, Bos	313	146	2.14	Smith Roy, Min	184	239	0.77
Dotson, ChA	206	202	1.02	Smith Z, Mon	278	96	2.90
Drabek, Pit	340	276	1.23	Smithson, Bos	193	215	0.90
Farrell, Cle	283	252	1.12	Smoltz, Atl	227	255	0.89
Fernandez S, NYN	151	310	0.49	Stewart D, Oak	310	308	1.01
Finley C, Cal	244	201	1.21	Stieb, Tor	292	213	1.37
Flanagan, Tor	291	180	1.62	Sutcliffe, ChN	337	216	1.56
Garrelts, SF	249	212	1.17	Swift, Sea	312	61	5.11
Glavine, Atl	291	209	1.39	Swindell, Cle	199	212	0.94
Gordon, KC	212	143	1.48	Tanana, Det	309	235	1.31
Gross K, Mon	250	203	1.23	Terrell, NYA	370	185	2.00
Gubicza, KC	451	182	2.48	Terry, StL	288	110	2.62
Hawkins, NYA	270	283	0.95	Valenzuela, LA	240	241	1.00
Heaton, Pit	200	180	1.11	Viola, NYN	331	257	1.29
Hershiser, LA	445	192	2.32	Walk, Pit	326	210	1.55
Hibbard, ChA	245	118	2.08	Welch, Oak	292	214	1.36
Hill K, StL	339	168	2.02	Whitson, SD	316	263	1.20
Holman B, Sea	300	198	1.52	Witt B, Tex	251	213	1.18
Hough, Tex	243	239	1.02	Witt M, Cal	355	219	1.62
Howell K, Phi	287	154	1.86				
Hurst, SD	325	235	1.38				
Johnson R, Sea	212	162	1.31				
Key, Tor	303	236	1.28				
Kilgus, ChN	263	160	1.64				
King E, ChA	273	137	1.99				
Knepper, SF	280	181	1.55				
LaCoss, SF	246	133	1.85				
Langston, Mon	295	242	1.22				
Leary, Cin	302	233	1.30				
Leibrandt, KC	221	214	1.03				
Lilliquist, Atl	217	229	0.95				
Maddux G, ChN	432	193	2.24				
Magrane, StL	415	213	1.95				
Mahler R, Cin	366	225	1.63				
Martinez De, Mon	360	233	1.55				

WHICH STARTERS ALLOW THE FEWEST BASERUNNERS?
(p. 158)

Both Leagues — Listed by Baserunners per Nine Innings
(140 or more innings)

Pitcher, Team	BR/9	IP	BR	Pitcher, Team	BR/9	IP	BR
Saberhagen, KC	8.71	262.1	254	Milacki, Bal	11.96	243.0	323
Garrelts, SF	9.08	193.1	195	Cerutti, Tor	11.97	205.1	273
DeLeon J, StL	9.53	244.2	259	King E, ChA	11.97	159.1	212
Scott M, Hou	9.63	229.0	245	Smith Z, Mon	12.00	147.0	196
Morgan M, LA	9.73	152.2	165	Leary, Cin	12.09	207.0	278
Fernandez S, NYN	9.77	219.1	238	Ojeda, NYN	12.14	192.0	259
Smith B, Mon	9.81	215.2	235	Smith Roy, Min	12.32	172.1	236
Smiley, Pit	9.95	205.1	227	Witt M, Cal	12.35	220.0	302
Whitson, SD	9.95	227.0	251	Mahler R, Cin	12.36	220.2	303
Ryan, Tex	10.12	239.1	269	Tanana, Det	12.43	223.2	309
Smoltz, Atl	10.13	208.0	234	Flanagan, Tor	12.48	171.2	238
Robinson D, SF	10.19	197.0	223	Anderson A, Min	12.54	196.2	274
Hurst, SD	10.30	244.2	280	Terrell, NYA	12.56	206.1	288
Perez P, Mon	10.30	198.1	227	Ballard, Bal	12.58	215.1	301
Blyleven, Cal	10.34	241.0	277	Dopson, Bos	12.60	169.1	237
Moore M, Oak	10.35	241.2	278	Gross K, Mon	12.61	201.1	282
Glavine, Atl	10.35	186.0	214	Boddicker, Bos	12.67	211.2	298
Deshaies, Hou	10.49	225.2	263	Walk, Pit	12.72	196.0	277
Belcher, LA	10.53	230.0	269	Smith P, Atl	12.74	142.0	201
Drabek, Pit	10.57	244.1	287	McWilliams, KC	12.80	153.1	218
Aguilera, Min	10.61	145.0	171	LaCoss, SF	12.87	150.1	215
Key, Tor	10.67	216.0	256	Lilliquist, Atl	12.93	165.2	238
Cone, NYN	10.69	219.2	261	Rasmussen D, SD	12.99	183.2	265
Bosio, Mil	10.70	234.2	279	Valenzuela, LA	13.04	196.2	285
Howell K, Phi	10.72	204.0	243	Holman B, Sea	13.08	191.1	278
Sutcliffe, ChN	10.73	229.0	273	Rosenberg, ChA	13.12	142.0	207
Hershiser, LA	10.73	256.2	306	Alexander, Det	13.16	223.0	326
Black, Cle	10.77	222.1	266	Morris Jk, Det	13.21	170.1	250
Swindell, Cle	10.79	184.1	221	Hill K, StL	13.27	196.2	290
Candiotti, Cle	10.79	206.0	247	Abbott, Cal	13.30	181.1	268
Bankhead, Sea	10.83	210.1	253	Hough, Tex	13.30	182.0	269
Reuschel, SF	10.84	208.1	251	Reuss, Mil	13.40	140.1	209
Martinez De, Mon	10.98	232.0	283	Schmidt D, Bal	13.44	156.2	234
Stieb, Tor	11.02	206.2	253	Smithson, Bos	13.47	143.2	215
Browning, Cin	11.10	249.2	308	Kilgus, ChN	13.47	145.2	218
Viola, NYN	11.17	261.0	324	Clancy, Hou	13.53	147.0	221
McCaskill, Cal	11.21	212.0	264	Davis Storm, Oak	13.71	169.1	258
Clemens, Bos	11.23	253.1	316	Perez M, ChA	13.75	183.1	280
Gubicza, KC	11.29	255.0	320	Johnson R, Sea	13.78	160.2	246
Langston, Mon	11.30	250.0	314	Witt B, Tex	13.80	194.1	298
Brown Kev, Tex	11.36	191.0	241	Hawkins, NYA	13.82	208.1	320
Bielecki, ChN	11.36	212.1	268	Robinson JD, Pit	14.07	141.1	221
Terry, StL	11.38	148.2	188	Leibrandt, KC	14.09	161.0	252
Magrane, StL	11.39	234.2	297	Rawley, Min	14.09	145.0	227
Heaton, Pit	11.48	147.1	188	Dotson, ChA	14.27	151.1	240
Finley C, Cal	11.49	199.2	255	Carman, Phi	14.52	149.1	241
Gordon, KC	11.54	163.0	209	Knepper, SF	14.62	165.0	268
Sanderson, ChN	11.56	146.1	188	August, Mil	14.86	142.1	235
Stewart D, Oak	11.70	257.2	335				
Maddux G, ChN	11.71	238.1	310				
Welch, Oak	11.80	209.2	275				
Farrell, Cle	11.86	208.0	274				
Darling, NYN	11.88	217.1	287				
Aquino, KC	11.91	141.1	187				

WHO WAS BETTER IN '89 — STORM DAVIS OR DOYLE ALEXANDER? (p. 160)

In the table below, Sup stands for run support provide for that pitcher by his club per nine innings pitched. RS is total run support for the season while the pitcher was in the game.

American League (20+ starts)

Pitcher, Team	W-L	ERA	Sup	IP	RS
Abbott, Cal	12-12	3.92	4.57	181.1	92
Alexander, Det	6-18	4.44	2.99	223.0	74
Anderson A, Min	17-10	3.80	6.86	196.2	150
August, Mil	12-12	5.31	5.63	142.1	89
Ballard, Bal	18-8	3.43	6.10	215.1	146
Bankhead, Sea	14-6	3.34	4.96	210.1	116
Black, Cle	12-11	3.36	3.89	222.1	96
Blyleven, Cal	17-5	2.73	5.04	241.0	135
Boddicker, Bos	15-11	4.00	5.14	211.2	121
Bosio, Mil	15-10	2.95	5.37	234.2	140
Brown Kev, Tex	12-9	3.35	4.66	191.0	99
Candiotti, Cle	13-10	3.10	3.54	206.0	81
Cerutti, Tor	11-11	3.07	4.16	205.1	95
Clemens, Bos	17-11	3.13	5.19	253.1	146
Davis Storm, Oak	19-7	4.36	6.48	169.1	122
Dopson, Bos	12-8	3.99	4.73	169.1	89
Dotson, ChA	5-12	4.46	3.93	151.1	66
Farrell, Cle	9-14	3.63	4.02	208.0	93
Finley C, Cal	16-9	2.57	4.33	199.2	96
Flanagan, Tor	8-10	3.93	4.09	171.2	78
Gubicza, KC	15-11	3.04	4.34	255.0	123
Hawkins, NYA	15-15	4.80	5.10	208.1	118
Hibbard, ChA	6-7	3.21	4.46	137.1	68
Higuera, Mil	9-6	3.46	3.72	135.1	56
Holman B, Sea	9-12	3.67	4.52	191.1	96
Hough, Tex	10-13	4.35	4.05	182.0	82
Jeffcoat, Tex	9-6	3.58	5.72	130.2	83
Johnson R, Sea	7-13	4.82	3.87	160.2	69
Key, Tor	13-14	3.88	4.54	216.0	109
King E, ChA	9-10	3.39	4.91	159.1	87
LaPoint, NYA	6-9	5.62	5.15	113.2	65
Leibrandt, KC	5-11	5.14	5.31	161.0	95
McCaskill, Cal	15-10	2.93	3.78	212.0	89
McWilliams, KC	4-13	4.11	3.29	153.1	56
Milacki, Bal	14-12	3.74	4.15	243.0	112
Moore M, Oak	19-11	2.61	4.25	241.2	114
Morris Jk, Det	6-14	4.86	3.54	170.1	67
Perez M, ChA	11-14	5.01	4.86	183.1	99
Rawley, Min	5-12	5.21	4.16	145.0	67
Reuss, Mil	9-9	5.13	5.00	140.1	78
Rosenberg, ChA	4-13	4.94	3.30	142.0	52
Ryan, Tex	16-10	3.20	4.66	239.1	124
Saberhagen, KC	23-6	2.16	4.87	262.1	142
Schmidt D, Bal	10-13	5.69	4.65	156.2	81
Smith Roy, Min	10-6	3.92	4.75	172.1	91
Stewart D, Oak	21-9	3.32	4.89	257.2	140
Stieb, Tor	17-8	3.35	5.18	206.2	119
Swindell, Cle	13-6	3.37	4.44	184.1	91
Tanana, Det	10-14	3.58	3.66	223.2	91
Terrell, NYA	11-18	4.49	4.14	206.1	95
Welch, Oak	17-8	3.00	5.15	209.2	120
Witt M, Cal	9-15	4.54	4.54	220.0	111
Witt B, Tex	12-13	5.14	4.77	194.1	103
Young C, Oak	5-9	3.73	2.84	111.0	35

National League (20+ starts)

Pitcher, Team	W-L	ERA	Sup	IP	RS
Belcher, LA	15-12	2.82	3.91	230.0	100
Bielecki, ChN	18-7	3.14	4.83	212.1	114
Browning, Cin	15-12	3.39	4.36	249.2	121
Carman, Phi	5-15	5.24	3.19	149.1	53
Clancy, Hou	7-14	5.08	3.86	147.0	63
Cone, NYN	14-8	3.52	5.20	219.2	127
Darling, NYN	14-14	3.52	4.43	217.1	107
DeLeon J, StL	16-12	3.05	3.79	244.2	103
Deshaies, Hou	15-10	2.91	4.07	225.2	102
Drabek, Pit	14-12	2.80	3.17	244.1	86
Fernandez S, NYN	14-5	2.83	4.88	219.1	119
Garrelts, SF	14-5	2.28	4.70	193.1	101
Glavine, Atl	14-8	3.68	5.23	186.0	108
Gross K, Mon	11-12	4.38	3.89	201.1	87
Hershiser, LA	15-15	2.31	3.61	256.2	103
Hill K, StL	7-15	3.80	3.80	196.2	83
Howell K, Phi	12-12	3.44	4.24	204.0	96
Hurst, SD	15-11	2.69	3.79	244.2	103
Jackson Dan, Cin	6-11	5.60	4.59	115.2	59
Kilgus, ChN	6-10	4.39	3.83	145.2	62
Knepper, SF	7-12	5.13	3.76	165.0	69
Langston, Mon	16-14	2.74	3.85	250.0	107
Leary, Cin	8-14	3.52	3.09	207.0	71
Lilliquist, Atl	8-10	3.97	3.37	165.2	62
Maddux G, ChN	19-12	2.95	4.87	238.1	129
Magrane, StL	18-9	2.91	4.64	234.2	121
Mahler R, Cin	9-13	3.83	3.67	220.2	90
Martinez De, Mon	16-7	3.18	4.77	232.0	123
Ojeda, NYN	13-11	3.47	4.69	192.0	100
Perez P, Mon	9-13	3.31	3.54	198.1	78
Rasmussen D, SD	10-10	4.26	4.31	183.2	88
Reuschel, SF	17-8	2.94	5.01	208.1	116
Robinson D, SF	12-11	3.43	4.34	197.0	95
Ruffin, Phi	6-10	4.44	4.58	125.2	64
Sanderson, ChN	11-9	3.94	5.78	146.1	94
Scott M, Hou	20-10	3.10	5.03	229.0	128
Smiley, Pit	12-8	2.81	3.81	205.1	87
Smith B, Mon	10-11	2.84	4.55	215.2	109
Smith P, Atl	5-14	4.75	3.36	142.0	53
Smoltz, Atl	12-11	2.94	3.50	208.0	81
Sutcliffe, ChN	16-11	3.66	4.83	229.0	123
Terry, StL	8-10	3.57	3.81	148.2	63
Valenzuela, LA	10-13	3.43	4.12	196.2	90
Viola, NYN	13-17	3.66	4.14	261.0	120
Walk, Pit	13-10	4.41	5.37	196.0	117
Whitson, SD	16-11	2.66	4.12	227.0	104

Who are the best relievers at holding the fort for their late men? (p. 164)

A hold ("H" in the chart below) is a save opportunity passed on to the next pitcher. If a pitcher comes into a game in a save situation and leaves the game without having blown the lead, this is a "passed-on" save opportunity and the pitcher is credited with a hold. The intent of this stat is to give credit to a relief pitcher who comes into a close game, pitches well, but leaves the game without giving up the lead — and has nothing to show for it! 'Til now.

Both Leagues — Listed Alphabetically (pitchers with 1 or more holds)

Pitcher, Team	H	Pitcher, Team	H	Pitcher, Team	H	Pitcher, Team	H
Aase, NYN	10	Fossas, Mil	13	Lancaster, ChN	8	Reed Jr, Sea	4
Acker, Tor	13	Franco Jn, Cin	1	Landrum B, Pit	3	Rodriguez Ro, Cin	1
Agosto, Hou	14	Fraser, Cal	1	Leach T, KC	2	Rogers, Tex	16
Aguilera, Min	1	Frey, Mon	1	Lefferts, SF	12	Rosenberg, ChA	1
Aldrich, Atl	1	Frohwirth, Phi	6	Leiper, SD	1	Sanderson, ChN	1
Alvarez J, Atl	2	Garcia M, Pit	2	Lilliquist, Atl	1	Schatzeder, Hou	3
Andersen L, Hou	16	Gardner W, Bos	1	Luecken, KC	1	Schiraldi, SD	16
Assenmacher, ChN	13	Gibson P, Det	2	Machado, NYN	1	Searage, LA	3
Atherton, Cle	5	Gideon, Mon	1	Maddux M, Phi	2	Sebra, Cin	1
Bailes, Cle	2	Gonzalez G, Min	1	McCarthy, ChA	2	Segura, ChA	1
Bair, Pit	13	Gooden, NYN	1	McClure, Cal	8	Shields, Min	1
Belcher, LA	1	Gordon, KC	3	McCullers, NYA	10	Smith Dv, Hou	1
Belinda, Pit	2	Gossage, NYA	2	McDowell R, Phi	2	Smith Le, Bos	4
Berenguer, Min	8	Grant, SD	5	McGaffigan, Mon	5	Smith MA, Bal	1
Boever, Atl	3	Guante, Tex	8	Medvin, Pit	1	Smith Z, Mon	6
Brantley J, SF	11	Guetterman, NYA	12	Meyer B, Hou	1	St.Claire, Min	1
Burns, Oak	9	Hall D, Tex	3	Mielke, Tex	8	Stanley B, Bos	7
Cadaret, NYA	6	Hammaker, SF	3	Minton, Cal	15	Stanton B, Atl	2
Camacho, SF	2	Harris Ge, Sea	1	Mirabella, Mil	1	Stoddard T, Cle	1
Carman, Phi	4	Harris GA, Bos	5	Mohorcic, NYA	4	Sutcliffe, ChN	1
Carpenter, StL	2	Harris GW, SD	6	Monteleone, Cal	1	Swift, Sea	2
Castillo T, Atl	6	Havens, Det	1	Montgomery, KC	11	Terry, StL	1
Charlton, Cin	8	Heaton, Pit	1	Morgan M, LA	1	Thurmond, Bal	5
Comstock, Sea	2	Henneman, Det	6	Mulholland, Phi	1	Trout, Sea	4
Cook D, Phi	1	Henry, Atl	1	Murphy R, Bos	13	Tunnell, Min	1
Cook M, Min	1	Hernandez X, Tor	1	Musselman J, NYN	3	Ward D, Tor	5
Corsi, Oak	2	Hesketh, Mon	3	Myers R, NYN	2	Wayne, Min	10
Costello, StL	12	Hickey, Bal	12	Nelson G, Oak	13	Wells, Tor	8
Crawford, KC	3	Hillegas, ChA	9	Niedenfuer, Sea	1	West, Min	2
Crews, LA	1	Holman B, Sea	1	Nunez E, Det	1	Weston, Bal	1
Crim, Mil	17	Holton, Bal	2	Olin, Cle	1	Wetteland, LA	1
Darwin, Hou	8	Honeycutt, Oak	24	Olson Gregg, Bal	1	Whitehurst, NYN	1
Davis Mrk, SD	1	Horton, StL	4	Orosco, Cle	12	Wilkens, ChN	3
Dayley, StL	22	Huismann, Bal	2	Pall, ChA	5	Williams F, Det	6
Dibble, Cin	23	Innis, NYN	1	Parrett, Phi	6	Williams Mitch, ChN	6
Dillard, Phi	1	Jackson M, Sea	9	Patterson K, ChA	3	Williamson, Bal	11
DiPino, StL	7	Jones Ba, ChA	1	Pena A, LA	5	Wills, Tor	1
Drummond, Min	1	Kilgus, ChN	1	Perry P, ChN	4	Wilson S, ChN	15
Dyer, Min	1	Kipper, Pit	12	Petry, Cal	3	Worrell, StL	3
Easley, Pit	1	Knudson, Mil	2	Pico, ChN	2	Young Mt, Oak	3
Eckersley, Oak	1	Kramer, Pit	3	Plunk, NYA	7		
Eichhorn, Atl	8	Krueger, Mil	4	Portugal, Hou	1		
Farr, KC	2	LaCoss, SF	1	Powell, Sea	10		
Fernandez S, NYN	1	Lamp, Bos	2	Quisenberry, StL	3		

WHICH RELIEVERS HAVE THE HIGHEST SAVE PERCENTAGES? (p. 166)

Both Leagues — Listed Alphabetically
(pitchers with 2 or more save opportunites)

Pitcher, Team	Saves	Opp	Save %	Pitcher, Team	Saves	Opp	Save %
Aase, NYN	2	3	66.7	Lamp, Bos	2	3	66.7
Acker, Tor	2	5	40.0	Lancaster, ChN	8	11	72.7
Agosto, Hou	1	5	20.0	Landrum B, Pit	26	29	89.7
Aguilera, Min	7	11	63.6	Lefferts, SF	20	24	83.3
Aldrich, Atl	1	2	50.0	McClure, Cal	3	3	100.0
Alvarez J, Atl	2	5	40.0	McCullers, NYA	3	6	50.0
Andersen L, Hou	3	6	50.0	McDowell R, Phi	23	28	82.1
Assenmacher, ChN	0	2	0.0	McGaffigan, Mon	2	5	40.0
Atherton, Cle	2	2	100.0	Mielke, Tex	1	2	50.0
Bair, Pit	1	2	50.0	Minton, Cal	8	11	72.7
Bedrosian, SF	23	31	74.2	Mohorcic, NYA	2	5	40.0
Berenguer, Min	3	7	42.9	Monteleone, Cal	0	2	0.0
Boever, Atl	21	30	70.0	Montgomery, KC	18	24	75.0
Burke, Mon	28	39	71.8	Murphy R, Bos	9	16	56.3
Burns, Oak	8	11	72.7	Myers R, NYN	24	29	82.8
Carpenter, StL	0	2	0.0	Nelson G, Oak	3	4	75.0
Costello, StL	3	6	50.0	Niedenfuer, Sea	0	3	0.0
Crews, LA	1	3	33.3	Nunez E, Det	1	3	33.3
Crim, Mil	7	14	50.0	Olson Gregg, Bal	27	33	81.8
Darwin, Hou	7	11	63.6	Orosco, Cle	3	7	42.9
Davis Mrk, SD	44	48	91.7	Pall, ChA	6	10	60.0
Dayley, StL	12	17	70.6	Parrett, Phi	6	12	50.0
Dibble, Cin	2	8	25.0	Pena A, LA	5	9	55.6
DiPino, StL	0	3	0.0	Pico, ChN	2	3	66.7
Eckersley, Oak	33	39	84.6	Plesac, Mil	33	40	82.5
Eichhorn, Atl	0	2	0.0	Plunk, NYA	1	3	33.3
Farr, KC	18	22	81.8	Powell, Sea	2	2	100.0
Fossas, Mil	1	3	33.3	Quisenberry, StL	6	7	85.7
Franco Jn, Cin	32	39	82.1	Reardon, Min	31	42	73.8
Fraser, Cal	2	3	66.7	Reed Jr, Sea	0	4	0.0
Gibson P, Det	0	2	0.0	Righetti, NYA	25	34	73.5
Gordon, KC	1	7	14.3	Robinson JD, Pit	4	8	50.0
Gossage, NYA	4	5	80.0	Rogers, Tex	2	5	40.0
Grant, SD	2	3	66.7	Russell Jf, Tex	38	44	86.4
Guante, Tex	2	5	40.0	Schatzeder, Hou	1	2	50.0
Guetterman, NYA	13	13	100.0	Schiraldi, SD	4	8	50.0
Harris Ge, Sea	0	2	0.0	Schooler, Sea	33	40	82.5
Harris GW, SD	6	8	75.0	Smith Dv, Hou	25	29	86.2
Harvey, Cal	25	32	78.1	Smith Le, Bos	25	30	83.3
Henke, Tor	20	24	83.3	Smith Z, Mon	2	3	66.7
Henneman, Det	8	12	66.7	Smithson, Bos	2	3	66.7
Henry, Atl	1	2	50.0	Stanley B, Bos	4	4	100.0
Hernandez G, Det	15	17	88.2	Stanton B, Atl	7	8	87.5
Hesketh, Mon	3	4	75.0	Tekulve, Cin	1	3	33.3
Hickey, Bal	2	2	100.0	Terry, StL	2	2	100.0
Hillegas, ChA	3	3	100.0	Thigpen, ChA	34	43	79.1
Honeycutt, Oak	12	16	75.0	Thurmond, Bal	4	4	100.0
Howell Jay, LA	28	32	87.5	Trout, Sea	0	2	0.0
Huismann, Bal	1	2	50.0	Ward D, Tor	15	27	55.6
Jackson M, Sea	7	10	70.0	Wayne, Min	1	3	33.3
Jones D, Cle	32	41	78.0	Wells, Tor	2	9	22.2
Kilgus, ChN	2	2	100.0	Williams F, Det	1	2	50.0
Kipper, Pit	4	8	50.0	Williams Mitch, ChN	36	47	76.6
Knudson, Mil	0	2	0.0	Williamson, Bal	9	15	60.0
Kramer, Pit	2	6	33.3	Wilson S, ChN	2	3	66.7
Krueger, Mil	3	3	100.0	Worrell, StL	20	23	87.0
LaCoss, SF	6	9	66.7				

WHO ARE THE TOUGHEST PITCHERS TO HIT? (p. 168)

Both Leagues — Listed by Opponent Batting Average
(140 or more innings pitched)

Pitcher, Team	AB	H	Opponent Batting Average	Pitcher, Team	AB	H	Opponent Batting Average
Ryan, Tex	867	162	.187	Smith Z, Mon	559	141	.252
DeLeon J, StL	878	173	.197	Terry, StL	561	142	.253
Fernandez S, NYN	794	157	.198	Milacki, Bal	919	233	.254
Gordon, KC	582	122	.210	McCaskill, Cal	795	202	.254
Smoltz, Atl	756	160	.212	Browning, Cin	946	241	.255
Garrelts, SF	704	149	.212	LaCoss, SF	560	143	.255
Scott M, Hou	848	180	.212	Dopson, Bos	647	166	.257
Howell K, Phi	722	155	.215	Martinez De, Mon	884	227	.257
Deshaies, Hou	829	180	.217	Darling, NYN	829	214	.258
Belcher, LA	838	182	.217	Gubicza, KC	973	252	.259
Saberhagen, KC	961	209	.217	Carman, Phi	584	152	.260
Langston, Mon	905	198	.219	Leary, Cin	786	205	.261
Stieb, Tor	748	164	.219	McWilliams, KC	587	154	.262
Moore M, Oak	880	193	.219	Holman B, Sea	739	194	.263
Cone, NYN	822	183	.223	Smith P, Atl	547	144	.263
Smith B, Mon	794	177	.223	Stewart D, Oak	987	260	.263
Smiley, Pit	770	174	.226	Perez M, ChA	708	187	.264
Clemens, Bos	929	215	.231	Tanana, Det	856	227	.265
Finley C, Cal	733	171	.233	Boddicker, Bos	813	217	.267
Heaton, Pit	544	127	.233	Smith Roy, Min	669	180	.269
Brown Kev, Tex	715	167	.234	Clancy, Hou	576	155	.269
Morgan M, LA	555	130	.234	Key, Tor	838	226	.270
Whitson, SD	841	198	.235	Rasmussen D, SD	704	190	.270
Perez P, Mon	752	178	.237	Walk, Pit	768	208	.271
Hurst, SD	903	214	.237	Aquino, KC	546	148	.271
Bielecki, ChN	789	187	.237	Cerutti, Tor	785	214	.273
Drabek, Pit	902	215	.238	Rosenberg, ChA	542	148	.273
Bankhead, Sea	784	187	.239	Sanderson, ChN	567	155	.273
Aguilera, Min	545	130	.239	Abbott, Cal	694	190	.274
Sutcliffe, ChN	842	202	.240	Anderson A, Min	777	214	.275
Hershiser, LA	942	226	.240	Alexander, Det	876	245	.280
Welch, Oak	793	191	.241	Mahler R, Cin	859	242	.282
Candiotti, Cle	778	188	.242	Morris Jk, Det	669	189	.283
Glavine, Atl	709	172	.243	Flanagan, Tor	658	186	.283
King E, ChA	591	144	.244	Robinson JD, Pit	569	161	.283
Farrell, Cle	803	196	.244	Kilgus, ChN	579	164	.283
Ojeda, NYN	731	179	.245	Ballard, Bal	836	240	.287
Hough, Tex	685	168	.245	Davis Storm, Oak	650	187	.288
Swindell, Cle	690	170	.246	Terrell, NYA	816	236	.289
Reuschel, SF	790	195	.247	Hawkins, NYA	820	238	.290
Gross K, Mon	760	188	.247	Witt M, Cal	864	252	.292
Robinson D, SF	743	184	.248	Knepper, SF	650	190	.292
Johnson R, Sea	593	147	.248	Rawley, Min	569	167	.293
Witt B, Tex	734	182	.248	Dotson, ChA	615	181	.294
Blyleven, Cal	907	225	.248	Smithson, Bos	573	170	.297
Bosio, Mil	905	225	.249	Lilliquist, Atl	671	202	.301
Maddux G, ChN	890	222	.249	August, Mil	579	175	.302
Viola, NYN	986	246	.249	Leibrandt, KC	644	196	.304
Valenzuela, LA	738	185	.251	Schmidt D, Bal	632	196	.310
Magrane, StL	871	219	.251				
Hill K, StL	739	186	.252				
Black, Cle	845	213	.252				

WHO HAS THE BEST STARTING STAFF IN BASEBALL? THE BEST RELIEF STAFF? (p. 170)

Team Pitching Statistics — Listed Alphabetically by Team

American League Starting Staffs

Team	ERA	W	L	IP	H	R	ER	HR	BB	K	BA
Baltimore	4.20	61	58	961.2	1031	479	449	98	323	387	.276
Boston	4.29	57	58	958.0	965	504	457	98	360	666	.262
California	3.42	70	55	1077.2	1078	449	409	85	317	645	.263
Chicago	4.54	45	68	910.0	988	511	459	88	348	469	.277
Cleveland	3.79	58	59	1029.2	1006	475	434	75	305	563	.255
Detroit	4.55	35	81	1000.2	1072	568	506	113	405	555	.275
Kansas City	3.75	63	53	1019.2	1035	465	425	65	274	630	.264
Milwaukee	3.96	60	63	954.2	1004	476	420	90	303	520	.269
Minnesota	4.23	57	65	984.0	1050	504	463	95	312	541	.274
New York	4.87	55	69	969.1	1095	573	525	110	353	491	.287
Oakland	3.34	82	46	1020.0	976	430	379	80	359	625	.252
Seattle	4.19	53	60	979.2	971	516	456	77	369	584	.260
Texas	4.07	63	63	1025.0	926	529	463	89	448	780	.239
Toronto	3.65	60	52	983.2	981	444	399	74	278	424	.263

National League Starting Staffs

Team	ERA	W	L	IP	H	R	ER	HR	BB	K	BA
Atlanta	3.81	47	62	967.2	940	480	410	81	298	572	.254
Chicago	3.67	73	51	986.0	943	456	402	73	321	590	.253
Cincinnati	3.88	50	65	986.0	993	482	425	92	352	554	.263
Houston	3.91	57	55	978.0	927	468	425	80	379	601	.250
Los Angeles	3.02	58	65	1060.1	929	403	356	72	374	730	.237
Montreal	3.44	58	60	1085.2	977	464	415	90	375	806	.240
New York	3.43	69	50	1052.1	918	442	401	96	376	809	.232
Philadelphia	4.23	44	75	920.1	938	493	433	88	397	552	.266
Pittsburgh	3.71	55	63	1008.2	964	478	416	94	335	513	.251
St. Louis	3.46	57	60	1016.0	931	433	391	57	341	584	.245
San Diego	3.46	68	60	1045.2	997	464	402	95	326	647	.252
San Francisco	3.42	68	49	954.2	897	397	363	77	268	513	.250

American League Relief Staffs

Team	ERA	W	L	IP	H	R	ER	HR	BB	K	BA
Baltimore	3.61	26	17	486.2	487	207	195	36	163	289	.263
Boston	3.46	26	21	502.1	483	231	193	33	188	388	.258
California	2.89	21	16	376.2	306	129	121	28	148	252	.223
Chicago	3.73	24	24	512.0	484	239	212	56	191	309	.253
Cleveland	3.32	15	30	423.1	417	179	156	32	147	281	.260
Detroit	4.51	24	22	426.2	442	248	214	37	247	276	.271
Kansas City	3.06	29	17	432.0	380	170	147	21	181	348	.238
Milwaukee	3.47	21	18	477.2	459	203	184	39	154	292	.256
Minnesota	4.39	23	17	445.1	445	234	217	44	188	310	.260
New York	3.80	19	18	445.1	455	219	188	40	168	296	.268
Oakland	2.63	17	17	428.1	311	146	125	23	151	305	.203
Seattle	3.63	20	29	458.1	451	212	185	37	191	313	.258
Texas	3.54	20	16	409.1	353	185	161	30	206	332	.236
Toronto	3.46	29	21	483.1	427	207	186	25	200	425	.239

Naitonal League Relief Staffs

Team	ERA	W	L	IP	H	R	ER	HR	BB	K	BA
Atlanta	3.51	16	35	480.0	430	200	187	33	170	394	.243
Chicago	2.90	20	18	474.1	426	167	153	33	211	328	.242
Cincinnati	3.46	25	22	478.1	411	209	184	33	207	427	.233
Houston	3.16	29	21	501.1	452	201	176	25	172	364	.241
Los Angeles	2.75	19	18	403.0	349	133	123	23	130	322	.236
Montreal	3.60	23	21	382.2	367	166	153	30	144	253	.259
New York	2.96	18	25	402.0	342	153	132	19	156	299	.230
Philadelphia	3.77	23	20	513.0	470	242	215	39	216	347	.245
Pittsburgh	3.49	19	25	479.0	430	202	186	27	204	314	.242
St. Louis	3.16	29	16	445.0	399	175	156	27	141	260	.240
San Diego	3.19	21	13	411.2	362	162	146	38	155	286	.239
San Francisco	3.08	24	21	502.1	423	203	172	43	203	289	.231

WHICH RELIEVERS HAVE THE BEST ENDURANCE? (p. 172)

Both Leagues — Listed Alphabetically (pitchers with 20 relief appearances and less than 5 starts with 20 batters faced after pitch 30)

Pitcher, Team	1-15 BFP Avg	16-30 BFP Avg	31+ BFP Avg	Pitcher, Team	1-15 BFP Avg	16-30 BFP Avg	31+ BFP Avg
Aase, NYN	157 .234	81 .194	23 .500	McCarthy, ChA	117 .291	65 .193	103 .320
Acker, Tor	274 .249	163 .204	62 .268	McClure, Cal	128 .217	55 .146	22 .333
Agosto, Hou	227 .281	104 .184	30 .308	McCullers, NYA	156 .284	114 .257	103 .211
Aldrich, Atl	83 .186	49 .275	28 .259	McDowell R, Phi	240 .234	118 .228	29 .250
Alvarez J, Atl	101 .200	73 .233	43 .333	McGaffigan, Mon	207 .296	104 .304	23 .250
Andersen L, Hou	187 .208	116 .194	48 .170	Minton, Cal	215 .205	121 .269	37 .250
Assenmacher, ChN	199 .266	93 .262	40 .189	Mohorcic, NYA	125 .296	96 .329	33 .133
Atherton, Cle	111 .307	45 .279	22 .250	Monteleone, Cal	72 .387	49 .167	49 .163
Bair, Pit	166 .201	77 .235	35 .233	Montgomery, KC	224 .232	103 .151	36 .118
Bedrosian, SF	214 .174	96 .205	32 .233	Murphy R, Bos	232 .220	151 .275	55 .320
Berenguer, Min	186 .259	143 .260	123 .208	Musselman J, NYN	88 .278	49 .439	40 .229
Birtsas, Cin	136 .331	90 .181	74 .233	Myers R, NYN	192 .202	121 .212	37 .206
Boever, Atl	210 .275	106 .198	33 .276	Nelson G, Oak	181 .198	84 .164	70 .262
Brantley J, SF	204 .221	141 .325	77 .304	Nunez E, Det	103 .250	81 .313	54 .174
Burns, Oak	180 .265	107 .089	87 .173	Olin, Cle	77 .243	48 .286	27 .240
Charlton, Cin	243 .229	108 .170	42 .103	Olson Gregg, Bal	206 .215	108 .133	42 .182
Clements P, SD	83 .250	58 .286	26 .280	Pall, ChA	208 .282	120 .236	42 .308
Corsi, Oak	77 .261	33 .143	39 .108	Parrett, Phi	245 .248	149 .213	50 .209
Costello, StL	149 .197	78 .236	26 .231	Patterson K, ChA	164 .275	68 .213	52 .261
Crawford, KC	93 .200	72 .279	59 .267	Pena A, LA	156 .200	112 .267	38 .162
Crews, LA	154 .299	91 .269	30 .250	Powell, Sea	119 .330	48 .250	34 .179
Crim, Mil	272 .269	134 .262	81 .219	Reed Jr, Sea	197 .253	139 .238	96 .195
Darwin, Hou	243 .199	168 .212	71 .258	Righetti, NYA	194 .272	85 .254	21 .400
Davis Mrk, SD	225 .204	110 .153	35 .323	Schatzeder, Hou	117 .276	80 .284	62 .310
Dayley, StL	193 .209	93 .225	24 .375	Schiraldi, SD	204 .188	112 .226	113 .196
Dibble, Cin	248 .183	126 .156	27 .200	Schooler, Sea	216 .294	86 .203	27 .250
DiPino, StL	204 .207	101 .232	42 .316	Stanley B, Bos	164 .286	108 .368	84 .329
Eichhorn, Atl	162 .243	85 .333	39 .286	Thigpen, ChA	201 .226	107 .216	28 .150
Farr, KC	167 .285	62 .291	50 .340	Thurmond, Bal	164 .291	127 .317	84 .237
Fossas, Mil	169 .248	61 .273	26 .261	Ward D, Tor	232 .223	166 .234	96 .244
Franco Jn, Cin	200 .226	102 .306	43 .297	Wayne, Min	178 .207	87 .187	37 .294
Fraser, Cal	166 .222	119 .245	90 .247	Wells, Tor	165 .215	93 .198	94 .202
Frohwirth, Phi	148 .241	79 .225	31 .276	Williams F, Det	150 .232	119 .265	61 .283
Grant, SD	206 .242	149 .296	111 .194	Williams Mitch, ChN	220 .232	110 .266	35 .185
Guante, Tex	159 .225	110 .298	42 .212	Williamson, Bal	222 .297	149 .226	74 .219
Guetterman, NYA	254 .258	114 .274	44 .220	Wills, Tor	91 .244	80 .268	131 .224
Hall D, Tex	105 .218	79 .231	58 .157	Young Mt, Oak	76 .286	42 .333	66 .255
Harris GA, Bos	191 .247	156 .230	95 .184				
Henke, Tor	207 .246	100 .132	49 .175				
Henneman, Det	195 .206	150 .300	56 .289				
Honeycutt, Oak	201 .219	80 .176	24 .200				
Jackson M, Sea	235 .259	132 .183	64 .170				
Jones D, Cle	209 .293	95 .193	27 .125				
Kipper, Pit	173 .150	99 .262	62 .179				
Lamp, Bos	150 .234	137 .214	158 .255				
Lancaster, ChN	137 .229	93 .253	58 .173				
Landrum B, Pit	196 .200	89 .259	40 .097				
Leach T, KC	162 .264	100 .270	151 .277				
Lefferts, SF	251 .263	137 .200	42 .162				

WHAT IS FIRST BATTER EFFICIENCY? (p. 174)

Both Leagues — Listed Alphabetically (40 or more games in relief)

Pitcher, Team	AB	H	HR	BB	SO	Avg
Aase, NYN	42	7	1	6	7	.167
Acker, Tor	54	16	1	2	5	.296
Agosto, Hou	66	22	1	3	14	.333
Andersen, Hou	55	11	0	3	19	.200
Assenmacher, ChN	57	16	0	4	11	.281
Bair, Pit	41	7	2	3	7	.171
Bedrosian, SF	57	8	1	11	6	.140
Berenguer, Min	53	13	0	2	10	.245
Birtsas, Cin	36	13	2	4	6	.361
Boever, Atl	62	16	2	4	12	.258
Brantley, SF	50	10	2	6	15	.200
Burke, Mon	63	14	0	3	11	.222
Burns, Oak	45	15	0	2	10	.333
Charlton, Cin	60	18	2	7	15	.300
Costello, StL	43	9	1	2	9	.209
Crews, LA	40	10	0	3	8	.250
Crim, Mil	69	26	2	3	10	.377
Darwin, Hou	60	17	2	4	16	.283
Davis, SD	62	12	1	5	20	.194
Dayley, StL	61	8	0	8	11	.131
Dibble, Cin	67	14	1	4	28	.209
DiPino, StL	58	10	1	4	7	.172
Eckersley, Oak	48	10	2	0	15	.208
Eichhorn, Atl	43	12	2	1	8	.279
Farr, KC	44	9	1	5	13	.205
Fossas, Mil	43	9	0	4	12	.209
Franco, Cin	55	12	0	3	9	.218
Fraser, Cal	41	9	1	1	3	.220
Frohwirth, Phi	38	9	0	5	8	.237
Grant, SD	45	8	1	2	9	.178
Guante, Tex	42	7	0	6	8	.167
Guetterman, NYA	63	10	0	4	15	.159
Harris GA, Bos	31	8	2	10	7	.258
Harris GW, SD	45	5	0	2	16	.111
Harvey, Cal	40	10	3	9	16	.250
Henke, Tor	61	19	3	2	23	.311
Henneman, Det	50	12	0	9	9	.240
Hesketh, Mon	39	9	0	4	10	.231
Hickey, Bal	42	11	2	8	8	.262
Honeycutt, Oak	57	9	1	4	10	.158
Howell, LA	52	9	0	4	9	.173
Jackson, Sea	52	13	0	10	14	.250
Jones, Cle	55	18	1	1	11	.327
Kipper, StL	48	6	0	3	6	.125
Lamp, Bos	38	16	1	2	4	.421
Lancaster, ChN	40	10	0	1	7	.250
Landrum, Pit	51	15	1	3	5	.294
Lefferts, SF	65	16	1	3	16	.246
McClure, Cal	41	7	1	5	3	.171
McCullers, NYA	43	7	1	5	15	.163
McDowell R, Phi	61	13	0	7	12	.213
McGaffigan, Mon	53	15	1	4	4	.283
Mielke, Tex	37	12	1	5	3	.324
Minton, Cal	58	10	0	3	6	.172
Montgomery, KC	59	17	1	3	17	.288
Murphy R, Bos	65	16	1	7	17	.246
Myers, NYN	58	9	1	6	18	.155
Nelson, Oak	44	4	0	2	14	.091
Olson, Bal	56	8	0	8	17	.143
Orosco, Cle	61	13	1	6	19	.213
Pall, ChA	48	9	1	2	10	.188
Parrett, Phi	64	18	1	6	14	.281
Patterson, Pit	40	13	3	8	7	.325
Pena A, LA	49	11	2	4	11	.224
Pico, ChN	45	9	0	2	6	.200
Plesac, Mil	47	10	0	4	15	.213
Plunk, NYA	36	8	2	7	10	.222
Powell, Sea	35	12	1	6	5	.343
Quisenberry, StL	61	13	0	1	8	.213
Reardon, Min	60	8	1	2	11	.133
Reed, Sea	44	11	1	5	9	.250
Righetti, NYA	49	11	1	3	13	.224
Rogers, Tex	58	15	1	10	16	.259
Russell, Tex	61	11	3	8	18	.180
Schiraldi, SD	46	6	0	8	8	.130
Schooler, Sea	63	19	1	2	12	.302
Searage, LA	35	9	0	4	10	.257
Smith D, Hou	47	12	1	5	7	.255
Smith Lee, Bos	56	11	0	8	14	.196
Stanley, Bos	40	14	0	3	4	.350
Thigpen, ChA	55	10	2	5	9	.182
Thurmond, Bal	44	15	1	3	7	.341
Ward, Tor	53	11	0	10	19	.208
Wayne, Min	52	12	2	7	12	.231
Wells, Tor	49	10	2	4	11	.204
Williams F, Det	33	9	1	7	5	.273
Williams M, ChN	58	15	2	13	15	.259
Williamson, Bal	57	18	0	4	6	.316
Wilson S, ChN	41	7	0	2	8	.171
Worrell, StL	45	9	1	0	4	.200

HOW MUCH REST IS BEST? (p. 176)

Both Leagues — Listed Alphabetically
(pitchers with at least three starts on three days rest)

	3 Days Rest			4 Days Rest		
Pitcher, Team	W-L	IP	ERA	W-L	IP	ERA
Anderson A, Min	1-2	22.1	2.42	9-7	111.2	4.27
Ballard, Bal	5-2	52.1	2.24	8-5	121.1	3.93
Bielecki, ChN	4-0	36.2	4.42	11-5	118.0	2.82
Browning, Cin	5-3	72.0	2.88	7-7	123.1	3.79
Carman, Phi	1-3	26.2	5.74	1-7	38.0	8.53
Clutterbuck, Mil	1-0	20.1	3.10	0-4	21.0	4.71
Cone, NYN	4-0	37.1	1.21	3-4	65.2	4.80
Davis Storm, Oak	6-0	42.1	2.76	7-4	74.0	4.26
DeLeon J, StL	1-2	33.2	1.87	14-6	177.0	3.25
Fernandez S, NYN	1-0	17.0	2.12	8-2	127.1	2.54
Gordon, KC	0-4	17.0	10.59	5-3	63.0	3.00
Gubicza, KC	3-1	47.1	3.23	9-9	165.1	3.32
Harnisch, Bal	2-1	25.2	3.16	2-6	58.0	4.97
Harris GW, SD	2-1	27.1	1.32	1-2	19.2	4.58
Hawkins, NYA	2-2	22.0	6.55	8-7	104.2	5.07
Heaton, Pit	0-0	17.0	1.59	2-6	66.1	3.80
Hill K, StL	1-1	29.2	3.94	4-11	122.2	4.11
Jackson Dan, Cin	1-2	22.2	4.37	2-7	61.0	6.34
Johnson D, Bal	2-3	46.2	4.05	1-3	27.0	5.00
Kilgus, ChN	0-1	17.1	6.23	3-4	55.2	4.04
Knepper, SF	1-2	14.0	10.93	4-5	88.3	4.70
Kramer, Pit	0-2	10.0	8.10	1-2	18.0	5.50
Leibrandt, KC	1-2	19.2	6.86	3-7	80.0	5.18
Lilliquist, Atl	1-1	26.0	4.15	3-5	74.2	3.38
Maddux G, ChN	2-3	40.1	4.69	11-6	126.2	2.63
Magrane, StL	2-4	39.1	2.97	12-4	153.1	2.88
Mahler R, Cin	2-6	66.0	4.77	5-5	97.1	3.33
McWilliams, KC	2-3	37.1	3.38	1-5	52.0	2.94
Milacki, Bal	7-1	72.0	2.50	6-7	115.1	3.90
Moore M, Oak	5-1	43.2	1.24	12-7	165.0	2.95
Portugal, Hou	2-0	20.0	1.35	3-0	56.0	2.57
Reuschel, SF	3-1	28.0	1.29	7-5	123.0	3.07
Rhoden, Hou	0-2	22.0	5.73	1-2	41.0	4.17
Rijo, Cin	2-1	30.0	2.10	4-4	62.0	3.34
Robinson D, SF	2-2	40.0	5.18	8-4	103.2	2.52
Saberhagen, KC	5-2	65.0	1.25	15-2	145.1	2.23
Schmidt D, Bal	0-3	6.0	22.50	7-7	89.1	4.63
Scott M, Hou	2-2	25.2	4.21	14-5	148.0	2.61
Smith Roy, Min	1-0	17.2	3.06	6-3	82.2	4.14
Smithson, Bos	1-4	28.0	7.71	3-5	51.0	4.24
Stewart D, Oak	2-1	30.0	2.10	15-5	182.2	3.30
Sutcliffe, ChN	2-1	31.2	3.98	7-8	133.1	3.85
Terry, StL	1-3	30.2	5.58	4-5	64.1	3.78
Welch, Oak	3-1	34.1	1.83	9-5	108.2	3.06

WHICH PITCHERS SHOULD NEVER LEAVE HOME? (p. 179)

Both Leagues — Listed Alphabetically
(60 or more innings at home and 60 or more innings on the road)

Pitcher, Team	Home W-L	Home ERA	Road W-L	Road ERA	ERA Diff.	Pitcher, Team	Home W-L	Home ERA	Road W-L	Road ERA	ERA Diff.
Abbott, Cal	5-5	4.84	7-7	3.06	1.78	King E, ChA	6-7	3.20	3-3	3.69	-0.49
Acker, Tor	1-3	1.97	1-4	2.90	-0.93	Knepper, SF	0-7	6.56	7-5	4.04	2.53
Aguilera, Min	6-5	2.61	3-6	2.97	-0.36	LaCoss, SF	6-4	2.90	4-6	3.40	-0.50
Alexander, Det	3-9	4.44	3-9	4.44	-0.00	Langston, Mon	8-5	3.58	8-9	2.04	1.55
Anderson A, Min	6-5	6.47	11-5	2.24	4.23	Leary, Cin	4-8	3.43	4-6	3.64	-0.21
Aquino, KC	4-3	3.03	2-5	3.91	-0.88	Leibrandt, KC	3-3	3.71	2-8	6.19	-2.49
Ballard, Bal	9-4	3.19	9-4	3.67	-0.48	Lilliquist, Atl	5-5	3.32	3-5	4.90	-1.58
Bankhead, Sea	7-3	3.40	7-3	3.28	0.12	Maddux G, ChN	10-5	3.03	9-7	2.87	0.15
Belcher, LA	10-4	2.10	5-8	3.66	-1.56	Magrane, StL	9-5	3.09	9-4	2.73	0.36
Bielecki, ChN	9-3	2.83	9-4	3.49	-0.66	Mahler R, Cin	6-6	4.43	3-7	3.13	1.30
Black, Cle	5-9	4.06	7-2	2.61	1.45	Martinez De, Mon	7-4	2.79	9-3	3.58	-0.79
Blyleven, Cal	8-1	2.64	9-4	2.81	-0.17	McCaskill, Cal	10-4	3.12	5-6	2.71	0.42
Boddicker, Bos	7-8	4.89	8-3	3.15	1.75	McWilliams, KC	3-8	4.21	1-5	3.97	0.23
Bosio, Mil	9-3	2.06	6-7	4.01	-1.96	Milacki, Bal	7-7	3.53	7-5	3.98	-0.45
Brown Kev, Tex	6-3	3.25	6-6	3.42	-0.17	Moore M, Oak	10-4	2.02	9-7	3.23	-1.21
Browning, Cin	7-8	4.14	8-4	2.62	1.52	Morgan M, LA	4-6	2.27	4-5	2.89	-0.63
Candiotti, Cle	7-3	2.95	6-7	3.25	-0.30	Morris Jk, Det	4-6	4.75	2-8	4.98	-0.23
Carman, Phi	4-5	4.26	1-10	6.26	-2.00	Ojeda, NYN	6-4	2.95	7-7	3.88	-0.93
Cerutti, Tor	5-5	2.63	6-6	3.51	-0.88	Perez M, ChA	4-6	5.06	7-8	4.97	0.08
Clancy, Hou	4-5	5.66	3-9	4.66	1.00	Perez P, Mon	6-9	2.80	3-4	4.19	-1.39
Clemens, Bos	9-3	2.90	8-8	3.29	-0.40	Rasmussen D, SD	5-4	3.42	5-6	4.86	-1.44
Cone, NYN	8-2	2.61	6-6	4.50	-1.89	Rawley, Min	2-7	6.18	3-5	4.07	2.11
Darling, NYN	8-6	3.04	6-8	4.13	-1.08	Reuschel, SF	8-5	2.79	9-3	3.10	-0.31
Davis Storm, Oak	9-3	4.70	10-4	4.03	0.67	Reuss, Mil	4-5	4.38	5-4	6.02	-1.63
DeLeon J, StL	8-6	2.55	8-6	3.67	-1.12	Robinson D, SF	9-4	2.10	3-7	5.49	-3.39
Deshaies, Hou	8-4	3.13	7-6	2.67	0.45	Robinson JD, Pit	3-6	4.16	4-7	4.92	-0.75
Dopson, Bos	6-5	4.07	6-3	3.86	0.21	Rosenberg, ChA	2-7	4.73	2-6	5.15	-0.41
Dotson, ChA	3-7	4.54	2-5	4.38	0.16	Ryan, Tex	9-6	3.68	7-4	2.52	1.16
Drabek, Pit	8-5	1.85	6-7	3.99	-2.13	Saberhagen, KC	11-1	1.71	12-5	2.61	-0.90
Farrell, Cle	5-6	3.21	4-8	4.10	-0.89	Sanderson, ChN	6-3	3.75	5-6	4.11	-0.36
Fernandez S, NYN	7-2	2.78	7-3	2.91	-0.13	Scott M, Hou	12-6	3.03	8-4	3.21	-0.18
Finley C, Cal	8-7	2.23	8-2	3.01	-0.78	Smiley, Pit	8-4	2.64	4-4	2.99	-0.35
Flanagan, Tor	5-4	3.51	3-6	4.34	-0.84	Smith B, Mon	5-5	2.73	5-6	2.99	-0.26
Garrelts, SF	10-2	1.57	4-3	3.19	-1.62	Smith P, Atl	2-7	4.48	3-7	5.04	-0.56
Gibson P, Det	2-3	3.49	2-5	5.92	-2.43	Smith Roy, Min	5-1	4.22	5-5	3.62	0.60
Glavine, Atl	6-4	3.72	8-4	3.63	0.09	Smith Z, Mon	1-5	2.81	0-8	4.24	-1.44
Gordon, KC	11-5	3.38	6-4	4.06	-0.68	Smithson, Bos	5-6	4.88	2-8	5.04	-0.16
Gross K, Mon	6-4	4.29	5-8	4.46	-0.16	Smoltz, Atl	6-4	2.63	6-7	3.23	-0.60
Gubicza, KC	8-6	3.17	7-5	2.87	0.30	Stewart D, Oak	11-4	2.77	10-5	3.91	-1.14
Harris GW, SD	6-4	2.36	2-5	2.80	-0.44	Stieb, Tor	7-4	3.34	10-4	3.36	-0.03
Hawkins, NYA	9-10	4.54	6-5	5.18	-0.65	Sutcliffe, ChN	5-7	4.80	11-4	2.78	2.03
Heaton, Pit	2-4	2.52	4-3	3.61	-1.09	Swindell, Cle	6-4	3.34	7-2	3.40	-0.06
Hershiser, LA	9-8	2.71	6-7	1.93	0.79	Tanana, Det	4-6	3.48	6-8	3.70	-0.22
Hibbard, ChA	4-3	2.86	2-4	3.57	-0.72	Terrell, NYA	4-9	4.73	7-9	4.33	0.40
Hill K, StL	2-5	3.80	5-10	3.79	0.01	Terry, StL	6-4	3.08	2-6	4.28	-1.20
Holman B, Sea	4-5	4.16	5-7	3.31	0.85	Valenzuela, LA	4-6	3.26	6-7	3.61	-0.34
Hough, Tex	5-6	4.88	5-7	3.94	0.93	Viola, NYN	6-9	3.52	7-8	3.79	-0.27
Howell K, Phi	4-5	3.19	8-7	3.69	-0.51	Walk, Pit	7-4	3.28	6-6	5.38	-2.11
Hurst, SD	9-6	2.58	6-5	2.83	-0.25	Welch, Oak	10-2	2.77	7-6	3.25	-0.49
Jeffcoat, Tex	5-1	3.60	4-5	3.57	0.03	Whitson, SD	9-6	2.98	7-5	2.27	0.70
Johnson R, Sea	2-6	4.76	5-7	4.86	-0.11	Witt B, Tex	5-7	4.74	7-6	5.49	-0.75
Key, Tor	7-8	3.81	6-6	3.95	-0.14	Witt M, Cal	5-7	4.85	4-8	4.25	0.60
Kilgus, ChN	3-4	3.68	3-6	5.40	-1.72						

WHICH PITCHERS MAKE THE LEAST OF THEIR INHERITANCE? (p. 182)

The table below shows the percentage (Pct) of inherited runners (IR) each relief pitcher allowed to scored (SC).

Both Leagues — Listed Alphabetically
(pitchers with 9 or more inherited runners)

Pitcher, Team	IR	SC	Pct	Pitcher, Team	IR	SC	Pct	Pitcher, Team	IR	SC	Pct
Aase, NYN	31	9	29.0	Guetterman, NYA	70	20	28.6	Olin, Cle	22	4	18.2
Acker, Tor	44	12	27.3	Hall D, Tex	41	9	22.0	Olson Gregg, Bal	44	10	22.7
Agosto, Hou	45	17	37.8	Hammaker, SF	13	4	30.8	Orosco, Cle	58	18	31.0
Aguilera, Min	19	10	52.6	Harris GA, Bos	42	21	50.0	Pall, ChA	47	23	48.9
Aldrich, Atl	16	1	6.3	Harris GW, SD	28	6	21.4	Parrett, Phi	41	19	46.3
Alvarez J, Atl	21	5	23.8	Harvey, Cal	40	9	22.5	Patterson K, ChA	41	10	24.4
Andersen L, Hou	34	14	41.2	Havens, Det	16	12	75.0	Pena A, LA	23	8	34.8
Aquino, KC	17	6	35.3	Henke, Tor	42	16	38.1	Pena R, Det	13	8	61.5
Arnsberg, Tex	24	10	41.7	Henneman, Det	38	10	26.3	Perry P, ChN	22	5	22.7
Assenmacher, ChN	50	17	34.0	Hernandez G, Det	31	12	38.7	Pico, ChN	41	19	46.3
Atherton, Cle	29	14	48.3	Hesketh, Mon	22	7	31.8	Plesac, Mil	42	12	28.6
Bailes, Cle	26	12	46.2	Hickey, Bal	48	13	27.1	Plunk, NYA	36	17	47.2
Bair, Pit	30	13	43.3	Hillegas, ChA	37	13	35.1	Powell, Sea	36	11	30.6
Bedrosian, SF	33	10	30.3	Holton, Bal	30	16	53.3	Price, Bos	36	16	44.4
Berenguer, Min	56	16	28.6	Honeycutt, Oak	42	10	23.8	Puleo, Atl	13	11	84.6
Birtsas, Cin	23	13	56.5	Horton, StL	25	8	32.0	Quisenberry, StL	29	8	27.6
Boever, Atl	23	4	17.4	Howell Jay, LA	28	7	25.0	Reardon, Min	47	14	29.8
Brantley J, SF	35	10	28.6	Innis, NYN	24	6	25.0	Reed Jr, Sea	47	12	25.5
Burke, Mon	37	14	37.8	Jackson M, Sea	65	20	30.8	Righetti, NYA	31	6	19.4
Burns, Oak	40	8	20.0	Jones Ba, ChA	23	5	21.7	Robinson JD, Pit	16	7	43.8
Cadaret, NYA	37	15	40.5	Jones D, Cle	40	9	22.5	Rogers, Tex	72	21	29.2
Candelaria, Mon	11	4	36.4	Kaiser, Cle	10	5	50.0	Rosenberg, ChA	20	8	40.0
Carman, Phi	22	5	22.7	Kipper, Pit	33	9	27.3	Russell Jf, Tex	65	22	33.8
Carpenter, StL	17	10	58.8	Knudson, Mil	23	12	52.2	Sanderson, ChN	14	5	35.7
Cary, NYA	16	9	56.3	Krueger, Mil	31	13	41.9	Schatzeder, Hou	22	10	45.5
Castillo T, Atl	25	5	20.0	LaCoss, SF	17	4	23.5	Schiraldi, SD	26	7	26.9
Charlton, Cin	23	5	21.7	Lamp, Bos	55	20	36.4	Schooler, Sea	41	17	41.5
Clements P, SD	13	6	46.2	Lancaster, ChN	39	12	30.8	Schwabe, Det	13	2	15.4
Comstock, Sea	30	8	26.7	Landrum B, Pit	31	11	35.5	Searage, LA	43	17	39.5
Cook M, Min	9	6	66.7	Leach T, KC	24	13	54.2	Smith Le, Bos	42	9	21.4
Corsi, Oak	17	9	52.9	Lefferts, SF	54	17	31.5	Smith MA, Bal	18	2	11.1
Costello, StL	37	12	32.4	Long B, ChA	31	12	38.7	Smith M, Pit	11	5	45.5
Crawford, KC	20	9	45.0	Luecken, KC	12	3	25.0	Smith Z, Mon	13	5	38.5
Crews, LA	31	17	54.8	Maddux M, Phi	15	9	60.0	Smithson, Bos	22	6	27.3
Crim, Mil	80	29	36.3	McCament, SF	23	6	26.1	Stanley B, Bos	53	23	43.4
Darwin, Hou	51	19	37.3	McCarthy, ChA	31	15	48.4	Stanton B, Atl	17	5	29.4
Davis Mrk, SD	75	16	21.3	McClure, Cal	50	7	14.0	Stoddard T, Cle	18	12	66.7
Davis Steve, Cle	14	1	7.1	McCullers, NYA	57	15	26.3	Swift, Sea	22	8	36.4
Dayley, StL	60	10	16.7	McDowell R, Phi	46	18	39.1	Tekulve, Cin	18	9	50.0
Dibble, Cin	61	12	19.7	McGaffigan, Mon	34	13	38.2	Thigpen, ChA	34	12	35.3
DiPino, StL	82	20	24.4	McMurtry, Tex	16	4	25.0	Thurmond, Bal	49	20	40.8
Eckersley, Oak	24	9	37.5	McWilliams, KC	16	6	37.5	Trout, Sea	16	9	56.3
Eichhorn, Atl	34	14	41.2	Mielke, Tex	61	20	32.8	Ward D, Tor	65	22	33.8
Farr, KC	11	4	36.4	Minton, Cal	60	25	41.7	Wayne, Min	54	15	27.8
Forsch B, Hou	17	5	29.4	Mirabella, Mil	11	6	54.5	Wells, Tor	40	12	30.0
Fossas, Mil	55	10	18.2	Mohorcic, NYA	36	13	36.1	Williams F, Det	39	13	33.3
Franco Jn, Cin	17	4	23.5	Monteleone, Cal	16	5	31.3	Williams Mitch, ChN	64	20	31.3
Fraser, Cal	39	14	35.9	Montgomery, KC	31	14	45.2				
Frey, Mon	11	6	54.5	Morgan M, LA	11	5	45.5	Williamson, Bal	65	27	41.5
Frohwirth, Phi	34	12	35.3	Murphy R, Bos	66	20	30.3	Wills, Tor	24	11	45.8
Gibson P, Det	36	11	30.6	Myers R, NYN	54	10	18.5	Wilson S, ChN	51	8	15.7
Gordon, KC	33	16	48.5	Nelson G, Oak	51	16	31.4	Worrell, StL	30	8	26.7
Gossage, NYA	22	6	27.3	Niedenfuer, Sea	10	5	50.0	Yett, Cle	23	8	34.8
Grant, SD	34	14	41.2	Nunez E, Det	28	5	17.9	Young Mt, Oak	30	9	30.0
Guante, Tex	63	14	22.2	O'Neal, Phi	19	3	15.8				

IS THE QUALITY START A QUALITY STAT? (p. 184)

Both Leagues — Listed Alphabetically (pitchers with 20 or more starts)

Pitcher, Team	Games Started	Quality Starts	%	Pitcher, Team	Games Started	Quality Starts	%
Abbott, Cal	29	17	58.6	Leary, Cin	31	18	58.1
Alexander, Det	33	20	60.6	Leibrandt, KC	27	10	37.0
Anderson A, Min	33	19	57.6	Lilliquist, Atl	30	12	40.0
August, Mil	25	10	40.0	Maddux G, ChN	35	21	60.0
Ballard, Bal	35	21	60.0	Magrane, StL	33	28	84.8
Bankhead, Sea	33	22	66.7	Mahler R, Cin	31	19	61.3
Belcher, LA	30	19	63.3	Martinez De, Mon	33	20	60.6
Bielecki, ChN	33	19	57.6	McCaskill, Cal	32	21	65.6
Black, Cle	32	22	68.8	McWilliams, KC	21	10	47.6
Blyleven, Cal	33	25	75.8	Milacki, Bal	36	18	50.0
Boddicker, Bos	34	14	41.2	Moore M, Oak	35	22	62.9
Bosio, Mil	33	22	66.7	Morris Jk, Det	24	11	45.8
Brown Kev, Tex	28	18	64.3	Ojeda, NYN	31	19	61.3
Browning, Cin	37	22	59.5	Perez M, ChA	31	15	48.4
Candiotti, Cle	31	20	64.5	Perez P, Mon	28	22	78.6
Carman, Phi	20	8	40.0	Rasmussen D, SD	33	16	48.5
Cerutti, Tor	31	18	58.1	Rawley, Min	25	9	36.0
Clancy, Hou	26	13	50.0	Reuschel, SF	32	21	65.6
Clemens, Bos	35	24	68.6	Reuss, Mil	26	10	38.5
Cone, NYN	33	20	60.6	Robinson D, SF	32	16	50.0
Darling, NYN	33	24	72.7	Rosenberg, ChA	21	9	42.9
Davis Storm, Oak	31	12	38.7	Ruffin, Phi	23	12	52.2
DeLeon J, StL	36	21	58.3	Ryan, Tex	32	20	62.5
Deshaies, Hou	34	21	61.8	Saberhagen, KC	35	30	85.7
Dopson, Bos	28	16	57.1	Sanderson, ChN	23	9	39.1
Dotson, ChA	26	15	57.7	Schmidt D, Bal	26	7	26.9
Drabek, Pit	34	24	70.6	Scott M, Hou	32	23	71.9
Farrell, Cle	31	18	58.1	Smiley, Pit	28	22	78.6
Fernandez S, NYN	32	22	68.8	Smith B, Mon	32	25	78.1
Finley C, Cal	29	21	72.4	Smith P, Atl	27	12	44.4
Flanagan, Tor	30	16	53.3	Smith Roy, Min	26	16	61.5
Garrelts, SF	29	21	72.4	Smoltz, Atl	29	21	72.4
Glavine, Atl	29	15	51.7	Stewart D, Oak	36	24	66.7
Gross K, Mon	31	17	54.8	Stieb, Tor	33	18	54.5
Gubicza, KC	36	22	61.1	Sutcliffe, ChN	34	22	64.7
Hawkins, NYA	34	16	47.1	Swindell, Cle	28	18	64.3
Hershiser, LA	33	27	81.8	Tanana, Det	33	21	63.6
Hibbard, ChA	23	10	43.5	Terrell, NYA	32	18	56.3
Higuera, Mil	22	11	50.0	Terry, StL	24	14	58.3
Hill K, StL	33	19	57.6	Valenzuela, LA	31	21	67.7
Holman B, Sea	25	11	44.0	Viola, NYN	36	21	58.3
Hough, Tex	30	15	50.0	Walk, Pit	31	16	51.6
Howell K, Phi	32	18	56.3	Welch, Oak	33	18	54.5
Hurst, SD	33	26	78.8	Whitson, SD	33	24	72.7
Jackson Dan, Cin	20	7	35.0	Witt B, Tex	31	11	35.5
Jeffcoat, Tex	22	13	59.1	Witt M, Cal	33	16	48.5
Johnson R, Sea	28	13	46.4	Young C, Oak	20	6	30.0
Key, Tor	33	17	51.5				
Kilgus, ChN	23	10	43.5				
King E, ChA	25	16	64.0				
Knepper, SF	26	12	46.2				
Langston, Mon	34	24	70.6				
LaPoint, NYA	20	6	30.0				

WHICH LEFTY RELIEVERS ARE TOUGHEST AGAINST LEFTHANDED HITTERS? (p. 186)

The table below shows lefty relievers and their performance against lefthanded and righthanded batters. Batters faced (BFP) and batting average (BA) are included.

Both Leagues — Listed by Batting Average against LHB
(pitchers with 1 or more games in relief)

Pitcher, Team	vs. LHB BFP	vs. LHB BA	vs. RHB BFP	vs. RHB BA	Pitcher, Team	vs. LHB BFP	vs. LHB BA	vs. RHB BFP	vs. RHB BA
Lovelace, Cal	2	.000	2	.000	Wells, Tor	85	.234	267	.198
Wickander, Cle	4	.000	11	.667	Plesac, Mil	50	.234	192	.207
Beatty, NYN	6	.000	19	.294	Guetterman, NYA	115	.236	297	.266
Mercker, Atl	3	.000	23	.444	Magrane, StL	148	.236	823	.254
Barfield Jn, Tex	12	.100	40	.378	Bailes, Cle	131	.238	342	.282
Patterson B, Pit	27	.120	82	.270	Davis Mrk, SD	54	.239	316	.194
Mirabella, Mil	21	.133	53	.340	Young Mt, Oak	56	.239	127	.307
Dubois, Det	33	.133	120	.243	Assenmacher, ChN	97	.247	234	.259
Heaton, Pit	132	.137	488	.260	Corbett, Cal	5	.250	15	.133
Orosco, Cle	98	.138	214	.226	Munoz, LA	5	.250	9	.500
Smith Z, Mon	156	.143	478	.289	Cadaret, NYA	138	.252	393	.290
Rodriguez Ro, Cin	8	.143	11	.222	Kilgus, ChN	123	.252	519	.290
West, Min	55	.146	239	.322	Williams Mitch, ChN	87	.254	278	.233
Charlton, Cin	99	.148	294	.212	Murphy R, Bos	119	.257	319	.249
McClure, Cal	76	.154	129	.244	Garcia M, Pit	26	.261	52	.404
Honeycutt, Oak	102	.156	203	.232	Lilliquist, Atl	108	.265	610	.308
Black, Cle	131	.158	781	.268	Gibson P, Det	135	.265	438	.257
Hall D, Tex	74	.159	168	.229	Wilson S, ChN	100	.267	264	.253
Candelaria, Mon	55	.160	219	.290	Rosenberg, ChA	112	.268	505	.274
Myers R, NYN	83	.164	266	.219	Righetti, NYA	71	.274	229	.277
Perry P, ChN	34	.167	107	.194	Hammaker, SF	75	.281	247	.268
Kipper, Pit	108	.170	226	.196	Ruffin, Phi	86	.281	490	.304
Rogers, Tex	99	.173	215	.258	Thurmond, Bal	111	.283	264	.290
Clements P, SD	52	.178	115	.307	Price, Bos	99	.286	265	.264
Fossas, Mil	92	.185	164	.296	Powell, Sea	71	.286	130	.284
Wayne, Min	91	.185	211	.225	Madden, Pit	18	.286	49	.342
Dayley, StL	110	.188	200	.251	Schatzeder, Hou	88	.287	171	.287
McWilliams, KC	113	.192	554	.277	Searage, LA	54	.289	98	.190
Johnson R, Sea	100	.195	615	.257	Guthrie, Min	48	.295	206	.291
Fernandez S, NYN	130	.197	753	.198	Davis Steve, Cle	32	.296	89	.325
Cary, NYA	71	.197	333	.212	Frey, Mon	32	.296	71	.339
Birtsas, Cin	89	.198	211	.289	Patterson K, ChA	76	.297	208	.243
Lefferts, SF	90	.200	340	.242	Hesketh, Mon	70	.298	149	.289
Tudor, LA	12	.200	50	.333	Knepper, SF	114	.301	632	.291
Franco Jn, Cin	55	.200	290	.269	Reuss, Mil	109	.317	508	.296
Rochford, Bos	6	.200	14	.300	Comstock, Sea	52	.333	59	.212
Edwards, ChA	11	.200	19	.313	Nolte, SD	12	.333	37	.387
Hernandez G, Det	44	.205	97	.333	Dillard, Phi	6	.333	13	.385
Havens, Det	43	.205	127	.369	Horton, StL	81	.343	233	.292
Hickey, Bal	74	.206	125	.229	Castillo T, Atl	36	.344	91	.274
Cook D, Phi	77	.206	422	.249	Leibrandt, KC	132	.347	580	.294
DiPino, StL	137	.209	210	.240	Rawley, Min	121	.363	517	.276
Mulholland, Phi	93	.212	420	.313	Musselman J, NYN	50	.366	127	.290
Young C, Oak	87	.213	408	.275	Leiper, SD	36	.370	107	.323
Stanton B, Atl	17	.214	77	.206	Searcy, Det	18	.375	82	.292
Cerutti, Tor	137	.218	719	.283	McElroy, Phi	9	.375	37	.265
Agosto, Hou	126	.220	235	.275	Buchanan, KC	7	.429	11	.250
Carman, Phi	121	.222	562	.269	Snyder B, Oak	3	.500	3	.500
Wilson Tr, SF	31	.222	136	.204	Kaiser, Cle	6	.600	16	.182
Krueger, Mil	104	.223	299	.278	Samuels, Pit	12	.625	11	.364
Trout, Sea	57	.231	91	.403	Mmahat, NYA	6	.750	38	.357
Gleaton, KC	16	.231	50	.378					

WHICH PITCHERS PERFORM BEST AGAINST THE TOP HITTERS? (p. 188)

Top American League hitters (runs created per game): A. Davis, Yount, McGriff, Boggs, Sierra, R. Henderson, Dw. Evans, Baines, Puckett, Esasky, Molitor, Franco, Whitaker, Mattingly and Tartabull.

Top National League hitters: Mitchell, W. Clark, L. Smith, H. Johnson, J. Clark, Grace, Guerrero, E. Davis, Hayes, Raines, Sandberg, G. Davis, Bonilla, Gwynn Bonds.

Both Leagues — Listed Alphabetically (62 or more opponent at bats)

Pitcher, Team	AB	H	HR	RBI	Avg	Pitcher, Team	AB	H	HR	RBI	Avg
Abbott, Cal	82	23	2	13	.280	Leary, Cin	107	31	4	16	.290
Alexander, Det	87	20	3	11	.230	Leibrandt, KC	89	33	0	12	.371
Anderson A, Min	76	24	3	16	.316	Lilliquist, Atl	99	28	2	7	.283
Ballard, Bal	96	32	4	15	.333	Maddux G, ChN	107	32	4	14	.299
Bankhead, Sea	95	19	2	8	.200	Magrane, StL	94	25	2	12	.266
Belcher, LA	113	29	4	6	.257	Mahler R, Cin	118	37	3	20	.314
Bielecki, ChN	110	25	3	9	.227	Martinez De, Mon	129	40	6	14	.310
Black, Cle	80	21	2	15	.262	McCaskill, Cal	103	29	3	11	.282
Blyleven, Cal	95	35	3	11	.368	Milacki, Bal	110	29	4	13	.264
Boddicker, Bos	77	21	4	13	.273	Moore M, Oak	81	23	1	7	.284
Bosio, Mil	96	19	2	11	.198	Morgan M, LA	85	28	1	13	.329
Brown Kev, Tex	75	17	2	10	.227	Morris Jk, Det	71	22	0	9	.310
Browning, Cin	113	39	11	25	.345	Mulholland, Phi	63	20	3	13	.317
Candiotti, Cle	89	25	1	5	.281	Ojeda, NYN	101	20	2	11	.198
Carman, Phi	74	22	3	11	.297	Perez M, ChA	97	37	9	23	.381
Cerutti, Tor	105	29	5	9	.276	Perez P, Mon	112	33	5	12	.295
Clancy, Hou	78	25	5	14	.321	Rasmussen D, SD	93	31	4	16	.333
Clemens, Bos	92	23	1	10	.250	Rawley, Min	66	24	2	9	.364
Cone, NYN	109	34	7	21	.312	Reuschel, SF	112	35	2	13	.313
Darling, NYN	110	29	2	17	.264	Robinson D, SF	103	29	8	21	.282
Davis Storm, Oak	82	25	5	17	.305	Robinson JD, Pit	69	18	5	16	.261
DeLeon J, StL	109	18	4	12	.165	Ruffin, Phi	64	18	2	7	.281
Deshaies, Hou	97	34	3	14	.351	Ryan, Tex	74	17	2	7	.230
Dopson, Bos	61	20	2	6	.328	Saberhagen, KC	101	25	3	10	.248
Drabek, Pit	114	36	5	13	.316	Sanderson, ChN	69	26	1	11	.377
Farrell, Cle	87	25	3	5	.287	Schmidt D, Bal	85	31	3	21	.365
Fernandez S, NYN	97	17	6	13	.175	Scott M, Hou	107	31	4	20	.290
Finley C, Cal	78	14	3	8	.179	Smiley, Pit	96	22	4	12	.229
Flanagan, Tor	82	27	1	11	.329	Smith B, Mon	98	26	4	13	.265
Garrelts, SF	92	29	5	19	.315	Smith P, Atl	81	27	2	13	.333
Glavine, Atl	86	23	4	14	.267	Smith Roy, Min	65	21	8	15	.323
Gordon, KC	74	23	3	17	.311	Smith Z, Mon	68	20	5	16	.294
Gross K, Mon	96	37	8	26	.385	Smoltz, Atl	113	28	7	19	.248
Gubicza, KC	123	36	2	7	.293	Stewart D, Oak	118	37	6	21	.314
Harnisch, Bal	63	15	1	5	.238	Stieb, Tor	88	28	2	11	.318
Hawkins, NYA	93	27	6	16	.290	Stottlemyre, Tor	63	26	2	12	.413
Hershiser, LA	142	40	5	16	.282	Sutcliffe, ChN	114	33	7	17	.289
Hibbard, ChA	62	15	1	6	.242	Swift, Sea	70	20	4	16	.286
Hill K, StL	80	31	1	13	.387	Swindell, Cle	73	16	3	7	.219
Holman B, Sea	73	21	2	10	.288	Tanana, Det	75	22	2	14	.293
Hough, Tex	62	16	1	6	.258	Terrell, NYA	103	29	5	18	.282
Howell K, Phi	97	21	3	15	.216	Terry, StL	77	25	6	15	.325
Hurst, SD	113	39	6	20	.345	Valenzuela, LA	84	28	4	14	.333
Johnson R, Sea	62	21	2	14	.339	Viola, NYN	133	42	5	15	.316
Key, Tor	77	28	1	10	.364	Walk, Pit	106	33	5	24	.311
Kilgus, ChN	74	12	0	6	.162	Welch, Oak	98	27	2	6	.276
King E, ChA	62	19	3	9	.306	Whitson, SD	102	27	4	8	.265
Knepper, SF	68	23	5	17	.338	Witt B, Tex	86	24	3	10	.279
LaCoss, SF	64	16	0	8	.250	Witt M, Cal	105	42	3	17	.400
Langston, Mon	95	18	3	7	.189						

WHICH PITCHERS ARE VICTIMIZED MOST BY THEIR OWN BULLPENS? (p. 190)

Both Leagues — Listed Alphabetically (140 or more innings pitched)

Pitcher, Team	GS/GR	ERA	BEQ	SCD	RS ERA	Pitcher, Team	GS/GR	ERA	BEQ	SCD	RS ERA
Abbott, Cal	29/0	3.92	28	15	0.74	Leary, Cin	31/2	3.52	18	8	0.35
Aguilera, Min	11/3	2.79	9	5	0.31	Leibrandt, KC	27/6	5.14	24	11	0.61
Alexander, Det	33/0	4.44	18	5	0.20	Lilliquist, Atl	30/2	3.97	34	10	0.54
Anderson A, Min	33/0	3.80	14	5	0.23	Maddux G, ChN	35/0	2.95	27	7	0.26
Aquino, KC	16/1	3.50	16	8	0.51	Magrane, StL	33/1	2.91	23	9	0.35
August, Mil	25/6	5.31	28	11	0.70	Mahler R, Cin	31/9	3.83	16	5	0.20
Ballard, Bal	35/0	3.43	35	12	0.50	Martinez De, Mon	33/1	3.18	15	6	0.23
Bankhead, Sea	33/0	3.34	21	8	0.34	McCaskill, Cal	32/0	2.93	21	2	0.08
Belcher, LA	30/9	2.82	21	11	0.43	McWilliams, KC	21/2	4.11	40	18	1.06
Bielecki, ChN	33/0	3.14	31	12	0.51	Milacki, Bal	36/1	3.74	36	12	0.44
Black, Cle	32/1	3.36	25	12	0.49	Moore M, Oak	35/0	2.61	20	5	0.19
Blyleven, Cal	33/0	2.73	12	4	0.15	Morgan M, LA	19/2	2.53	14	3	0.18
Boddicker, Bos	34/0	4.00	39	13	0.55	Morris Jk, Det	24/0	4.86	19	5	0.26
Bosio, Mil	33/0	2.95	23	7	0.27	Ojeda, NYN	31/0	3.47	28	7	0.33
Brown Kev, Tex	28/0	3.35	23	10	0.47	Perez M, ChA	31/0	5.01	30	12	0.59
Browning, Cin	37/0	3.39	19	8	0.29	Perez P, Mon	28/5	3.31	8	5	0.23
Candiotti, Cle	31/0	3.10	27	6	0.26	Rasmussen D, SD	33/0	4.26	33	10	0.49
Carman, Phi	20/2	5.24	36	21	1.27	Rawley, Min	25/2	5.21	22	9	0.56
Cerutti, Tor	31/2	3.07	29	11	0.48	Reuschel, SF	32/0	2.94	19	4	0.17
Clancy, Hou	26/7	5.08	22	12	0.73	Reuss, Mil	26/4	5.13	18	7	0.45
Clemens, Bos	35/0	3.13	24	11	0.39	Robinson D, SF	32/2	3.43	19	4	0.18
Cone, NYN	33/1	3.52	20	3	0.12	Robinson JD, Pit	19/3	4.58	18	8	0.51
Darling, NYN	33/0	3.52	19	5	0.21	Rosenberg, ChA	21/1	4.94	41	22	1.39
Davis Storm, Oak	31/0	4.36	19	3	0.16	Ryan, Tex	32/0	3.20	23	7	0.26
DeLeon J, StL	36/0	3.05	22	13	0.48	Saberhagen, KC	35/1	2.16	8	2	0.07
Deshaies, Hou	34/0	2.91	20	11	0.44	Sanderson, ChN	23/3	3.94	26	11	0.68
Dopson, Bos	28/1	3.99	30	9	0.48	Schmidt D, Bal	26/1	5.69	23	8	0.46
Dotson, ChA	26/2	4.46	24	9	0.54	Scott M, Hou	32/1	3.10	5	2	0.08
Drabek, Pit	34/1	2.80	16	3	0.11	Smiley, Pit	28/0	2.81	8	2	0.09
Farrell, Cle	31/0	3.63	28	6	0.48	Smith B, Mon	32/1	2.84	14	5	0.21
Fernandez S, NYN	32/3	2.83	18	6	0.25	Smith P, Atl	27/1	4.75	27	10	0.63
Finley C, Cal	29/0	2.57	22	5	0.23	Smith Roy, Min	26/6	3.92	24	5	0.26
Flanagan, Tor	30/0	3.93	33	8	0.42	Smith Z, Mon	17/3	3.49	20	7	0.43
Garrelts, SF	29/1	2.28	14	4	0.19	Smithson, Bos	19/2	4.95	24	12	0.75
Glavine, Atl	29/0	3.68	20	12	0.58	Smoltz, Atl	29/0	2.94	11	3	0.13
Gordon, KC	16/3	3.64	22	7	0.39	Stewart D, Oak	36/0	3.32	22	6	0.21
Gross K, Mon	31/0	4.38	25	16	0.72	Stieb, Tor	33/0	3.35	16	9	0.39
Gubicza, KC	36/0	3.04	17	10	0.35	Sutcliffe, ChN	34/1	3.66	26	13	0.51
Hawkins, NYA	34/0	4.80	35	14	0.60	Swindell, Cle	28/0	3.37	21	11	0.54
Heaton, Pit	18/2	3.05	14	4	0.24	Tanana, Det	33/0	3.58	16	4	0.16
Hershiser, LA	33/2	2.31	4	2	0.07	Terrell, NYA	32/0	4.49	20	9	0.39
Hill K, StL	33/0	3.80	30	7	0.32	Terry, StL	24/7	3.57	10	4	0.24
Holman B, Sea	25/8	3.67	18	8	0.38	Valenzuela, LA	31/0	3.43	18	7	0.32
Hough, Tex	30/0	4.35	31	10	0.49	Viola, NYN	36/0	3.66	10	4	0.14
Howell K, Phi	32/1	3.44	17	9	0.40	Walk, Pit	31/2	4.41	23	14	0.64
Hurst, SD	33/0	2.69	9	1	0.04	Welch, Oak	33/0	3.00	23	8	0.34
Johnson R, Sea	28/1	4.82	26	6	0.34	Whitson, SD	33/0	2.66	12	2	0.08
Key, Tor	33/0	3.88	19	7	0.29	Witt B, Tex	31/0	5.14	32	14	0.65
Kilgus, ChN	23/1	4.39	35	15	0.93	Witt M, Cal	33/0	4.54	24	12	0.49
King E, ChA	25/0	3.39	24	7	0.40						
Knepper, SF	26/9	5.13	16	6	0.33						
LaCoss, SF	18/2	3.17	23	8	0.48						
Langston, Mon	34/0	2.74	13	5	0.18						

Note: RS ERA = "Runs Scored" ERA

WHO ARE THE TOUGHEST (AND EASIEST) PITCHERS TO STEAL ON? (p. 194)

Both Leagues — Listed Alphabetically (140 or more innings pitched)

Pitcher, Team	SB	CS	CS %	SB per 9 Inn	Pick-offs
Abbott, Cal	29	8	78.4	1.44	0
Aguilera, Min	9	5	64.3	0.56	0
Alexander, Det	16	10	61.5	0.65	1
Anderson A, Min	12	8	60.0	0.55	0
Aquino, KC	4	6	40.0	0.25	1
August, Mil	12	7	63.2	0.76	0
Ballard, Bal	14	14	50.0	0.59	1
Bankhead, Sea	17	8	68.0	0.73	0
Belcher, LA	22	14	61.1	0.86	0
Bielecki, ChN	5	7	41.7	0.21	0
Black, Cle	15	8	65.2	0.61	1
Blyleven, Cal	18	5	78.3	0.67	0
Boddicker, Bos	16	6	72.7	0.68	1
Bosio, Mil	16	4	80.0	0.61	1
Brown Kev, Tex	6	5	54.5	0.28	2
Browning, Cin	15	9	62.5	0.54	1
Candiotti, Cle	24	5	82.8	1.05	6
Carman, Phi	4	4	50.0	0.24	0
Cerutti, Tor	12	14	46.2	0.53	1
Clancy, Hou	14	2	87.5	0.86	0
Clemens, Bos	19	17	52.8	0.68	0
Cone, NYN	27	10	73.0	1.11	0
Darling, NYN	26	11	70.3	1.08	2
Davis Storm, Oak	8	10	44.4	0.43	1
DeLeon J, StL	13	12	52.0	0.48	0
Deshaies, Hou	27	6	81.8	1.08	1
Dopson, Bos	28	5	84.8	1.49	0
Dotson, ChA	9	3	75.0	0.54	0
Drabek, Pit	24	9	72.7	0.88	8
Farrell, Cle	20	3	87.0	0.87	0
Fernandez S, NYN	11	4	73.3	0.45	0
Finley C, Cal	17	12	58.6	0.77	0
Flanagan, Tor	15	5	75.0	0.79	0
Garrelts, SF	15	5	75.0	0.70	1
Glavine, Atl	12	11	52.2	0.58	0
Gordon, KC	7	3	70.0	0.39	0
Gross K, Mon	34	13	72.3	1.52	1
Gubicza, KC	9	8	52.9	0.32	0
Hawkins, NYA	8	11	42.1	0.35	0
Heaton, Pit	12	3	80.0	0.73	1
Hershiser, LA	11	8	57.9	0.39	0
Hill K, StL	19	9	67.9	0.87	0
Holman B, Sea	11	4	73.3	0.52	0
Hough, Tex	26	9	74.3	1.29	2
Howell K, Phi	26	15	63.4	1.15	1
Hurst, SD	15	14	51.7	0.55	4
Johnson R, Sea	32	5	86.5	1.79	4
Key, Tor	9	4	69.2	0.38	2
Kilgus, ChN	5	5	50.0	0.31	1
King E, ChA	13	7	65.0	0.73	1
Knepper, SF	17	6	73.9	0.93	0
LaCoss, SF	8	8	50.0	0.48	0
Langston, Mon	23	18	56.1	0.83	4
Leary, Cin	19	8	70.4	0.83	0
Leibrandt, KC	14	9	60.9	0.78	1
Lilliquist, Atl	6	6	50.0	0.33	0
Maddux G, ChN	11	12	47.8	0.42	0
Magrane, StL	24	11	68.6	0.92	0
Mahler R, Cin	21	17	55.3	0.86	0
Martinez De, Mon	23	13	63.9	0.89	2
McCaskill, Cal	5	5	50.0	0.21	1
McWilliams, KC	6	7	46.2	0.35	0
Milacki, Bal	19	6	76.0	0.70	0
Moore M, Oak	7	10	41.2	0.26	2
Morgan M, LA	7	4	63.6	0.41	2
Morris Jk, Det	24	6	80.0	1.27	0
Ojeda, NYN	28	10	73.7	1.31	0
Perez M, ChA	18	12	60.0	0.88	0
Perez P, Mon	16	9	64.0	0.73	0
Rasmussen D, SD	10	6	62.5	0.49	0
Rawley, Min	11	7	61.1	0.68	1
Reuschel, SF	9	7	56.3	0.39	1
Reuss, Mil	5	7	41.7	0.32	0
Robinson D, SF	18	10	64.3	0.82	0
Robinson JD, Pit	25	5	83.3	1.59	2
Rosenberg, ChA	11	4	73.3	0.70	0
Ryan, Tex	36	6	85.7	1.35	0
Saberhagen, KC	5	9	35.7	0.17	3
Sanderson, ChN	15	5	75.0	0.92	0
Schmidt D, Bal	13	4	76.5	0.75	0
Scott M, Hou	39	2	95.1	1.53	0
Smiley, Pit	29	9	76.3	1.27	0
Smith B, Mon	24	4	85.7	1.00	1
Smith P, Atl	17	9	65.4	1.08	0
Smith Roy, Min	10	9	52.6	0.52	0
Smith Z, Mon	14	7	66.7	0.86	1
Smithson, Bos	10	4	71.4	0.63	1
Smoltz, Atl	14	6	70.0	0.61	3
Stewart D, Oak	11	8	57.9	0.38	0
Stieb, Tor	11	6	64.7	0.48	1
Sutcliffe, ChN	25	7	78.1	0.98	2
Swindell, Cle	18	13	58.1	0.88	0
Tanana, Det	22	12	64.7	0.89	2
Terrell, NYA	8	3	72.7	0.35	0
Terry, StL	11	4	73.3	0.67	0
Valenzuela, LA	15	15	50.0	0.69	1
Viola, NYN	16	11	59.3	0.55	0
Walk, Pit	24	11	68.6	1.10	4
Welch, Oak	22	7	75.9	0.94	2
Whitson, SD	8	5	61.5	0.32	0
Witt B, Tex	30	4	88.2	1.39	0
Witt M, Cal	14	7	66.7	0.57	0

WHOSE HEATER IS THE HOTTEST? (p. 199)

Both Leagues — Listed Alphabetically
(pitchers with 25 starts or 50 relief appearances)

Pitcher, Team	K	IP	K/9	Pitcher, Team	K	IP	K/9	Pitcher, Team	K	IP	K/9
Abbott, Cal	115	181.1	5.7	Garrelts, SF	119	193.1	5.5	Orosco, Cle	79	78.0	9.1
Acker, Tor	92	126.0	6.6	Glavine, Atl	90	186.0	4.4	Pall, ChA	58	87.0	6.0
Agosto, Hou	46	83.0	5.0	Grant, SD	69	116.1	5.3	Parrett, Phi	98	105.2	8.3
Alexander, Det	95	223.0	3.8	Gross K, Mon	158	201.1	7.1	Pena A, LA	75	76.0	8.9
Andersen L, Hou	85	87.2	8.7	Guante, Tex	69	69.0	9.0	Perez M, ChA	141	183.1	6.9
Anderson A, Min	69	196.2	3.2	Gubicza, KC	173	255.0	6.1	Perez P, Mon	152	198.1	6.9
Assenmacher, ChN	79	76.2	9.3	Guetterman, NYA	51	103.0	4.5	Plesac, Mil	52	61.1	7.6
August, Mil	51	142.1	3.2	Harris GA, Bos	76	103.1	6.6	Quisenberry, StL	37	78.1	4.3
Ballard, Bal	62	215.1	2.6	Harvey, Cal	78	55.0	12.8	Rasmussen D, SD	87	183.2	4.3
Bankhead, Sea	140	210.1	6.0	Hawkins, NYA	98	208.1	4.2	Rawley, Min	68	145.0	4.2
Bedrosian, SF	58	84.2	6.2	Henke, Tor	116	89.0	11.7	Reardon, Min	46	73.0	5.7
Belcher, LA	200	230.0	7.8	Henneman, Det	69	90.0	6.9	Reed Jr, Sea	50	101.2	4.4
Berenguer, Min	93	106.0	7.9	Hershiser, LA	178	256.2	6.2	Reuschel, SF	111	208.1	4.8
Bielecki, ChN	147	212.1	6.2	Hickey, Bal	28	49.1	5.1	Reuss, Mil	40	140.1	2.6
Black, Cle	88	222.1	3.6	Hill K, StL	112	196.2	5.1	Righetti, NYA	51	69.0	6.7
Blyleven, Cal	131	241.0	4.9	Holman B, Sea	105	191.1	4.9	Robinson D, SF	96	197.0	4.4
Boddicker, Bos	145	211.2	6.2	Honeycutt, Oak	52	76.2	6.1	Rogers, Tex	63	73.2	7.7
Boever, Atl	68	82.1	7.4	Hough, Tex	94	182.0	4.6	Russell Jf, Tex	77	72.2	9.5
Bosio, Mil	173	234.2	6.6	Howell Jay, LA	55	79.2	6.2	Ryan, Tex	301	239.1	11.3
Brantley J, SF	69	97.1	6.4	Howell K, Phi	164	204.0	7.2	Saberhagen, KC	193	262.1	6.6
Brown Kev, Tex	104	191.0	4.9	Hurst, SD	179	244.2	6.6	Schiraldi, SD	71	100.0	6.4
Browning, Cin	118	249.2	4.3	Jackson M, Sea	94	99.1	8.5	Schmidt D, Bal	46	156.2	2.6
Burke, Mon	54	84.2	5.7	Johnson R, Sea	130	160.2	7.3	Schooler, Sea	69	77.0	8.1
Candiotti, Cle	124	206.0	5.4	Jones D, Cle	65	80.2	7.3	Scott M, Hou	172	229.0	6.8
Cerutti, Tor	69	205.1	3.0	Key, Tor	118	216.0	4.9	Smiley, Pit	123	205.1	5.4
Charlton, Cin	98	95.1	9.3	King E, ChA	72	159.1	4.1	Smith B, Mon	129	215.2	5.4
Clancy, Hou	91	147.0	5.6	Kipper, Pit	58	83.0	6.3	Smith Dv, Hou	31	58.0	4.8
Clemens, Bos	230	253.1	8.2	Knepper, SF	64	165.0	3.5	Smith Le, Bos	96	70.2	12.2
Cone, NYN	190	219.2	7.8	Landrum B, Pit	51	81.0	5.7	Smith P, Atl	115	142.0	7.3
Crim, Mil	59	117.2	4.5	Langston, Mon	235	250.0	8.5	Smith Roy, Min	92	172.1	4.8
Darling, NYN	153	217.1	6.3	Leary, Cin	123	207.0	5.3	Smoltz, Atl	168	208.0	7.3
Darwin, Hou	104	122.0	7.7	Lefferts, SF	71	107.0	6.0	Stewart D, Oak	155	257.2	5.4
Davis Mrk, SD	92	92.2	8.9	Leibrandt, KC	73	161.0	4.1	Stieb, Tor	101	206.2	4.4
Davis Storm, Oak	91	169.1	4.8	Lilliquist, Atl	79	165.2	4.3	Sutcliffe, ChN	153	229.0	6.0
Dayley, StL	40	75.1	4.8	Maddux G, ChN	135	238.1	5.1	Swindell, Cle	129	184.1	6.3
DeLeon J, StL	201	244.2	7.4	Magrane, StL	127	234.2	4.9	Tanana, Det	147	223.2	5.9
Deshaies, Hou	153	225.2	6.1	Mahler R, Cin	102	220.2	4.2	Terrell, NYA	93	206.1	4.1
Dibble, Cin	141	99.0	12.8	Martinez De, Mon	142	232.0	5.5	Thigpen, ChA	47	79.0	5.4
DiPino, StL	44	88.1	4.5	McCaskill, Cal	107	212.0	4.5	Valenzuela, LA	116	196.2	5.3
Dopson, Bos	95	169.1	5.0	McCullers, NYA	82	84.2	8.7	Viola, NYN	211	261.0	7.3
Dotson, ChA	69	151.1	4.1	McDowell R, Phi	47	92.0	4.6	Walk, Pit	83	196.0	3.8
Drabek, Pit	123	244.1	4.5	McGaffigan, Mon	40	75.0	4.8	Ward D, Tor	122	114.2	9.6
Eckersley, Oak	55	57.2	8.6	Milacki, Bal	113	243.0	4.2	Wayne, Min	41	71.0	5.2
Farrell, Cle	132	208.0	5.7	Minton, Cal	42	90.0	4.2	Welch, Oak	137	209.2	5.9
Fernandez S, NYN	198	219.1	8.1	Montgomery, KC	94	92.0	9.2	Wells, Tor	78	86.1	8.1
				Moore M, Oak	172	241.2	6.4	Whitson, SD	117	227.0	4.6
Finley C, Cal	156	199.2	7.0	Murphy R, Bos	107	105.0	9.2	Williams Mitch, ChN	67	81.2	7.4
Flanagan, Tor	47	171.2	2.5	Myers R, NYN	88	84.1	9.4				
Fossas, Mil	42	61.0	6.2	Nelson G, Oak	70	80.0	7.9	Williamson, Bal	55	107.1	4.6
Franco Jn, Cin	60	80.2	6.7	Ojeda, NYN	95	192.0	4.5	Witt B, Tex	166	194.1	7.7
				Olson Gregg, Bal	90	85.0	9.5	Witt M, Cal	123	220.0	5.0

WHO THROWS TO FIRST? (p. 200)

Both Leagues — Listed Alphabetically (140 or more innings pitched)

Pitcher, Team	PkOf Throws	IP	PkOf per 9 IP	SB per 9 IP	Pitcher, Team	PkOf Throws	IP	PkOf per 9 IP	SB per 9 IP
Abbott, Cal	119	181.1	5.9	1.44	Leibrandt, KC	147	161.0	8.2	0.78
Aguilera, Min	22	145.0	1.4	0.56	Lilliquist, Atl	76	165.2	4.1	0.33
Alexander, Det	178	223.0	7.2	0.65	Maddux G, ChN	109	238.1	4.1	0.42
Anderson A, Min	90	196.2	4.1	0.55	Magrane, StL	62	234.2	2.4	0.92
Aquino, KC	42	141.1	2.7	0.25	Mahler R, Cin	114	220.2	4.6	0.86
August, Mil	98	142.1	6.2	0.76	Martinez De, Mon	251	232.0	9.7	0.89
Ballard, Bal	147	215.1	6.1	0.59	McCaskill, Cal	186	212.0	7.9	0.21
Bankhead, Sea	240	210.1	10.3	0.73	McWilliams, KC	8	153.1	0.5	0.35
Belcher, LA	134	230.0	5.2	0.86	Milacki, Bal	153	243.0	5.7	0.70
Bielecki, ChN	143	212.1	6.1	0.21	Moore M, Oak	196	241.2	7.3	0.26
Black, Cle	126	222.1	5.1	0.61	Morgan M, LA	101	152.2	6.0	0.41
Blyleven, Cal	41	241.0	1.5	0.67	Morris Jk, Det	41	170.1	2.2	1.27
Boddicker, Bos	133	211.2	5.7	0.68	Ojeda, NYN	66	192.0	3.1	1.31
Bosio, Mil	111	234.2	4.3	0.61	Perez M, ChA	61	183.1	3.0	0.88
Brown Kev, Tex	157	191.0	7.4	0.28	Perez P, Mon	10	198.1	0.5	0.73
Browning, Cin	103	249.2	3.7	0.54	Rasmussen D, SD	169	183.2	8.3	0.49
Candiotti, Cle	247	206.0	10.8	1.05	Rawley, Min	91	145.0	5.6	0.68
Carman, Phi	24	149.1	1.4	0.24	Reuschel, SF	89	208.1	3.8	0.39
Cerutti, Tor	249	205.1	10.9	0.53	Reuss, Mil	61	140.1	3.9	0.32
Clancy, Hou	112	147.0	6.9	0.86	Robinson D, SF	176	197.0	8.0	0.82
Clemens, Bos	295	253.1	10.5	0.68	Robinson JD, Pit	77	141.1	4.9	1.59
Cone, NYN	129	219.2	5.3	1.11	Rosenberg, ChA	154	142.0	9.8	0.70
Darling, NYN	161	217.1	6.7	1.08	Ryan, Tex	53	239.1	2.0	1.35
Davis Storm, Oak	60	169.1	3.2	0.43	Saberhagen, KC	93	262.1	3.2	0.17
DeLeon J, StL	11	244.2	0.4	0.48	Sanderson, ChN	78	146.1	4.8	0.92
Deshaies, Hou	355	225.2	14.2	1.08	Schmidt D, Bal	134	156.2	7.7	0.75
Dopson, Bos	147	169.1	7.8	1.49	Scott M, Hou	121	229.0	4.8	1.53
Dotson, ChA	46	151.1	2.7	0.54	Smiley, Pit	166	205.1	7.3	1.27
Drabek, Pit	143	244.1	5.3	0.88	Smith B, Mon	175	215.2	7.3	1.00
Farrell, Cle	68	208.0	2.9	0.87	Smith P, Atl	217	142.0	13.8	1.08
Fernandez S, NYN	42	219.1	1.7	0.45	Smith Roy, Min	73	172.1	3.8	0.52
Finley C, Cal	20	199.2	0.9	0.77	Smith Z, Mon	164	147.0	10.0	0.86
Flanagan, Tor	149	171.2	7.8	0.79	Smithson, Bos	110	143.2	6.9	0.63
Garrelts, SF	107	193.1	5.0	0.70	Smoltz, Atl	108	208.0	4.7	0.61
Glavine, Atl	185	186.0	9.0	0.58	Stewart D, Oak	123	257.2	4.3	0.38
Gordon, KC	39	163.0	2.2	0.39	Stieb, Tor	138	206.2	6.0	0.48
Gross K, Mon	84	201.1	3.8	1.52	Sutcliffe, ChN	222	229.0	8.7	0.98
Gubicza, KC	122	255.0	4.3	0.32	Swindell, Cle	68	184.1	3.3	0.88
Hawkins, NYA	126	208.1	5.4	0.35	Tanana, Det	196	223.2	7.9	0.89
Heaton, Pit	120	147.1	7.3	0.73	Terrell, NYA	104	206.1	4.5	0.35
Hershiser, LA	145	256.2	5.1	0.39	Terry, StL	17	148.2	1.0	0.67
Hill K, StL	106	196.2	4.9	0.87	Valenzuela, LA	156	196.2	7.1	0.69
Holman B, Sea	148	191.1	7.0	0.52	Viola, NYN	109	261.0	3.8	0.55
Hough, Tex	277	182.0	13.7	1.29	Walk, Pit	172	196.0	7.9	1.10
Howell K, Phi	111	204.0	4.9	1.15	Welch, Oak	161	209.2	6.9	0.94
Hurst, SD	253	244.2	9.3	0.55	Whitson, SD	122	227.0	4.8	0.32
Johnson R, Sea	177	160.2	9.9	1.79	Witt B, Tex	125	194.1	5.8	1.39
Key, Tor	121	216.0	5.0	0.38	Witt M, Cal	48	220.0	2.0	0.57
Kilgus, ChN	55	145.2	3.4	0.31					
King E, ChA	124	159.1	7.0	0.73					
Knepper, SF	200	165.0	10.9	0.93					
LaCoss, SF	91	150.1	5.4	0.48					
Langston, Mon	180	250.0	6.5	0.83					
Leary, Cin	99	207.0	4.3	0.83					

WHICH PITCHERS THROW THE MOST DOUBLE PLAY GROUNDERS? (p. 202)

The table below shows the percentage of GDP opportunities turned into a groundball double play for each pitcher. A GDP oppotunity is defined as a man on first with less than two outs.

Both Leagues — Listed Alphabetically
(pitchers with 81 or more GDP opportunities)

Pitcher, Team	Op	DP	DP%	Pitcher, Team	Op	DP	DP%	Pitcher, Team	Op	DP	DP%
Abbott, Cal	154	23	14.9	Hanson, Sea	91	11	12.1	Perez P, Mon	118	14	11.9
Alexander, Det	184	15	8.2	Harnisch, Bal	90	9	10.0	Price, Bos	81	8	9.9
Anderson A, Min	160	22	13.8	Hawkins, NYA	153	25	16.3	Rasmussen D, SD	166	19	11.4
Aquino, KC	131	12	9.2	Heaton, Pit	102	9	8.8	Rawley, Min	137	17	12.4
August, Mil	131	15	11.5	Henneman, Det	82	10	12.2	Reuschel, SF	138	10	7.2
Bailes, Cle	99	17	17.2	Hershiser, LA	192	29	15.1	Reuss, Mil	124	13	10.5
Ballard, Bal	169	24	14.2	Hibbard, ChA	103	16	15.5	Robinson D, SF	102	11	10.8
Bankhead, Sea	151	15	9.9	Higuera, Mil	104	10	9.6	Robinson JD, Pit	84	6	7.1
Belcher, LA	170	9	5.3	Hill K, StL	169	13	7.7	Rogers, Tex	81	6	7.4
Berenguer, Min	92	8	8.7	Hillegas, ChA	95	7	7.4	Rosenberg, ChA	100	14	14.0
Bielecki, ChN	151	18	11.9	Holman B, Sea	166	19	11.4	Ruffin, Phi	117	13	11.1
Black, Cle	150	19	12.7	Holton, Bal	92	11	12.0	Ryan, Tex	132	4	3.0
Blyleven, Cal	170	25	14.7	Hough, Tex	129	10	7.8	Saberhagen, KC	136	13	9.6
Boddicker, Bos	170	19	11.2	Howell K, Phi	144	17	11.8	Sanderson, ChN	107	9	8.4
Bosio, Mil	192	15	7.8	Hurst, SD	158	12	7.6	Schmidt D, Bal	128	8	6.3
Brantley J, SF	83	9	10.8	Jackson Dan, Cin	106	9	8.5	Scott M, Hou	115	10	8.7
Brown Kev, Tex	142	22	15.5	Jeffcoat, Tex	104	11	10.6	Smiley, Pit	120	12	10.0
Browning, Cin	161	18	11.2	Johnson R, Sea	126	10	7.9	Smith B, Mon	133	20	15.0
Burns, Oak	83	10	12.0	Key, Tor	130	16	12.3	Smith P, Atl	90	11	12.2
Cadaret, NYA	122	14	11.5	Kilgus, ChN	125	16	12.8	Smith Roy, Min	129	10	7.8
Candiotti, Cle	122	11	9.0	King E, ChA	131	25	19.1	Smith Z, Mon	132	13	9.8
Carman, Phi	122	6	4.9	Knepper, SF	136	13	9.6	Smithson, Bos	125	9	7.2
Cerutti, Tor	140	22	15.7	Knudson, Mil	86	14	16.3	Smoltz, Atl	151	13	8.6
Clancy, Hou	114	14	12.3	Kramer, Pit	95	10	10.5	Stanley B, Bos	86	13	15.1
Clemens, Bos	175	23	13.1	LaCoss, SF	142	14	9.9	Stewart D, Oak	187	19	10.2
Cone, NYN	118	6	5.1	Langston, Mon	186	17	9.1	Stieb, Tor	156	18	11.5
Crim, Mil	117	20	17.1	LaPoint, NYA	110	12	10.9	Stottlemyre, Tor	95	11	11.6
Darling, NYN	148	10	6.8	Leary, Cin	165	20	12.1	Sutcliffe, ChN	150	13	8.7
Darwin, Hou	94	4	4.3	Lefferts, SF	88	9	10.2	Swift, Sea	130	26	20.0
Davis Mrk, SD	88	12	13.6	Leibrandt, KC	139	15	10.8	Swindell, Cle	124	10	8.1
Davis Storm, Oak	174	24	13.8	Lilliquist, Atl	110	13	11.8	Tanana, Det	166	20	12.0
DeLeon J, StL	145	12	8.3	Long B, ChA	82	7	8.5	Terrell, NYA	162	26	16.0
Deshaies, Hou	149	12	8.1	Maddux G, ChN	203	17	8.4	Terry, StL	89	9	10.1
Dopson, Bos	139	19	13.7	Magrane, StL	166	24	14.5	Thurmond, Bal	85	16	18.8
Dotson, ChA	132	13	9.8	Mahler R, Cin	144	14	9.7	Valenzuela, LA	151	9	6.0
Drabek, Pit	134	13	9.7	Martinez De, Mon	143	21	14.7	Viola, NYN	195	16	8.2
Dunne, Sea	103	11	10.7	McCaskill, Cal	170	32	18.8	Walk, Pit	131	12	9.2
Farrell, Cle	143	5	3.5	McDowell R, Phi	88	12	13.6	Ward D, Tor	119	9	7.6
Fernandez S, NYN	124	8	6.5	McWilliams, KC	129	11	8.5	Welch, Oak	139	17	12.2
Finley C, Cal	138	14	10.1	Milacki, Bal	171	29	17.0	Whitson, SD	135	16	11.9
Flanagan, Tor	138	23	16.7	Minton, Cal	86	11	12.8	Williams F, Det	84	6	7.1
Forsch B, Hou	104	9	8.7	Moore M, Oak	153	18	11.8	Williams Mitch, ChN	93	3	3.2
Garrelts, SF	109	9	8.3	Morgan M, LA	100	17	17.0				
Gibson P, Det	111	7	6.3	Morris Jk, Det	124	15	12.1	Williamson, Bal	100	12	12.0
Glavine, Atl	118	14	11.9	Mulholland, Phi	109	11	10.1	Witt B, Tex	175	13	7.4
Gordon, KC	139	20	14.4	Murphy R, Bos	98	12	12.2	Witt M, Cal	154	17	11.0
Grant, SD	90	15	16.7	Navarro, Mil	87	10	11.5	Yett, Cle	81	6	7.4
Gross K, Mon	138	5	3.6	Ojeda, NYN	147	13	8.8				
Gubicza, KC	174	20	11.5	Parker C, NYA	86	13	15.1				
Guetterman, NYA	93	18	19.4	Perez M, ChA	126	10	7.9				

WHICH PITCHERS ARE THE BEST "LONG DISTANCE RUNNERS?" (p. 204)

Both Leagues — Listed Alphabetically (162 or more innings pitched)

Pitcher, Team	Inning 1-6 CG IP ERA	Inning 7+ IP ERA	Diff	Pitcher, Team	Inning 1-6 CG IP ERA	Inning 7+ IP ERA	Diff
Abbott, Cal	4 157.0 3.96	24.1 3.70	-0.26	Key, Tor	5 182.1 3.80	33.2 4.28	0.48
Alexander, Det	5 187.2 4.36	35.1 4.84	0.48	Knepper, SF	1 152.3 5.21	13.3 4.15	-1.06
Anderson A, Min	4 168.1 4.01	28.1 2.54	-1.47	Langston, Mon	8 196.2 2.84	53.1 2.36	-0.48
Ballard, Bal	4 182.1 3.70	33.0 1.91	-1.79	Leary, Cin	2 175.3 3.14	32.0 5.63	2.49
Bankhead, Sea	3 185.1 3.45	25.0 2.52	-0.93	Lilliquist, Atl	0 155.2 4.05	10.0 2.70	-1.35
Belcher, LA	10 168.1 2.78	61.2 2.92	0.14	Maddux G, ChN	7 198.1 3.22	40.0 1.58	-1.64
Bielecki, ChN	4 185.2 3.10	26.2 3.38	0.28	Magrane, StL	9 186.2 2.84	48.0 3.19	0.34
Black, Cle	6 184.2 3.17	37.2 4.30	1.13	Mahler R, Cin	5 187.1 3.80	33.1 4.05	0.25
Blyleven, Cal	8 193.1 2.70	47.2 2.83	0.13	Martinez De, Mon	5 191.0 2.92	41.0 4.39	1.47
Boddicker, Bos	3 183.0 4.23	28.2 2.51	-1.72	McCaskill, Cal	6 175.3 3.13	36.2 1.96	-1.17
Bosio, Mil	8 189.0 2.90	45.2 3.15	0.25	Milacki, Bal	3 196.1 3.71	46.2 3.86	0.15
Brown Kev, Tex	7 151.1 3.51	39.2 2.72	-0.79	Moore M, Oak	6 201.1 2.68	40.1 2.23	-0.45
Browning, Cin	9 204.1 3.74	45.1 1.79	-1.95	Morris Jk, Det	10 132.0 5.18	38.1 3.76	-1.42
Candiotti, Cle	4 170.2 3.11	35.1 3.06	-0.05	Ojeda, NYN	5 162.0 3.61	30.0 2.70	-0.91
Cerutti, Tor	3 175.0 2.83	30.1 4.45	1.62	Perez M, ChA	2 163.2 5.11	19.2 4.12	-0.99
Clemens, Bos	8 200.0 3.06	53.1 3.38	0.32	Perez P, Mon	2 162.2 2.55	35.2 6.81	4.26
Cone, NYN	7 175.2 3.64	44.0 3.07	-0.57	Rasmussen D, SD	1 165.0 4.31	18.2 3.86	-0.45
Darling, NYN	4 183.1 3.53	34.0 3.44	-0.09	Reuschel, SF	2 179.2 3.01	28.2 2.51	-0.50
Davis Storm, Oak	1 157.0 4.24	12.1 5.84	1.60	Robinson D, SF	5 163.2 3.63	33.1 2.43	-1.20
DeLeon J, StL	5 199.2 3.02	45.0 3.20	0.18	Ryan, Tex	6 188.2 3.29	50.2 2.84	-0.45
Deshaies, Hou	6 191.2 2.82	34.0 3.44	0.62	Saberhagen, KC	12 205.0 1.93	57.1 2.98	1.05
Dopson, Bos	2 149.0 4.17	20.1 2.66	-1.51	Scott M, Hou	9 184.0 3.38	45.0 2.00	-1.38
Drabek, Pit	8 196.0 2.98	48.1 2.05	-0.93	Smiley, Pit	8 164.1 2.52	41.0 3.95	1.43
Farrell, Cle	7 170.2 3.74	37.1 3.13	-0.61	Smith B, Mon	3 184.0 2.98	31.2 1.99	-0.99
Fernandez S, NYN	6 183.1 2.60	36.0 4.00	1.40	Smith Roy, Min	2 148.1 3.94	24.0 3.75	-0.19
Finley C, Cal	9 161.2 2.23	38.0 4.03	1.80	Smoltz, Atl	5 169.2 3.08	38.1 2.35	-0.73
Flanagan, Tor	1 152.2 4.13	19.0 2.37	-1.76	Stewart D, Oak	8 207.0 3.22	50.2 3.73	0.51
Garrelts, SF	2 163.2 2.20	29.2 2.73	0.53	Stieb, Tor	3 181.0 3.23	25.2 4.21	0.98
Glavine, Atl	6 152.3 3.60	33.1 4.05	0.45	Sutcliffe, ChN	5 189.2 3.23	39.1 5.72	2.49
Gordon, KC	1 91.0 3.66	72.0 3.63	-0.03	Swindell, Cle	5 150.1 3.29	34.0 3.71	0.42
Gross K, Mon	4 172.2 4.33	28.2 4.71	0.38	Tanana, Det	6 182.2 3.74	41.0 2.85	-0.89
Gubicza, KC	8 200.2 3.36	54.1 1.82	-1.54	Terrell, NYA	5 178.2 4.08	27.2 7.16	3.08
Hawkins, NYA	5 177.2 4.81	30.2 4.70	-0.11	Valenzuela, LA	3 173.1 3.17	23.1 5.40	2.23
Hershiser, LA	8 196.0 2.62	60.2 1.34	-1.28	Viola, NYN	9 211.1 4.17	49.2 1.45	-2.72
Hill K, StL	2 179.0 3.67	17.2 5.09	1.42	Walk, Pit	2 165.0 3.93	31.0 6.97	3.04
Holman B, Sea	6 156.3 3.75	35.1 3.31	-0.44	Welch, Oak	1 182.2 2.86	27.0 4.00	1.14
Hough, Tex	5 154.2 4.13	27.1 5.60	1.47	Whitson, SD	5 183.0 2.75	44.0 2.25	-0.50
Howell K, Phi	1 175.1 3.70	28.2 1.88	-1.82	Witt B, Tex	5 162.0 5.56	32.1 3.06	-2.50
Hurst, SD	10 190.0 3.08	54.2 1.32	-1.76	Witt M, Cal	5 183.2 4.12	36.1 6.69	2.57

WHICH CATCHERS THROW OUT THE MOST BASERUNNERS? (p. 208)

Both Leagues — Listed Alphabetically (250 or more innings caught)

Catcher, Team	SB	CS	CS %	SB per 9 innings	Pickoffs
Allanson, Cle	76	30	28.3	0.76	1
Benedict, Atl	41	28	40.6	0.76	0
Berryhill, ChN	36	29	44.6	0.42	0
Biggio, Hou	140	29	17.2	1.18	0
Boone, KC	60	44	42.3	0.50	2
Borders, Tor	38	21	35.6	0.79	3
Bradley S, Sea	61	15	19.7	0.97	0
Carter G, NYN	46	20	30.3	1.12	1
Cerone, Bos	84	32	27.6	1.01	0
Daulton, Phi	78	39	33.3	0.73	1
Davis Jody, Atl	37	26	41.3	0.62	0
Dempsey, LA	26	25	49.0	0.62	1
Diaz B, Cin	29	7	19.4	0.82	0
Fisk, ChA	57	25	30.5	0.70	0
Fitzgerald, Mon	74	26	26.0	1.06	1
Gedman, Bos	73	24	24.7	0.99	0
Geren, NYA	20	14	41.2	0.37	1
Girardi, ChN	36	21	36.8	0.73	0
Harper B, Min	53	26	32.9	0.63	0
Hassey, Oak	51	22	30.1	0.74	0
Heath, Det	78	42	35.0	0.75	0
Karkovice, ChA	26	25	49.0	0.46	2
Kennedy, SF	61	36	37.1	0.63	0
Kreuter, Tex	64	14	17.9	1.09	0
Lake, Phi	27	26	49.1	0.62	0
Laudner, Min	46	20	30.3	0.83	0
Lavalliere, Pit	65	14	17.7	1.12	0
Lyons Bar, NYN	54	20	27.0	0.87	2
Macfarlane, KC	17	12	41.4	0.45	0
Manwaring, SF	31	18	36.7	0.55	0
Melvin, Bal	50	20	28.6	0.71	0
Nokes, Det	38	19	33.3	0.88	0
O'Brien C, Mil	32	18	36.0	0.55	5
Oliver, Cin	25	11	30.6	0.65	1
Ortiz, Pit	74	23	23.7	1.12	0
Parent, SD	20	12	37.5	0.55	0
Parrish Ln, Cal	72	29	28.7	0.62	0
Pena T, StL	90	45	33.3	0.75	1
Petralli, Tex	33	13	28.3	0.96	0
Reed Jf, Cin	84	46	35.4	0.98	1
Russell Jn, Atl	21	17	44.7	0.66	0
Santiago, SD	46	32	41.0	0.38	14
Santovenia, Mon	75	40	34.8	0.92	1
Sasser, NYN	41	17	29.3	0.88	0
Schroeder, Cal	29	8	21.6	0.96	0
Scioscia, LA	73	47	39.2	0.62	1
Skinner J, Cle	41	17	29.3	0.72	0
Slaught, NYA	52	33	38.8	0.57	0
Steinbach, Oak	38	26	40.6	0.42	3
Sundberg, Tex	34	21	38.2	0.67	0
Surhoff BJ, Mil	81	28	25.7	0.81	0
Tettleton, Bal	56	22	28.2	0.78	0
Valle, Sea	48	34	41.5	0.55	1
Whitt, Tor	61	28	31.5	0.62	1

WHO LED THE LEAGUE IN FUMBLES? (p. 210)

The chart below shows games per error (G/E) by defensive position. Defensive innings are converted to games by dividing by nine.

**Both Leagues — Listing the Top and Bottom Five from each Position
(750 or more defensive innings played)**

	Top Five				Bottom Five		
Player, Team	Inn	E	G/E	Player, Team	Inn	E	G/E
Catcher				**Catcher**			
Pena T, StL	1086.1	2	60.4	Santiago, SD	1087.2	20	6.0
Parrish Ln, Cal	1053.1	5	23.4	Harper B, Min	756.2	11	7.6
Valle, Sea	783.1	4	21.8	Daulton, Phi	965.1	11	9.8
Berryhill, ChN	764.1	4	21.2	Steinbach, Oak	823.0	9	10.2
Whitt, Tor	889.1	5	19.8	Scioscia, LA	1063.0	11	10.7
First Base				**First Base**			
Brett, KC	892.1	2	49.6	Clark Jk, SD	1093.2	15	8.1
Joyner, Cal	1373.0	4	38.1	McGriff F, Tor	1412.0	17	9.2
Murray E, LA	1418.2	6	26.3	Guerrero, StL	1290.1	15	9.6
Esasky, Bos	1322.1	6	24.5	Palmeiro, Tex	1236.1	12	11.4
Grace, ChN	1240.1	6	23.0	Davis A, Sea	1078.1	10	12.0
Second Base				**Second Base**			
Oquendo, StL	1360.2	5	30.2	Alomar R, SD	1399.1	28	5.6
Sandberg, ChN	1339.1	6	24.8	Lind, Pit	1302.0	18	8.0
Herr, Phi	1212.0	7	19.2	Reynolds H, Sea	1298.1	17	8.5
Thompson Ro, SF	1247.1	8	17.3	Jefferies, NYN	1007.0	12	9.3
Randolph, LA	1240.2	9	15.3	Treadway, Atl	1041.2	12	9.6
Third Base				**Third Base**			
Howell Jk, Cal	1211.0	11	12.2	Bonilla B, Pit	1382.0	35	4.4
Gaetti, Min	1055.1	10	11.7	Johnson H, NYN	1140.0	24	5.3
Buechele, Tex	1153.1	12	10.7	Gruber, Tor	1045.1	22	5.3
Pendleton, StL	1390.0	15	10.3	Pagliarulo, SD	881.0	17	5.8
Lansford, Oak	1123.2	13	9.6	Molitor, Mil	968.1	17	6.3
Shortstop				**Shortstop**			
Fernandez T, Tor	1243.0	6	23.0	Ramirez R, Hou	1229.1	30	4.6
Ripken C, Bal	1433.1	8	19.9	Thomas A, Atl	1210.2	29	4.6
Trammell, Det	1010.2	9	12.5	Rivera L, Bos	772.0	16	5.4
Schofield, Cal	774.2	7	12.3	Fermin, Cle	1311.0	26	5.6
Owen S, Mon	1211.1	13	10.4	Fletcher S, ChA	757.1	15	5.6
Left Field				**Left Field**			
Raines, Mon	1223.0	1	135.9	Gladden, Min	953.0	9	11.8
Smith Lo, Atl	1142.2	2	63.5	Bell Geo, Tor	1188.2	10	13.2
Bradley P, Bal	1197.0	3	44.3	Jackson B, KC	954.0	8	13.2
Hatcher B, Pit	792.0	2	44.0	Coleman, StL	1194.2	10	13.3
Henderson R, Oak	1271.0	4	35.3	McReynolds, NYN	1254.0	10	13.9
Center Field				**Center Field**			
Young G, Hou	1252.2	1	139.2	Griffey Jr, Sea	1057.2	10	11.8
Gallagher, ChA	1169.1	2	65.0	Martinez Da, Mon	772.0	7	12.3
Shelby, LA	826.1	2	45.9	Wilson W, KC	830.2	6	15.4
Puckett, Min	1329.1	4	36.9	Burks, Bos	855.1	6	15.8
Walton, ChN	987.1	3	36.6	Henderson D, Oak	1298.1	9	16.0
Right Field				**Right Field**			
Snyder C, Cle	1076.1	1	119.6	Brooks, Mon	1163.0	9	14.4
Dawson, ChN	937.0	3	34.7	Deer, Mil	1059.0	8	14.7
Lemon, Det	897.1	3	33.2	Strawberry, NYN	1096.2	8	15.2
O'Neill, Cin	980.0	4	27.2	Wilson G, Hou	923.1	6	17.1
Marshall, LA	855.1	4	23.8	Maldonado, SF	769.2	5	17.1

CAN CATCHERS HELP A PITCHER'S ERA? (p. 212)

Both Leagues — Listed Alphabetically (250 or more innings caught)

Catcher, Team	Innings Caught	Staff ERA when catching	Staff ERA with others catching	Difference
Allanson, Cle	902.1	3.60	3.74	-0.14
Benedict, Atl	488.2	3.48	3.83	-0.35
Berryhill, ChN	764.1	2.88	4.01	-1.13
Biggio, Hou	1064.2	3.42	4.25	-0.83
Boone, KC	1083.0	3.55	3.54	0.01
Borders, Tor	435.0	3.31	3.71	-0.40
Bradley S, Sea	563.2	4.28	3.84	0.44
Carter G, NYN	369.1	2.97	3.41	-0.44
Cerone, Bos	748.2	4.33	3.67	0.66
Daulton, Phi	965.1	3.99	4.23	-0.24
Davis Jody, Atl	539.2	3.62	3.77	-0.15
Dempsey, LA	380.1	2.34	3.16	-0.82
Diaz B, Cin	318.0	3.57	3.79	-0.23
Fisk, ChA	730.0	3.80	4.72	-0.92
Fitzgerald, Mon	625.2	3.32	3.60	-0.28
Gedman, Bos	661.1	3.67	4.28	-0.61
Geren, NYA	487.2	4.67	4.47	0.20
Girardi, ChN	443.1	4.36	3.01	1.35
Harper B, Min	756.2	3.95	4.66	-0.71
Hassey, Oak	618.0	3.45	2.89	0.56
Heath, Det	938.1	4.55	4.53	0.02
Karkovice, ChA	506.0	4.75	3.97	0.78
Kennedy, SF	870.0	3.43	3.11	0.32
Kreuter, Tex	528.0	3.56	4.12	-0.56
Lake, Phi	389.0	4.51	3.90	0.61
Laudner, Min	500.2	4.84	3.98	0.86
Lavalliere, Pit	522.2	3.22	3.87	-0.65
Lyons Bar, NYN	557.0	3.36	3.26	0.10
Macfarlane, KC	339.2	3.50	3.56	-0.06
Manwaring, SF	510.1	3.17	3.38	-0.21
Melvin, Bal	633.0	3.73	4.22	-0.49
Nokes, Det	390.2	4.10	4.71	-0.61
O'Brien C, Mil	527.0	3.59	3.92	-0.33
Oliver, Cin	347.0	4.15	3.62	0.53
Ortiz, Pit	594.1	3.85	3.51	0.34
Parent, SD	328.2	3.31	3.40	-0.09
Parrish Ln, Cal	1053.1	3.33	3.14	0.19
Pena T, StL	1086.1	3.30	3.58	-0.28
Petralli, Tex	310.0	4.62	3.72	0.90
Reed Jf, Cin	770.1	3.63	3.86	-0.23
Russell Jn, Atl	286.1	4.05	3.63	0.42
Santiago, SD	1087.2	3.43	3.24	0.21
Santovenia, Mon	737.2	3.72	3.24	0.48
Sasser, NYN	417.0	3.41	3.25	0.16
Schroeder, Cal	271.0	3.45	3.24	0.21
Scioscia, LA	1063.0	3.17	2.34	0.83
Skinner J, Cle	509.2	3.80	3.58	0.22
Slaught, NYA	827.0	4.63	4.41	0.22
Steinbach, Oak	823.0	2.91	3.43	-0.52
Sundberg, Tex	457.1	3.99	3.88	0.11
Surhoff BJ, Mil	899.1	3.91	3.60	0.31
Tettleton, Bal	646.2	4.26	3.79	0.47
Valle, Sea	783.1	3.96	4.07	-0.11
Whitt, Tor	889.1	3.64	3.51	0.13

WHICH INFIELDERS HAVE THE BEST RANGE? (p. 215)

1989 Infielders — Listed By Zone Rating
(600 or more defensive innings)

FIRST BASE

Player, Team	Innings	P	A	E	Range Factor	In Zone	Outs	Zone Rating
Magadan, NYN	682.1	574	59	6	---	141	134	.950
Hrbek, Min	734.1	723	60	4	---	156	147	.942
Clark W, SF	1374.0	1445	111	10	---	350	320	.914
Brock, Mil	822.0	850	58	5	---	196	179	.913
Joyner, Cal	1373.0	1487	99	4	---	292	265	.908
Milligan, Bal	926.0	914	83	5	---	219	198	.904
Mattingly, NYA	1223.2	1274	87	7	---	306	274	.895
McGwire, Oak	1231.1	1170	114	6	---	280	250	.893
McGriff F, Tor	1412.0	1460	115	17	---	287	256	.892
O'Brien P, Cle	1331.0	1359	114	9	---	292	260	.890
Esasky, Bos	1322.1	1317	107	6	---	390	347	.890
Grace, ChN	1240.1	1230	126	6	---	326	290	.890
Murray E, LA	1418.2	1316	137	6	---	362	321	.887
Galarraga, Mon	1288.2	1335	91	11	---	288	250	.868
Benzinger, Cin	1413.0	1417	73	7	---	305	264	.866
Brett, KC	892.1	896	80	2	---	241	208	.863
Davis A, Sea	1078.1	1106	81	10	---	253	218	.862
Palmeiro, Tex	1236.1	1167	119	12	---	312	268	.859
Davis G, Hou	1377.2	1347	113	12	---	355	303	.854
Bergman, Det	900.0	912	85	7	---	210	178	.848
Clark Jk, SD	1093.2	1135	88	15	---	246	207	.841
Jordan, Phi	1165.0	1271	61	9	---	275	229	.833
Perry G, Atl	618.2	618	51	9	---	156	128	.821
Guerrero, StL	1290.1	1445	72	15	---	326	243	.745

SECOND BASE

Player, Team	Innings	P	A	E	Range Factor	In Zone	Outs	Zone Rating
Thompson Ro, SF	1247.1	307	425	8	5.34	643	637	.991
Oquendo, StL	1360.2	346	500	5	5.63	680	657	.966
Sax S, NYA	1352.2	312	460	10	5.20	691	667	.965
Foley T, Mon	795.1	188	295	6	5.53	428	411	.960
Phillips, Oak	687.0	140	252	6	5.21	377	362	.960
Liriano, Tor	1068.0	267	330	12	5.13	544	518	.952
Ripken B, Bal	903.2	255	335	9	5.97	533	507	.951
Gantner, Mil	953.0	241	362	8	5.77	524	496	.947
Whitaker, Det	1179.0	327	393	11	5.58	620	585	.944
Ray, Cal	1157.1	279	403	11	5.39	623	586	.941
Oester, Cin	763.2	211	239	7	5.39	392	368	.939
Randolph, LA	1240.2	260	412	9	4.94	612	574	.938
Barrett M, Bos	703.0	152	245	10	5.21	383	359	.937
Franco Ju, Tex	1199.1	256	386	13	4.92	615	574	.933
Herr, Phi	1212.0	281	415	7	5.22	602	561	.932
Sandberg, ChN	1339.1	294	466	6	5.15	747	691	.925
Browne J, Cle	1325.2	305	380	15	4.75	682	629	.922
Treadway, Atl	1041.2	271	336	12	5.35	529	486	.919
Reynolds H, Sea	1298.1	311	506	17	5.78	770	705	.916
White F, KC	1059.1	238	407	10	5.56	638	584	.915
Lind, Pit	1302.0	309	438	18	5.29	690	627	.909
Alomar R, SD	1399.1	341	472	28	5.41	755	686	.909
Jefferies, NYN	1007.0	223	254	12	4.37	444	403	.908
Backman, Min	657.2	146	187	6	4.64	313	283	.904
Doran, Hou	1157.0	254	345	12	4.75	620	554	.894

THIRD BASE

Player, Team	Innings	P	A	E	Range Factor	In Zone	Outs	Zone Rating
Gaetti, Min	1055.1	104	251	10	3.11	364	330	.907
Caminiti, Hou	1414.2	126	335	22	3.07	458	414	.904
Buechele, Tex	1153.1	106	264	12	2.98	358	321	.897
Howell Jk, Cal	1211.0	95	322	11	3.18	426	381	.894
Boggs W, Bos	1339.1	123	264	17	2.71	362	322	.890
Molitor, Mil	968.1	78	243	17	3.14	353	311	.881
Wallach, Mon	1357.1	113	302	18	2.87	405	356	.879
Jacoby, Cle	1267.0	92	268	17	2.68	379	331	.873
Hamilton J, LA	1255.1	139	233	19	2.80	379	331	.873
Pendleton, StL	1390.0	113	392	15	3.37	529	461	.871
Law V, ChN	952.2	76	168	13	2.43	247	214	.866
Salazar L, ChN	615.0	45	143	8	2.87	209	180	.861
Gruber, Tor	1045.1	86	291	22	3.44	402	342	.851
Lansford, Oak	1123.2	104	183	13	2.40	291	247	.849
Sabo, Cin	660.1	36	145	11	2.62	219	185	.845
Hayes C, Phi	703.2	51	174	22	3.16	269	227	.844
Seitzer, KC	1357.1	112	272	20	2.68	423	351	.830
Worthington, Bal	1273.2	113	277	20	2.90	414	341	.824
Bonilla B, Pit	1382.0	125	330	35	3.19	532	435	.818
Presley, Sea	730.2	54	154	17	2.77	239	191	.799
Pagliarulo, SD	881.0	44	205	17	2.72	311	248	.797
Johnson H, NYN	1140.0	63	180	24	2.11	289	229	.792

SHORTSTOP

Player, Team	Innings	P	A	E	Range Factor	In Zone	Outs	Zone Rating
Ripken C, Bal	1433.1	276	531	8	5.12	827	793	.959
Templeton, SD	1193.0	232	409	20	4.99	628	597	.951
Weiss, Oak	651.0	106	195	15	4.37	341	324	.950
Trammell, Det	1010.2	188	396	9	5.28	608	576	.947
Fernandez T, Tor	1243.0	260	475	6	5.37	739	697	.943
Guillen, ChA	1341.2	272	512	22	5.41	821	772	.940
Espinoza, NYA	1225.1	237	471	22	5.36	732	688	.940
Smith O, StL	1336.1	209	483	17	4.78	726	680	.937
Gallego, Oak	730.1	152	255	14	5.19	390	365	.936
Dunston, ChN	1159.1	213	379	17	4.73	606	567	.936
Elster, NYN	1208.1	235	374	15	4.65	623	579	.929
Griffin Alf, LA	1128.1	208	333	14	4.43	578	536	.927
Thon, Phi	1024.0	174	380	16	5.01	582	539	.926
Fermin, Cle	1311.0	247	512	26	5.39	840	773	.920
Spiers, Mil	705.2	138	264	16	5.33	428	393	.918
Vizquel, Sea	1125.0	208	388	18	4.91	606	556	.917
Uribe, SF	1215.2	225	436	18	5.03	642	589	.917
Fletcher S, ChA	757.1	133	201	15	4.15	362	330	.912
Owen S, Mon	1211.1	232	387	13	4.70	624	568	.910
Thomas A, Atl	1210.2	231	400	29	4.91	697	634	.910
Stillwell, KC	1088.1	179	334	16	4.37	608	553	.910
Bell Jay, Pit	649.1	109	197	10	4.38	355	322	.907
Reed Jd, Bos	650.1	107	213	11	4.58	347	312	.899
Gagne, Min	1144.1	218	389	18	4.92	671	594	.885
Larkin B, Cin	690.0	142	267	10	5.47	440	388	.882
Rivera L, Bos	772.0	126	240	16	4.45	391	344	.880
Ramirez R, Hou	1229.1	189	326	30	3.99	636	546	.858
Quinones R, Pit	626.0	99	193	22	4.51	350	295	.843

WHICH OUTFIELDERS ARE THE TOUGHEST TO RUN ON?
(p. 220)

Both Leagues — Listed by Hold Percentage
(25 or more baserunner opportunites)

Right Field				Center Field				Left Field			
Player, Team	Opp	XB	%	Player, Team	Opp	XB	%	Player, Team	Opp	XB	%
Gwynn T, SD	62	20	32.3	Dascenzo, ChN	37	16	43.2	Felder, Mil	25	4	16.0
Buhner, Sea	71	26	36.6	Finley S, Bal	30	13	43.3	James D, Cle	46	10	21.7
Finley S, Bal	44	18	40.9	Sosa, ChA	30	13	43.3	Smith Dw, ChN	55	12	21.8
Barfield Je, NYA	152	63	41.4	Henderson D, Oak	124	57	46.0	Cotto, Sea	35	8	22.9
Sierra, Tex	116	49	42.2	Anderson B, Bal	76	35	46.1	Eisenreich, KC	25	6	24.0
Canseco, Oak	44	19	43.2	Carter J, Cle	123	57	46.3	Leach R, Tex	35	9	25.7
Felix, Tor	73	32	43.8	Thompson M, StL	106	50	47.2	Bell Geo, Tor	118	31	26.3
Washington C, Cal	83	37	44.6	Griffey Jr, Sea	148	70	47.3	Roberts Bip, SD	34	9	26.5
Coles, Sea	112	50	44.6	Cotto, Sea	25	12	48.0	Martinez Crm, SD	48	13	27.1
Tartabull, KC	62	28	45.2	Butler, SF	149	72	48.3	Lynn, Det	58	16	27.6
Brunansky, StL	145	66	45.5	Shelby, LA	91	44	48.4	Hatcher M, LA	25	7	28.0
Snyder C, Cle	103	48	46.6	Dykstra, Phi	150	74	49.3	Braggs, Mil	131	38	29.0
Winters, KC	30	14	46.7	Van Slyke, Pit	132	66	50.0	Ward G, Det	31	9	29.0
Dawson, ChN	94	44	46.8	Young G, Hou	174	88	50.6	Henderson R, Oak	134	40	29.9
O'Neill, Cin	102	48	47.1	Winningham, Cin	55	28	50.9	Incaviglia, Tex	123	37	30.1
Wilson G, Hou	82	39	47.6	Wilson W, KC	100	51	51.0	Briley, Sea	76	23	30.3
Reynolds RJ, Pit	46	22	47.8	Gwynn T, SD	77	40	51.9	Hatcher B, Pit	92	28	30.4
Eisenreich, KC	33	16	48.5	Espy, Tex	156	82	52.6	James C, SD	82	25	30.5
Heep, Bos	43	21	48.8	Kelly, NYA	192	102	53.1	Bonds, Pit	134	42	31.3
Puhl, Hou	46	23	50.0	Puckett, Min	205	109	53.2	Greenwell, Bos	124	39	31.5
Evans Dw, Bos	84	42	50.0	Devereaux, Bal	77	42	54.5	Davis C, Cal	120	38	31.7
Deer, Mil	156	80	51.3	Samuel, NYN	139	76	54.7	Mitchell K, SF	122	39	32.0
Armas, Cal	35	18	51.4	McGee, StL	53	29	54.7	Hall M, NYA	52	17	32.7
Orsulak, Bal	99	51	51.5	Wynne, ChN	40	22	55.0	Williams K, Det	27	9	33.3
Strawberry, NYN	91	47	51.6	Burks, Bos	138	76	55.1	McDowell O, Atl	75	25	33.3
Castillo C, Min	38	20	52.6	Reynolds RJ, Pit	27	15	55.6	Roomes, Cin	35	12	34.3
Bush, Min	66	35	53.0	Pettis, Det	152	86	56.6	Coleman, StL	99	34	34.3
Sheridan, SF	43	23	53.5	Davis E, Cin	134	76	56.7	Ready, Phi	26	9	34.6
Hayes V, Phi	76	41	53.9	Romine, Bos	49	28	57.1	Boston, ChA	48	17	35.4
Javier, Oak	44	24	54.5	Martinez Da, Mon	82	47	57.3	Webster M, ChN	31	11	35.5
Lemon, Det	112	62	55.4	Nixon O, Mon	61	35	57.4	Smith Lo, Atl	103	37	35.9
Murphy Dl, Atl	65	36	55.4	Gonzalez Jo, LA	33	19	57.6	McClendon, ChN	50	18	36.0
Tabler, KC	36	20	55.6	Moseby, Tor	156	91	58.3	Johnson L, ChA	33	12	36.4
Maldonado, SF	61	35	57.4	Gallagher, ChA	153	90	58.8	Polonia, NYA	130	48	36.9
Lusader, Det	26	15	57.7	White D, Cal	163	96	58.9	Gladden, Min	111	41	36.9
Calderon, ChA	104	61	58.7	Yount, Mil	160	96	60.0	Jones Tr, Det	34	13	38.2
Marshall, LA	75	44	58.7	McDowell O, Atl	75	45	60.0	Winningham, Cin	26	10	38.5
Roomes, Cin	27	16	59.3	Felix, Tor	25	15	60.0	Jackson B, KC	85	33	38.8
Baines, Tex	28	17	60.7	Felder, Mil	38	23	60.5	McReynolds, NYN	121	47	38.8
Belle, Cle	31	19	61.3	Murphy Dl, Atl	77	48	62.3	Bradley P, Bal	162	63	38.9
Brooks, Mon	110	75	68.2	Wilson M, Tor	43	27	62.8	Gibson K, LA	59	23	39.0
Bass K, Hou	40	28	70.0	Walton, ChN	128	81	63.3	Daniels, LA	40	16	40.0
Berroa, Atl	27	20	74.1	Williams K, Det	49	32	65.3	Carter J, Cle	54	22	40.7
Wilson M, Tor	30	23	76.7	Komminsk, Cle	52	34	65.4	Raines, Mon	121	50	41.3
				Eisenreich, KC	42	29	69.0	Heep, Bos	28	12	42.9
								Orsulak, Bal	30	13	43.3
								Kruk, Phi	73	32	43.8
								Tabler, KC	28	13	46.4
								Pasqua, ChA	50	24	48.0
								Griffey, Cin	32	16	50.0

WHO ARE THE PRIME PIVOT MEN? (p. 222)

All Major League Second Basemen, 1989 — Listed Alphabetically

Player, Team	DP Opp	DP	Pct	Player, Team	DP Opp	DP	Pct
Aguayo, Cle	6	5	83.3	Litton, SF	6	4	66.7
Alomar R, SD	90	51	56.7	Lombardozzi, Hou	4	3	75.0
Anderson K, Cal	1	1	100.0	Lyons S, ChA	48	31	64.6
Backman, Min	44	26	59.1	Manrique, Tex	36	17	47.2
Baker Dg, Min	2	2	100.0	McLemore, Cal	19	13	68.4
Barrett M, Bos	40	24	60.0	Miller K, NYN	8	4	50.0
Barrett Tom, Phi	11	7	63.6	Molitor, Mil	10	4	40.0
Bates, Mil	8	6	75.0	Newman A, Min	35	24	68.6
Belliard, Pit	6	5	83.3	Noboa, Mon	2	1	50.0
Blankenship L, Oak	7	6	85.7	Oberkfell, SF	3	1	33.3
Blauser, Atl	17	9	52.9	Oester, Cin	47	26	55.3
Booker R, StL	2	2	100.0	Oquendo, StL	93	57	61.3
Briley, Sea	4	3	75.0	Pecota, KC	3	2	66.7
Brookens, NYA	1	1	100.0	Pedrique, Det	8	3	37.6
Browne J, Cle	81	40	49.4	Phillips, Oak	41	20	48.8
Brumley, Det	10	8	80.0	Polidor, Mil	12	4	33.3
Buechele, Tex	8	4	50.0	Quinones L, Cin	18	8	44.4
Cochrane, Sea	2	2	100.0	Randolph, LA	59	43	72.9
Doran, Hou	51	29	56.9	Ray, Cal	89	59	66.3
Duncan, Cin	6	4	66.7	Ready, Phi	5	3	60.0
Felder, Mil	4	3	75.0	Reed Jd, Bos	45	31	68.9
Fletcher S, ChA	36	27	75.0	Reynolds C, Hou	7	6	85.7
Foley T, Mon	46	23	50.0	Reynolds H, Sea	108	59	54.6
Franco Ju, Tex	70	33	47.1	Riles, SF	5	1	20.0
Gallego, Oak	15	7	46.7	Ripken B, Bal	76	47	61.8
Gantner, Mil	79	49	62.0	Rivera L, Bos	1	0	0.0
Garcia D, Mon	23	14	60.9	Roberts Bip, SD	10	7	70.0
Gonzales R, Bal	37	23	62.2	Romero E, Mil	1	1	100.0
Hale, Min	9	5	55.6	Romero E, Mil	20	11	55.0
Harris L, LA	29	15	51.7	Sandberg, ChN	88	49	55.7
Herr, Phi	87	50	57.5	Sax S, NYA	101	59	58.4
Hinzo, Cle	2	1	50.0	Schaefer, ChA	1	1	100.0
Hoffman, Cal	3	2	66.7	Schu, Det	1	1	100.0
Hubbard, Oak	30	15	50.0	Sharperson, LA	2	2	100.0
Hudler, Mon	7	5	71.4	Smith G, ChN	2	0	0.0
Hulett, Bal	13	6	46.2	Speier, SF	2	2	100.0
Huson, Mon	4	3	75.0	Spiers, Mil	2	1	50.0
Infante, Tor	1	0	0.0	Strange, Det	6	3	50.0
Javier, Oak	1	1	100.0	Teufel, NYN	12	7	58.3
Jefferies, NYN	41	20	48.8	Thompson Ro, SF	73	43	58.9
Jeltz, Phi	7	6	85.7	Tolleson, NYA	4	4	100.0
Jones Tim, StL	6	1	16.7	Treadway, Atl	72	49	68.1
Jurak, SF	1	0	0.0	Trillo, Cin	5	1	20.0
King J, Pit	5	2	40.0	Wellman, KC	23	17	73.9
Kunkel, Tex	3	3	100.0	Whitaker, Det	105	55	52.3
Lawless, Tor	4	3	75.0	White F, KC	68	40	58.8
Lee M, Tor	31	17	54.8	Wilkerson, ChN	6	4	66.7
Lemke, Atl	6	3	50.0	Yelding, Hou	5	3	60.0
Lind, Pit	78	46	59.0				
Liriano, Tor	71	36	50.7				

WHICH CATCHERS ARE BEST AT BLOCKING PITCHES?
(p. 224)

Both Leagues — Listed Alphabetically (all catchers)

Catcher, Team	Innings Caught	WP	PB	Games per Miscue
Allanson, Cle	902.1	19	12	3.2
Alomar S, SD	41.0	3	0	1.5
Ashby, Hou	150.2	8	1	1.9
Bando, Det	4.1	0	0	0.0
Bathe, SF	12.0	0	0	0.0
Beane, Oak	1.0	0	0	0.0
Benedict, Atl	488.2	9	5	3.9
Berryhill, ChN	764.1	22	5	3.1
Biggio, Hou	1064.2	33	9	2.8
Bilardello, Pit	222.1	8	4	2.1
Boone, KC	1083.0	43	3	2.6
Borders, Tor	435.0	25	3	1.7
Bradley S, Sea	563.2	27	2	2.2
Brenly, SF	130.4	7	3	1.4
Cabrera, Atl	7.0	1	0	0.8
Carter G, NYN	369.1	11	3	2.9
Cerone, Bos	748.2	26	4	2.8
Cochrane, Sea	3.0	0	0	0.0
Datz, Det	18.0	0	0	0.0
Daulton, Phi	965.1	60	5	1.7
Davis Jody, Atl	539.2	21	6	2.2
Dempsey, LA	380.1	15	3	2.3
Diaz B, Cin	318.0	5	2	5.0
Distefano, Pit	6.0	1	1	0.3
Dorsett, NYA	54.0	2	0	3.0
Engle, Mil	6.0	0	0	0.0
Fisk, ChA	730.0	21	9	2.7
Fitzgerald, Mon	625.2	16	6	3.2
Fletcher D, LA	20.0	0	1	2.2
Gedman, Bos	661.1	11	6	4.3
Geren, NYA	487.2	17	3	2.7
Girardi, ChN	443.1	9	5	3.5
Harper B, Min	756.2	13	5	4.7
Hassey, Oak	618.0	23	4	2.5
Heath, Det	938.1	27	2	3.6
Hoiles, Bal	12.0	0	0	0.0
Jones Tim, StL	1.0	0	0	0.0
Karkovice, ChA	506.0	22	4	2.2
Kennedy, SF	870.0	23	2	3.9
Kreuter, Tex	528.0	27	21	1.2
Kutcher, Bos	2.2	0	0	0.0
Lake, Phi	389.0	27	0	1.6
Laudner, Min	500.2	27	2	1.9
Lavalliere, Pit	522.2	19	4	2.5
Lawless, Tor	1.0	0	0	0.0
Litton, SF	3.0	0	0	0.0
Lombardi, NYN	111.0	4	1	2.5
Lyons Bar, NYN	557.0	24	5	2.1
Lyons S, ChA	1.0	0	0	0.0
Macfarlane, KC	339.2	12	9	1.8
Magrann, Cle	34.0	3	0	1.3
Mann, Atl	58.2	1	0	6.5
Manwaring, SF	510.1	11	7	3.2
Marzano, Bos	47.2	3	1	1.3
McClendon, ChN	8.1	2	0	0.5
McGriff T, Cin	29.0	1	0	3.2
McGuire, Sea	88.0	3	2	2.0
Melvin, Bal	633.0	9	1	7.0
Mercado, Min	111.0	4	1	2.5
Merullo, ChA	185.0	12	3	1.4
Mizerock, Atl	67.1	2	1	2.5
Moreland, Bal	0.1	0	0	0.0
Myers G, Tor	72.0	3	0	2.7
Nichols C, Hou	22.0	2	0	1.2
Nieto, Phi	77.1	4	1	1.7
Nokes, Det	390.2	20	7	1.6
O'Brien C, Mil	527.0	8	1	6.5
Oliver, Cin	347.0	3	1	9.6
Olson Greg, Min	5.0	0	0	0.0
Ortiz, Pit	594.1	22	9	2.1
Orton, Cal	118.0	4	0	3.3
Pagnozzi, StL	186.2	3	2	4.1
Palacios, KC	29.0	1	0	3.2
Pardo, Phi	1.2	0	0	0.0
Parent, SD	328.2	10	0	3.7
Parrish Ln, Cal	1053.1	39	12	2.6
Pena T, StL	1086.1	31	5	3.4
Petralli, Tex	310.0	21	7	1.2
Pevey, Mon	93.0	6	1	1.5
Prince, Pit	142.1	5	1	2.6
Quirk, Bal	204.2	8	4	1.9
Reed Jf, Cin	770.1	30	5	2.4
Reyes, Mon	12.0	0	0	0.0
Russell Jn, Atl	286.1	14	2	2.0
Salas, Cle	7.0	0	0	0.0
Santiago, SD	1087.2	29	14	2.8
Santovenia, Mon	737.2	18	4	3.7
Sasser, NYN	417.0	11	2	3.6
Schroeder, Cal	271.0	7	2	3.3
Scioscia, LA	1063.0	38	6	2.7
Sinatro, Det	80.0	3	1	2.2
Skinner J, Cle	509.2	20	5	2.3
Slaught, NYA	827.0	21	4	3.7
Spilman, Hou	2.0	2	0	0.1
Stanley M, Tex	139.0	6	4	1.5
Steinbach, Oak	823.0	48	9	1.6
Sundberg, Tex	457.1	11	10	2.4
Surhoff BJ, Mil	899.1	27	10	2.7
Tettleton, Bal	646.2	23	3	2.8
Tingley, Cal	12.0	0	0	0.0
Trevino, Hou	240.0	5	4	3.0
Valle, Sea	783.1	17	6	3.8
Virgil, Tor	1.0	0	0	0.0
Webster L, Min	56.0	2	0	3.1
Whitt, Tor	889.1	26	12	2.6
Wrona, ChN	244.1	11	2	2.1
Zeile, StL	187.0	6	5	1.9

WHICH FIRST BASEMEN RECORD THE MOST 3-6-3 DOUBLE PLAYS? (p. 228)

Games per 3-6-3 doubleplay below is determined by using a "9-inning" game, rather than actual games played. Defensive innings played are divided by nine to get the number of games. This allows for better comparison between starting players and players who are often used as defensive replacements.

All First Basemen — Listed by Games per 3-6-3 Doubleplay
(first basemen with 1 or more 3-6-3 DP, 1987-1989)

Player, Team	363 DPs	Innings	Games per 363 DP	Player, Team	363 DPs	Innings	Games per 363 DP
Melvin, Bal	1	7.0	0.8	Joyner, Cal	12	4028.1	37.3
Gaetti, Min	1	14.0	1.6	Stubbs, LA	4	1357.1	37.7
Bradley S, Sea	1	18.0	2.0	Bream, Pit	7	2393.1	38.0
Sheets, Bal	1	34.1	3.8	Ward G, Det	1	343.0	38.1
Medina, Cle	3	129.2	4.8	McGwire, Oak	11	3782.1	38.2
Fisk, ChA	1	53.1	5.9	King J, Pit	1	361.0	40.1
Canale, Mil	1	70.0	7.8	Davis A, Sea	9	3419.1	42.2
Adduci, Phi	1	34.0	3.8	Robidoux, ChA	1	387.2	43.1
Calderon, ChA	2	177.0	9.8	Hayes V, Phi	5	2083.1	46.3
Oberkfell, SF	1	114.0	12.7	Galarraga, Mon	9	3935.2	48.6
Schroeder, Cal	1	145.1	16.1	Evans Da, Atl	4	1810.0	50.3
Hendrick, Cal	1	147.2	16.4	Palmeiro, Tex	3	1391.0	51.5
Hrbek, Min	15	2797.0	20.7	Marshall, LA	1	463.2	51.5
Larkin G, Min	6	1158.1	21.5	Buckner, KC	2	981.0	54.5
Traber, Bal	5	971.1	21.6	Benzinger, Cin	4	1981.1	55.0
Kittle, ChA	1	204.0	22.7	Knight, Det	1	510.0	56.7
Mattingly, NYA	18	3722.2	23.0	Brett, KC	5	2686.2	59.7
Upshaw, Cle	11	2399.2	24.2	Milligan, Bal	2	1110.1	61.7
Murray E, LA	16	3687.0	25.6	Clark Jk, SD	4	2283.1	63.4
Magadan, NYN	5	1265.0	28.1	Davis G, Hou	7	4043.1	64.2
Carter J, Cle	3	791.1	29.3	Grace, ChN	4	2373.0	65.9
Durham, StL	5	1330.1	29.6	Esasky, Bos	5	3080.2	68.5
Morman, ChA	1	271.2	30.2	Kruk, Phi	2	1375.1	76.4
Clark W, SF	14	3939.2	31.3	Francona, Mil	1	724.1	80.5
Martinez Crm, SD	3	849.0	31.4	Brock, Mil	4	2967.0	82.4
Aldrete, Mon	1	295.2	32.9	Walker G, ChA	3	2552.1	94.5
Tabler, KC	3	911.2	33.8	Moreland, Bal	1	866.2	96.3
Nelson Rob, SD	1	312.0	34.7	McGriff F, Tor	3	2831.0	104.9
Hernandez K, NYN	8	2558.1	35.5	Guerrero, StL	2	2042.0	113.4
Laga, SF	1	325.1	36.1	Balboni, NYA	1	1071.2	119.1
O'Brien P, Cle	12	3938.1	36.5	Jordan, Phi	1	1762.0	195.8
Bergman, Det	5	1662.1	36.9	Perry G, Atl	1	2978.2	331.0

WHICH OUTFIELDERS HAVE THE BEST RANGE (p. 230)

Range Factors and Zone Ratings, 1989 — Outfielders
(600 or more defensive innings)

LEFT FIELD

Player, Team	Innings	P	A	E	Range Factor	In Zone	Outs	Zone Rating
Henderson R, Oak	1271.0	335	8	4	2.46	385	325	.844
Coleman, StL	1194.2	248	5	10	1.98	271	227	.841
Incaviglia, Tex	994.1	199	6	6	1.91	231	191	.835
Smith Lo, Atl	1142.2	290	3	2	2.32	344	284	.828
Braggs, Mil	1053.2	252	7	7	2.27	303	247	.822
Bell Geo, Tor	1188.2	257	4	10	2.05	313	256	.821
McReynolds, NYN	1254.0	307	10	10	2.35	376	305	.809
Jackson B, KC	954.0	223	10	8	2.27	274	218	.807
Bonds, Pit	1337.0	364	13	6	2.58	432	347	.803
Davis C, Cal	1302.0	270	5	6	1.94	330	263	.803
Briley, Sea	701.1	164	5	7	2.26	195	157	.800
Bradley P, Bal	1197.0	284	4	3	2.19	357	284	.796
Raines, Mon	1223.0	252	7	1	1.91	307	243	.792
Hatcher B, Pit	792.0	199	1	2	2.30	252	194	.774
Greenwell, Bos	1227.0	221	10	8	1.75	287	220	.774
James C, SD	705.1	153	4	3	2.04	193	149	.772
Polonia, NYA	857.1	232	9	4	2.57	297	228	.771
Gladden, Min	953.0	238	9	9	2.42	310	237	.765
Mitchell K, SF	1280.1	303	8	7	2.24	389	289	.743

CENTER FIELD

Player, Team	Innings	P	A	E	Range Factor	In Zone	Outs	Zone Rating
White D, Cal	1365.2	426	10	5	2.91	498	446	.898
Henderson D, Oak	1298.1	386	5	9	2.77	482	415	.865
Devereaux, Bal	621.2	203	1	1	2.97	252	217	.865
Gallagher, ChA	1169.1	346	4	2	2.71	431	374	.861
Shelby, LA	826.1	224	3	2	2.49	272	235	.860
Dykstra, Phi	1117.0	333	10	4	2.80	391	334	.859
Espy, Tex	986.1	274	5	3	2.57	353	304	.858
Martinez Da, Mon	772.0	187	7	7	2.34	229	195	.856
Davis E, Cin	1017.1	286	3	4	2.59	372	313	.841
Thompson M, StL	1022.0	303	5	7	2.77	380	318	.834
Samuel, NYN	1146.2	339	6	4	2.74	447	373	.830
Walton, ChN	987.1	285	3	3	2.65	380	316	.829
Griffey Jr, Sea	1057.2	298	12	10	2.72	379	319	.828
Moseby, Tor	1048.1	286	3	4	2.52	391	325	.826
Puckett, Min	1329.1	439	13	4	3.09	572	472	.822
Burks, Bos	855.1	243	7	6	2.69	324	266	.821
Butler, SF	1293.1	408	11	6	2.96	515	423	.819
Young G, Hou	1252.2	411	15	1	3.07	551	450	.808
Wilson W, KC	830.2	255	2	6	2.85	331	266	.807
Murphy Dl, Atl	729.0	194	2	4	2.47	265	211	.804
Yount, Mil	1217.2	362	8	7	2.79	505	402	.798
Gwynn T, SD	745.2	212	7	4	2.69	277	220	.798
Kelly, NYA	1161.2	351	8	6	2.83	468	372	.793
Pettis, Det	1021.2	323	1	4	2.89	420	331	.790
Carter J, Cle	883.1	257	5	6	2.73	348	277	.790
Van Slyke, Pit	1065.0	336	10	4	2.96	468	366	.776

RIGHT FIELD

Player, Team	Innings	P	A	E	Range Factor	In Zone	Outs	Zone Rating
Felix, Tor	700.1	184	7	7	2.54	209	182	.871
Sierra, Tex	1402.1	310	13	9	2.13	362	309	.854
Hayes V, Phi	967.2	215	8	5	2.12	237	200	.840
Dawson, ChN	937.0	227	4	3	2.25	262	219	.836
O'Neill, Cin	980.0	218	6	4	2.09	251	208	.829
Barfield Je, NYA	1183.2	300	18	7	2.47	362	300	.826
Brunansky, StL	1309.0	289	7	7	2.08	316	261	.823
Snyder C, Cle	1076.1	294	18	1	2.62	344	286	.823
Wilson G, Hou	923.1	214	10	6	2.24	253	207	.818
Gwynn T, SD	633.0	138	8	2	2.10	168	137	.815
Washington C, Cal	821.0	181	6	5	2.10	221	180	.814
Marshall, LA	855.1	177	2	4	1.93	217	174	.806
Murphy Dl, Atl	613.2	137	3	1	2.07	159	128	.805
Deer, Mil	1059.0	267	9	8	2.41	328	265	.805
Evans Dw, Bos	657.1	152	6	3	2.20	188	152	.803
Orsulak, Bal	707.1	205	8	3	2.75	251	198	.789
Strawberry, NYN	1096.2	272	4	8	2.33	333	261	.787
Coles, Sea	716.0	180	9	4	2.43	207	164	.783
Brooks, Mon	1163.0	235	6	9	1.93	296	230	.780
Calderon, ChA	737.2	181	7	3	2.33	227	177	.775
Maldonado, SF	769.2	178	6	5	2.21	229	176	.764
Lemon, Det	897.1	190	6	3	2.00	239	181	.757

Note: Putouts, assists and errors by outfield position are unofficial.